RORKE'S DRIFT

ADRIAN GREAVES

CASSELL

In Memory of Norman Holme
Whose original research fired my own interest

Cassell Military Paperbacks

an imprint of Orion Books Ltd,
Orion House, 5 Upper St Martin's Lane,
London WC2H 9EA

An Hachette UK company

ISBN 978-0-3043-6641-5

Designed by Gwyn Lewis

Printed and bound in Great Britain by
CPI Group (UK) Ltd, Croydon, CR0 4YY

Paper used in the production of this book is a natural,
recyclable product made from wood grown in sustainable forests.
The manufacturing process conforms to the environmental
regulations of the country of origin.

www.orionbooks.co.uk

Contents

PART TWO

APPENDICES

List of Illustrations and Maps

MAPS AND PLANS

Acknowledgements

An account of 'The Defence of Rorke's Drift', signed by Major J.R.M. Chard VC, RE, at the personal request of Queen Victoria and first published in *The Silver Wreath*, copyright reserved. By gracious permission of Her Majesty Queen Elizabeth II.

I also gratefully acknowledge the kind and generous permission of the following people without whose co-operation and assistance this work would have been incomplete: Freda Holme who kindly allowed me to reproduce the nominal rolls and associated material from *The Silver Wreath*; Dr Lita Webley of the Albany Museum, Grahamstown, South Africa, for kind permission to reproduce parts of her archaeological report concerning Rorke's Drift; Jack Karran and Tony Lucking for the Curling letters; Nicky von der Heyde for the drawings of Rorke's Drift, and Brian Best for his generous assistance relating to the Victorian period and medals.

For the use of photographs, I gratefully acknowledge Major Martin Everett of the 24th Regimental Museum; Ian Knight; the Curator of the British Empire and Commonwealth Museum; Ron Sheeley; Brian Best; the Anglo Zulu War Historical Society and the Killie Campbell Library in Durban.

For general guidance and advice, I gratefully acknowledge Ian Knight. I also owe much to David and Nicky Rattray and to David and Sue Charles at Fugitives' Drift for their assistance and wonderful hospitality. I especially acknowledge Consultant Surgeon Clifford Stossel and his wife Katie who have supported me with their professional skill and human kindness during a long and painfull period of my life.

Needless to say, no one else had any direct control or influence over the final draft. I alone accept responsibility for any factual errors or omissions.

I know others more expert and learned in the field will regard some of my conclusions as errors of interpretation but it is the uncertainty of knowing exactly what happened at Rorke's Drift that enhaces the excitment of the event.

Finally, I acknowledge the sacrifice of precious family time due to my reclusive study in preparation for this book. My wife, Debbie, and our three sons have all been especially patient and stoically accepted my need for frequent visits to Rorke's Drift for yet more research.

Chronology

11 December 1878 British ultimatum to Zulu King Cetshwayo.

11 December onwards British assemble along Zulu border in preparation for invasion.

11 January 1879 British invade Zululand leaving small garrison and hospital at Rorke's Drift.

20/21 January British establish camp at Isandlwana.

22 January Zulu army defeats British at Isandlwana; Zulu reserves attack Rorke's Drift.

Rorke's Drift battle timetable

8 a.m. Lt Chard RE rides the 10 miles to Isandlwana to check his orders. On hearing of the reports of approaching Zulus from mounted sentries and seeing that a party of Zulus was moving across the Nqutu Plateau towards Rorke's Drift, Chard starts back, arriving at the Drift at noon. Chard holds a brief discussion with Maj. Spalding but no action is taken.

2 p.m. Maj. Spalding, the officer commanding Rorke's Drift, leaves for Helpmekaar to speed the relieving companies to the mission station. Lt Chard given command at the mission station but stays at the river crossing. Distant rifle fire is then heard and men are seen crossing the Buffalo river.

2.30 p.m. At the river crossing, Lts Vane and Adendorff report the defeat at Isandlwana to Lt Chard. They carry Chard's orders to Lt Bromhead at the mission station, and then ride off to Helpmekaar.

3 p.m. Lt Chard assumes command of the mission station while Mr Dalton organizes the construction of defence walls of bags of mealies and boxes of biscuits strengthened with two wagons built into the south wall.

3.30 p.m. Chard returns to the Drift to urge his men to retire with the water cart and tools. Lt Henderson with a large party of Durnford's Horse appears and is ordered to guard the ferry.

4.30 p.m. Chard returns to the mission station and orders six men to guard the hospital, reserve ammunition is made ready and bayonets are fixed. A lookout is posted on the ridgepole of the store.

5 p.m. On the approach of the Zulus, Lt Henderson and the native horse depart whereupon Capt. Stevenson and his native contingent also desert. The effective strength is now reduced from 350 to about 139 (including 30 sick). Men now taken from the line to construct a wall between the perimeter and the corner of the store (this became the famous wall of biscuit boxes providing the second and final line of defence).

5.30 p.m. The Zulus appear on the terraces of the Oskarsberg. The initial attack on the south of the defences is contained and the leading ranks of Zulus are pinned down by rifle fire. The main attack is diverted to the west of the hospital and along the thinly held northern wall. Zulu sniping from the Oskarsberg begins.

6 p.m. In desperate hand-to-hand fighting the defenders are forced to retire into the yard – the hospital becomes vulnerable.

Hospital 6.20 p.m. to 7.15 p.m. Pte Cole (suffering from claustrophobia), Gnr Howard and Ptes Beckett and Waters flee the hospital; Cole, Adams (who had remained inside the hospital) and Beckett are killed, Howard and Waters survive the night in bushes. John Williams cuts a hole through the wall whilst Joseph Williams and Horrigan hold the Zulus at bay. John Williams pulls two patients through the hole before the Zulus burst in; they kill the four men in the room. The two Joneses help four patients to escape through the window in the corner room. The sick are assisted to safety by Pte Hitch and Cpl Allen (both already wounded).

6.45 p.m. Thatch fired.

7 p.m. until midnight The Zulus continue to attack in intermittent waves.

4 a.m. The Zulus retire.

8 a.m. Mission station is relieved by Lord Chelmsford and remnants of his Centre Column.

Brannigan: Tell the boys to hold their fire too. (*To the two houses*) Stay four minutes. Let's see if anything is visible in the corner room. Frank can watch it ... (*To the blonde girl*) Alice, you come in here. Go ...

6.15 p.m. taken a break.

2 p.m. interrogation. The information is much too important to ...

Brannigan: Okay, okay, okay ...

2 p.m. Alice can confirm that he had just arrived and suspects of treachery again ...

PART ONE

Introduction

*It is more than probable that active steps will have to be taken to check
the arrogance of Cetywayo, Chief of the Zulus.*[1]

LORD CHELMSFORD. COMMANDER-IN-CHIEF, SOUTH AFRICA.

Since prehistoric times the area of land around Rorke's Drift has been of considerable importance to mankind, primarily because it is one of the few crossing points of the Buffalo River, which in 1879 formed the 200 mile border between Zululand and British controlled Natal. Immediately down stream of Rorke's Drift the Buffalo river becomes impassable where it enters a precipitous gorge that speeds it into a fast-flowing torrent until its confluence with the predominant Tugela river. From this gorge onwards the Tugela surges through a steep-sided valley that hems it in until it reaches the sea. This physical barrier ensured that there were only two points of access into Zululand, either at Rorke's Drift some 60 miles from the sea, or at the coast where the Tugela river meets the Indian Ocean. At Rorke's Drift a rocky outcrop in the riverbed provided a reasonably safe and level crossing point for wagons, as well as a series of small islands that can, even today, be traversed by people jumping from rock to rock at low water. When the river was in flood, Rorke's Drift was the one place where a small boat could still be rowed across. This natural crossing point, or drift, and the comparatively level nature of the country on both sides have jointly contributed to the settlement of the area since prehistoric times. On the dominating rocky hillock that overlooks the river, rock paintings, stone artefacts and the remains of ancient human dwellings evidence a long history of human occupation.

The area was named after James Rorke, a settler who started a trading store in addition to his farming activities. Born in 1821, James Rorke was the son of an Irish immigrant to South Africa who had fled the poverty of his homeland. At the age of 28 years the young Rorke made his way inland and purchased a remote farm called 'Tyeana' bordering the Buffalo river and towards the end of 1849 he established a small trading store known to the Zulus as *KwaJimu* (Kwa 'of', hence *KwaJimu*, *KwaZulu* etc.). Rorke led an uneventful life that ended when he committed suicide on 24 October 1875, allegedly by shooting himself when his source of gin ran dry. In accordance with Rorke's final wishes, his body was placed in a rough wooden coffin and buried under a yard of concrete. Rorke fully understood the Zulu penchant for excavating European graves for 'treasure' or body parts for their '*muti*' or medicine. Rorke's funeral was attended by the few local white people in the area, some having travelled 40 miles to attend the burial service that was conducted by a Scottish missionary from the settlement of Dundee, some 25 miles distant. Rorke's penniless wife was forced to sell the farm and a Swedish missionary, Otto Witt, purchased the property on behalf of the Swedish Missionary Service. The farm possessed two small buildings and was protected by a hill known to the local Zulus as *Shiyane*, meaning eyebrow. Witt renamed the hill 'Oskarsberg' after his Swedish king and the missionaries' patron saint – Saint Ansgar (Oscar). Rorke's Drift remains an active mission station to this day.

The surrounding area of Rorke's Drift is also historically important. It witnessed the events that led to the onset of the Zulu War and the river crossing that took its name formed the start line of the initial British invasion of Zululand on 11 January 1879. A few days later, on 22 January, two of the most famous military battles in the history of the British Army were fought to the death; a stunning British victory took place at the mission station itself while, within sight at nearby Isandlwana, the British suffered the humiliation of both a total defeat and the massacre of its invasion force. Without doubt, little would have been known of this isolated yet picturesque location but for the fierce and bitter war that broke out at the beginning of 1879 when Britain invaded Zululand. Rorke's Drift was also destined to play an ongoing role in the harshly fought series of Boer Wars that followed the Zulu War.

Very few people, even those born in South Africa, know much about the Anglo-Zulu War of 1879. South Africans tend to have a hazy idea that, once upon a time, there was a short war between the Zulu people and red-jacketed Imperial troops reinforced by locally recruited Colonial units. They may also know that the war produced, on the very same day, a terrible British defeat at Isandlwana followed by an equally spectacular victory at nearby Rorke's Drift. Most South Africans would maintain that these events were purely British in their nature and the consequences of the war had little to do with their own domestic history. Indeed, even today, over 70 per cent of visitors to the relatively unchanged battlefields of Zululand are from Britain.

By the 1960s the Zulu War had long been forgotten within the British Isles. Only military men and historians would be able to recall that the battle of Rorke's Drift had resulted in the highest number of Victoria Crosses ever awarded to one regiment for one battle, a unique feat unsurpassed by events in either of the World Wars. Beyond that fact little was known. Then, in 1964, the highly successful feature film *ZULU* was released; it recreated the battle of Rorke's Drift using spectacular South African scenery and a group of highly competent actors that included Michael Caine, Stanley Baker and Jack Hawkins in the lead roles, supported by Prince Mangosuthu Buthelezi. Due to a combination of other crucial factors such as the powerful storyline, haunting music and psychological tension, the film had a dramatic effect on the public that ensured that the film enjoyed lasting popularity. The history of Rorke's Drift had been resurrected; sadly, numerous myths and falsehoods within the film became firmly established in the minds of the public and some historians.

At the time news of the battle of Rorke's Drift reached home, hardly anyone in Britain knew of King Cetshwayo or where Zululand was. Judging from comments made in the press and Parliament, even the nation's leaders were temporarily unsure of its exact geographical location. They and the British people were soon to find out. On 11 February 1879 the official dispatch containing the news of the terrible military defeat of the British invasion force, including the loss of the 1st Battalion 24th (2nd Warwickshire) Regiment,[2] finally reached London and the press. The magnitude of the catastrophe had a stunning effect on the nation; no one could understand how an unsophisticated army of Zulus could inflict such a crushing defeat on a highly trained British force armed with the most modern rifles and supported with equally modern artillery. Many questions were asked, all were difficult to answer; the defeat was totally incomprehensible. Not since the sanguinary events of the Indian Mutiny in 1857 had such devastating and humiliating losses been reported to an incredulous and previously overconfident British public.

The loss of fifty British officers and virtually a whole battalion of the famous 24th Regiment stunned the nation and created a hive of activity in the press. The *Daily News* commented:

Death had prematurely visited hundreds of peaceful and happy homes in England. British treasure and blood would now be expended on a scale the authors of the war had not contemplated, and burdens, heavy in all cases and ruinous in many, will be inflicted on struggling industries, and all for what? Lord Beaconsfield's answer was awaited.

Almost overlooked, as it came at the end of the dispatch, came the news that on the very same day, and within sight of the British massacre at Isandlwana, another vicious engagement had been fought. At the tiny Mission Station at Rorke's Drift, a company of soldiers from the same regiment had beaten off a determined Zulu attack, the British having been outnumbered in the ratio of 40:1. In the absence of a full report from Rorke's Drift it was too soon for Lord Chelmsford and the establishment to realize the significant political advantages that could be wrung out of this separate engagement.

The reaction to the defeat at Isandlwana came immediately. 'The dead could not be brought to life' affirmed the leading English newspaper *The Times*, at that period usually referred to as *The Thunderer*. The newspaper reported:

Their names would be imperishably inscribed on the Death Roll of England's illustrious heroes, but swift and terrible retribution must be exacted. It was clear that the Zulus were even more formidable than the military authorities anticipated. It was known they were well drilled and that numbers of them were armed with modern breech-loaders and that they could fight courageously, but it was only now realised how large a force they could mass at one point. Sad as the loss of a British regiment was, still graver peril would arise to the colonists in Natal if immediate action were not taken to forward adequate reinforcements.

The *Standard* opined that the British would not renew the war until reinforcements were available. Although the actual British losses amounted to scarcely one twentieth of the troops on the spot, such a success for the Zulus, together with their acquisition of guns, rifles and ammunition, was bound to hearten the Zulus and materially improve their defensive strength. In the House of Lords that same evening the Earl of Beaconsfield responded:

It is a military disaster, a terrible military disaster, but I think we may say it is no more. It is not a military defeat which arises either from the failing energies or resources of the country, but it arises accidentally, and, at this moment, we do not accurately understand the circumstances which have occurred in the course of the campaign.

Nothing indeed is certain at this moment respecting this disaster, except the valour of our troops. They have shown, as they have ever shown, the utmost devotion. Those who have fallen will be remembered, but we must not forget also that there has been an exhibition of heroic valour by those who have been spared, and the recollection of the conduct of those eighty men, who for twelve hours, in a forlorn post, kept at bay four thousand of the enemy, and ultimately repulsed them, will prove that the stamina of the English soldiery has not diminished or deteriorated. (Cheers.)

We have taken steps, such as any persons entrusted with the management of the affairs of this great country would necessarily and promptly take, to send reinforcements to the Cape. These reinforcements are far beyond the number which the General in command thought was required:

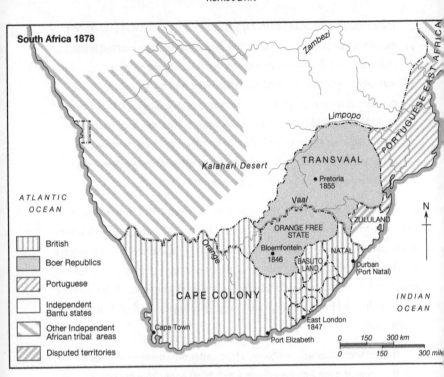

South Africa 1878

| British |
| Boer Republics |
| Portuguese |
| Independent Bantu states |
| Other Independent African tribal areas |
| Disputed territories |

and I hope that the measures which have been taken, and the valour of our troops, will soon put a different aspect upon the conditions of affairs in South Africa to that which they assume at the present moment.[3]

During the sixty-four year reign of Queen Victoria the British Army, with its ubiquitous red-jacketed soldiers, had fought in sixty-three campaigns throughout the British Empire. Military defeat was virtually unknown to the English-speaking world and, with two further disastrous British defeats at the hands of the Zulus at Ntombe Drift and Hlobane about to occur, the Zulu War thereafter dominated the attention of the press and public imagination. In a determined endeavour to salve the nation's prestige, more famous British regiments were mobilized throughout the country and empire and dispatched to fight Britain's former ally, King Cetshwayo and his most ferocious and feared Zulu army. Further political disaster followed with the death of the heir to the Napoleonic dynasty, Louis Napoleon, the Prince Imperial. This young prince had been exiled to England with his father, Napoleon III (who died in 1873) and his mother, Empress Eugénie. Both the empress and the young prince continued to enjoy the protection and patronage of Queen Victoria; then, at the age of 21, the prince volunteered to fight with the British in Zululand, only to be killed by a Zulu scouting party. Britain had to act; her reputation of invincibility was rapidly becoming tarnished.

The Zulu people

By the time of his death in 1828, King Shaka of the Zulus had successfully trained the nation's warriors in the art of tactical warfare. This tradition had been passed down to his brother, King Mpande, who had two principal sons, Mbulazi and Cetshwayo. Mbulazi was intellectually inclined while the more flamboyant Cetshwayo had moulded himself on Shaka and had carefully studied the art of war. These two princes had strong followings and each regarded himself as heir apparent but Mpande favoured Mbulazi, which was curious as he lacked any leadership qualities.

On 3 December 1856 the faction that supported Cetshwayo made a raid on European traders in Zululand, confiscating all their goods and other possessions and murdering their native servants. This molestation of Europeans was highly provocative and challenged King Mpande's authority, now vested in Mbulazi who rallied his followers. What followed was probably the greatest battle for supremacy that Africa has ever witnessed. The battle took place at Ndondakusuka on the Zulu side of the Tugela river. Cetshwayo, who had inherited the military ability and savage ferocity of his uncle Shaka, overcame his brother's army and slew Mbulazi and five of his relatives who supported his cause, together with, it has been estimated, more than 30,000 men, women and children. Thousands of their bodies were thrown into the fast-flowing river and for weeks afterwards, the ocean beaches from the mouth of the Tugela were strewn with the innumerable corpses of Cetshwayo's victims.

After this brutal exhibition of power by Cetshwayo King Mpande relinquished the reins of active authority to his victorious son, and on his demise in 1872 Cetshwayo proclaimed himself King of Zululand. Probably to gain favour with his British neighbours, Cetshwayo conceived the idea of soliciting the assistance of the Secretary for Native Affairs, Sir Theophilus Shepstone, to perform the coronation ceremony.

Shepstone, presumably on the advice or instruction of Sir Henry Bulwer, Lieutenant Governor of Natal, acceded to Cetshwayo's request. In August 1872 Shepstone proceeded to the royal palace to carry out the investment and in the presence of a vast assemblage of Zulu warriors, the Secretary for Native Affairs proclaimed Cetshwayo as King of Zululand in the name of Her Majesty Queen Victoria. The 'coronation' was a farce with Shepstone placing a golden cape and a tinsel crown, made for the occasion by a tailor of the 75th Regiment, on Cetshwayo's head and the firing of a salute, which bore no resemblance to that required for a monarch.

During the ceremony Shepstone, who was a fluent Zulu speaker, had made a series of requests, ostensibly for the king's guidance in his future relations with his subjects. Cetshwayo should prohibit indiscriminate bloodshed, no person should be condemned without open trial and condemned persons had the right of appeal to the king; none of his subjects' lives should be sacrificed without the king's personal sanction, and fines should be imposed in the place of death sentences for all minor offences. To these requests the king and his councillors apparently acquiesced and, being well satisfied with the 'agreement', Shepstone returned to Natal. The British authorities thereafter ignored the matter and in any event, they had no effect on Cetshwayo. Zululand was left to the Zulus and Britain concentrated its attention on the commercial development of Natal.

On a broader scale during the 1870s, Britain had successfully developed the policy of confederation as a means of self-financing and administering her numerous colonies around the world. Previously, Britain supplied her colonies with troops from within the British Army and also bore the heavy financial and administrative burden. Under the new policy the defence and laws of each colony were brought under one accepted form of administration. Local administrators were trained and soldiers recruited, though the military system was supervised and commanded by British officers. The system was highly successful and relieved Britain of the expensive responsibility for maintaining British military garrisons worldwide. During the years immediately leading up to the Zulu War, this policy was seen as the obvious solution in uniting southern Africa's fragile colonies into one cohesive country, including the Boer Republics and Zululand.

In October 1867 the discovery of diamonds in the Boer Orange Free State saw thousands of prospectors from all over the world converge on the area. In 1871, after several years of chaos, and with obvious wealth still to be won, Britain annexed the whole area to the British Crown, including Basutoland. The total cost to the Crown was the sum of £90,000 – paid in the form of compensation. The Secretary of State for the Colonies, Lord Carnarvon, then appointed Sir Henry Bartle Edward Frere (popularly known as Sir Bartle Frere) as High Commissioner to South Africa and Governor of the Cape. Although the Boers actively disliked the British, the threat, real or imagined, of a Zulu uprising had long dominated Boer thinking. It was this deep-seated Boer fear, based on years of bloodshed and conflict with the Zulus, that gave Britain the opportunity to coerce the Boer leaders into accepting British rule.

The 1830s saw a great trek of Boers away from British domination in the Cape; thousands of Boer families loaded their possessions into columns of heavy ox-drawn wagons to undertake the quest for the Promised Land. They sought new lands that would be free from British rule with its stifling legislation – particularly with regard to keeping slaves – and punitive taxation. The trek was an undertaking of biblical proportions and Boer wagon trains spread far and wide across and beyond southern Africa in their quest for freedom. The first party of Boers crossed the Drakensberg Mountains in 1837 and discovered the lush green pastures and hills of Zululand. The word quickly spread and hundreds of Boer families rapidly followed to settle the area. There were savage conflicts between the Boers and Zulus but little could be done to prevent the steady settlement across Zululand, limited only by the natural boundary that crossed the country, the Tugela river. By the mid 1870s the pressure for more farming land encouraged Boer settlers to move even further into Zululand, a process that the Zulus successfully resisted with increasing vigour and violence.

The area of greatest tension lay between the Buffalo and Blood rivers immediately north of the river crossing point known locally as Rorke's Drift. In the meantime, the Zulu king, Cetshwayo, was growing increasingly agitated by the violent land-hungry Boers; due to their constant seizure of tracts of Zululand for their farms, Cetshwayo naturally viewed them as an invading enemy. Cetshwayo had never experienced any difficulty with his British neighbours whom he regarded as allies. During August 1876, as crisis loomed along the Boer border, Theophilus Shepstone, Secretary for Native Affairs in Natal, was on home leave in London to receive a knighthood for his loyal services. He then travelled to Wales for a holiday where he learned from a newspaper that a force of Boers had been defeated by Chief Sekhukune of the baPedi people who lived to the north of Zululand. Having crowned Cetshwayo in 1873, Shepstone realized the political and military implications for Britain of the Boer defeat; namely that Germany, France and Holland might arm the Boers thus upsetting British military domination in South Africa and thwart Britain's desire to gain the Transvaal goldfields. Shepstone immediately returned to London where he received an unsigned draft charter to annex the Transvaal. He was also given certain orders, the exact contents of which remain a mystery; on the following day he set sail for South Africa with the intention of annexing the Transvaal to Britain.

His written charter was unambiguous; he was to secure the Transvaal, but only after he had gained the consent of the majority of the Transvaalers. Upon Shepstone's arrival in South Africa, his superior, Sir Bartle Frere, the Governor General for Native Affairs and High Commissioner to South Africa, revised Shepstone's orders and gave him permission to make the annexation without this consent – if the circumstances of the case were such that in his opinion made it necessary to issue a proclamation forthwith. Shepstone then travelled to neighbouring Natal where he made secret plans for the annexation of the Transvaal. He delayed his plans for several months while he waited for the revised authority from London to reach him; he also reflected on his good relationship with King Cetshwayo and pondered the implications of the proposed annexation on the Zulu king.

By early 1877 relationships between the Zulus and Boers deteriorated still further as Boer trekkers forced their way onto traditional Zulu farmland, displacing the local Zulus by force. Out of sheer frustration at this blatant theft of Zulu grazing land, Cetshwayo decided to attack the Boers and

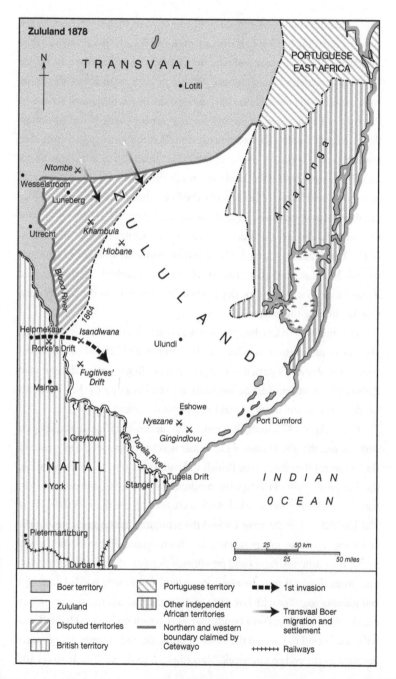

Zululand 1878

N

TRANSVAAL

• Lotiti

PORTUGUESE
EAST AFRICA

Ntombe ✕

Wesselstroom

Luneberg

Utrecht

Khambula ✕

Hlobane ✕

Z
U
L
U
L
A
N
D

A
m
a
t
o
n
g
a

Blood River

1864

Helpmekaar

Rorke's Drift ✕

Isandlwana ✕

Ulundi •

Fugitives'
Drift ✕

Msinga •

Eshowe •

Nyezane ✕

Gingindlovu ✕

Port Durnford •

Greytown •

Tugela River

NATAL

York •

Tugela Drift

Stanger •

INDIAN

OCEAN

Pietermaritzburg •

| 0 | 25 | 50 km |
| 0 | 25 | 50 miles |

Durban •

	Boer territory		Portuguese territory	■■■▶	1st invasion
	Zululand		Other independent African territories	➔	Transvaal Boer migration and settlement
	Disputed territories		Northern and western boundary claimed by Cetewayo		
	British territory			+++++	Railways

27

openly sent his combined impis, amounting to over 30,000 warriors, to the Boers' Transvaal border. It is documented in official British records that there was already intense political activity between Shepstone and King Cetshwayo to defuse the situation.[4] With only days to go before the Zulus were expected to launch their attack against the Boers, Shepstone arrived in Pretoria with an escort of twenty-four members of the Natal Mounted Police together with eight administrators. It is therefore highly probable that Shepstone was fully aware of the Zulus' intention to attack the Boers and that they were poised ready to attack the Transvaal. Shepstone certainly used this knowledge to terrify the Boer leaders into agreeing to succumb to British rule and its concomitant protection. However, before Cetshwayo could give the order to attack, the principle of British annexation of the Transvaal was agreed. Shepstone immediately ordered Cetshwayo to withdraw his army; Cetshwayo reluctantly complied. To this day, the Zulus believe that Shepstone duped them into massing on the Boer border, thus facilitating the annexation.

The intention of Cetshwayo to make an attack on the Transvaal, in the absence of annexation, is evidenced by a number of official British documents: Cetshwayo's patience with the Boers' illegal encroachment into Zululand ran out and he accordingly moved his army to the Transvaal border with the intention of making a punitive strike.[5]

On 12 April 1877, using the excuse of an impending Zulu attack, coupled with the fact that the Transvaal exchequer was bankrupt, Shepstone annexed the Transvaal Republic to the British Crown. At the time of the annexation, the debentures debt of the republic amounted to £156,883, the national debt was £138,238 and the salaried staffs were owed more than £3,000. There was less than £1 in the treasury and the republic's banknotes were rapidly becoming worthless. In representing the British Crown, Shepstone was viewed by the Boer administrators and pro-British element of Pretoria as their saviour from financial ruin; he also represented desperately needed commercial stability together with law and order. Credit and commerce were immediately restored, the railway bonds that were worth nothing in Holland rose with one bound to par and the value of domestic and commercial property doubled by the end of that week. Nevertheless, while the Boer bankers and tradesmen accepted the agreement with relief, annexation was not a popular move with the Boer people. In years to come they would once again simmer with discontent under British rule, but only until after the coming Zulu War when they would rebel with ferocity against the British Crown in a series of vicious Anglo–Boer Wars.

At home, the government was well aware of the effect of the annexation on British relations with the Zulus. A Colonial Office confidential memo, No. 164, states:

> It will be urged in Parliament that the present difficulty with the Zulus, and the necessity (if necessity there was) of coercing them, are due to the annexation of the Transvaal Republic by Sir Theophilus Shepstone on the 12th of April 1877, without the consent of the Republican Government, a step which, though not perhaps contemplated by the Government at home, was ratified and approved by the Secretary of State on behalf of the Government in a despatch, dated 21st June 1877. (Blue Books C–1883)

With the Transvaal now constitutionally annexed to the Crown, British support for the Zulus began to wane. Likewise, by annexing the Transvaal, Britain destroyed the very motive that formally prompted Cetshwayo to be Britain's friend, namely, his desire to play the British off against the Boers. Within days of the annexation it was widely realized that Britain had inadvertently assumed responsibility for the long-running border conflict between the numerous Boer settlers and Zulu farmers. Boer citizens were now legally British subjects and they were quick to demand that the British authorities should act offensively on their behalf. Faced with the deteriorating situation between the Boers and Zulus, the British allied themselves with the Boers and ordered King Cetshwayo to abandon his claim to the 'disputed territory'. The Zulu king was distressed by the British action; he had naively believed that British annexation of the Transvaal would protect Zululand from further Boer settlement. He had poignantly written to Shepstone: 'I am glad to know now that the Transvaal is English ground; perhaps now there may be rest'.

On the contrary, there was to be no rest and it was not long before the Boers took advantage of the situation. In early 1878 a number of Boer and displaced native settlers joined those Boer families already occupying the area directly to the north of Rorke's Drift. The Zulus especially prized this well-watered land for its winter grazing, especially after the serious droughts of 1877 and 1878. It was clear that King Cetshwayo would not accept the increasing flow of settlers and time was running out for the British: urgent action was required.

The British High Commissioner to South Africa, Sir Bartle Frere, had previously been a highly respected Governor of Bombay and he had long since come to the conclusion that the Zulus were a threat and should be absorbed by confederation, at least as a British protectorate and by war if necessary. Direction from the British government was weak and Frere was given a free hand to use his initiative. Frere's communications with the British Colonial Secretary, Sir Michael Hicks Beach (who had succeeded Lord Carnarvon), were vague and led the Colonial Secretary to believe Frere would solve any problems without recourse to military action. This situation is understandable as Britain was on the verge of war in Afghanistan and the long-running series of frontier wars against the Xhosa people around the South African Cape were finally coming to an end, due in no small part to the determination and skill of the British military commander, Lord Chelmsford. A memorandum in July of 1878 from Chelmsford to the Duke of Cambridge at the War Office should have alerted the British government to the threat of war against the Zulus. He wrote: 'It is more than probable that active steps will have to be taken to check the arrogance of Cetywayo, Chief of the Zulus'.

Frere believed that war against the Zulus was the sole solution to a number of problems he faced before South Africa was united. Defeating the Zulus, Frere reasoned, would be an easy task for the British. A quick victory would intimidate the black population into accepting white domination, and remind the Boers that British military rule was not to be challenged. It would also reassure the Boer and settler communities that they would be secure and prosperous under British rule, but Frere needed time to allow Chelmsford to concentrate his troops around Zululand. Frere's civilian administrator, Sir Henry Bulwer, was greatly alarmed by Frere's quest for war: he argued that military action would severely damage Britain's reputation, antagonize the neighbouring black nations and damage the colony's economic foundation. Bulwer proposed an independent commission to examine the border issue. Frere concurred in the belief that such a Boundary Commission would neatly defer the settler problem by adjudicating, once and for all, on title to the disputed territory. The proposal was submitted to Cetshwayo who immediately agreed; his reply shows his grasp of the subtleties of British diplomacy:

> Before sending for people across the sea for the settlement of the boundary, Cetywayo would be glad if the Governor of Natal would send his representatives to see what the claims of Cetywayo are, and to hear what he says, and to hear what others say, and if these cannot come to an understanding on the matter, then a letter can be sent across the sea for other people to see what can be done.

All parties generally agreed the notion of a Commission; the principal members consisted of Michael Gallwey, a barrister who, although only 31, had become the Attorney-General of Natal in 1857; Lieutenant Colonel Anthony Durnford RE, a distinguished and experienced army officer who had served in South Africa for many years and who represented the military; and John Shepstone, brother and deputy of the Secretary for Native Affairs. The local Boers were represented by Piet Uys, a farmer who had lost several relatives in skirmishes with the Zulus; Adrian Rudolph, the Boer Landdrost of Utrecht; and Henrique Shepstone who served on his father's staff in Pretoria. King Cetshwayo was fully consulted; he was also invited to send some of his advisors to attend the Commission and local Zulu chiefs would be permitted to submit evidence. Confident of his people's case and in the appointed officials, Cetshwayo readily agreed to abide by the Commission's decision. The actual terms of the Commission were laid down in a letter of instruction to the Commissioners, who were to report on the matter of the disputed border and make recommendations, as they deemed advisable to settle the dispute.[6]

Sub-Inspector Campbell and a troop of the Natal Mounted Police escorted the members of the Commission to the nominated venue of Rorke's Drift. The location was ideal, being situated on one of the few crossing points on the Buffalo river that formed the largely unmapped border of Natal with Zululand. It was also just within the disputed territory, making the venue easily accessible to witnesses from both sides. The Commission was provided with eighteen marquees and accommodation tents together with the necessary staff of cooks, servants, scribes and guards, over which the British flag was flown.

The Commission sat for nearly five weeks during which time they considered voluminous verbal and written representations; it was a difficult task because each Boer claim resulted in a Zulu counterclaim. The Boer cause was weakened as their legal case relied on documents that were either unsigned or blatantly fraudulent. Boundaries claimed by the Boers were frequently hand-drawn onto maps, and no two maps concurred. In the final analysis the Commission focused upon two main issues: who owned the land prior to the dispute and whether any land under dispute had been properly purchased or ceded. The Commission also noted that it had long been Boer policy, if policy it may be called, gradually to force the Zulus from their rich pasturelands. The Commissioners concluded:

> that no cession of territory was ever made by the Zulu people, and that even had such a cession been made by either Panda [Mpande] or Cetywayo it would have been null and void, unless confirmed by the voice of the nation according to the custom of the Zulus.

The Commissioners held that the Boers never acquired and the Zulus never lost dominion over the disputed territory, and that the disputed territory was still properly a portion of Zululand and, furthermore, the developing Boer settlement at Utrecht must also be surrendered. The Boundary Commission eventually delivered their unexpected verdict in July 1878 to an astonished Sir Bartle Frere who determinedly sought to coerce the Commissioners to amend their findings, without success.

On 24 June Durnford had written home: 'I think our views will be maintained – at least I hope so. You see we have gone in for fair play'.

Although the Commission's findings were not legally binding, Frere was nevertheless devastated by the result; again, he secretly sought to have the Commissioners' findings modified, again without success. Realizing his prime reason for the invasion of Zululand had been annulled by the Commission, he decided to ignore the findings and keep the decision secret so as to allow Lord Chelmsford time to prepare and mass his troops ready for battle. In the meantime another reason for the invasion of Zululand had to be found. Frere requested the British Government to send massive military reinforcements but his request was refused. Hicks Beach made matters worse for Frere by sending him a dispatch that stated: 'All the information that has hitherto reached them [Parliament] with respect to Zululand appears to them to justify a confident hope that by the exercise of prudence, and by meeting the Zulus in a spirit of forbearance and reasonable compromise, it will be possible to avert the very serious evil of a war with Cetshwayo'. Clearly, Frere had been warned off declaring war on the Zulus.

Frere would also have known that he was now acting illegally. As recently as the Ashanti War Britain had found itself in a remarkably similar 'ultimatum' situation when its Gold Coast Governor unilaterally threatened war. The response of the Home Government was unambiguous and stated that the principle of military proceedings:

> … should be that of defence and not aggression. It is upon this principle alone that the Governors are authorized to make war, and no invasion of neighbouring territories can be sanctioned unless it can be shown that it is really a defensive measure, safer, and less costly in blood and money, and more likely to be decisive in its results, than waiting for an attack that is being prepared, and which no measure can ward off without loss of that position and dignity which are essential to our security.
> (Hansard 27 March 1879)

Furthermore, Frere would have been fully aware of Regulation 35 of the Colonial Service, which stated that Governors of Colonies are ordinarily expected to confine themselves to the internal government of their colony, and distinctly forbids them to proclaim war against foreign states. It reads:

General Powers of an Officer appointed to conduct a Colonial government.
He is not to declare or make war against any foreign state, or against the

subjects of any foreign state. Aggression he must at all times repel to the
best of his ability.
(Functions and duties of High Commissioner. C–2242)

Unable to alter the results of the Boundary Commission, Frere knew
that he could not delay the publication of the Commission's findings beyond
a few months. He was also aware that the eventual publication of the findings would seriously antagonize the Boers; worse still, there was every like-
lihood that the Boers would be required to surrender their farms in Zululand.
Frere realized that the Boers might retaliate by taking military action against
British-controlled Natal. From his days in India, Frere also knew only too
well that at a time when Britain faced war in Afghanistan, Russia would
be watching events in South Africa. If Russia detected any British weakness, there was the distinct possibility that Russian warships would arrive off
the Cape and sever Britain's supply line to India and beyond; Frere had to act
decisively.

On 28 July a minor incident occurred which Frere used to generate
widespread anti-Zulu sentiment. Two of Chief Sihayo's sons crossed the
river into Natal to capture two of their father's adulterous wives. One wife
was duly returned across the border at Rorke's Drift and clubbed to death
in sight of the Mission Station. The following day the second wife was
recovered and suffered the same fate. Adultery in Zululand was a serious
offence against Zulu tradition, especially when committed by the wives of
an important chief, and the punishment for being caught was invariably
instant death. This situation was widely accepted by the Zulus and, prior to
current times, would have been ignored by the British on the grounds that
matters within Zululand were outside their jurisdiction. On this occasion the
incident received officially orchestrated publicity throughout Natal in order
to inflame public opinion against Cetshwayo. On 9 October a further incident occurred; a local chief of Swazi origin, Mbilini, led his warriors through
the Pongola valley in the very area under dispute. Immigrant Boers and
local natives were attacked and their herds of cattle were driven off. This
action played straight into Frere's hands; he was already preparing the terms
of an ultimatum and he secretly made Mbilini's raid the third item in the
ultimatum.

Frere and Shepstone both encouraged the press to promulgate the belief that Cetshwayo possessed a standing army of 50,000 warriors, which was poised to invade the developing British colony of Natal and its principal towns of Pietermaritzburg and Durban. The civilian population was encouraged to believe that a quick campaign was all that was needed; after all, the British Army had wide experience gained during several years of suppressing native insurrections. King Cetshwayo would quickly be defeated and obliged to understand that Queen Victoria ruled all of Africa and, furthermore, relationships between the British and Boer communities could be mended – all this could be achieved once the Zulu army which 'threatened' both white communities was defeated.

The Ultimatum

Frere reasoned that a British invasion of Zululand would solve the majority of the growing 'problems' relating to Zululand. Not only would the defeat of the Zulu army facilitate confederation, it would also placate the argumentative Boers and a display of British military might would deter other Bantu-speaking nations from hindering Britain's territorial and commercial expansion. Defeat of the Zulu army would also eliminate the long-standing threat to Natal while at the same time freeing the Zulu men to work for both British and Boer commercial ventures. Frere ordered his General Commanding British Forces in South Africa, Sir Frederic Thesiger (shortly to become Lord Chelmsford), to prepare his forces secretly for an immediate and brief war against the Zulus. Both men were fully aware that success on the battlefield, even a quick and easy result, would bring them considerable personal success. Frere had enjoyed a truly glittering career and another success could advance his position even further. Chelmsford was already secure in every respect but he remained a relatively poor man; he was popular, both with his men and his Queen. Chelmsford knew that a victory would enable him to return home with even greater glory and acclaim. Frere knew that to achieve his objectives, war against the Zulus was necessary. He accordingly decided to deal with the Boundary Commission's findings by initiating a policy of inactivity; the files were placed in a locked drawer and even his staff officers were not permitted to discuss the subject.

Frere forwarded a new request for troop reinforcements to protect Natal and those Boer families still within the disputed area; the request went to Sir Michael Hicks Beach. Frere also sent a short dispatch to the home government in which he stated that he would make 'certain demands' of the Zulu king. Curiously, the last four points of the ultimatum served on Cetshwayo were omitted from Frere's dispatch. Sent on 13 November, this dispatch did not reach Hicks Beach until 2 January; neither did it specify the nature of the demands. Frere justified his troop request and 'demands' in two short paragraphs:

> Zululand is surrounded landward by the territory of the British Government or its allies. They are all peaceful, non-aggressive people, and would never interfere with Cetywayo, nor attempt to harm him or his subjects, unless Cetywayo first meddled with them, but whilst he keeps up a large standing army, useless for all but purposes of tyranny or aggression, it is quite impossible for his peaceful neighbours to feel secure. The English Government is forced to keep large numbers of her Majesty's troops in Natal and the Transvaal, and even then the people do not feel secure that Cetywayo will not attack them to 'wash his spears'.
>
> It is, therefore, absolutely necessary for the peace and quiet of Natal or the Transvaal that Cetywayo should alter his military system, and reduce the size of his army to such dimensions as shall be considered by the Great Council of Zulus and the British Government sufficient to secure the internal peace of the country.[7]

The average time taken for a return message to travel between London and Natal was six weeks; Frere therefore knew that Hicks Beach's official reply could not reach him before his British troops invaded Zululand. Likewise, the home government would remain in the dark about the ultimatum and Frere's intentions until 25 January 1879, three days after the invasion of Zululand by Chelmsford's invasion force. The War Office and numerous politicians would later protest that Frere's primary purpose of his journey to Natal was solely to arbitrate on the boundary dispute under the instructions of the Secretary of State; he had no authority to wage war. Meanwhile, on 11 December 1878, Zulu representatives were summoned to the site of a shady tree on the Natal bank of the Tugela river to learn the result of the Boundary Commission's deliberations. Cetshwayo sent three of his senior generals together with eleven chieftains and their retainers to listen to the findings, which were interpreted by Mr Fynney, a Border Agent and Zulu-speaker. John Shepstone, brother and deputy of the Secretary for Native Affairs, Sir Theophilus Shepstone, was appointed to announce the findings on behalf of Britain. John Shepstone was a curious choice, as the Zulus knew he was one of the Boers' representatives during the Boundary Commission's deliberations. He was also despised by the Zulus for having once led a party which tracked down a wanted Zulu chief, Matyana; Shepstone had arranged a truce with Matyana's followers but on meeting Matyana, Shepstone drew a hidden revolver and shot the chief causing him a minor wound. Matyana escaped and John Shepstone's reputation with the Zulus was lost for ever.

During the morning session, the findings of the Boundary Commission were relayed to the Zulu officials but in heavily worded terms designed to cause confusion. Writing was unknown to the Zulus, who were accomplished at memorizing even lengthy speeches. Nevertheless the Zulus realized they had 'won their case' and were well satisfied with the final judgement that defined the Blood and Pongola rivers as the border between Zululand and the Transvaal. Any Zulus located on the Transvaal side of the new border, who might wish to move back into Zululand, and British or Boer subjects located on the Zulu side wishing to move back across the border, would be permitted to do so, in peace, and with compensation where 'circumstances warranted the expenditure'. At midday the Zulu dignitaries were invited to remain for a lunch of roast beef and their favourite sugar-water as a prelude to a further 'short announcement'. This was to be Frere's ultimatum; worded in such terms that it would be impossible for Cetshwayo to accept. Frere knew the ultimatum would render the Boundary Commission's report obsolete and Cetshwayo's non-compliance would justify his war against the Zulus.

When the time came for the announcement, both groups reassembled and the content of the hitherto secret ultimatum was then read to the astonished Zulus, translated again by Mr Fynney. In customary style the Zulus listened impassively, until in the midst of the proceedings the noted Durban photographer, Mr James Lloyd, took their photograph, when they became agitated by the intrusion.

The main requirements of the ultimatum included:

1   The surrender of Chief Sihayo's brother and two sons (for crossing the river border into Natal, abducting and then murdering two of Sihayo's adulterous wives) to the Natal Government plus a fine of 500 cattle for not complying with the original order for their surrender, made in August 1878.

2   A fine of 100 cattle for having hustled and insulted two British surveyors, Deighton and Smith, at the Middle Drift border crossing.

3   The surrender to the Transvaal Courts of the Swazi chief, Mbilini, (for cattle raiding in the (now) British territory).

4   That the king should observe promises made by him at his coronation to the British Government. These promises were:
    i   Indiscriminate executions should cease.
    ii   No Zulu should be condemned without open trial and the public examination of witnesses, for and against, and there should be a right of appeal to the king.
    iii   No Zulu's life should be taken without the previous knowledge and consent of the king, after a trial and after the right of appeal to the king.
    iv   That for minor crimes, the loss of property should be substituted for the death penalty.
    v   A number of prominent Zulus were to be surrendered for trial (no names were specified).

5   The Zulu army was to disband and every Zulu was to be free to marry [see p. 61 for Zulu controls on marriage].

6   A British resident official was to oversee Zulu affairs.

7   Missionaries were to be readmitted to Zululand without let or hindrance. Any dispute involving a European was to be dealt with under British jurisdiction.

Having respectfully listened to the ultimatum, the Zulu deputation then expressed their horror at the terms. They were united in their protest that Cetshwayo had never given any such assurances but Shepstone stifled their protests. The Zulus requested an extension of the deadline but this was also refused. By the middle of the afternoon, Shepstone drew the meeting to a close and the perplexed Zulus were ferried back across the Tugela to take the terms of the ultimatum to Cetshwayo. A local white trader, John Dunn, managed to obtain a copy of the ultimatum and, being on good terms with Cetshwayo, sent a copy directly to the king. There followed a succession of futile attempts by the Zulus to placate the British, all to no avail.

Cetshwayo sent a letter denying that he had broken any vows; interestingly, the letter was not made public until after the invasion of Zululand. Cetshwayo wrote:

> Did I ever tell Mr Shepstone I would not kill? Did he tell the white people I had made such an arrangement? If he did, he has deceived them. I do kill, but do not consider that I have done anything yet in that way. Why do the white people start at nothing? I have not yet begun. I have yet to kill. It is the custom of our nation and I shall not depart from it. Why does the Government of Natal speak to me about my laws? Do I go to Natal and dictate to him [Shepstone] about his laws?
>
> I shall not agree to any laws or rules from Natal, and by so doing throw the large kraal, which I govern, into the water.
>
> My people will not listen unless they are killed; and while wishing to be friends with the English, I do not agree to give my people over to be governed by laws sent to me by them.
>
> Have I not asked the English to allow me to wash my spears since the death of my father Mpande? And they have kept playing with me all the time, treating me like a child.
>
> Go back and tell the English that I shall now act on my own account, and if they wish me to agree to their laws, I shall leave and become a wanderer, but, before I go it will be seen, as I shall not go without having acted.
>
> Go back and tell the white men this, and let them hear it well. The Government of Natal and I are equal. He is the Governor of Natal and I am the governor here.

Frere would have realized that this poignant but angry letter was a virtual declaration that Cetshwayo would fight a defensive war if Zululand were attacked.

The ultimatum posed serious problems for both the British government at home and the Zulu king. The British government, still not aware of the full terms of the ultimatum, had to be content with awaiting news of the outcome of events. Cetshwayo responded by sending conciliatory messages to Sir Bartle Frere while he reluctantly prepared his army to oppose British troops now massing along his border. Yet, for Cetshwayo, the time was opportune; the whole Zulu army was shortly due to assemble at Cetshwayo's royal homestead at Nodwengu, near Ulundi, for the *umKhosi*, the annual festival of first fruits. With the Zulu warriors already preparing to travel to the event, a further instruction was issued for the warriors to attend, not to celebrate a festival, but with their arms and shields ready to defend their country. Lord Chelmsford had not appointed an intelligence officer to his staff; seeing no need for such an appointment, the omission unfortunately resulted in the expiry of the ultimatum and the invasion of Zululand both coinciding with the one occasion in the year when the whole Zulu army would be assembled before Cetshwayo at Ulundi. Just three days before the British ultimatum was due to expire, each regiment in turn began the process of being 'doctored' for war by special war-doctors who administered potions (*muti*) to make the warriors believe they would be bullet proof, or would rapidly heal in the unlikely event of sustaining injury.

Zulu accounts reveal that Cetshwayo was genuinely distressed by the prospect of war; after all, the Zulus had been faithful allies of the British for many years and had not engaged in warfare during the previous twenty-two years since the battle of Ndondakusuka, although they were, nevertheless, highly trained. In the final weeks leading up to the British invasion Cetshwayo sent no fewer than six pleas for more time to be given. The British received his final request on 11 January; the reply was curt – Cetshwayo should contact Lieutenant General Lord Chelmsford, whose forces were already invading Zululand. Cetshwayo responded by addressing his army with the words:

I am sending you out against the whites, who have invaded Zululand and driven away our cattle. You are to go against the column at Rorke's Drift and drive it back into Natal, and if the state of the river will allow, follow it up through Natal right up to the Drakensberg. You will attack by daylight as there are enough of you to eat it up, and you will march slowly so as not to tire yourselves.[8]

The Zulus' determination to defend their country was to produce the most unexpected result. From this point onwards the news from South Africa was to dominate the British press. Curiously, the Swedish government had realized the outcome of the coming conflict was not a foregone conclusion; prior to the ultimatum, the British Foreign Office had received an application from the Swedish government asking 'that steps might be taken to afford protection in the event of a Zulu war to the Mission Station at Rorke's Drift'. Apparently the Swedish government's dispatch was not considered worthy as no reply was sent or considered necessary; it was merely noted internally.[9]

As far as the white population of Natal was concerned, the rumblings of war meant little to them other than an opportunity of making profit by supplying the British Army. With Christmas coming, life in Natal proceeded as normal; the possibility of war with the Zulus did not unduly concern the civilian population who were more interested in the coming festivities and the price of their market commodities. Both towns were prospering from the influx of the military that consumed vast quantities of provisions. Several new buildings in both Durban and Pietermaritzburg had second floors, which reflected the colony's new wealth, and their shops and stores were well provisioned. Good beef could be obtained for 5d. per pound, lamb for 6d., sugar 4d., and coffee 1s. 4d. There was plenty of Christmas fare specially imported from Europe and most popular were English hams and bacon, Stilton cheese and a variety of sherries and champagne. Private houses were decorated with local ferns, flowers and lilies. The social scene thrived with concerts, theatres and music halls all well attended. All transactions were in British coinage – sovereigns and half-sovereigns, crowns and half-crowns, florins, shillings, fourpenny and threepenny bits, copper pence, halfpence and farthings.

These two towns each had a small hospital to cater for their growing populations, people who generally regarded the function of such places as purely to receive dead and dying people. Illness and injury were much dreaded, patent medicines known as 'cure-alls' being all that was available to the population. Better-off families usually owned a medicine chest complete with a book of instructions and phials of lotions and potions for every known ailment. The Zulu War would bring a flood of British medical teams to Natal, and the women of Natal who generously assisted with nursing the military sick and wounded would likewise quickly gain their expertise.

CHAPTER 1

The Invaders of Zululand

For a shilling a day.

During the reign of Queen Victoria, there were more than enough recruits to make conscription unnecessary and taking the queen's shilling, and all it stood for, was a legally binding contract between the recruit and the army. Recruiting sergeants knew where to find hungry and unemployed young men and consequently frequented the public houses and taverns where they collected, although any recruit who could be proved to have been drunk at the time of his 'enlistment' could be released from the commitment on payment of £1. Recruits were normally 'sworn in' within twenty-four hours before being medically examined and posted to a regiment or to join a draft being sent abroad. Most young men joined the army to escape unemployment, poverty and wretched squalor. Many were initially unfit or suffering from poor physique due to the ravages of illness and disease that swept the civilian population of the time; tuberculosis, cholera, influenza, whooping cough, scarlet fever, measles, syphilis and a variety of lesser infectious diseases were rife. The life expectancy of the working classes was as low as 38 years – with only the well-off having any hope of reaching their mid-fifties. The average height of an army recruit had fallen over the previous ten years to a skinny 5ft 4in and yet, in spite of their poor physical condition, several weeks of sustained military training usually sufficed to transform the recruits into competent soldiers. A comparison of contemporary statistics reveals that in 1869 there were 12,000 recruits to the army with 3,341 desertions, or 27 per cent. In 1878 the recruits numbered 28,325 and the desertions 5,400, or 19 per cent. Despite these figures, the British soldiers about to face Cetshwayo's Zulus were resilient fellows hardened by the African weather and by six years' constant campaigning, although most had little or no idea why they would be fighting the Zulus. They amused themselves with a variety of sports such as wrestling and spear throwing and soldiers with less than fifteen years' service were expected to undertake three half-mile runs each week. At first sight a soldier's pay appeared to be reasonable, but from the daily shilling, official deductions ensured his continued poverty. A married soldier could have maintenance deducted from his wages and paid to his wife or family though no official help, other than charity, was available to the widow of a soldier killed in action, or who died of disease on campaign. It was not until after 1881 that any form of widow's benefit became payable.

Letters from soldiers in the Zulu War tended to concentrate on worries about their families and friends rather than the conditions they were experiencing in Africa. At the time of the invasion of Zululand their life centred on staying dry and comfortable, a difficult task during the heavy thunderstorms of the four-month rainy season. The older and more experienced soldiers knew how to look after themselves and their equipment; they knew to sleep among rocks rather than on the damp ground to keep clean and dry, to dry out their wet kit when the sun shone and to swill out their boots daily with their own urine to fight athlete's foot. Preventative medicine as such was not knowingly practised and so dysentery, enteric fever and tuberculosis all took their relentless toll, especially when the soldiers were coughing and spitting in squalid and overcrowded conditions. Close contact with infected animals and drinking contaminated milk resulted in tuberculosis spreading rapidly among the soldiers while the common practice of drawing drinking water from the same source used by animals and local people spread enteric fever. Likewise, it was not realized until after the war that sick oxen and dying Zulus tended to make for water; the many decomposing carcasses polluted the watercourses, but unfortunately this was ignored by water-collecting parties.

Disease was one problem, staying out of trouble was another; most soldiers quickly learned to obey every order instantly as flogging was still regularly practised. Of the 12,000 soldiers who took part in the two invasions of Zululand, 545 were flogged between 11 January and 4 July 1879; the standard punishment for insubordination or similar minor offences was twenty-five lashes, sleeping on duty or theft merited fifty lashes. It appears from their letters that soldiers accepted the necessity of corporal punishment though a number described it as 'a sorry sight'. Following furious protests in the British press, flogging was eventually banned at the end of 1879, even for active service offences.

The British officers who led their men to Zululand were generally taller and fitter than their men. They usually came from the middle and upper classes and most had purchased their commissions prior to the Cardwell reforms that abolished the purchase system. Most officers enjoyed the benefits of family wealth but on campaign officers were expected to display a high level of fitness, loyalty, team spirit and physical bravery. By the time of the Zulu War many officers had adopted a more paternal attitude towards their men; they were more concerned for their men's welfare and many readily assisted with the vital task of letter writing and reading.

By 1874 communications and trade throughout Natal were so severely hampered by impassable roads, a complete lack of navigable rivers and the absence of a transport system that a government enquiry had taken place to examine the feasibility of creating a unified infrastructure throughout Natal. The enquiry considered developing an integrated rail and road network but, due to a lack of finance, the recommendations of the enquiry were never implemented. The commerce of Natal continued to depend on a network of dirt roads and inaccurate maps; and with regard to neighbouring Zululand, no reliable maps existed as much of the country remained unexplored.

By mid 1878 plans were well advanced for the invasion of Zululand, but one practical problem remained – there was no established system of transport within the British Army. Lord Chelmsford's invasion force would amount to an estimated total of 12,500 fighting men who would need many hundreds of wagons with thousands of oxen, mule carts, mules and horses.

Lord Chelmsford requested the imposition of martial law in order that his army could commandeer all the wagons, oxen and horses needed for the invasion but the civilian Governor of Natal, Sir Henry Bulwer, refused the request. The officer in charge of supplies, Commissary General Strickland, had a peacetime establishment of twenty junior officers and thirty men under his command, a woefully inadequate staff for such an enormous undertaking. Chelmsford quickly realized his invasion could not take place without sufficient transport and appointed a Board, under Colonel Sir Evelyn Wood, to advise him. Chelmsford telegraphed the War Office for an urgent draft of experienced captains to be sent to Natal to supplement the commissariat; he then ordered the unopened railway line that was still under construction from Durban to Pietermaritzburg to be made available. While the commissariat pondered the merit of purchase as an alternative to the hire of transport, Chelmsford ordered the purchase of 200 wagons on the open market. This decision caused a dramatic increase in prices across the country and the army was soon at the mercy of speculative contractors. Chelmsford had even less luck with oxen and horses as Natal had only recently come through a two-year drought and healthy animals were already being traded at a premium. Horses in poor condition, that would previously have sold for as little as £2 each, were being traded for £40 while oxen could only be hired at exorbitant rates, but not purchased as the owners realized they could levy monthly hire charges that were in excess of the animals' true value.[1]

Without the imposition of martial law to control prices, the cost of mounting the invasion soared by the day. At last, exasperated and frustrated by the profiteering and lack of progress, Chelmsford took control of the commissariat and immersed himself in the task of resolving the situation. It was to his credit that, within weeks, he brought the situation back under control and had established an effective commissariat team under Commissary General Strickland, shortly to be reinforced by the specially drafted officers now en route from England. The Commissariat and Transport Department was still a young department of the army, having come into existence only on 9 December 1875 by royal warrant. Its officers held commissions identical to other army officers although their rank structure set them apart. On operations the senior officer was the commissary general; his deputy held the equivalent rank to a lieutenant colonel, a commissary as a major, a deputy commissary to a captain and an assistant commissary to a lieutenant. Sadly, other officers in the British Army looked down on their commissary brothers; even Wolseley wrote that 'to rely upon a Commissariat officer is to be destroyed, and so it must always be until the Commissariat men are gentlemen, or at least as much gentlemen as the average British Officer'. At Rorke's Drift, Commissary officers were shortly to prove they were more than an equal match for their brother officers.

Within the regiments and units preparing for the invasion, Chelmsford ordered each unit to appoint its own officers of transport to assist the commissariat. These officers were required to coordinate and take responsibility for their unit's transport requirements, assisted by a sub-conductor for every ten wagons. The total number of wagons allocated per infantry battalion amounted to seventeen, including one HQ (Headquarters) wagon; a battery of artillery had ten wagons and a squadron of mounted infantry had four. The overall responsibility for transport fell on the appointed transport officer, one per invading column. By September Chelmsford had created an effective and efficient supply system and advanced planning for the invasion was finalized. Fate then intervened; the two-year drought suddenly came to an end with incessant torrential rain and, within a matter of days, the dusty rutted tracks of Natal had become impassable quagmires.

It soon became obvious to Chelmsford that his plan for five invasion columns was totally impracticable; there were simply not enough wagons to carry the necessary stores. The list of stores was enormous and wide-ranging; it included tents, ammunition, cooking equipment, mobile hospitals and medicines, tools, spare boots and uniforms and food for the whole campaign. Chelmsford wisely decided to reduce the number of invasion columns from five to three, and also instructed that a series of supply depots be established at intervals along each column's line of march; the column could then be 'drip-fed' on a daily basis from the nearest depot. For the Centre Column, which Chelmsford would accompany, depots were prepared and stocked with one month's supplies at Helpmekaar and Rorke's Drift. By 11 January when the invasion commenced, Chelmsford was satisfied that he had enough stores in place to sustain his columns; each could theoretically carry fifteen days' supplies enabling them to move at 10 miles per day. Chelmsford had achieved an apparently impossible task.

The average soldier was probably unaware of all the administrative arrangements necessary for him to fight the Zulus; he was probably more concerned with the availability of his daily rations and bottled beer. His daily entitlement was a minimum of 1 pound of fresh meat, 1.5 pounds of fresh bread or its equivalent in biscuits, plus fresh vegetables and fruit or lime juice and sugar in lieu; this regulatory ration allowance gives an indication of the logistical planning necessary just to feed the 12,500 strong invasion force.

Chelmsford's invasion date in early January 1879 was carefully chosen; the timing would interfere with the Zulu harvest and demoralize the Zulu population unable to gather their crops. Chelmsford was advised that from January onwards the rivers forming the Natal boundary with Zululand would be in full flood and create a natural defence for Natal against Zulu attacks. The recent rains would also provide natural grazing for the invasion force's numerous oxen and horses, the absence of which precluded invading during the later dry season.

Both Frere and Chelmsford fully expected a rapid defeat of the Zulu army. The British and Colonial officers and their troops were all experienced in African warfare and Chelmsford's main fear was that the Zulus would not fight – although he had been warned by Boer leaders, remembering their own defeats at the hands of the Zulus, that he faced a powerful adversary. He realzed his columns would be vulnerable to sudden attacks and he accordingly ordered a high state of readiness to be observed during the advance; overnight, every camp must be laagered ready to resist attack. In planning his strategy, Chelmsford had to leave the border of Natal virtually unprotected while the columns advanced into Zululand. He reasoned that by an advance on Ulundi in a three-pronged attack, the Zulus would be forced to attack one or all invading columns rather than Natal; he also reasoned that the simultaneous advance would force Cetshwayo to commit all his *amabutho* (regiments), leaving him without reserves. Orders were given for every Zulu homestead and food store in the path of the invasion force to be destroyed; this laying waste would systematically remove supplies from any Zulu force, and it would break the will of the Zulu people[2] and provoke their army into attacking Chelmsford. And when they attacked, they would be no match for his calm and experienced troops with their sophisticated firepower. Well-aimed rifle volley fire supported by rockets, artillery and Gatling guns would, in Chelmsford's opinion, ensure the swift defeat of such an unsophisticated adversary. He accordingly gave priority to the implementation of regulations relating to the availability of ammunition. Each artillery battery of two guns carried sixty-eight rounds together with twelve rockets and additional reserves were to be readily available in accompanying carts and wagons. Rifle ammunition was calculated at 270 rounds per soldier, 70 in the possession of each man and 200 rounds in easily recognized colour-coded ammunition wagons. All column commanders had received written instructions that 'a commanding officer would incur a heavy responsibility should required supplies fail to arrive in time, through any want of foresight and arrangement on his part'.

During October Chelmsford undertook a tour of inspection of the proposed route to be taken by the Centre Column to the Zulu border. He rode from Greytown to Helpmekaar and then down the escarpment overlooking the Zulu border to the Drift itself. He noted that there were two routes from Helpmekaar, a 'good one which makes a wide detour and may be considered as two days' march distant' (the modern road today), 'and a bad one which takes a direct line, and could easily be accomplished in one day'. Chelmsford gave orders for the 'bad road' to be improved 'as its importance for both offence and defence, would be very great.' From his meeting with local people along the route, he became so convinced that the Zulus would shrink from his force that he also considered the establishment of camps to deal with Zulu refugees. By November the store depot at Helpmekaar was sufficiently stocked that supplies for the front line could begin to be forwarded to the advance supply depot at Rorke's Drift.

Everyone settled down to await the expiry of the ultimatum, and in order to retain harmony within the growing camp it was decreed by commanding officers that sports should be encouraged but all sports involving physical contact were temporarily banned from Christmas Day onwards. In reporting the ban, the *Natal Witness* reporter wrote from Helpmekaar on 1 January:

> At sports, as is not unusual, disputes arise, and partisanship will be demonstrative; the consequences might be a quarrel, which under the present circumstances for which the forces are collected, would prove a most unhappy and untoward event. If the prohibition of sport is attributed, therefore, to severe military discipline, there is a very good reason and excuse for it.

Harmony was further enhanced with the arrival of the Revd George Smith in his new capacity of military chaplain; he was a huge and bearded man and was formally of the local Estcourt parish. The same reporter wrote of him:

> It is an impressive scene to witness 1,000 warlike men, in various uniforms, form square, and join a robed priest, standing in the centre, with a band of musicians – vocal and instrumental, in the worship of Almighty God. This is one of the greatest civilising influences which the forces could carry with them.

Within a week of the expiry date of the ultimatum on 11 January 1879, the three columns were fully equipped and ready to invade Zululand. The main attacking Centre Column, commanded by Colonel Glyn with 1,600 Europeans and 2,500 natives, had moved down during November from Helpmekaar to Rorke's Drift. Colonel Pearson's Coastal Column consisted of 1,800 Europeans and 2,000 natives and Colonel Wood VC commanded the Northern Column, with 1,700 Europeans and 300 natives. There were two small columns held in reserve: one was commanded by Colonel Rowlands VC just inside the Transvaal border while the other, commanded by Colonel Durnford, was at Middle Drift to protect the Natal border from any Zulu incursion. Theoretically Durnford had a force of 3,000 natives but his actual establishment amounted to only 500, of which half were the élite and very loyal (to Durnford) Natal Native Horse. He also had at his disposal a small rocket battery commanded by Major Russell RA.

On 10 January a general order was read to the patiently waiting troops; the Centre Column was to prepare to strike tents at 3 a.m. the following day, cross the Buffalo river and march into Zululand. At that time, the camp was aroused by the trumpet calls of the different corps to feed their horses, and after a very early breakfast, tents were struck; 'boot and saddle' was sounded followed by 'prepare to mount', and then 'mount and fall in'. By 4 a.m. not a vestige of the cavalry camp could be seen; tents and baggage were all packed on wagons, and each corps was standing in line, formed ready to march. Once under way the trumpet call 'trot' was sounded, and then the stillness of the moonlit scene was broken by that martial sound of activity that only a body of cavalry can make when in rapid motion. The cavalry reached Rorke's Drift as dawn approached and joined the waiting columns of the 24th Regiment.

The main Centre Column of the invasion force was to be spearheaded by the two battalions of the 24th (2nd Warwickshire) Regiment. Both battalions were enthusiastic at the prospect of leading operations against the Zulus and it was a coincidence that both battalions of this regiment were to serve together in the Zulu War. The very experienced 1st Battalion had not seen home service since arriving in South Africa on 4 February 1875 after a series of Mediterranean postings. They were tough and battle-hardened after four years' active campaigning during the Ninth Frontier War at the Cape. The 2nd Battalion, with 24 officers and 849 other ranks, had arrived in South Africa on 28 February 1878 and shortly afterwards commenced their duties at King William's Town. Both battalions were then engaged in quelling small pockets of rebellion throughout the Cape area when news of a threatened Boer insurrection at Kimberley reached Natal. The 1/24th were already battle-hardened and extremely fit; on one occasion, under the command of Colonel Richard Glyn, they were ordered to march the 650 miles to Kimberley. On their arrival the Boers had a change of heart so the regiment promptly marched back to the Cape. This added experience helped to toughen the regiment in preparation for the arduous campaign looming in Natal.

By the middle of 1878 rumours were beginning to spread throughout Natal that King Cetshwayo was threatening to invade Natal; consequently the 2nd Battalion was directed to Pietermaritzburg where they assembled on 6 August 1878. The 1st Battalion was not long in following the 2nd; it had been back at King William's Town about a month when C and D Companies, under Brevet Lieutenant Colonel Henry Pulleine, were also ordered to Pietermaritzburg.

During the operations against the local tribes, neither battalion had sustained significant casualties. Only two officers, Captains Frederick Carrington and Frederick Goodwin-Austen, were wounded, one man was killed and a few wounded, though from disease the loss was higher: eighteen men of the 1st Battalion and twenty-one of the 2nd. General Thesiger (later Lord Chelmsford) spoke in the highest terms of both battalions, emphasizing how well the younger soldiers, of whom the 2/24th was in large measure composed, had come through this severe ordeal of hard work in the face of difficult conditions. Likewise, the soldiers respected Chelmsford, the *Natal Witness* reported (5 January):

> The headquarter staff camp is pitched to the right of all the others, almost in the centre as you walk from one end to the other. The Union Jack flies in front of the tent of the General, and his mule wagons are placed in position behind; otherwise there is nothing to show the difference between it and the other camps. His Excellency is much liked, and sets a good example to the men under him. He rises at daylight, and when on the march assists in striking and pitching his own tent. His manner is exceedingly affable to all, and he seems to have the happy knack of thoroughly understanding at once what is meant to be conveyed to him, although it may be wrapped up either in eloquence or long-windedness. His love of punctuality is well known through the camp, and of course leads to the same system in others.

It was to be the fate of the 1st Battalion and one company of the recently arrived 2nd Battalion to face the Zulu attack at Isandlwana where almost all the men and officers involved would be killed. On the very same day, B Company of the 2nd Battalion would initially suffer the ignominy of being left behind at Rorke's Drift to guard the stores and then, within hours, find themselves facing potentially overwhelming numbers of Zulus seeking to destroy the position.

In addition to the two battalions of the 24th, Chelmsford's main fighting force was to consist of the 90th, and single battalions of the 3rd, 4th, 13th and 99th regiments, with a battalion of the 80th held in reserve at Luneburg. This force amounted to a total of nearly 9,000 professional and well-armed soldiers, with a similar number of native troops, – known disparagingly as the 'untrained untrainables' – divided into seven battalions and led by white officers. To this force were added irregular units based on the quasi-military Natal police together with frontier guards and local defence groups with such grand names as the Natal Horse, Natal Carbineers and Durban Mounted Rifles.

By Christmas everything was ready for the invasion; kit was cleaned and polished, wagons were loaded and the regimental bands rehearsed the stirring themes that would spur on the columns of soldiers as they marched into Zululand. On 6 January 1879, four days before the expiry of the ultimatum, troops of Wood's Northern column began crossing into Zululand. Everyone's fervent hope was that the Zulus would stand and fight.[3]

CHAPTER 2

The Zulus

I have no fears myself that Natal will be overrun by hostile Zulus, but much fear that Zululand should be overrun by hostile Britons.

ANTHONY TROLLOPE

Like the British soldiers, the Zulus had also originally invaded southern Africa. Over several thousand years the Bantu-speaking people spread laterally across central Africa from the equatorial West Coast and slowly progressed south and east around the wastes of the Kalahari desert. One tribe, the *Nguni*, settled the area known today as Natal, probably between 1500 and 1700 AD. The remaining *Xhosa* tribe continued south, eventually reaching the Great Fish River; they were only 500 miles from the Cape, which, unbeknown to them, was in the process of being colonized by the Boers. It is ironic that a migration of such magnitude and over such a long span of time should have failed to reach the Cape and that Europeans should fill that vacuum at exactly the same point in time.

An insignificantly small group of Nguni people lived near the coast on the banks of the White Mfolozi river. Their chief, named *Zulu*, was succeeded by his two brothers who then gave way to Senzangakona. At the same time the Xhosa first came into conflict with the Boers at the Battle of Kaffirkop. During this embryonic stage of their development the group adopted the title 'Zulu' and had grown in size to well over 1,000. Around 1787 Senzangakona fathered the child of a neighbouring *eLangeni* chief's

54

daughter, Nandi. Senzangakona reluctantly appointed Nandi as his unofficial third wife but refused to recognize her son *Shaka*. In due course Nandi and her children were evicted back to the unwelcoming eLangeni who treated the family as outcasts.

In 1802 the whole land was suffering widespread famine; nevertheless the eLangeni banished the luckless family into destitution. Nandi fled to the *Qwabe* clan where she had once given birth to a son by a Qwabe warrior named Gendeyana. Under Gendeyana's patronage the family again received shelter and the young Shaka developed into such a skilled warrior that Senzangakona eventually sought his return. Shaka's reputation increased and legend records both his fearlessness when hunting wild animals and great prowess with the spear. At the age of 24 Shaka was called to join King Dingiswayo's IziCwe *ibutho* (guild or regiment of 'national service' warriors). During the next five years he closely studied the king's strategy of control over other tribes by the use of brutal and aggressive tactics, a policy frequently but incorrectly attributed to Shaka.

Under Dingiswayo Shaka was appointed to lead the IziCwe regiment; he taught his warriors the close combat for which he became famous and caused the ineffective throwing spears to be melted down and recast as the long, sharp, flat-bladed stabbing spear[1] or *Ikwa*, the onomatopoeic term for the sucking sound of the blade being withdrawn from a body. He ordered his regiment's traditional large shields to be cut down in size and made stronger, so that in close combat the new shield could be hooked under that of an opponent and, when twisted sideways, revealed the opponent's body exposed and vulnerable to the deadly *Ikwa* thrust.

His re-trained regiment was soon pitched against the nearby *Buthelezi* tribe and in due course both regiments lined up for the traditional *giya,* a bloodless confrontation of taunts and abuse with victory going to the most impressive side. The unsuspecting Buthelezi, led by Shaka's Chief Bakaza, commenced to *giya* but Shaka instantly killed Bakaza whereupon the IziCwe fell upon the unsuspecting Buthelezi and slaughtered them to a man. Dingiswayo thereupon appointed Shaka to lead the northern Zulu tribe. On Senzangakona's death, Shaka annexed the Zulu clan and deposed his half-brother Dingane by sending him back to his own distant clan, an offshoot of the Qwabe tribe.

Shaka was in his early thirties when he commenced his ruthless reign. Opponents and dissenters were mercilessly executed, as were warriors who did not reach the exacting physical standards required for a Zulu *impi*, the Zulu fighting force usually of regimental strength. He perfected the *Ikwa* and developed the *Impondo Zankhomo*, the encircling technique known as the 'horns of the bull' whereby the fast-running horns on each flank encircled an enemy. The main Zulu body would then engage and slaughter the surrounded enemy using the close combat techniques of shield and stabbing spear. Shaka drilled his Zulus remorselessly in order to attack the resurgent and belligerent Buthelezi clan. When the two sides met, Shaka's warriors encircled the Buthelezi and slaughtered them before their distraught onlookers. Shaka then ordered the massacre of the Buthelezi non-combatants.

By 1818 Shaka's impi had grown to more than 2,000 warriors and his sphere of influence was steadily increasing. The struggle for power now focused on another powerful chief, Zwide. Zwide attacked Shaka at Gqokli Hill but the battle was inconclusive and both sides withdrew to their own territory. Shaka's army was still intact and warriors from other clans immediately flocked to swell his ranks. Zwide attacked the Zulus again in the summer of 1819 with a massive army of nearly 20,000 warriors but this time Shaka was even better prepared.

Shaka teased Zwide's army into following a number of feints across barren terrain until, several days later, Shaka attacked and destroyed Zwide's starving men. Shaka thereafter ruled unchallenged. His army grew to over 20,000 trained warriors and was based in a heartland that extended from the Indian Ocean to the Drakensberg and from the Pongola river in the north to the Tugela river in the south. Shaka forced his ruthless influence still further and by 1822 his clan had grown into an empire that extended into the Kalahari desert, north to the shores of Lake Malawi and south to the northern Cape.

In early 1824 Shaka heard of the handful of white men living at a small coastal enclave known to the whites as Port Natal and, to satisfy his curiosity, sent them an invitation to visit his kraal at *kwaBulawayo* (the place of him who kills). The party consisted of Lieutenant Francis Farewell RN; Henry Fynn, the British resident in Zululand; four hardy pioneers, John Cane, Henry Ogle, Joseph Powell and Thomas Halstead; and a large number of gifts. After various displays and feasts, Farewell and Fynn finally met with Shaka and during one of their meetings they sought and were granted trading rights for the Farewell Trading Company. The party returned to Port Natal but without Fynn who remained at Shaka's request – not as a hostage, but to enable Shaka to learn more of the white men. Fynn was residing at the royal kraal when an attempt was made on Shaka's life. He was stabbed through his left arm and ribs by an unknown assailant and lay at death's door for a week. During this time, Fynn cleaned and bandaged the wound and generally watched over Shaka who quickly recovered. Shaka believed that members of the distant Qwabe tribe were responsible for the attempt; accordingly, two impis were dispatched which captured the Qwabe cattle and destroyed their kraals. The settlers' position was assured and Shaka allegedly signed an agreement granting Farewell nearly 4,000 square miles of land around Port Natal.

During 1826 Farewell and Fynn accompanied Shaka's army of over 40,000 warriors on an expedition against the distant Ndwandwe clan. The result was a total slaughter of the Ndwandwe; an event that distressed even Farewell and Fynn, though Shaka was delighted with the 60,000 captured cattle. Shaka's absolute disregard for the sanctity of human life was difficult for the Europeans to comprehend; on a daily basis a dozen executions were normal.

Shaka's rule was total until 1827 when his mother, Nandi, suddenly died. It is said that Shaka's grief was so intense that he required every Zulu to experience his loss. At a gathering of some 20,000 souls within the homestead, enforced wailing and summary executions commenced and continued for more than a day until well over 1,000 of the multitude lay dead. Shaka then decreed that during the next twelve months no crops could be grown, children were not to be conceived, or milk drunk – all on pain of death. The situation continued for three months until Shaka tired of mourning, whereupon some normality returned.

The damage and carnage was such that Shaka's half-brothers, Dingane and Mhlangana, clandestinely agreed that Shaka must die. They waited until the army was on campaign and stabbed Shaka to death during a meeting with his remaining advisers. His body was unceremoniously buried in a pit weighted down with stones. Many years later the site was purchased by a farmer, and today Shaka's grave lies somewhere under Cooper Street in the small town of Stanger, north of Durban.

Within days the exhausted and anxious army returned in expectation of Shaka's wrath, only to be relieved when Dingane welcomed his army back, fed them and then authorized their leave. Dingane thus ensured their loyalty and, being unchallenged, he assumed the mantle of king. Curiously, the title 'king' appears to have evolved from a spontaneous gesture by Lt Farewell during an earlier meeting between Shaka and Farewell. In awe of Shaka, Farewell took a smear of grease from one of his cannon wheel hubs and ceremonially anointed Shaka on his forehead – after which, he was referred to as 'the king'.

At no more than 30 years of age, Dingane settled into a life of luxury and security. He enjoyed singing and dancing and clearly had an artistic inclination. Unlike Shaka, Dingane spent most of his time in the *isiGodlo* (harem) or reviewing parades of warriors and cattle. He reduced the size of the Zulu army and Shaka's previous policy of random butchery ceased, though miscreants were still summarily executed without trial or mercy.

In 1838 a Boer trek leader, Piet Retief, took a party of Boers to Dingane's royal homestead kraal to seek permission to settle; instead of gaining permission they were massacred. Dingane immediately sent his warriors to destroy the unsuspecting waiting Boer families and in a further night of slaughter, another 523 souls died, mainly women and children. The Boers exacted revenge in their victory at Blood River towards the end of 1838. After this defeat Dingane withdrew his army and regrouped his forces at umGungundhlovu. The following Boer trekkers streamed across the Drakensberg mountain range and began settling on the central plateau. They named the settled area the 'Free Province of New Holland in South East Africa' and its centre of crowded wagons became known as 'Pietermaritzburg' after two Boer notables, Piet Retief and Gert

Maritz. At the same time the British formally occupied Port Natal and renamed it 'Durban' after Sir Benjamin D'Urban, Governor of the Cape Colony. They negotiated a truce with Dingane but then abandoned the port to the Boers.

Having controlled the advancing Boers, Dingane decided to re-establish his control over the non-Zulu tribes by undertaking a punitive expedition against his younger half-brother, Mpande, who promptly fled to the Boers for protection with nearly 20,000 of his people. The Boers realized the Zulus were in disarray and mounted a massive counter-expedition, which included Mpande's Zulus in support of the Boers, mainly to recapture their lost cattle and horses.

Dingane sent two ambassadors to plead for a truce with the Boers who were camped at the site of the Blood River battle, but the two were promptly executed out of vengeance for their suspected complicity in Retief's murder. During the protracted skirmishing which followed, the Boers recovered most of their cattle and Dingane was forced to flee across the northern Pongola river where his own people, eager for a return to peace, murdered him.

The news of Dingane's death swept across Natal and then beyond to the many tribes who had been displaced by Shaka and Dingane. These commenced their own steady trek back to their homelands, only to discover the Boers were settling on their lands. The Boer Volksraad (Council) decreed that the natives, now starving and homeless, were to be rounded up and moved into a native homeland well away from the Boer sphere of influence. The British at the Cape heard of the plan towards the end of 1841 and forbade the Boer action. British troops re-seized Durban and quickly dispatched sufficient administrators to govern the area while the Volksraad endeavoured to regain control over the increasingly contrary Boers, who had even endeavoured, unsuccessfully, to enlist the support of the King of Holland. Unbeknown to the Boers, it was a wasted exercise, as Holland had no intention of provoking Britain.

In 1845 Britain annexed the whole of Natal into the Cape Colony, including Boer-held territory. Reluctantly the Boer Volksraad acquiesced. The Boers had overreached themselves and, by provoking the British, lost sovereignty over lands won by their great sacrifice. Settlers continued arriving from Europe and Durban rapidly prospered as the influence of Pietermaritzburg declined. During the European upheaval in Natal the Zulus, under their new king Mpande, had decided to avoid further confrontation with the whites and had withdrawn to the north side of the Buffalo and Tugela rivers.

During the relatively peaceful years that followed, Mpande ruled the Zulu nation fairly but firmly according to Zulu custom. It was a period of consolidation after the internecine wars of 1838 and 1840 and the Zulus were also recovering from the economic impoverishment resulting from white settlers' encroachment. Mpande turned his attention to the *isiGodlo*, and to feasting until he became too obese to walk. His activities in the *isiGodlo* produced nearly thirty sons; the firstborn was named Cetshwayo and was followed shortly by a brother named Mbulazi. As Mpande aged, schisms developed within the Zulu nation and gradually the subservient chiefs and clans gradually inclined to either Cetshwayo or Mbulazi. The two brother princes were now in their early twenties and led the *uThulwana* and *amaShishi* regiments respectively. Cetshwayo was a traditionalist and hankered after the regal days of Shaka whereas Mbulazi was more inclined to intellectual matters, though equally devious and powerful; it was 1856 and both sought to be king.

As usual, resolution came through bloody conflict, perhaps the worst seen or recorded in African history. Near Ndondakusuka hill Cetshwayo mustered 20,000 warriors, the *uSuthu*, and pitted them against Mbulazi's army of 30,000, the *iziGqoza*, which included many women and old men. The confrontation took place on the banks of an insignificant stream, the Thambo, which fed into the Tugela river. The battle lasted no more than an hour with Mbulazi's army being heavily defeated. In customary Zulu fashion, Cetshwayo gave orders for their total slaughter and only a handful of survivors escaped. Cetshwayo was later song-praised for his victory as being the victor who 'Caused people to swim against their will, for he made men swim when they were old'.[2]

Following the battle Cetshwayo effectively took over the running of the Zulu nation, leaving Mpande a mere figurehead. Cetshwayo had long since observed the underlying tension between the British in Natal and the Transvaal Boers and knew he was in a position of considerable strength. He now had full control of Zululand and in order to strengthen his grip further he astutely courted friendship with the British, whereupon Shepstone, Secretary for Native Affairs, went to Mpande and suggested that, in the name of Queen Victoria, Cetshwayo should be appointed heir apparent. Mpande accepted the proposal on behalf of the Zulus though Cetshwayo was aware that his future now depended, to a degree, on British support. Mpande died in 1872 after thirty relatively peaceful years on the Zulu throne, a reign marred only by his two sons' recent battle by the Tugela. Mpande was the only Zulu king of the era to die of natural causes.

Cetshwayo became king in his mid forties and immediately sought British confirmation of his position. Shepstone readily agreed and, in a sham ceremony on 1 September 1873, Cetshwayo was crowned king of the Zulu nation – in the name of Queen Victoria. Cetshwayo, perhaps the most intelligent of all the Zulu kings, now ruled a united nation, his army was at its strongest and the Zulus had a most powerful friend, Queen Victoria - and no apparent enemies.

With his military position secure, Cetshwayo began to strengthen his economic and political control. Since the reign of Shaka young men had been obliged to serve in the army as a means of binding the nation together. The units or *amabutho* were the king's active service units and in peacetime gave service at the king's command, often as tax officials or by undertaking policing duties. Apart from drawing young men into an amabutho or unit for military and work purposes, this arrangement also served to accustom warriors into identifying the Zulu king as their leader, regardless of their origins. However, when young men came from an outlying area or had recently been absorbed into the Zulu nation, they were allocated menial work and were known as *amalala* (menials), *amanhlwenga* (destitutes) or *iziendane* (unusual hairstyles).

These warriors remained in their regimental *amabutho* until the king authorized their 'marriage'; this was another misunderstood concept that has often led to confusion. Zulu marriage has invariably been interpreted through European eyes with overtones of repressed Freudian sexuality and transposed with European values of marriage. To a Zulu man, marriage denoted the most significant event of his life by giving him the right to take a number of wives; he was free to establish his personal kraal and he could own land for his cattle and crops. The king controlled marriage as a means of keeping his young men under arms and out of the economic structure of Zululand. Had every warrior been permitted to establish his own kraal at will, the effect on various Zulu social processes, including production and reproduction, would have resulted in economic instability. Concomitantly, by delaying the time when Zulu women could marry, the growth and pressure of an increasing population could be strictly controlled and the Zulu birth rate maintained in line with economic production.

The Zulu army and its weapons.

British intelligence led Chelmsford to believe that the total strength of the Zulu army amounted to between 40,000 and 50,000 men immediately available for action. The total Zulu population at the time only amounted to some 350,000 people and so this figure is probably correct. Each year young men of the age of 16 were formed into a regiment, which after a year's probation was placed in a military kraal or headquarters. This first year also symbolized the transition from boyhood to manhood as a warrior. This kraal might belong to another regiment with which the young one was incorporated, or it might be newly formed. As a rule several regiments of different ages were combined at the same kraal, so that the young soldiers might have the benefit of the experience of their seniors and, when the latter died out, might take their place and maintain the name and prestige of the military kraal. In this manner corps were formed, occasionally some thousands strong.

The Zulu army consisted of twelve such corps and two regiments, each with its own military kraal. These corps necessarily contained men of all ages, some being married, others unmarried, some being old men scarcely able to walk, and others mere boys. Five of these corps each consisted of a single regiment, while the remaining corps was composed of several regiments. Each corps or regiment possessed its own military kraal and had one commander, one second in command, and several junior commanders who controlled the flanks in action. The uniform of the Zulu army was clearly laid down and was somewhat different, as a rule, in each corps. The great distinction was between the married and unmarried regiments. The former were obliged to shave the crown of the head, and to wear a ring made of hemp and coated with a hardened paste of gum and grease; they also carried shields with predominantly white colouring, whereas the unmarried regiments wore their hair naturally and had coloured shields.

In 1878 the total number of regiments in the Zulu army was thirty-four, of which eighteen were married and sixteen unmarried. Seven of the former were composed of men over 60 years of age, so that for practical purposes there were only twenty-seven Zulu regiments fit to take the field, amounting to some 41,000 warriors. Intelligence figures of the day break these down as 17,000 between 20 and 30 years of age, 14,500 between 30 and 40, 5,900 between 40 and 50 and 4,500 between 50 and 60.

In the ordinary European acceptation of the word, drill was unknown in the Zulu army. They could, however, perform a number of movements with some accuracy, such as forming a circle of companies or regiments. Their skirmishing skills were extremely good, and could even be performed under a heavy fire with the utmost determination. The officers had their duties and responsibilities according to their rank, and discipline was most rigidly enforced. Commodore Sullivan, writing in August 1878, gave a high account of the discipline of the Zulu army. He stated that the regiments were so well disciplined that 'the men never fell out of the ranks on the march under any pretext; they marched at the double, and were said to keep up from 50 to 60 miles daily, carrying their own provisions'.

The Zulu army required but little commissariat or transport. Three or four days' provision, in the shape of maize or millet, and a herd of cattle proportionate to the distance to be traversed, accompanied each regiment. The older boys followed each regiment and assisted in driving the cattle; they also carried the provisions and camp equipage, which consisted of sleeping mats and blankets. The Zulus would also avoid rivers that were impassable to the British Army but when necessary the Zulus adopted a remarkable method to get across. When they came to a river, which was out of their depth, they would plunge into it in a dense mass, holding on to one another, those behind forcing the others forward, and thus they would succeed in crossing, with the loss of only a few of their number.

When hostilities were decided upon, messengers were sent out by the king, travelling night and day if necessary, to order the men to assemble in regiments at their respective kraals where their commanding officers were ready to receive them. When corps or regiments were assembled at the headquarters they were usually ordered to proceed to the king's royal homestead. Before marching a circle, or *umkumbi*, was formed inside the homestead, each company together, and their officers in an inner ring with the first and second in command at the centre. The regiment then proceeded to break into companies, beginning from the left-hand side; each company formed a circle, and marched off, followed by boys carrying provisions, mats and food supplies. The company officers marched immediately in rear of their men, the second in command in rear of the left wing, and the commanding officer in rear of the right. On arriving at the king's royal homestead certain important ceremonies took place, and various medicines were administered to the warriors to enhance their fighting capacity and render them immune from British firepower. On the third day after their assembly at the king's homestead they were sprinkled with medicine by the doctors and, after all necessary formalities were completed, the warriors started on their expedition.

Prior to marching off, the regiments re-formed companies under their respective officers, and the corps selected by the king to take the lead advanced. The march was in the order of companies for the first day, after which it was continued in the *umsila* or path, which may be explained by likening it to a British division advancing in line of brigade columns, each brigade in mass; each regiment in close column. The line of provision-bearers moved on the flank; the intervals between the head of columns varied, according to circumstances, from several miles to within sight of each other, constant communication being kept up by runners.

The march was then continued in this order, but the baggage and provision-bearers fell in rear of the column on the second day, and the cattle composing the commissariat were driven between them and the rearmost regiment until the force approached the enemy. When the latter appeared in sight the whole army formed an *umkumbi* for the purpose of enabling the commander-in-chief to address the men, and to give his final orders for attack.

When the enemy were sighted, the Zulus advanced in a long thick line with the bulk of their force remaining out of sight; the line then broke up in apparent confusion on approaching the enemy. The flanks moved off rapidly to the right and left and, circling round, formed the horns or claws that gripped the enemy, while the centre body now attacked. By 1878 Zulu weapons of aggression consisted of both traditional Zulu spears and obsolete European rifles. Cetshwayo's generals still drilled their soldiers using Shaka's shock tactics of the mass charge and close-quarter fighting to the death; the thrust of the stabbing spear underarm into the belly of the opponent was the final act. There were a number of different types of throwing spears common in 1879, most of which had 6-inch blades with the iron shank visible for several inches before being set into the long shaft.

The manufacture of stabbing spears was a highly skilled craft. It was entrusted to particular clans such as the *Mbonambi* and the *Cube*. The iron ore was collected at surface deposits and smelted in a clay forge with the aid of goatskin bellows. The blade was hammered into shape, tempered with fat and sharpened on a stone before being set into a short wooden shaft. It was glued with strong vegetable glues and bound with wet cane fibre. A tube of hide, cut from a calf's tail, was rolled over the join and allowed to shrink. At its best, such a weapon was tough and sharp and well designed for its purpose. However, by 1879 there is a suggestion that the importation of iron implements from white traders had led to a decline in the indigenous iron industry. Certainly there are a number of stories of blades bending or buckling in use.

Warriors were responsible for their own weapons, but the king initially received the spears in bulk from those clans that made them, distributing them to warriors who had distinguished themselves. Most warriors carried clubs or knobkerries, the *iWisa*, which were simple polished sticks with a heavy bulbous head. Zulu boys carried them for everyday protection and their possession at all times became second nature. A number of axes were used; these were often ornamental and were imported from the tribes in the north.

In any battle or confrontation a large body of troops were also always kept in hand as a reserve; they were usually seated with their backs to the enemy so as not to get excited; the commanders and staff assembled to some eminence, and retained one or two of the older regiments as extra reserves. All orders were delivered by runners. No great changes had been introduced into Zulu tactics or movements consequent on the introduction of firearms though, in addition to firearms, each man usually carried four or five spears. One short and heavy-bladed spear was used solely for stabbing, and was never parted with; the others were lighter, and sometimes thrown. The men armed with firearms rarely carried a shield. The Zulus made great use of spies, had an elaborate system for obtaining and transmitting intelligence, and were efficient at outpost duty. The following notes on engaging the enemy come from a memo published under the direction of Lord Chelmsford in 1879.

> Although the Zulus will often meet their enemy in a fair fight in the open, like all savages they are fond of ambuscades and other ruses.
>
> In going through bush, remember that the natives will often lie down to let you pass, and then rise and fire on you.
>
> In moving through bush advance and rear guards and flanking parties are necessary.
>
> They should look well under the bushes, and notice all footmarks and sounds, such as the cracking of bushes, &c, and note whether the twigs have been lately bent or broken, or the grass trodden down, all indications of men having recently passed. When the bush is too thick for flanking parties, the leading file should turn to the right and enter the bush as far as he can, kneel, and look well under the bushes; the next file, after about five paces, turn to his left, and the next to his right, and so on. The whole body may do this or only the advanced guard, according to circumstances. As the rear of the force in question approaches, the files rise in succession and close by sections, moving along between the halted sentries, and when the foremost of these is reached the process is repeated.
>
> When waylaying or surprising an enemy make no noise until the enemy finds you, rise, and move, not along the path, but just inside the bush.

When moving near an enemy, or reconnoitring, do not return to the camp by the route you left it.

A common ruse with the natives is to hide a large force in the bush and show a few solitary individuals to invite an attack. When the troops enter the bush in pursuit of the latter the hidden men rise and attack them.

In advancing through bush a herd of cattle is seen feeding with only a small guard, which runs as soon as our troops appear. The mounted men push on to capture the former, and when they are well separated from the rest, the natives, who were hidden all the time in the bush, rise and cut them off before the infantry can come to their rescue.

Native advance guards and flanking parties cannot be trusted, the former will cluster together, and the latter will often lie down.

Natives always know when an enemy is in the bush, but they often forget to report it, thinking the white men know as well as themselves.

The Boers found that the Zulus could not stand repeated cavalry charges on the flanks, and that a very effective method of attack was to gallop upon their flanks, dismount, and fire into them; retreating to reload, or when attacked.

When the wagons of a force are parked at night, if the Zulus attack they always try to make the cattle, which are kept within the park, stampede, in order to break a hole in the line of defence.

The same applies to cavalry, who should take every precaution against their horses being stampeded by a sudden attack.

By the time of the British invasion the Zulu army possessed firearms in large numbers. A trusted English trader, John Dunn, had imported them in large quantities for Cetshwayo. During the 1870s as many as 20,000 guns entered southern Africa through Mozambique alone, most of them intended for the Zulu market. The majority of these firearms were obsolete military muskets, dumped on the unsophisticated 'native market'. More modern types were available; particularly the percussion Enfield, and a number of chiefs had collections of quality sporting guns. Individuals like Prince Dabulamanzi and Chief Sihayo of Rorke's Drift were recognized as good shots but most Zulus were untrained and highly inaccurate; numerous accounts of Zulu War battles note both the indiscriminate use of their fire-power and its general inaccuracy.

By the time the Zulu War commenced, successive Zulu kings had efficiently controlled the development of Zulu social organization and ensured a comparatively healthy and prosperous population. Anthony Trollope travelled through southern Africa and parts of Zululand during 1878 just as European hysteria was mounting; yet he viewed the Zulus as being perceptive and living in sympathy with their time and environment. He wrote, 'I have no fears myself that Natal will be overrun by hostile Zulus, but much fear that Zululand should be overrun by hostile Britons'.

CHAPTER 3

Springboard to War

*I am inclined to think that the first experience of the power of
the Martini-Henrys will be such a surprise to the Zulus that they will
not be formidable after the first effort.*

DISPATCH FROM LORD CHELMSFORD AT PIETERMARITZBURG TO
COLONEL WOOD, 23 NOVEMBER 1878

Apart from the 24th Regiment that had previously been stationed at King
William's Town, all other troops and stores for the Centre Column's invasion of Zululand had commenced their African journey at the port of Durban. Everything then travelled by dirt road to Pietermaritzburg, thence to
Greytown and to the main invasion column's store area situated on the
crest of a range of hills, the Biggarsberg, at Helpmekaar.[1] The roadways
between the towns were nothing more than rough tracks and passage was
at the mercy of heavy rain that regularly made them unnavigable even
though gangs of locally recruited natives toiled to make passable the numerous bogs of slime along the route. Prior to the build-up for the invasion
there was little at Helpmekaar, just two rough stone-built farmers' houses
and, nearby, a tiny church built in 1874 by another farming family, the Ver-
maaks. The area was isolated, desolate and windswept but the end of 1878
saw vast columns of red-coated soldiers and laden wagons laboriously
winding along the valleys and toiling up the long slope towards Helpmekaar.
The army commandeered the two houses and erected three sheds constructed

of zinc sheets to protect the column's perishable supplies of grain, forage and ammunition boxes from the rain. As soon as the zinc sheds were full, a neat row of thatched huts was built to cope with the ever-increasing overflow of stores. Within days a sea of white tents covered the whole area and extended more than a mile towards the pass that led down the steep spur towards the Zulu border at Rorke's Drift, some 10 miles further down the track. As the troops gathered, the daily activities of the camp included butchering and baking, cooking and cleaning, drill, polishing equipment, parades and either sheltering from the rain or drying wet clothes in the hot sun. The centre of the position was a confusing mass of stores surrounded by wagons and horse- and ox-pens. Due to the heavy rains and troop movements, much of the area had already become a deep quagmire of foul smelling sticky mud; furthermore, dysentery broke out among the troops. To make matters worse, the wagons bringing Christmas supplies to the troops remained firmly stuck in the mud at Umsinga, some 20 miles away, and only reached Helpmekaar the following week. The British weekly magazine, the *Graphic*, reported the appalling conditions, (8 March):

> Nothing, on first landing in South Africa, impresses the newcomer more than the immense teams of animals used for drawing a single wagon. We have seen as many as twenty-four thus yoked together, and although the driver at the shafts has a phenomenally long whip, yet he cannot reach the leader, so there is generally a gentleman on horseback, also armed with a whip, to stimulate the energies of the foremost cattle. These long teams are necessitated by the rugged nature of the country. Some of the roads are more like walls than roads for steepness, and the bullocks have to hang on like houseflies.

The Centre Column's advance from Rorke's Drift was to be spearheaded by the two very experienced battalions of the 24th Regiment whose men were battle seasoned and fresh from engagements during the recently ended Cape Frontier War. Both had received high praise for their 'cheerfulness in facing hardships and discomforts and by their good conduct and good discipline in the field'.[2] Chelmsford had spoken of them 'in the highest terms', indeed, the soldiers were hardened to both battle and the climate; they were fighting fit and suntanned, most were bearded and their patched and repaired uniforms were evidence of many months of constant combat. Their officers were equally fit, enthusiastic about the coming campaign and totally familiar with the tactics of the unsubdued native tribes, or so they thought. It was not until early January that both battalions eventually met up again at Helpmekaar, which in itself was unusual as it was War Office policy to maintain one battalion of each regiment on a home posting. The 1/24th Regiment had marched to Helpmekaar leaving D and F Companies at Durban, much to their annoyance due to a plague of bugs, fleas, ticks and mosquitoes,[3] though F Company was to follow on in time for their fateful meeting with the Zulu army. The 2/24th Regiment had already arrived at Helpmekaar in the beginning of January and on 9 January, just a few days short of the thirtieth anniversary of the 24th's unfortunate experience at the battle of Chillianwallah, the officers of both battalions, sitting on supply boxes, shared a mess dinner at which a toast was proposed: 'That we may not get into such a mess and have better luck next time'.[4]

The following day the remaining troops still at Helpmekaar marched the 12 miles off the high escarpment and down along the deeply rutted track to the border with Zululand at Rorke's Drift. The whole area was a hive of activity; they passed a large party of natives under the supervision of a detachment of Royal Engineers who were repairing the roadway down the escarpment to Rorke's Drift. On arrival at the campsite they saw the Royal Engineers detachment commanded by their officer, Lieutenant Francis MacDowel, the Centre Column's only RE officer, testing the two barrel ponts that would carry them across the river to the Zulu bank. MacDowel was well known for his ingenuity; he had initially been attached to Wood's Northern Column until Glyn commandeered him to improve the efficiency of the ponts.

Chelmsford had already visited Rorke's Drift on 4 January and was impressed with the readiness and enthusiasm of the gathering invading force. His intelligence officers reported that a large force of Zulus was assembled to oppose the invasion; Chelmsford informed his subordinates that he hoped the reports were true. Back at Helpmekaar he was presented with three emissaries from Cetshwayo who requested more time to consider the ultimatum; Chelmsford ignored them just as he had the ignored six previous pleas from Cetshwayo, and, fearing the emissaries were spies, banned further Zulu messengers from entering British positions.

Unexpectedly, and equally unbelievably, Chelmsford was faced with the threat of mutiny by his previously loyal Colonial troops. He had unthinkingly given command of the Natal Mounted Police and all the Natal volunteer units to Brevet Major John Russell of the Mounted Infantry, ignoring their own commandant, Major Dartnell. Chelmsford had previously decreed that all commanders were to be Imperial officers and had given an instruction to this effect in para.144 of his *Regulations for Field Forces in South Africa*. The effect of this regulation debarred any colonial officer, regardless of his rank, from having command over Imperial troops. The severely disgruntled colonials paraded at Helpmekaar and took a vote on the matter; it was unanimously decided that they would not enter Zululand under the command of an unknown British officer, especially as they respected Major Dartnell's proven experience in native warfare. Chelmsford was forced to compromise and promoted Dartnell to the rank of lieutenant colonel and appointed him to his own staff, which gave him authority over Russell. The decision was grudgingly accepted by the Colonials who then obeyed their orders and moved down to Rorke's Drift.

Just a half-mile from the Buffalo river crossing of Rorke's Drift and on a rising outcrop of rock was the Swedish mission station run by the Reverend Otto Witt. It consisted of the missionary's house and a small church; both made of local stone with thatched roofs. The station lay in the lea of the Oskarsberg hill. The 700ft high hill commanded a magnificent view over the Buffalo river and gave a clear view for some 5 miles into Zululand. The homestead itself consisted of three acres of cultivated land that included an orchard of grapevines and orange, apricot, apple, peach, fig, pomegranate and other fruit trees. There was a vegetable garden protected on one side by a 130ft long and 5ft high wall, the whole being surrounded by an assortment of lime trees and quince bushes. The main building, Witt's home, was nearly 30 yards long and airy and spacious. Witt's small, dignified church, 40yds away, was used by the missionary in his daily work with the local native community. Immediately beyond the church was a small cattle kraal and then, below the rock terrace on which the buildings nestled, there was a larger stone cattle kraal that could hold 100 cattle. The mission station was connected to the rest of Natal by a dirt track that led westwards towards the high escarpment of the Biggarsberg and thence to Helpmekaar. In the other direction the track continued down towards the Buffalo river and was the only route into Zululand for hunters and itinerant traders plying their wares among the Zulus.

Since 9 January, the influx and noise of British troops and all the impedimenta of Chelmsford's invasion force had shattered the tranquillity and beauty of Rorke's Drift. The Imperial troops and white volunteers erected their tents in neat formations between the river bank and the mission station while the Natal Native Contingent (NNC) were instructed to camp downstream of the Europeans; their domestic and cleansing habits left much to be desired, even to campaign-experienced troops. Notwithstanding the protestations of Otto Witt, Assistant Commissary Chermside had commandeered the two buildings on behalf of the Crown. On the day before the invasion, Chermside swiftly converted Witt's twelve-roomed house into a makeshift hospital to cater for several cases of fever and soldiers with damaged limbs caused by a number of incidents where wagons had slid into some marching troops. The church became an ammunition store and in despair at the damage caused to his home and church, Witt dispatched his wife and small children to stay with friends at nearby Umsinga, some 10 miles south of Helpmekaar.

The previously tranquil mission station now seethed with activity as over 5,000 men of the invasion force and a similar number of oxen and horses were assembled on the sloping area between the mission station and the river. It rained incessantly and the area soon became a muddy quagmire strewn with effluent and rubbish, yet spirits remained high as the hours passed towards the expiry of the ultimatum.

The *Natal Witness* published two reports (5 January):

No attempt to cross the river will be made if opposed, except under the
protection of the battery. These Zulus do not yet know what a shell is like or

what effect it will have upon them. May they soon learn, and the larger the quantity that is present the better the effect will be.

On arrival I was sorry to hear of the accident which had occurred during our absence. An order had been issued some days ago, that no one was to bathe above the drift, probably because it is all deep water above the stream – an order which rather excited the ire of the numerous good swimmers among the volunteers, especially the Carbineers, but which, from the sad occurrence of this morning, was only too plainly needed. One of the Newcastle Rifles, by name Dixon, got into a hole below the drift, and, being unable to swim, was drowned. A volunteer party attempted to recover his body, but failed. It has cast a considerable gloom over the portion of the force to which he belonged. Health in camp generally good.

On the evening of 10 January, Chelmsford arrived with his entourage of staff officers and the word quickly spread that the invasion would take place the following morning. The troop's level of excitement was high; the final adjustments had been made to the ponts and few men had slept. During the night the six guns of N Battery commanded by Colonel Harness RA were moved through the camp and relocated to an adjacent small rise overlooking the river. Shortly after 2 a.m. reveille was sounded, men dressed and gathered their equipment, wagons were coupled to their oxen and within the hour the column approached the river crossing point; everyone was ready to commence the invasion. One minor diversion occurred when it was discovered that a trader's supply wagon had been looted and a cursory search failed to discover the culprits or the stolen stores. As dawn came the whole area was covered in a heavy wet mist so that the Zulu river bank could not be seen; eyes peered into the mist but no sound of massing Zulus could be heard. As the mist gradually lifted, the opposing bank and surrounding countryside was bathed in bright sunshine; there was no sign of the Zulus. Unbeknown to Chelmsford, the nation's warriors were already assembled 60 miles away at Ulundi and were being prepared for the defence of their country.

The invasion of Zululand began on 11 January with a simultaneous advance of the three main columns in a crescent formation. The Coastal

Column progressed slowly northwards hugging the coastline of the Indian Ocean. The Centre Column advanced from Rorke's Drift while the Northern Column advanced from Luneburg across the Blood river. At Rorke's Drift, the mounted troops cautiously rode their horses through the swirling waters using the submerged flat rocks of the original traders' crossing point. Once across, they spread out in a wide semicircle in anticipation of a Zulu attack. All they saw were three startled Zulu boys tending their cattle. The mounted troopers held their defensive position while the infantry were slowly ferried across the river. The Native forces had been assembled downstream of the main crossing point and were cajoled by their officers towards the fast flowing muddy river. They began the crossing in their customary style by linking arms and entering the water in a 'V' formation, those in the front apex being pushed across by those in the rear. When the front ranks reached the far bank, they then pulled their colleagues over; the Native contingent lost several men in the crossing but, as their officers didn't know how many natives they commanded, little concern was shown.

Once across, the force spread out in a defensive formation until the mounted patrols confirmed the absence of Zulu defenders. A few hundred yards from the crossing point a new campsite was prepared, and by noon the slow process of bringing stores and wagons across from Rorke's Drift was well under way. It is unlikely that, during the crossing, any of the troops would have noticed the prominent rocky outcrop of Isandlwana that dominated the skyline some 7 miles away. It is equally unlikely that they would have known its name, with which their relatives would shortly become familiar: the Zulus called it *Isandlwana*.

Chelmsford was delighted with the progress of the invasion and rode off to liaise with Colonel Wood, commander of the Northern Column, as it, too, was crossing into Zululand some 30 miles distant. By the following day all necessary supplies had been brought across the river and the column commenced the slow advance towards Ulundi. Within sight of the advancing troops, some 5 miles away, was a high row of steep cliffs that formed the backdrop to the *umuzi*, or homestead, of Chief Sihayo. Notwithstanding that the chief was an anglophile, wore European clothes and had been a good friend of James Rorke, it was Sihayo who had, unwittingly, outraged polite Natal society with the murder of his two adulterous wives within sight of the mission station. Of greater significance to the British commander was the fact that Sihayo's homestead would lie directly across the invading column's main supply route. Retribution was in the air and Chelmsford needed the stronghold neutralized; during the early hours of 12 January Chelmsford and his staff watched as the 'untrained untrainables' of the NNC spearheaded the first attack of the invasion against Sihayo's homestead.

Lieutenant Harford, a popular young officer on loan to the NNC from the 99th Regiment and a noted entomologist, led the attack. The attacking force advanced towards Sihayo's homestead; they crossed the Batshe stream and approached the steep cliffs, coming under distant rifle fire from scattered Zulus sheltering in caves. Under fire from the Zulus, Harford enhanced his reputation by gathering a rare beetle; whilst he was on his hands and knees it was thought by watching senior officers that Harford had been wounded and the cry reverberated round the hills, 'Harford is down, Harford is down'. With the beetle safely in his pocket, Harford continued with the attack. The NNC had been given specific orders not to harm non-combatants or their property on pain of severe punishment. The NNC formed up, and then stormed the stronghold supported by the 2/24th. It was weakly defended as Sihayo and his warriors were assembling with the main Zulu army at Ulundi. The NNC lost less than a dozen natives with a similar number wounded while the 24th sustained no casualties. Several of Sihayo's men were captured and roughly interrogated, by necessity an unpleasant process and one that was to rebound on the British a few days later. Released the following day, the Zulus took comfort at the neighbouring village at Sothondose's Drift, soon to be known as Fugitives' Drift. Angered by the destruction of their village, the death of one of Sihayo's sons and their own treatment, they were not well disposed to the British fugitives who were to flee through Sothondose's Drift a few days later. The *Natal Times* enthusiastically reported the engagement at Sihayo's homestead:

THE FIRST ENGAGEMENTS AT RORKE'S DRIFT, VICTORIOUS REPULSE, SIXTY
TO EIGHTY ZULUS KILLED, LARGE CAPTURE OF CATTLE

Up to 9 o'clock last night no intimation had been received from the front of
shots being fired in any quarter; but at that hour we received the following
important telegram, notifying the repulse and flight of the Zulus, with great
loss on their side, at the first encounter. It will be seen that the initiative in
attack came from the enemy, and, as has been expected, it was from Uirajo's
[Sihayo's] people. We regret to see that one of Lonsdale's officers has been
killed, and, we fear, two of the Natal Mounted Police; but the telegram leaves
room for a probability that the latter have only been wounded. They were
probably chasing the flying enemy. The prediction of those best acquainted
with the Zulus, that they would never stand the fire of regular forces, has
been abundantly verified.

Chelmsford's headquarters staff issued its own dispatch:

Despatches from Lord Chelmsford's headquarters, up to the 13th, state that
the Rorke's Drift column (Colonel Glynn's) was taken out to reconnoitre on
the 12th. In passing under the Neguda Hill, one of Usirajo's strongholds, Lord
Chelmsford ordered Colonel Glyn, with four companies 1-24 and 1-3rd Natal
Native Contingent, in skirmishing order, to advance towards the hill. They
were fired on from krantzes and caves, which were cleared in about half an
hour, and about 500 cattle taken. Colonel Degacher, with half a battalion
2-24 and 400 2-3rd Natal Native Contingent, was then ordered to Usirajo's
own kraal, under a very steep krantz full of caves, which were found empty.
Usirajo's own kraal was burnt, but none of the other huts touched. Lord
Chelmsford says "the Native Contingent behaved very well; not a native
touched a woman or child, or killed the wounded men." Lieut.-Colonel
Russell was sent along the Isupezi Hill road, to ascend the high ground
above the krantz, where nearly at the top, about 60 of the enemy opened
fire, at a distance of about 100 yards, with little effect. Colonel Russell
dismounted his men and drove off the enemy with a loss of 9 or 10 killed,
among whom was one of Usirajo's sons, shot by Sergt. Steele, and distinctly
recognised after his death. Total loss of enemy about 30. On our side, two of
the Natal Native Contingent killed, 12 wounded; Corporal Meyor, N.N.C.,

severely wounded in the thigh, Lieut. Purvis, N.N.C., severely wounded in the arm. Usirajo's men behaved with great courage. The wounded, prisoners included, are well cared for. Progress very difficult from heavy rains. Soldiers of all arms and force in good health. The result of the action gave great confidence to camp followers and natives of all classes. Commandant Lonsdale recovering from effects of a bad fall.

Following the skirmish at Sihayo's homestead, the subject of captured Zulu cattle caused much discontent among column troops who all expected a fair share of the plunder. Evidently, the cattle captured at Sihayo's and the surrounding area had been sold cheaply to contractors and word spread quickly through the column.[5]

The *Natal Witness* correspondent at Rorke's Drift sensed the widespread disquiet among the troops and sent the following report on the subject, published on 22 January:

The captured cattle, than which a finer lot I have rarely seen, a large portion being oxen fit for the butcher, and milk cows with calves, were absolutely sold to the contractor by the prize committee, who consisted (I believe) of two captains in the N.N.C. – though it does not much matter who they were – for the sum of £2 head, the goats for 2s 6d and the sheep for 6s a head. There will be very considerable discontent among all ranks if the bulk of our prize money goes to enrich contractors.

After destroying Sihayo's homestead, the invasion force made a temporary camp halfway between Rorke's Drift and Isandlwana to enable the Royal Engineers to repair the wagon track that ran through two swampy areas along the invasion route. Lieutenant MacDowel RE had been brought from Rorke's Drift to supervise the repairs, there being no further need for an officer at the ponts. The following morning Chelmsford, accompanied by his staff and escorted by fifty mounted infantry, made a reconnaissance along the roadway leading towards Isandlwana. The morning was fine and dry, and until the heat became great – which it very soon did – the ride was a pleasant one. The first part of the ride was over the section of road that had been lately undergoing repairs. The soil was of a dark alluvial nature, and so soft that the wheels of a wagon would stick fast in it. The worst places had to be filled up with stones and deep trenches had to be cut on each side of the track to permit drainage. Nearby Zulu huts were found to be most useful: they were pulled down and the wattles and supports, of which they were composed, were spread over the roadway.

That morning several natives came into the camp with a warning for Chelmsford that Cetshwayo intended to decoy the British and lure them into the bush; the Zulu army would then make for Natal. On his return Chelmsford dismissed their warning; he believed the drifts were adequately covered and resolved to push on deeper into Zululand without delay. The *Natal Witness* reporter with the Carbineers submitted the following dispatch to his newspaper on 18 January; it was published on 23 January.

> We have already had three different patrols into the enemy's quarters. Rumour had it that there were thousands near to us: but, though we hunted up hill and down dale, "saw we never none." It is impossible to know what to believe. The Zulus must assuredly be somewhere, but wherever we go, we only come across deserted huts. It is evident that a large number of the people have taken to flight, but whether they have done so through fear of us, or of their own "noble savage" defenders, I cannot undertake to say. As a change, however, on the last occasion we came across a Zulu, whom we took prisoner. On questioning him as to why there were so few men about, he said that they were quite scared away at the manner in which we had taken their mountain fortress [Sihayo's] from them – as they had not ever dreamt that we should venture up it. This amount of fear does not look very much like the wonderful prowess of the Zulus, of which we heard so much in Natal. I imagine they are much like other natives – very great at bragging, but easily depressed and panic-stricken by any sudden reverse.

The camp at Rorke's Drift now lay silent, guarded by a token force; only B Company of the 2/24th with 100 men had been left behind to guard the advancing column's reserve of stores and the hospital. The soldiers were under the command of 33-year-old Lieutenant Gonville Bromhead, an officer from a famous military family. Bromhead has unfairly been portrayed elsewhere as a 'duffer' with poor mental acuity and little enthusiasm for activity; in reality he was very popular with his men, being a champion boxer, a wrestler and an accomplished top scoring regimental cricketer. He did suffer from recurring deafness that caused him embarrassment on parade when he misheard orders. Although B Company had been left behind to guard the mission station, the men knew they would follow their regiment as soon as their relief arrived; the company from the 2/4th Regiment designated for the protection of Rorke's Drift were still marching to the front.

The company's senior NCO was 24-year-old, 5ft 3in tall Colour Sergeant Bourne, who had originally joined the army under age as a 16-year-old. He ran away from home, probably to avoid becoming a farm labourer, and on hearing that the 24th Regiment were visiting Brighton he walked the 16 miles to join them. His father later tried to buy him out on the grounds of his age and lack of stature, but as he was doing so well his army service continued.[6] The young Bourne made rapid progress and his three promotions to lance sergeant, sergeant and his present rank had been made within the last year. He had, nevertheless, experienced command in action on several occasions during the recent Cape Frontier wars. Due to his youthful looks the men knew him as 'the lad', a nickname that always amused him. After the main invasion force departed, there was little for the men of B Company to do other than assist with moving stores as and when wagons from Helpmekaar arrived and otherwise occupy themselves as best they could. Their tents were neatly pitched in two rows between the church and the small cattle kraal, well away from Witt's house; and the men's favourite haunt was the cooking area where they could lounge about, when it wasn't raining hard.

Bromhead had a number of officers to keep him company. Lieutenant Smith-Dorrien was in charge of a small wagon repair unit that was situated next to the large cattle kraal. The hospital building was commanded by Surgeon Reynolds who, with one member of the Army Hospital Corps and a soldier of B Company, looked after the fifteen or so hospital patients and were in the process of preparing the building in anticipation of casualties when the Zulus were eventually encountered. The Column's chaplain, the Revd George Smith, a veteran of the Bushman's Pass fiasco in 1873, had also remained at Rorke's Drift, uncertain of his role with the advancing column. Finally, the stores were organized by three hard-working officers of the Commissariat; their senior officer was Assistant Commissary Walter Dunne who was supported by Acting Assistant Commissary Dalton, a very experienced officer with over twenty years' previous service with the 85th Regiment from which he had retired as a sergeant before moving to South Africa. Dalton had joined the Commissariat as a civilian at the end of 1877 and participated in the Ninth Border War, being the only civilian mentioned in dispatches during the campaign. He had been in sole command of the forward stores depot at Ibeka, which came under direct attack on two occasions; he then successfully supervised the logistics for Colonel Glyn's fighting column. It was on Glyn's strong personal recommendation that Dalton was appointed to the Centre Column's Commissariat. Dalton's deputy was 21-year-old Acting Storekeeper Louis Byrne from Pietermaritzburg who joined the Commissariat at Dalton's request; he was still technically a civilian pending confirmation of his appointment. Due to their lower status in the army, these three lived apart and dined separately from Bromhead and the other officers. Assisting the Commissariat officers at Rorke's Drift was 32-year-old Corporal Attwood of the Army Service Corps. Attwood was an argumentative individual who had been transferred from Helpmekaar to Rorke's Drift as a punishment for his behaviour.

During the day preceding the invasion, another officer arrived at Rorke's Drift: he was 31-year-old Lieutenant John Rouse Merriott Chard of the Royal Engineers. Chard had arrived at Durban a few days earlier as the result of a request from Chelmsford for an additional detachment of engineers. In the absence of any direct orders and accompanied by his batman Sapper Robson[7], Chard had taken a horse-trap ride to Helpmekaar in a worthy attempt to arrive before the column advanced into Zululand.[8] Having arrived at Rorke's Drift he was, again, without orders. He made contact with Major Spalding of the 104th Regiment, Chelmsford's deputy assistant adjutant and quartermaster general, who was also the commanding officer at Rorke's Drift and responsible for communications and supplies from the front line. Spalding instructed Chard to plan a sturdy redoubt overlooking the river and to supervise its construction as soon as further reinforcements of the 24th, still at Helpmekaar, arrived to undertake the work. In the meantime there was little for Chard to do so he erected his tent near the ponts where MacDowell and his engineers had previously camped. His interaction with Bromhead and the other officers was minimal, probably because Royal Engineers officers were, like the Commissariat officers, not considered to be 'proper' officers. There was another officer present who, being considered by the line officers to be socially inferior, kept apart from all others; he was Captain William Stephenson, a Colonial officer of the NNC who commanded some 300 natives whose task was the completion of all menial tasks around the camp at Rorke's Drift. All settled down to await events.

In the meantime, and in order to justify the invasion of Zululand and to reassure the European population of Natal, Frere issued a statement that appeared in the *Natal Times* on 18 January 1879:

> The British Forces are crossing into Zululand to exact from Cetywayo reparations for violations of British territory committed by the sons of Sihayo and others, and to enforce compliance with the promises made by Cetywayo at his Coronation for the better government of his people.
>
> The British government has no quarrel with the Zulu people. All Zulus who come in unarmed, or lay down their arms, will be provided for until the troubles of their country are over. And will then, if they please, be allowed to return to their own land; but all who do not submit will be treated as enemies.
>
> When the war is finished, the British Government will make the best arrangements in its power for the future good government of the Zulus in their own country, in peace and quietness, and will not permit the killing and oppression they have suffered from Cetywayo to continue.

Referring to the British invasion force, the Biggarsberg correspondent of the *Natal Mercury* wrote for his newspaper, 'This army could not be beaten the world over'.

CHAPTER 4

Isandlwana, 22 January 1879

There will be an awful row at home about this.[1]

Having witnessed the derisory effect of Zulu marksmanship at Sihayo's homestead, where the Zulus had been unable to hit the extended column of mounted troops and marching men at 200 yards, Chelmsford was even more enthusiastic to confront the Zulu army. Beating the Zulus had proved to be so easy; getting the wagons from Rorke's Drift to the next campsite at Isandlwana was now proving to be more difficult.

Reconnaissance had shown that the route between Rorke's Drift and Isandlwana lay along a rough traders' track that crossed two marshy areas and a number of dongas, or watercourses. To undertake the work of making the track passable to the army's heavy wagons, four companies of the 2/24th were detailed to undertake the work and to make a depot for firewood, assisted by native levies, under the command of the regiment's senior staff officer, Major William Dunbar. Dunbar was ordered to pitch his tents beneath a rock outcrop close to Sihayo's homestead amidst heavy thorn with no field of fire. He did his best to clear the ground but was obliged to mount strong guards every night with men who had been working all day. On the 16th the position was inspected by Lord Chelmsford and his staff who were accompanied by Glyn and other officers; Dunbar made his fears known to them and asked for permission to move his camp to the other side of the stream. In the discussion that followed, Chelmsford's senior staff officer, Lieutenant Colonel Crealock, seems to have lost his temper and remarked impatiently 'if Maj. Dunbar is afraid to stay there, we could send someone who was not'.[2] Dunbar, a big imposing man, resigned his commission on the spot and walked off in a rage, but was later persuaded by Chelmsford to postpone his decision for the time being. This incident must soon have become known to his fellow officers. Until his promotion in 1874, Dunbar had been the senior captain of the 1/24th and had the most distinguished war record of any officer in the two battalions. The embarrassment caused to both Chelmsford and Glyn, whose relationship was already difficult, should not be underestimated.

There can be little doubt that, thereafter, even battle-experienced officers of the invasion force were reluctant to challenge or query any order from one of Chelmsford's staff officers for fear of humiliation. This might also explain why, at the moment of the main Zulu attack on the column a few days later at Isandlwana, all the 24th officers totally obeyed their orders to hold their exposed positions even as the Zulu army closed in and overwhelmed them.

Nevertheless, Dunbar's work was successfully completed by 20 January and the whole column moved through to the new campsite next to the long rock outcrop at Isandlwana. In the final approach to the camp the wagons constituted a column of 110 great Cape wagons, each drawn by up to sixteen oxen. Lieutenant Penn Symons wrote a description of Isandlwana:

> The hill was at its highest at its southern end, beyond which was a neck over which the track passed, and beyond that again an isolated kopje [hill] 500 yards from the main hill. In front, facing Eastward, open ground sloped gently down from Isandhlwana Hill, forming a plain about four miles from North to South and eight from East to West. Beyond that were hills and to the North of the plain a steepish ridge ran from East and West, at one point coming within a mile of the site chosen for the camp just in front of Isandhlwana Hill. To the right flank the ground between the camp and the Buffalo river was undulating and much broken.

Chelmsford intended that the column, once restocked with supplies, would move towards Isipezi hill and thence to Ulundi to confront Cetshwayo and his army. During the establishment of the camp on 20 January Chelmsford received a number of intelligence reports that the Zulu army was approaching his position from the direction of Ulundi. This made perfect sense and he accordingly dispatched a large reconnaissance party under Major John Dartnell towards the Mangeni falls to locate the Zulus, with orders to bring his force back to Isandlwana before nightfall. During the day Dartnell reported seeing numerous Zulu scouting parties and after dark he saw countless Zulu cooking fires across the distant hills towards Ulundi. He accordingly requested further reinforcements from Chelmsford, who mistakenly presumed that Dartnell had found the Zulu army. At 1.30 a.m. on 22 January Chelmsford divided his force; he accompanied the force now tasked with supporting Dartnell.

The camp was left with six companies of the 1/24th, one company of the 2/24th, two guns of the Royal Artillery and some 600 members of the NNC, a total force of over 1,700 men under the command of Lieutenant Colonel Henry Pulleine who had only just arrived at Isandlwana from Pietermaritzburg to take over the command of the 1/24th from Glyn. Pulleine was an accomplished administrator, and, rare for a senior officer at that time, he totally lacked any combat experience. His orders were to 'defend the camp' while at the same time he was to pack the camp ready to move to the next campsite at Isipezi.

Pulleine inherited a camp that was totally undefended; no defensive measures had been taken although Glyn and several of his officers had expressed concern that the camp was 'as vulnerable as an English village'.[3] Despite the instructions in the *Regulations for Field Forces in South Africa*, the Isandlwana camp had not been entrenched nor had the wagons been formed into a laager; Chelmsford's staff had overruled the junior officers' concern on the grounds that the precaution of laagering was unnecessary and that the wagons had to return to Rorke's Drift for further supplies.

It is impossible to pass over this matter because a terrible disaster resulted from the decision. The official records of the 24th Regiment state:

> The point has to be considered in the light of the methods and ideas then prevalent in the Army. In those days "theirs is not to reason why" was the

accepted gospel of the majority, for a subordinate officer to criticise or protest or even make suggestions wanted a marked degree of self-confidence and moral courage, while individual initiative and independence of thought was hardly encouraged in the highest circles. An order was an order, what was not ordered was not done.

A field officer of the 2nd Battalion on duty with the pickets on the previous day had expressed strong misgivings about the protective arrangements to the staff officer on duty, pointing out the poor defensive position of the camp and that there were no guards to the rear of it. Another officer, Lieutenant Melvill, adjutant of the 1/24th, stated at the time:

> These Zulus will charge home and with our small number we ought to be in laager, or, at any rate, prepared to stand shoulder to shoulder.[4]

Pulleine's orders were to 'keep his men in camp, to act strictly on the defensive, draw in the infantry and extend the cavalry picquets'[5]. Accordingly, Pulleine ordered the combatant troops out in a defensive line some 800 yards beyond the outer edge of the tented camp. The line ran along the crest of a low ridge, forming a quarter circle subtending the north-east of the Isandlwana position. The men were deployed in skirmishing order, i.e. between 3 and 5 yards apart. Two 7 pound guns (N Battery, 5th Brigade) of the Royal Artillery were placed on the knuckle of the line.

At about 10 a.m. parties of Zulus were seen looking down on the Isandlwana camp from the Nqutu plateau to the north; this confused Pulleine who believed the Zulu army was still approaching from Ulundi in the east. In fact the Zulu army was camped in a great hidden valley, the *Ngwebeni*, in the north-east and only 5.5 miles from the British camp; its fighting strength was between 23,000 and 25,000 men and the clusters of Zulus watching the camp were the Zulu commanders and their escorts.

Before leaving Isandlwana Chelmsford had ordered Colonel Durnford and his 2nd Column, consisting mainly of mounted native troops, to move towards Mangeni from Rorke's Drift where he had been held in reserve. By 10.30 a.m. Durnford and his mounted men reached Isandlwana – just as the observing Zulus appeared to move away from the ridge towards Chelmsford's position. The Zulus already on the edge of the plateau were in sufficient numbers to cause the experienced Durnford some concern; he was clearly puzzled as to why the camp was being observed from the north if the Zulu army was still many miles off to the south. As a precaution, he dispatched two of his mounted troops under the command of Lieutenants Raw and Roberts to ascend the plateau by the nearest ridge to ascertain the situation. At the same time Durnford moved off towards Mangeni in a due easterly direction, past the prominent conical hill and onto the plain beyond towards Ulundi. Durnford was followed by his rocket battery under Major Russell RA and presumably their intention was to protect Chelmsford and his highly exposed force.

When Lieutenant Raw and his men reached the top of the plateau the Zulus had disappeared; all that remained about 2 miles across the plateau was a small herd of cattle being led by several Zulu boys. Forgetting that this was a classic Zulu decoy, Raw and his men set off to investigate. They ascended a small rise only to ride into the advance guard of the approaching main Zulu army. They immediately opened fire on the Zulus with a series of rapid volleys. Stimulated by the sound of these volleys, the main Zulu force immediately sped up its advance towards the British position. The Zulu force, superbly disciplined and under the command of the chieftains Ntshingwayo ka Mahole Khoza and Mavumengwana ka Ndlela Ntuli emerged swiftly from the hidden valley, deploying into the tactic of the 'horns of the bull'. The first inkling the British force at Isandlwana had of their coming crisis was when they saw the Zulu, right horn descend from the plateau and destroy the rocket battery under the command of Major Russell. More Zulus then descended off the plateau to engage Colonel Durnford on the plain below, and they began to push Durnford's men obliquely back towards Isandlwana. Durnford's force made a valiant stand in a dry watercourse east of the camp, known thereafter as 'Durnford's Donga'.

The two guns of the Royal Artillery were then unlimbered and accurately fired several shells into the right horn of the Zulu army who were now pinned down by Durnford on the far side of the donga. This action elicited 'three cheers' from the watching infantrymen.

It was only then that the terrifying sight of the main Zulu force massing on the heights to the north and north-east of the camp became visible to the British.

A large wing of the Zulu army (the right horn) broke away from this force and moved down the valley that extends north-west from a point north of Isandlwana, and the British forces up on the ridge fired into them, eliciting little or no response. These warriors then turned south, threatening the road back to Rorke's Drift.

The Zulu commanders sat on the great bluff of rocks known as *iNyoni*, from where they directed the movements of Zulu forces, and when the 'horns of the bull' were in position the main body of the Zulu army descended into the killing field. Within half an hour the whole Zulu force had deployed and commenced its attack on the British front line. Due to the distance of the British firing line from the camp, it is unlikely that the camp commander, Colonel Pulleine, could even see their position or predicament. There was something of an impasse when the Zulu force came up against the concentrated Martini-Henry rifle fire of disciplined British troops; the Zulus sustained heavy casualties in the depression below the British firing line, but they bravely held their position.

Zulu warriors began to edge their way around the south of Durnford's position in the donga; this threatened G Company 2/24th who, having been detached from the southern extremity of the British firing line to assist Durnford, got caught out in the open and were swiftly overrun and slaughtered. Durnford retired to a position to the right (south) of the Isandlwana camp and made a determined last stand near the north-eastern base of the 'Stony Koppie' (Black's Koppie).

A bugler sounded the 'retire', whereupon a tactical withdrawal of the line commenced towards the camp. It failed, and the retreat became a rout when the soldiers were forced to fight the advancing Zulus through the chaos of their own camp, the tents of which had not been struck. Some British soldiers fought their way in small pockets down what is today known as the 'Fugitives' Trail', and the last stand of the 24th was probably fought on the banks of the Manzimyama river a mile south-west of Isandlwana.

At least one company of men, thought to be C Company of the 1/24th under the command of Captain Reginald Younghusband, made a last stand high up on the shoulder of the Isandlwana hill, and the last man to die on the British side is thought to have taken up a position in the cave high on the side of Isandlwana itself, immediately above Younghusband's position where he is believed to have kept off his enemy for some considerable time. Within half an hour the Zulus breached the British defences, forced Colonel Durnford's survivors back towards the camp and completed their encirclement. Within a further half-hour the camp and its occupants were completely destroyed. Trooper W. Barker of the Natal Carbineers later commented in a letter home: 'Zulus seemed to be behind, before, and on each side of us, and as we hurried on we had to leave poor fugitives crying and begging us not to leave them'.

The scene across the British position, as stabbing Zulus fought hand to hand with desperate soldiers, was unimaginably terrifying. British discipline had been replaced by rout; it was every man for himself amidst the carnage. Nevertheless, some acts of selflessness were recorded; the Hon. Standish Vereker gave his horse to an injured man, which resulted in his own death moments later. Surgeon Major Peter Shepherd would have escaped on his horse had he not stopped to assist a severely wounded soldier; Shepherd was stabbed through the neck by a passing Zulu. With the British force so outnumbered, it was remarkable that anyone could have escaped back to the safety of Natal, although of the fifty-five Europeans who did escape, the majority were camp followers who departed before the battle was under way, or Colonials who were mounted and could outrun the Zulus. Lieutenant Horace Smith-Dorrien, who was one of only five Imperial officers to escape, was in camp as the Zulus attacked and wrote of his escape to his father:

> I was out with the front companies of the 24th handing them spare ammunition. Bullets were flying all over the place, but I never seemed to notice them. The Zulus nearly all had firearms of some kind and lots of ammunition. Before we knew where we were, they came right into the camp, assegaing everybody right and left. Everybody then who had a horse turned to fly. The enemy were going at a kind of very fast half walk and half run. On looking round we saw that we were completely surrounded and the

road to Rorke's Drift was cut off. The place where they seemed thinnest was where we all made for. Everybody went pell-mell over the ground covered with huge boulders and rocks until we got to a deep spruit or gully. How the horses got over, I have no idea. I was riding a broken kneed old crock which did not belong to me, and which I expected to go on its head every minute. We had to go bang through them at the spruit. Lots of our men were killed there. I had lots of marvellous escapes, and was firing away at them with my revolver as I galloped along. The ground there down to the river was so broken that the Zulus went as fast as the horses and kept killing all the way. There were very few white men; they were nearly all mounted niggers of ours flying. This lasted until we came to a kind of precipice down to the river Buffalo. I jumped off and led my horse down. There was a poor fellow of the Mounted Infantry, a Private, struck through the arm, who said as I passed that if I could bind up his arm and stop the bleeding he would be alright. I accordingly took out my handkerchief and tied up his arm. Just as I had done it, Maj. Smith of the Artillery came down by me wounded, saying, "*For God's sake get on, man, the Zulus are on the top of us*". I had done all I could for the wounded man as I turned to jump on my horse. Just as I was doing so, the horse went with a bound to the bottom of the precipice, being struck with an assegai. I gave up all hope, as the Zulus were all round me, finishing off the wounded, the man I had helped and Maj. Smith among the number. However, with the strong hope that everybody clings to that some accident would turn up, I rushed off on foot and plunged into the river, which was little better than a roaring torrent.

Lieutenant William Cochrane was also in the camp when it was overrun by the Zulus; he echoed the desperate attempts to escape when he wrote to his family:

I made in the direction which I had seen taken by the mounted men, guns and Royal Artillery, and natives on foot. I was cut off by the enemy, who had now reached the line of retreat; but with a good horse, hard riding, and good luck, I managed to reach the Buffalo River. The Zulus seemed perfectly fearless; they followed alongside, having desperate fighting with those retreating, mostly our natives on foot. On several occasions they were quite close to me, but I was fortunate enough to escape, while others dropped at my side. They fired at us the whole way from the camp to the river, but having mounted the bank on the opposite side we were safe.

With the exception of Lieutenant Curling who vainly tried to save the artillery guns, no British frontline soldier or officer survived. This situation caused much controversy when, a few days after the battle, it was discovered that two mounted officers of the 24th Regiment, Lieutenants Coghill and Melvill, had not only managed to escape from the camp but had reached Natal on horseback before being killed. Their departure from the battle-field while their regiment's soldiers were still fighting for their lives, and the circumstances in which the two officers died, were to become the subject of much speculation, debate and a harsh statement from Chelmsford's successor, Sir Garnet Wolseley.[6]

In the closing moments of the battle Lieutenant Melvill tried to rally his men to the Queen's Colour of his battalion. He quickly realized the futility of his actions and instead tried to save the Colour from the Zulus. He made an epic ride over some 5 miles of boulder-strewn, bush-clad broken country down to the Buffalo river. He and Lieutenant Nevill Coghill both crossed the river but were both killed high up on the lip of the gorge on the Natal side of the river, having saved each other's lives but lost the Queen's Colour to the waters of the flooded river in a gallant attempt to get the Colour to the Natal bank. Both officers were killed by previously friendly locals from Sihayo's homestead – angry at the British attack on their village and their brutal treatment under questioning when taken prisoner.

Only three Isandlwana Victoria Crosses were awarded; curiously, each recipient had fled the battlefield. Private Samuel Wassall's VC was presented to him in September 1879; Coghill and Melvill were honoured posthumously in 1907, after a delay of nearly thirty years.[7]

As part of the Zulus' battle ritual, warriors invariably disembowelled, and occasionally mutilated, the bodies of their slain enemy. It was an act that horrified British soldiers who initially believed that disembowelment was a process of torture. In fact it was a post-combat ritual which reflected the

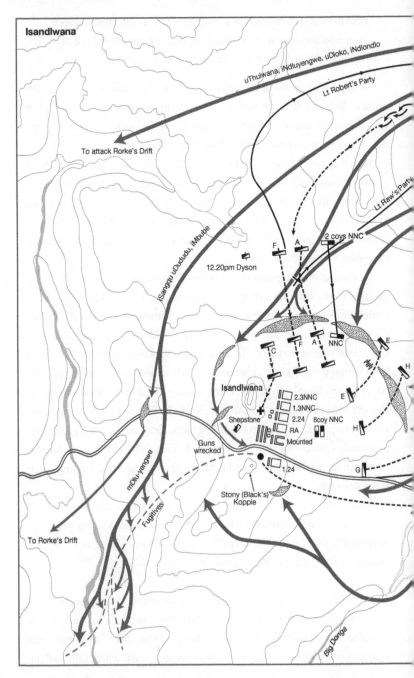

Isandlwana

uThulwana, iNdluyengwe, uDloko, iNdlondlo

Lt Robert's Party

To attack Rorke's Drift

Lt Raw's Party

2 coys NNC

F   A

12.20pm Dyson

iSangqu uDududu, iMbube

F   A   NNC   E

C   F   A   E

H

Isandlwana   2.3NNC

1.3NNC

Shepstone   2.24   6coy NNC   E

Guns   RA
wrecked   Mounted   H

1,24

Stony (Black's)   G
Koppie

To Rorke's Drift

mDlu-yengwe

Fugitives

Big Donga

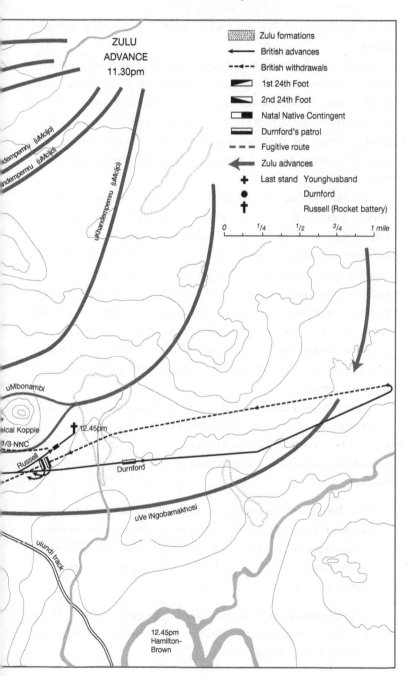

extent to which death in combat was linked to the spiritual world of the Zulus.

After battle, freshly slain bodies were repeatedly stabbed in a practice known as *ukuhlomula*. The practice of *hlomula*ing a fallen enemy was a ritual to mark a participating warrior's role in the kill. Warriors who had been involved in the fighting but had not actually killed an enemy were still entitled to share the glory that was attached to the victory – stabbing the corpse after it was dead and 'washing the spear' in blood acknowledged this.

The associated custom of disembowelling a fallen enemy – *qaqa* – was directly related to the Zulu view of the afterlife and its relationship with the world of the living. Part of this ritual involved slitting open the stomach of the slain enemy. Under the African sun any corpse will quickly putrefy and the gases given off by the early stages of decay cause the stomach to swell. In Zulu belief this was the soul of the dead warrior vainly trying to escape to the afterlife. The victor was obliged to open the stomach of his victim to allow the spirit to escape, failing which, the victor would be haunted by the ghost of his victim, who would inflict unmentionable horrors upon him, including causing his own stomach to swell until, eventually, the victor went mad.

Mehlokazulu kaSihayo, son of Sihayo and an attendant of King Cetshwayo, was present at Isandlwana with the *iNgobamakhosi* regiment. In his account of the war, which was recorded in September 1879, he made various references to the subject of stripping and disembowelling the dead:

> As a rule we took off the upper garments, but left the trousers, but if we saw blood upon the garments we did not bother. All the dead bodies were cut open, because if that had not been done the Zulus would have become swollen like the dead bodies. I heard that some bodies were otherwise mutilated.[8]

At Isandlwana, some bodies were disembowelled immediately. Trooper Richard Stevens of the Natal Mounted Police survived the battle, and recorded his shock at the practice:

> I stopped in the camp as long as possible, and saw one of the most
> horrid sights I ever wish to see. The Zulus were in the camp, ripping our men
> up, and also the tents and everything they came across, with their assegais.
> They were not content with killing, but were ripping the men up
> afterwards.[9]

One aspect of Zulu ritual that did result in mutilation of the dead was the removal of body parts from a fallen enemy that could be added to the ritual medicines used to prepare the Zulu army before a campaign. These medicines were known as *intelezi*, and were sprinkled on the warriors by *izinyanga*, war-doctors, before the army set off on campaign. Parts from a dead enemy, especially one who had fought bravely, would be an enormous boost to Zulu morale thus ensuring supremacy in battle. Since a number of *izinyanga* accompanied the army that triumphed at Isandlwana, they would certainly have taken the opportunity to collect the raw materials for such medicine from dead soldiers. Archibald Forbes's graphic account of the state of the bodies at the time of the first burial expedition to Isandlwana in May 1879 is highly suggestive:

> Every man had been disembowelled, some were scalped, and others
> subject to yet ghastlier mutilations.[10]

At Isandlwana these mutilations included the disarticulation by the Zulus of the dead soldiers' jawbones for trophies, complete with beards. Facial hair was relatively unknown to the warriors and the luxurious beards worn by the soldiers fascinated them. Despite the soldiers' deep-seated fears that these mutilations were carried out before death, and therefore amounted to torture, there is no evidence that this was in fact the case. Interestingly, after Isandlwana the practice of shaving became widespread throughout the army; soldiers accepted the necessity of dying for their country but were reluctant to be disarticulated after death on the battlefield.

The gulf of cultural misunderstanding was so wide that, after Isandlwana, any Zulu who fell into British hands was doomed.

Oblivious of the drama and slaughter at Isandlwana, Chelmsford and his reconnaissance force had met up with Dartnell's force and both groups then experienced a day of intense frustration some 15 miles out on the plain towards Ulundi. The Zulu army had not materialized but a number of large Zulu groups had repeatedly given the British the slip in and around the Magogo hills near the Mangeni falls. The Zulus would appear in force on a distant hilltop, only to have disappeared when the weary troops reached the position; it was a cat-and-mouse tactic repeated throughout the day and resulted in Chelmsford's force becoming angry and exhausted by the effort. It was after 12 noon and while lunching at Mangeni that Chelmsford received reports that Isandlwana was under attack, but due to the fact that the British at Isandlwana did not strike the tents, the distant and blurred view through the heat haze suggested that the camp was intact. Chelmsford presumed that, had an attack occurred, the British were in sufficient numbers to win the day.

It was only at about 3 p.m. that Chelmsford decided to return to Isandlwana to ascertain events for himself. He took with him a small escort; en route he met Colonel Hamilton-Browne who, having watched the defeat of the camp from a hillock 3 miles from Isandlwana, tried to persuade Chelmsford that the camp was lost. While the two officers discussed the situation, Commandant Lonsdale arrived from Isandlwana and confirmed the camp was in the hands of the Zulus.

Chelmsford ordered his scattered force around Mangeni to assemble for the 12 mile march back to Isandlwana; by the time they arrived back at Isandlwana, the camp was silent and in darkness. Chelmsford ordered the artillery to fire several rounds into the previously tented area in case the Zulus had occupied it. Major Black and his company then stormed the small hill opposite the shattered wagon park. The Zulus had long since departed having totally smashed and looted the camp.

On the southern slope of Isandlwana lay some 5,000 bodies; the British lost 1,500 defending the camp, the remainder were Zulus who had been killed during the battle. The devastation in the camp was reflected by the entry in the 24th Regiment's official history.

There were no 'wounded' or 'missing', only 'killed'. From the 1st Battalion the twenty-fourth lost 16 officers and 407 NCOs and men, including R.S.M. Gapp, Q.M.S. Leitch, five other Staff Sergeants and five Colour Sergeants. Of the 2nd Battalion there perished five officers and 127 other ranks, including Bandmaster Ballard and Q.M.S. Davis. It was a worse blow than Chilianwala; even 1914–1918 was not to produce such another casualty list.

Through the darkness that now descended on Isandlwana, an eerie red glow began to lighten the sky from the direction of Rorke's Drift. Chelmsford and his weary survivors were quickly forced to realize that their base camp and hospital at Rorke's Drift were under Zulu attack. Due to the utter exhaustion of his men, Chelmsford was powerless to intervene. He paced up and down throughout the night while his men caught what sleep they could until dawn.

CHAPTER 5

Rorke's Drift; The Prelude

Nothing will happen.

MAJOR SPALDING, ON DEPARTING FROM RORKE'S DRIFT

Having arrived at Rorke's Drift too late to accompany the invasion force, Lieutenant John Chard of the Royal Engineers had pitched his tent at the site of the river ponts previously occupied by his engineer colleagues. Chard's superior and the senior Royal Engineers officer at Rorke's Drift, Lieutenant Francis MacDowel, had sufficiently impressed Chelmsford and Glyn with his engineering skills that he and his detachment had been ordered to join the invasion column for road-building purposes. Meanwhile, the ponts at Rorke's Drift were in the care of Sergeant Milne of the 2/3rd Regiment and six Natal natives. Chard was disappointed that there were no specific orders for him, especially since he had made a spirited dash on horseback from Durban in anticipation that he would be in time to accompany the invasion force. In the absence of orders he glumly assumed responsibility for the ponts and awaited events. Being a good half-mile from the mission station, Chard kept to himself and had little to do with anyone else, apart from Major Spalding who was in overall command. For several days Chard was content to await his orders and spent his time making minor adjustments to the ponts; soon there was nothing for him to do. During the evening of 21 January, an ambiguous order arrived from the Centre Column ordering the engineers to Isandlwana;

The party of R.E. now at Rorke's Drift are to move at once to join the Column under the charge of the NCO.

Chard was evidently sufficiently confused by the reference to the NCO being in charge of the party instead of himself to raise the matter with Major Spalding in an attempt to clarify his role and responsibilities. Spalding knew that a fortified position to protect the river crossing was due to be built on the small rise immediately overlooking the ponts; but this work was scheduled to be undertaken by the five companies of the 2/4th Regiment who were still marching to the front. Spalding had little idea of their whereabouts or when he could expect them. Not knowing what to do with this underemployed officer, Spalding agreed that Chard should ride to Isandlwana the following morning to ascertain his duties from the column commander.

Since the invasion column had departed, life at Rorke's Drift had become unusually comfortable for those who remained behind, including Lieutenant Bromhead and the eighty-five members of B Company of the 2/24th. Only the surgeon and his small team were occupied with an ever-increasing number of sick or injured. There were now thirty-five hospital patients who occupied the three largest rooms in what was formerly the Revd Witt's home. The senior ranking patient, Sergeant Maxfield, was given Witt's bed as he was delirious with fever. The remaining patients had been allocated straw beds on wooden pallets propped up on bricks. Even accounting for the British attack on Sihayo's stronghold, there were only three men, all from the NNC, who were suffering from actual war wounds. Corporal Schiess, a Swiss national, had serious blisters on his foot and Corporal Mayer was suffering from a leg injury. One of Sihayo's Zulus had been shot through his leg and, as a prisoner, he had been isolated from the other hospital patients. The remaining cases related to fever, trench foot, lumbago and rheumatism in addition to several cases of injuries sustained from wagon accidents; all were under the care of Surgeon Reynolds and his three orderlies from the Army Hospital Corps. On loan to the surgeon was Private Henry Hook from B Company 2/24th, a 28-year-old teetotaller from Gloucestershire and an excellent cook; his main responsibility was to feed the patients.

On 22 January the day dawned dry and bright. By breakfast time it was obviously going to be a hot day and, with no wagons to be loaded, Bromhead gave most of his men free time; a section of eight men were detailed to guard the ponts, not in itself an onerous task. Captain Stephenson's NNC company, camped next to the river to the right of the old drift, merely sat in the sun and avoided any form of physical activity as did their officer and six white NCOs. The commissaries should have been reloading empty wagons from Isandlwana in order to transfer further stores forward to Glyn's column but, in the absence of the wagons, there was nothing to do; they also enjoyed a quiet morning free of any responsibilities.

Before dawn the transport officer of Glyn's column, Lieutenant Horace Smith-Dorrien, had ridden back to Rorke's Drift from Isandlwana to deliver an order to Colonel Durnford, who had arrived at the drift the previous evening; Durnford was to move his force forward to support Chelmsford. Smith-Dorrien took breakfast with the commissaries to discuss the reprovisioning of the column and during the meal he informed them that a major engagement against the Zulus was expected later that day. He then returned to Isandlwana.[1]

At daybreak Chard had ordered his small detachment, consisting of Corporal Gamble and Sappers Cuthbert, MacLaren, Wheatley and Robson, to load the engineering equipment onto their mule wagon and set off for Isandlwana. Not wishing to be further delayed, Chard impatiently rode on ahead of his men. On arriving at Isandlwana he found the main camp in some disarray; Chelmsford had taken half the force to support Major Dartnell who had, or so he thought, discovered the advancing Zulu army. Isandlwana camp was now defended by the 1/24th who were manning their forward line over half a mile away from the camp; this was in response to groups of Zulus congregating about 2 miles distant on the Nqutu Plateau overlooking the British position. There were several teams of men taking down tents while the remainder, clerks, cooks and bakers, bandsmen, farriers and other camp staff went about their daily business, all seemingly oblivious of the Zulus observing them from the plateau overlooking the camp. Chard initially went to the officers' mess and obtained some breakfast. He then sought out the headquarters staff to ascertain his orders, which were disappointing: he was to return to Rorke's Drift to supervise the ponts and keep the road between Rorke's Drift and Isandlwana in good working order. Before he departed from Isandlwana, he learned that another large group of Zulus had been seen observing the camp from the high Nqutu plateau. Using his binoculars he could clearly see the Zulus silhouetted against the distant skyline; he observed a number of them move away from the ridge. One group moved off to the west and, thinking they might approach Rorke's Drift and cut him off, Chard decided to return to the drift to deny the Zulus access to his ponts. One mile from Isandlwana, he met Colonel Durnford's column advancing towards Isandlwana. Chard ordered his men to offload their stores onto one of Durnford's wagons and to march the remaining mile to Isandlwana, and to their deaths later that day; he took the wagon and Sapper Robson back with him to Rorke's Drift where he arrived at midday to be given a copy of the daily orders.

Camp Rorke's Drift
22nd January 1879.

Camp Morning Orders.

1   The force under Lt. Col. Durnford RE. having departed, a guard of 6 Privates and 1 N.C.O. will be furnished by the detachment 2/24th Regiment on the ponts. A guard of 50 armed natives will likewise be furnished by Capt. Stevenson's detachment at the same spot – the ponts will be invariably drawn over to the Natal side at night. This duty will cease on the arrival of Capt. Rainforth's Company, 1/24th Regiment.
2   In accordance with para. 19 Regulations for Field Forces in South Africa, Capt. Rainforth's Company 1/24th Regiment, will entrench itself on the spot assigned to it by Column Orders.

H. Spalding, Major
Commanding.

There was still no sight of Rainforth's company, now several days overdue. This new order posed Chard a problem; he knew that if the Zulus arrived at the drift, he could not possibly defend the ponts with seven men and a handful of natives. Rainforth's company should have been in

position at Rorke's Drift well before the main column crossed into Zululand and Glyn had since dispatched three sets of orders to Rainforth requiring him to move down from Helpmekaar; as the commander at Rorke's
Drift, Spalding knew of Glyn's orders and he presumed they, or Rainforth,
had failed to arrive. In fact the orders had been at Helpmekaar awaiting
Rainforth whose company had fortuitously arrived the previous day having
been severely delayed by the deep mud and storm damage to the Helpmekaar road. There were now two companies of the 1/24th at Helpmekaar,
Rainforth's and Upcher's G and D Companies, and both made preparations, presumably to comply with the awaiting orders, to march on to
Rorke's Drift later that day.[2]

At about 1 p.m. Chard reported to Spalding and told him of the Zulus
at Isandlwana; he also explained his difficulty in complying with the order
in the absence of Rainforth's company. Spalding was clearly irritated by
the situation as he had sent two additional written orders to Helpmekaar and
could not understand Rainforth's non-arrival.[3] Spalding decided to ride to
Helpmekaar to clarify matters; as he was about to depart, he asked Chard:
'Which of you is senior, you or Bromhead?' Chard didn't know so Spalding
returned to his tent and examined his copy of the Army List. Spalding then
told Chard 'I see you are senior, so you will be in charge, although, of course,
nothing will happen, and I shall be back again this evening, early'. It was
2 p.m. when Spalding rode out of Rorke's Drift and with his departure he
abandoned his chance of glory; Chard casually returned to his riverside
tent for a late lunch with Commissary Dunne and the intention of spending
the remainder of the afternoon writing letters home.

It is strange that Chard did not consider it necessary to inform Bromhead, the commander of the only fighting troops at Rorke's Drift, that he had
earlier seen Zulus heading in their direction. To be fair to him, Chard was
the only officer at Rorke's Drift without any campaign experience in Africa
and may not have understood Zulu tactics. Bromhead was oblivious of
what Chard had seen; Chard sought out Commissary Dunne and after
lunch, the pair rested in the shade of their tarpaulin shelter while the rest
of the garrison quietly went about their own duties.

Colour Sergeant Bourne, accompanied by Sergeants Gallagher, Smith,

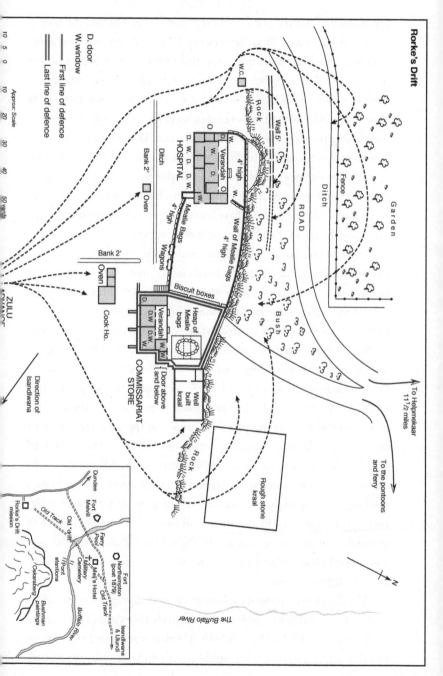

Rorke's Drift

D. door
W. window

First line of defence
Last line of defence

Approx. Scale
0 5 10 20 30 40 50 yards

Windridge and Wilson, first visited the Shiyane summit behind the mission station on 12 January. From here they had a magnificent view into Zululand and on a daily basis they were able to watch the Centre Column progress into Zululand; they even followed the Column's successful attack on Sihayo's stronghold in the Batshe valley. The same group were on the summit at midday of the 22nd when they heard the distant sound of artillery fire coming from the direction of Isandlwana. They strained to see the 6 miles to Isandlwana but could see nothing of note and then returned to camp. A few minutes later the muffled sound of gunfire could be heard at Rorke's Drift from the direction of Isandlwana, but not by Bromhead due to his deafness. Chard could not have heard this either; his campsite was in a depression by the river and out of sight of Isandlwana.

Eager to find out more, and with nothing else to do that afternoon, the Swedish missionary Witt, the Revd George Smith with his telescope, and Surgeon Reynolds took some horses and set out to ride to the summit of the Oskarsberg in the hope of seeing what was happening. From their vantage point they could see three distant columns of natives approaching the Buffalo river from the direction of Isandlwana. Revd Smith's first impressions were that these columns were detachments of the NNC returning to Rorke's Drift until, half an hour later, Smith noticed that there were two natives on white horses leading an obvious *impi* of Zulus. Ahead of the main *impi* they saw scouting patrols of Zulus who appeared to be searching in wide sweeps and occasionally firing into the bush. They remained watching the advancing Zulus until Surgeon Reynolds noticed some riders approaching the mission station from the direction of the river; thinking that they might need medical attention, he set off down the hillside, quickly followed by the others. All four were in no doubt that an unusual event must have occurred to allow a large Zulu force to bypass Chelmsford's main column and head for Rorke's Drift, completely unhindered by British troops.

The Zulu force consisted of elements of the iNdluyengwe, uThulwana, iNdlondlo and uDloko *ibutho* and collectively they crossed the Buffalo river some 4 miles below Rorke's Drift. The river was in flood and running fast through this stretch; it was studded with rocks between the precipitous sides of the ravine and it was here, no doubt, that the Zulus jumped across. Having successfully crossed the river they then advanced along the Natal bank and climbed onto the plateau behind Rorke's Drift where they rested and took snuff. It is popularly believed that King Cetshwayo had ordered his generals to stay out of Natal but this belief overlooks Cetshwayo's address to his army.[4] Either way, orders in the heat of battle and those that went against the warriors' immediate instincts were often disregarded during the Zulu War. After all, three hours earlier, the Zulus had attacked the position at Isandlwana in defiance of the king's orders not to attack the British when encamped; crossing the border into Natal against orders was no worse, especially if serious damage could be caused along the border and Natal cattle looted. The commander of the approaching Zulus, Prince Dabulamanzi, was certainly more concerned with gaining glory than obeying his half-brother the king. Having crossed the border into Natal, Dabulamanzi's force was intent on some serious plunder and 'spear washing' to compensate for not having participated at the battle of Isandlwana. They could still gain prestige and glory by killing any Natal natives they came across between Helpmekaar and the river, and by burning their farms and plundering their cattle. Rorke's Drift was incidental to Dabulamanzi's plan – the garrison was not his main objective, it just happened to be in his way. After taking snuff and quenching their thirst, the Zulus divided into several groups; some headed off to plunder towards the distant hills near Helpmekaar. The main body continued towards Rorke's Drift where they came across the recently abandoned farm belonging to a white farmer, Edward Woodroffe; this was burnt to the ground.

Meanwhile, just as Witt and his party rode back to the mission station, Chard was enjoying his afternoon rest on the river bank. Chard's peace was disturbed when at about 3.30 p.m. he noticed two horsemen galloping towards the drift from the direction of Isandlwana. The pair plunged their horses into the river shouting to Chard that the Zulus were approaching; the two riders were Lieutenants Vane and Adendorff of the NNH, both being survivors of the battle at Isandlwana; this unbelievable news was the first intimation Chard had of the disaster at Isandlwana. There can be little doubt that Chard was bemused by the news and before he had time to react, another messenger arrived from Bromhead suggesting that Chard should strike his tents, inspan his wagon, load his tools and return immediately to the mission station. It transpired that a native horseman of the Edendale Contingent had just delivered a note to Bromhead, written by Captain Essex who had survived Isandlwana, reporting the loss of the British camp to the Zulus. Chard dispatched Vane and Adendorff with his reply to Bromhead stating that he would return to the Post once he had collected his working party. As Adendorff rode off, he called back to Chard that he would stay on at the mission station and fight.

Chard then had a water cart filled with water and, with what tools he could load on his wagon, set off to join Bromhead. At the mission station, Lieutenants Vane and Adendorff had arrived just as Dalton and Bromhead were in deep discussion; both Natal Native Horse (NNH) officers volunteered that, with the Zulus so close, the garrison should move out with all speed. Vane was ordered by Bromhead to ride on to warn the garrison at Helpmekaar; meanwhile, the dreadful news from Isandlwana had been re-confirmed by three more breathless horsemen, all survivors from the battle, including Private Frederick Evans 2/24th on loan to the Mounted Infantry. Having made their report, they too made off at the gallop towards Helpmekaar. Bromhead's first reaction was to make a fighting withdrawal back to Helpmekaar; he ordered all tents to be struck and the two available wagons to be made ready to convey the hospital patients away from danger.

It was at this point that Commissary Dalton intervened. He had realized the serious implications of the news and then quietly and respectfully pointed out to Bromhead that trying to outrun the Zulus over a distance of 12 miles with a slow-moving convoy was extremely dangerous; also, there was the long and steep winding track up the ridge to Helpmekaar. Bromhead knew full well that Dalton was an experienced campaigner and heeded his suggestions. Dalton suggested that the only course of action was to fortify the post and defend it until Major Spalding returned with Rainforth's company – they were due back at Rorke's Drift within a matter of hours.

Dalton's advice and obvious leadership convinced Bromhead to stay and fight; Bromhead gave orders for a 4ft high wall of mealie sacks and boxes to be built around the perimeter of the mission station buildings, to be supervised by Dalton, who set the men to work linking the two buildings. Readily available from the piles of commissariat stores were a large number of 200 pound mealie sacks and hundredweight biscuit and meat boxes. The north side wall overlooking the garden and track to Helpmekaar was made to follow a 5ft high rocky ledge; this gave added height to the barricade as it grew. The decision to stay and fight came during the transfer of the hospital sick and wounded to the wagons; there was a short period of indecision before the process was reversed and all were returned to the hospital.

The quick and perceptive reaction by Dalton to the possibility of a Zulu attack indicates that he may well have anticipated such an event. He also recognized that Rorke's Drift garrison was undefended, something that neither Spalding nor Bromhead had realized. The officers had unwittingly failed to comply with Chelmsford's standing orders to laager every camp. With nearly 100 men of B Company and some 300 natives from Captain Stephenson's NNC, there was more than sufficient manpower to complete the work quickly. Once work began, Dalton instructed that the external doors of the hospital were to be barricaded and its walls loopholed for the defenders to fire through. There are sufficient contemporary accounts and letters, many written by private soldiers, which acknowledge Dalton's overall leadership; the soldiers would certainly have been aware that he had served as a sergeant[5] in the 85th Regiment (later the King's Shropshire Light Infantry). Dalton clearly controlled events even at this early stage, and he obviously did so with Bromhead's approval; not only did Dalton make sense, he was a natural leader with a sound reputation earned during the Ninth Border War.

It was during this period of high activity and confusion that Adendorff quietly slipped away, his absence going unnoticed by Chard. To be fair to Adendorff, he had already survived the British disaster at Isandlwana and, knowing that Rorke's Drift was about to be attacked by the same Zulus, his desertion is understandable. Curiously, Chard believed that Adendorff stayed to fight, and wrote in both of his official reports that Adendorff 'stayed to assist in the defence'. Not so; there is sufficient evidence from contemporary letters that indicate Adendorff not only departed from Isandlwana before the main battle occurred but then also made a timely flight from Rorke's Drift. When Adendorff initially reported to Chard he stated that he had fled Isandlwana by the 'Rorke's Drift road'. This was not possible; the Zulus had completely blocked the road in question before their attack on Isandlwana took place. Vane escaped alone from Isandlwana and only met with Adendorff as he approached the river crossing. The mystery of Chard's misidentification is solved in Chard's own report and nominal roll of the Rorke's Drift survivors – both presented to Queen Victoria. Corporal Francis Attwood of the Army Service Corps was one of five soldiers who received the Distinguished Conduct Medal for bravery at Rorke's Drift. In his report, Chard describes certain actions of Adendorff but these were well known by those present to have been performed by Attwood. It was a straightforward case of mistaken identity by Chard; Attwood was awarded his DCM at Pietermaritzburg on 15 November 1879. By then Adendorff had disappeared into obscurity although weeks later, news reached the garrison at Rorke's Drift that both Vane and Adendorff had been arrested at Pietermaritzburg for desertion. The pair were due to face an enquiry but there is no evidence this ever took place. Chard's report that Adendorff had 'stayed to fight' had already been submitted to higher authority and had the trial taken place, Chard would certainly have been called to give evidence, against his own report – and so the matter of Adendorff's desertion appears to have been quietly dropped.

In the midst of these preparations, Witt and his party returned off the hill and blurted out the news of the imminent arrival of the Zulus. When Witt saw his house being prepared for battle and his furniture being used in the barricade, he became, in the words of Surgeon Reynolds, 'excitable, and in broken English, demanded an explanation'.[6] As soon as Witt grasped the desperation of the situation, he muttered something about his family, remounted his horse and sped off towards Helpmekaar. The Revd Smith also thought the time had arrived for him to depart; he frantically sought his horse only to discover that both his horse and native groom had disappeared. With the Zulus now approaching, Smith chose to assist with the defence rather than fleeing on foot.

As Witt departed in a cloud of dust, Chard arrived to find the site being barricaded, a wall of sacks being erected and the two buildings in the process of being loopholed. There was an urgent discussion between Chard, Bromhead and Dalton, whereupon Chard, now the senior officer, gave his approval to remain and fight. Although command was passed to Chard, he, like Bromhead, let Dalton get on with the work.

An interesting and most unusual chain of command now developed at Rorke's Drift. The senior officer present, Captain Stephenson, was a Colonial officer and therefore had no authority over Imperial troops. The senior Imperial officer, Lieutenant Chard, was a Royal Engineer; he lacked fighting experience and even with his marginal seniority, he could not have commanded Bromhead's company without Bromhead's explicit approval, which Bromhead readily gave. In any event, both Chard and Bromhead permitted Dalton to give the actual orders; this is odd, as Dalton was both socially and militarily 'inferior' being a mere Commissary 'officer', a former NCO and, worse, now a Colonial.[7]

By 4 p.m. the perimeter wall linking the two main buildings, the storehouse and the hospital was complete. Along the 50 yard front of the buildings was a steep 5ft drop off the ledge overlooking the Helpmekaar road, the orchard and Witt's walled garden. Along the top of the ledge, another wall of mealie bags was laid to a height of 3ft; this resulted in a barrier some 8ft high along the entire front of the position. The wagons, which Bromhead had brought up to evacuate the wounded now formed part of the impenetrable mealie bag wall facing the Oskarsberg hill. The whole defensive perimeter now stood at a height of at least 4ft, which Dalton considered high enough to afford the defending soldiers adequate protection and still enable them to fight.

Chard now made a curious decision; he apparently wanted to ensure that the ponts were moored in the middle of the river and out of reach of the Zulus; also, his men had still not arrived back from the ponts. Instead of sending an NCO, he left the mission station and returned to the river where he declined an offer from Sergeant Milne to defend the ponts and hurried his men back to the safety of the mission station. He then met Lieutenant Henderson and his troop of mounted NNH. Henderson and his men had escaped from Isandlwana and readily accepted Chard's request to cover the ponts and engage any Zulus that approached. This would give those at the mission station sufficient warning of the Zulus' approach from the direction of the river. Vause was then to report back to Chard and assist however he could. Chard then returned to the mission station. At about 4.20 p.m. the first rank of Zulu skirmishers approached the river and were engaged by Henderson's NNH. After an initial exchange of shots, the NNH then rode up the hill and, bypassing the mission station, headed off towards Helpmekaar; Lieutenant Henderson shouted his apologies to Chard and then rode off to join his men. This was too much for Stephenson's NNC who were already agitated by the sound of gunfire; seeing the NNH departing towards apparent safety, they jumped the barricades as one body and ran after the fleeing riders. Sadly, their white NCOs and Captain Stephenson followed suit; whilst the departure of the natives was never likely to be considered a loss to the defenders, the defection of their white officer and NCOs seriously annoyed Bromhead's men who were now lining the barricade. They fired a spatter of shots at the fleeing deserters and Corporal Anderson fell dead as he was running away towards the road. No order to fire had been given and no questions were subsequently asked.[8]

The defection of so many suddenly left the garrison severely depleted and it was obvious that the perimeter was now too long for the remaining 104 able-bodied fighting men. Chard gave orders for the remaining biscuit boxes to be used to build a dividing wall across the position, effectively cutting it in two and isolating the hospital. With only minutes to go before the Zulus arrived, Chard made yet another strange decision: instead of abandoning the now isolated hospital and concentrating his defenders and the sick into the newly created and more easily defended smaller compound, he decided to try and defend the original perimeter. Meanwhile Colour Sergeant Bourne supervised the opening of ammunition boxes and initiated a supply system that ensured every defender had a pile of rounds readily available. He was then directed to take a small party of skirmishers beyond the mission station to deter the approaching Zulus.

The approaching Prince Dabulamanzi and his remaining force of some 4,500 Zulus had sent scouts ahead; these were the first Zulus to come face to face with the Rorke's Drift defenders, albeit from a distance of about half a mile. The Zulu scouts quickly reported back to Dabulamanzi that a small and weakly defended British position lay immediately behind Shiyane. It was an unexpected prize with piles of stores, food and soldiers' rifles ready for the taking. Dabulamanzi gave orders for the attack to begin and the warriors spread out into their traditional 'horns' battle formation.[9] The Zulus were unaware that the British were ready for them or that, within the next few hours, the Zulus would need their whole scavenging force just to maintain the attack – thus curtailing their previous intention of plundering the whole area. As the Zulus advanced, they pushed Bourne's skirmishes back to the mission station; Bourne later wrote: 'I was instructed … to take out and command a line of skirmishers … and about 4.30 the enemy came in sight round the hill to our south and driving in my thin red line of skirmishers, made a rush at our south wall'. The attack on Rorke's Drift had begun.

CHAPTER 6

The Battle of Rorke's Drift

From Officer Commanding B/Co. 2/24th Regiment Rorke's Drift
22nd January 1879

To Officer Commanding 1/24th Regiment Helpmakaar

Sir,
Intelligence has just reached camp that the camp at Isandula Hill is
taken by the enemy.

Lt. G Bromhead, Lieutenant
Commanding B Company 2/24th Regt.[1]

By 4 p.m. Lieutenant Chard was in no doubt that his unexpected command at Rorke's Drift was about to be attacked by an apparently overwhelming number of Zulu warriors. He could hear the muffled sound of gunshots coming from behind the Oskarsberg, and the firing was coming steadily closer. All around him the work to defend the outpost was nearing completion, and Commissary Dalton was industriously opening ammunition boxes and supervising distribution of rounds to the soldiers manning its defensive wall. In his blue jacket and slouch hat Dalton, a big man and well over 6ft tall, must have stood out among the red-coated soldiers whose average height was less than 5ft 6in. Chard suddenly remembered that there were several casks of medicinal rum in the store building and knowing only too well the British soldiers' insatiable desire for alcohol, gave orders to Sergeant Windridge that the spirit was not to be touched. Windridge was in temporary charge of the storeroom and he detailed the nearest soldier to guard the rum with orders that, after giving the standard military warning of 'Stop or I fire', he was to shoot anyone who attempted to touch the spirit. Having given the order, Windridge continued supervising the defence of the commissariat store, cutting loopholes through the walls and strengthening barricades around the building.

In the other building, originally Witt's house but now the hospital, lay twenty bed patients. Bromhead directed six soldiers of B Company to take up defensive positions in the hospital; they were Privates Joseph Williams, John Williams (real name Fielding), Robert Jones and William Jones, Henry Hook and Thomas Cole. Those patients who were 'walking sick' were issued with rifles; they were Gunner Howard and Privates Adams, Horrigan and Waters. Under the supervision of Dalton, each defender was given a haversack full of ammunition and allocated a room to defend; then all the doors and windows were barred and sealed with sacks and boxes and final improvements were made to the loopholes. Due to the intensive activity, no one questioned the fact that access from each room was only to the outside; there was no access to the other rooms within the hospital, so once barricaded in, the defenders and patients were effectively trapped inside their allotted rooms.

At the commissariat store, Private Hitch had been detailed to act as lookout from the top of the thatched roof of the building when, at about 4.30 p.m., he urgently shouted a warning that the Zulus were approaching. These first thirty or so Zulus were the iNdluyengwe scouts who had probed ahead of Dabulamanzi's marauding force. The scouts began to spread out in front of the far end of the mission station beyond the hospital and, as Hitch watched, another 500 or 600 in number arrived and silently joined the scouts in the classic 'horns' attack formation. Once in position they began to advance at a run towards the outpost's south wall between the hospital and storeroom. The defenders immediately opened fire with

Rorke's Drift hospital at 4 p.m. (before the attack)

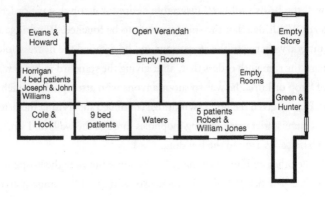

controlled volleys; the distance was between 300 and 400 yards and a scattering of warriors fell. As the defenders warmed to their task they became more accurate with their fire, which was fortuitous because, as the warriors ran forwards, they darted from whatever cover they could find while wildly firing their own guns, albeit ineffectively. The Zulus were highly skilled at using their shields to distract the soldiers' aim; they ran with their shields held away from their bodies in the anticipation that the soldiers would fire at the steadily held shields and not the darting bodies holding them. In this way, many Zulus got to within 50 yards of the outpost with their very first charge before the British volleys forced them to take cover behind the numerous boulders that littered the area. The warriors then retreated and regrouped some 40 yards away behind the 5ft high garden wall facing the ledge in front of the mission station. They soon came under a heavy crossfire from the two buildings and those warriors unprotected by the wall sought whatever cover they could find in the orchard and stream beds while those Zulus behind the buildings who bore the brunt of the initial volleys took cover in the area of the cookhouse ovens in front of the Oskarsberg.

The Zulus in the orchard then charged at the mealie bag barrier along the ledge to the front of the hospital. They were met with devastating blasts of volley fire at close range; as warriors fell, those behind jumped over them and crashed against the barrier. A fierce and desperate struggle ensued before the Zulus suddenly retreated leaving scores of their dead and wounded warriors lying several deep against the defensive wall of sacks. In the mêlée Dalton, a former army marksman, shot a Zulu who was in the act of stabbing a corporal of the Army Hospital Corps; the Zulu had seized the corporal's rifle muzzle rendering the soldier momentarily defenceless. The impetus and ferocity of the Zulus' attack began forcing the soldiers back from the barrier immediately in front of the hospital and, with no time to reload their rifles, the defenders desperately fought with their bayonets. Although the Zulus relished close combat, they had a fearful respect for the British bayonet and after suffering very severely in the struggle they suddenly retreated back into the cover of the garden wall and orchard. In the midst of the initial attack, one of the two mounted Zulu chiefs was shot from his horse by Private Dunbar; according to his comrades, Dunbar then calmly hit another six Zulus with as many shots.

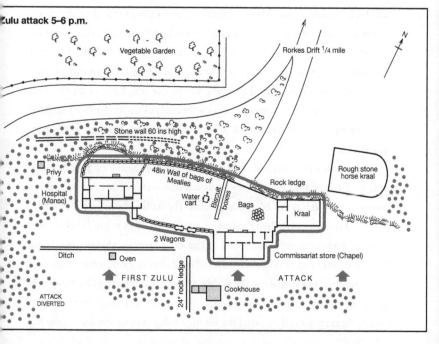

The defenders had but a momentary respite before the main Zulu body appeared to the rear of the outpost across the forward ridge of the Oskarsberg. As the soldiers watched, the Zulus formed into skirmishing order and advanced down the steep slope towards the mission station. Their marksmen took up sniping position in the Oskarsberg caves and from behind the hill's rocky ledges less than 300 yards from the defenders; the Zulus commenced firing directly at the backs of the soldiers manning the far barrier overlooking the orchard. Fortunately for the British, the Zulus were poor shots. Meanwhile the strongest mass of Zulus concentrated in the area of the garden and orchard and began creeping forward through the rough bush that grew right up to the front defensive line. Although Dalton had given orders for the garden wall and bush to be cleared, there had been insufficient time even to commence the task. Consequently the British defended their side of the mealie bag wall; the Zulus commanded the other side. There can be little doubt that an organized rush by the Zulus at this early stage of the battle would have resulted in a rapid overwhelming of the British position. However, the Zulus were not organized and their mounted chief, Dabulamanzi, now sheltering behind a tree, seemed unable to co-ordinate their attacks even though he was less than 100 yards from the front of the hospital. Dabulamanzi had earlier seen his *induna* shot from his horse and this may well have encouraged him to keep out of sight during the remaining period of daylight. For the next hour or so, the Zulu attacks evolved into a series of uncoordinated rushes at the front wall; all were beaten back by the British who, so far, had not incurred any serious casualties.

The Zulus then turned their attention to the mealie bag walls either side of the hospital, which they attacked in a series of brave but reckless assaults. As each wave of Zulus reached the walls, they were met with a volley of rifle fire and then the line of waiting soldiers behind their blood-covered bayonets; with the speed of the Zulu attacks, there was no time for the soldiers to reload their rifles. The Zulus suffered greatly: as each wave reached the British position they first had to jump or climb over the growing pile of dead and wounded Zulus and then, sliding on their comrades' slippery gore, they faced the 6ft high ledge supporting the mealie bag

116

wall. The ferocity of such close combat was totally new to the British soldiers whose experience of native warfare had been limited to distant volley fire, before which previous native adversaries had always retreated. Now they were desperately fighting for their lives, their forward vision clouded by the acrid smoke from their own volleys as deafened by the combination of gunfire and screaming Zulus, they shot and furiously stabbed at the terrifying black mass while desperately seeking to hold their position. Through the smoke and noise of battle, Chard, Bromhead and Dalton skilfully maintained control over the outpost and concentrated their small force to meet each fresh attack. When a gap appeared, one or other of these officers would step forward and join the fight. This pattern of assault continued for the next hour or so with each repulsed wave of Zulus being forced to retreat back into the scrub and undergrowth of the orchard. Meanwhile the Zulu marksmen positioned in the Oskarsberg caves maintained sporadic but mostly ineffective rifle fire into the British position.

At about 6 p.m. and with daylight rapidly fading, the area of the orchard and road, screened as it was by the original garden wall and thick bush, was now swarming with Zulus. Dabulamanzi abandoned his horse and, while controlling the Zulu attack from the cover of a nearby gully, directed his warriors to divide their attack against the north (front) wall and the south (rear) wall facing the Oskarsberg. This tactic put the British under severe pressure; Dalton was in the forefront of each attack using his rifle with deadly effect on any Zulu who got close. He moved up and down his section of the wall calmly directing fire and encouraging everyone as they fought the spear-slashing Zulus who, if they could, would try and wrench the defenders' rifles from them – usually without success. It is no wonder that he inspired the admiration which caused ordinary soldiers to remember and write, as did Private Hook: 'Mr Dalton was one of the bravest men who ever lived', or remarked later, like Corporal John Lyons, 'Mr Dalton, who has since received a commission, deserved any amount of praise'. Dalton was then shot at close range through his shoulder; without comment he handed his rifle to Chard before collapsing. Surgeon Reynolds quickly pulled Dalton from the firing line and dressed the wound. Within a matter of minutes, Dalton was back on his feet encouraging the defenders and, where necessary, giving orders. Surgeon Reynolds, separated from the hospital and his patients, also actively assisted with the defence; he repeatedly carried ammunition to the hospital, a Zulu bullet once striking his helmet as he did so.

Corporal Schiess of the NNC, a Swiss national, had been hospitalized with blisters on his foot following the initial British attack against Sihayo's homestead. Nevertheless, he joined the defensive line at the front of the outpost and fought alongside his British colleagues. He noticed a cluster of Zulus, who had hidden themselves on the far side of the mealie bag wall and who were taking close-range but ineffective shots at Schiess and those around him. Infuriated, Schiess mounted the barrier to shoot the Zulus, only to find himself looking down the barrel of a Zulu rifle. The Zulu fired and the round missed Schiess but pierced his hat; now face to face with the startled Zulu, Schiess bayoneted the warrior, reloaded his rifle and shot a second, only to be attacked by a third warrior, whom he also bayoneted off the wall. Schiess later received the Victoria Cross for his bravery. Another hospital patient, Corporal Scammell of the NNC, had joined the line only to be shot in the back by a Zulu sniper firing from the Oskarsberg. Scammell fell to the ground and was quickly attended to by Acting Commissariat Officer Byrne.

Having played a leading part in building up the original barricades, the young Byrne had put himself in the forefront of the firing line. Noticing that Corporal Scammell was wounded and calling for some water, Byrne opened his water bottle and, bending down to give him a drink, was shot dead by a Zulu sniper and fell on top of Scammell. The corporal pulled himself free of the body and, seeing Chard with Dalton's empty rifle, he crawled over to Chard and gave him the rounds in his pouch before reporting to Surgeon Reynolds.

One Zulu attack nearly succeeded in breaking over the south wall of biscuit boxes. Chard and Bromhead rushed forward with half a dozen men but they were too few; Chard realized they could no longer hold that part of the position and, in a fortuitous brief lull, he gave the order to abandon the position and to withdraw to within the inner wall of boxes – the wall that had been erected across the outpost almost as an afterthought. No sooner

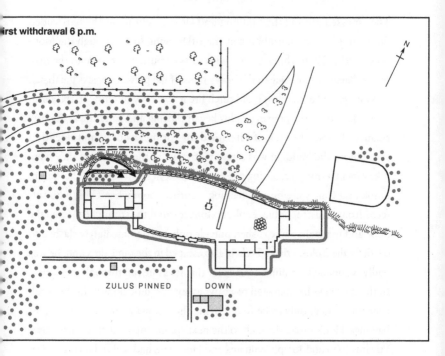

First withdrawal 6 p.m.

ZULUS PINNED   DOWN

had Chard's men run back to the entrenchment than the Zulus occupied the far side of the wall just abandoned; the Zulus now used the wall as a protective breastwork to fire over. The British retreat had both halved the size of the area to be defended and left the hospital and its six able-bodied men and twenty-four patients isolated and virtually surrounded by Zulus.

Chard now took stock of his defenders; his men were beginning to suffer serious casualties and apart from two fatalities, Byrne and Private Cole, another four were seriously wounded – Corporal Allen and Privates Chick, Fagan and Scanlon. Chard's main fighting force was now concentrated in the small entrenchment but he had lost control and communication with those trapped in the hospital some 40 yards away. Officers and soldiers alike were becoming wearied by the constant attacks but all knew it was a fight to the death – the Zulus would take no prisoners.

It was now that a series of dramatic and heroic events occurred. The hospital veranda and far end of the hospital could not be covered by fire from Chard's new position, a situation that the Zulus were quick to exploit.

They massed around the building and closed right up to the barricaded doors and windows, grabbing at the rifles being fired through the loopholes. Other Zulus threw spears with tufts of burning grass onto the hospital's thatched roof. Due to the heavy rains of the previous weeks the thatch was damp, and even when it did catch fire it was slow to burn. To the alarm of the defenders, the pressing Zulus began clawing and battering at the barricaded doors. The lack of interior doors or means of communication throughout the building was already obvious to the defenders; they were 'like rats in a trap', according to Private Hook in his account of the action. Hook and Cole were busy defending a corner room when Cole, who suffered from claustrophobia, could no longer stand the strain; he opened the door and in a wild panic rushed outside only to be immediately slashed to death by the Zulus. Private Beckett also escaped in the same direction; he was badly wounded by a number of spear thrusts as he ran through the enemy. In the darkness he managed to crawl away and hide himself in the scrub near the garden, only to be found dying the following morning. Using his bayonet, Hook broke through to the next room where the three defenders, Privates John and Joseph Williams and Horrigan, had realized their predicament; not only were they and their patients trapped, the Zulus could break through at any moment and the roof fire was beginning to fill the room with thick choking smoke. While Hook kept the Zulus at bay with his bayonet, Williams hacked a hole into the next room in the hope they might reach the far end of the building before the Zulus broke in. They eventually cut their way through and managed to pull three sick men after them before the Zulus broke in and killed the remaining patients.

The wounded Zulu (taken prisoner during the attack on Sihayo's stronghold) was still in his room when Hook thought to rescue him; Hook realized the Zulus had already gained access to the room and, thinking they would assist their comrade, Hook left him. His charred body was discovered the following morning in the hospital ruins.

Then the process began all over again, Hook firing and wielding his bayonet by the hole and Williams swinging his pick to break into the next room where they joined up with Private Waters who, when the time came to crawl through into the final room, chose to hide in a wardrobe. Later, when the Zulus broke into the same room, they ignored the wardrobe, Waters was not detected and he later escaped into the darkness outside and was able to hide until dawn, when he rejoined his comrades. Two defenders holding this last room brought the total trapped inside to eighteen. One patient, Private Connolly, had suffered a dislocated knee and in dragging him through a hole his knee was again dislocated causing him to scream with pain. It took a further fifteen long minutes for the final wall to be breached; all the time Hook guarded the last escape hole and every time a Zulu tried to get through, the warrior would be skewered by Hook's bayonet; the Zulus would then pull the twitching victim back to enable another warrior to receive the same treatment. Once in the last room, the survivors had a few seconds' respite; the Zulus could not breach the hole guarded by Hook and the roof fire had not yet reached their end of the building. There were no doors and the only possible exit point was a window high up in the wall; to their relief, they saw that it overlooked open space between the hospital and the defended position some 40 yards away. The window was, however, too small for a man to climb through and the frame had to be smashed out before the process of lowering the injured to the ground could begin.

At Chard's position, the defenders saw the plight of the hospital survivors; they could clearly see from the light of the hospital flames that the Zulus were only yards away from the escape window and the end wall. Chard called for two volunteers and as the first patient was lowered from the window, Private Hitch and Corporal Allen raced across the no-man's-land to render assistance. Their actions were all the more remarkable as Hitch had already been shot through the shoulder and Allen through the arm. As the two raced towards the hospital Chard ordered covering fire. The patients were gently lowered to the ground and Hitch and Allen, in turn, carried or dragged each one to safety.

Rifle fire from Chard's inner wall kept most of the Zulus behind their position, but one managed to leap over the wagon and kill a patient, Trooper Hunter of the Natal Mounted Police, as he hesitatingly crawled on all fours towards safety. Hunter was repeatedly stabbed before the defenders' eyes; the Zulu who killed him was then shot dead by a furious British

Rorke's Drift hospital at time of attack

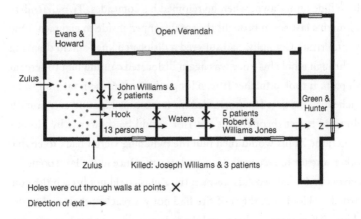

Holes were cut through walls at points ✗

Direction of exit ⟶

Patients were saved through the high window **Z** where Cpl Allen and Pte Hitch, both already wounded, gave invaluable assistance getting the patients down from the window and, while keeping the Zulus at bay, ferried the wounded to safety.

volley. Having reached the outside of the building, one of the defenders realized that the delirious and fever-ridden Sergeant Maxfield was still inside and climbed back into the blazing building to rescue him. Maxfield's rescuer tried to dress him but in his delirium he refused to co-operate and fought the attempt to save him. Maxfield had to be abandoned and was killed as the Zulus broke into the room. A partial collapse of the hospital roof gave Gunner Howard an opportunity to escape. With Private Adams he had been cut off in an isolated room throughout the fight; now he dashed and dived for cover where he lay in the darkness and survived to tell the tale; Adams stayed behind and died. Within the hospital building the terrifying ordeal in the darkness, thick smoke and deafening noise had lasted well over two hours. Commissary Dunne later wrote: 'overhead, the small birds disturbed by the turmoil and smoke flew hither and thither confusedly'.

The smouldering thatched roof of the hospital now blazed and illuminated the surrounding Zulus.

With the fall of the hospital the final desperate phase of the battle began.

For Chard and his men, squeezed into the compound round the storehouse and the adjoining cattle kraal, it was simply a fight for survival. Dabulamanzi was also in serious trouble, albeit of a different nature. He had already ignored Cetshwayo on two counts, firstly by crossing into Natal and secondly by attacking the British in a defensive position; to make matters worse, his men had suffered enormous casualties with nothing to show for their bravery and efforts. The other Zulu skirmishers who had been burning local farms had since been drawn back to Rorke's Drift by the flames and sounds of constant firing; they joined Dabulamanzi's force and in the light from the burning hospital the Zulus increased their pressure all round. The Zulus had not yet realized that the same light illuminated their massing ranks and made them easy targets for Chard's marksmen. Then Dabulamanzi changed tactics: he ordered the firing of the storehouse thatched roof. As soon as Chard realized that the Zulus were making a determined effort to set fire to the storehouse roof, presumably to force out the defenders, he ordered Commissary Dunne to construct a redoubt from two

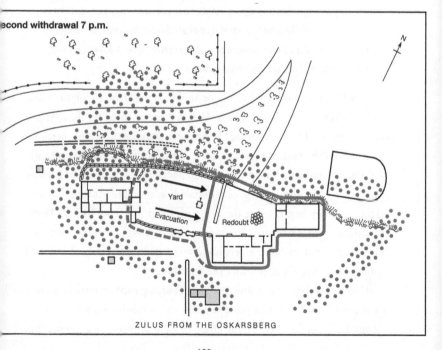

Second withdrawal 7 p.m.

Yard

Evacuation

Redoubt

ZULUS FROM THE OSKARSBERG

huge piles of mealie bags that had been previously stacked at the front of the store. Chard knew that if the storehouse fell the Zulus would be able to surround the defenders at a distance of less than 20 yards; Dunne, a quiet young man, directed the work without thought for his personal safety. He stood on the mound of sacks and encouraged the weary soldiers to construct the final redoubt. In so doing he attracted steady fire from the Zulus on all sides, but he remained unscathed throughout.

As the construction of the final redoubt progressed, an excited shout rang out from a soldier facing towards the Helpmekaar road. He claimed to have seen marching redcoats approaching from the direction of Helpmekaar but although the officers peered through the gloom, they saw nothing to indicate help was at hand. The rumour quickly spread and a loud cheer rang out. This confused the Zulus who slackened their attack as if to await events. For ten minutes everything was quiet; but no relieving troops came. The Zulus regrouped and darkness finally fell. Chard wrote about this incident:

> It is very strange that this report should have arisen amongst us, for the two companies 24th Regiment from Helpmekaar did come down to the foot of the hill, but not, I believe, in sight of us. They marched back to Helpmekaar on the report of Rorke's Drift having fallen.

It will be remembered that Major Spalding, the Officer Commanding Rorke's Drift, had earlier ridden to Helpmekaar to speed up the overdue reinforcements. He was nearing Helpmekaar at about 3.30 p.m. when he encountered the two companies of the 24th marching to Rorke's Drift. Spalding accompanied them to the steep pass and went on ahead accompanied by a Mr Dickson of the local Buffalo Border Guard. As they descended the pass they began seeing the first native fugitives from Rorke's Drift; puzzled, they rode on until they met the first fugitives from the Mounted Infantry. All told the same story: Isandlwana had fallen to the Zulus and Rorke's Drift was about to suffer the same fate.

Uncertain of the best course of action, Spalding rode on until he gained a low crest; from his vantage point he could see the mission station in flames. He and Dickson then saw a large group of Zulu skirmishers approaching;

the Zulus came on to within 100 yards and then began to form into their traditional encircling attack formation whereupon Spalding and Dickson
retreated back to the marching column, now only a mile distant. Spalding
was in a dilemma; should he proceed to relieve Rorke's Drift or return to
Helpmekaar? On reaching the column, Spalding was informed that Zulu
raiding parties had been seen approaching the pass they had just descended;
in the light of this information, Spalding decided to retreat. He ordered the
column to 'about turn' and the two companies, along with all their wagons, laboriously turned round and began the ascent of the pass. All safely
reached Helpmekaar at about 9 p.m. whereupon they formed a defensive
laager using the wagons and all available stores. During the evening numerous fugitives rode past Helpmekaar and all confirmed the British disaster.
Spalding and his men spent the night in anticipation of a full Zulu attack
but it never materialized. There can be little doubt that the defenders at
Rorke's Drift, even in the failing light, had seen the approaching column;
indeed, Spalding reached a position less than 2 miles from Rorke's Drift
before he retreated: this would have placed the marching column less than
3 miles from Rorke's Drift – due to its size and associated dust from the
marching men, wagons and oxen, the relieving force would all have been
comparatively easy to see at that distance, especially by the attacking Zulus.[2]

Meanwhile the Zulus had begun to concentrate on the one remaining
building still defended by the British, the storehouse. Corporal Attwood of
the Army Service Corps had defended a window in the building throughout the action and now performed the vital task of shooting at the warriors
trying to fire the thatch above him. Until the end of the battle he held his
position and kept the Zulus from firing the roof. Nevertheless, the pressure of hand-to-hand fighting continued unabated and eventually the British
holding the outer wall of the cattle kraal were forced to retire, first to an
intermediate wall which divided the kraal and then finally behind the wall
which actually joined onto the storehouse. This was to be the final British
position; there was nowhere else to go and there could be no further retreat.

Chard and Dunne, assisted by four soldiers, then began the task of converting the two large pyramids of bagged maize into an oblong redoubt.
The purpose of their endeavours was to construct a final position for the

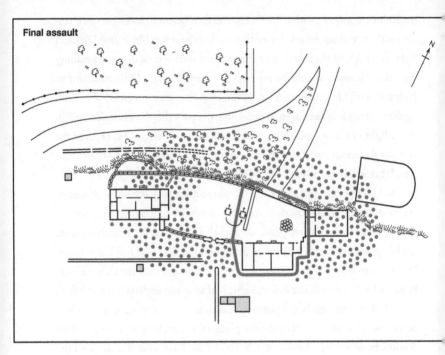

Final assault

wounded and, if the final wall was surrendered to the Zulus, the few survivors could occupy the redoubt. Chard supervised the work and in ten minutes their final position was ready. Access to the core of the pile was by a narrow entrance that could be sealed from the inside; the wounded were then placed inside the new position and Chard detailed marksmen to occupy the upper rampart. This gave them an elevated field of fire, which with the dying glow of the hospital building enabled them to pour several volleys into the massed Zulu ranks now pressing up against the final wall of boxes and mealie bags. Within the British position Allen and Hitch, regardless of their wounds, continued to supply ammunition around the perimeter; it was now about 10.30 p.m. and still the attacks came. Then the glow from the hospital fire began to dwindle and, as it did so, the Zulus' enthusiasm for close combat showed the first signs of waning. By midnight the battle had transformed from a constant Zulu attack into a series of isolated but determined attacks; this change in Zulu tactics enabled the

British to anticipate more accurately the direction of each attack, each being repulsed with the same vigour that had characterized the whole British defence. The defenders had been without water for over eight hours and all were suffering from a raging thirst. Chard could see the water cart that he had earlier filled from the river and brought to the position; with bayonets fixed, he led four men, including Private Hook, in an almost suicidal charge over the wall to reach the water cart that had been abandoned halfway between the two buildings. Not recognizing the cart for what it was, the Zulus had ignored it, even though they were also desperate for water. The Zulus retreated before the advancing line of bayonets, thus enabling Chard to drag the cart back to the defenders' wall. The cart was too heavy to lift over the wall so they improvised by means of leather hose, and drained the water through a hole in the wall into an assortment of containers.

After midnight the Zulus were clearly more exhausted than the British; not only had they run from Isandlwana, they had been without food for two days and had last drunk water when they crossed the river some nine hours earlier. Their attacks became sporadic but their marksmen continued to fire into the British position. The final flickering from the remains of the burning hospital died out at about 4 a.m. and thereafter there were no more Zulu attacks. Not knowing what the Zulus were doing under the cover of darkness and fearing an attack at any moment, Chard ordered his battle-weary men to remain at their posts. Shortly after 5 a.m. the early dawn lightened the sky and the British realized that the only Zulus in sight were the dead and wounded. The Zulu force had vanished.

After satisfying himself that the Zulus had retreated, Chard sent out a patrol to flush out any hidden Zulu marksmen and to put the wounded Zulus out of their misery; all round the British outpost lay nearly 400 dead with many more human remains still visible in the smouldering hospital building. One Zulu had remained in hiding about 100 yards from the mission station; why he had not retreated with his colleagues was a mystery – some later presumed he might have fallen asleep. He rose to his feet and fired a shot at the startled defenders. The shot passed harmlessly over their heads whereupon the Zulu ran off in the direction of the river. Some of the defenders fired after him but he survived to tell a remarkable story. Another native appeared and because he was unarmed and walked straight into the British position, he was not fired upon. Chard had him interviewed by Daniells the pontman who could speak some Zulu. Daniells had armed himself with Spalding's sword in order to overawe the terrified native though he appeared to have been in the NNC and claimed to have escaped from Isandlwana. Chard took pity on the man; he was rescued from Daniels's theatrical interrogation and was dispatched to the officer commanding at Helpmekaar with a situation report and a request for assistance.

Chard's wagon driver, a Cape black man, had panicked when firing was first heard and let his oxen free. He ran from the outpost and climbed the slope of the Oskarsberg before secreting himself in the back of a cave. His situation worsened when Zulu marksmen entered the cave and then spent several hours firing into the British position. When the British returned fire one Zulu marksman was killed by a well-aimed shot. Chard's driver remained undetected and left his hiding place only when the Zulus finally departed.

Obviously no one at Rorke's Drift had any definite knowledge of Chelmsford's column or its fate or even whether the general had survived. Neither did they know whether Helpmekaar had been attacked. Shortly after 7 a.m. the Zulus reappeared on the western slope of the Oskarsberg; the defenders waited, but the Zulus had lost the will to fight: they rested for several minutes, took snuff and then Dabulamanzi led them at a safe distance back towards the drift and Zululand. Chard later wrote that he was glad to seize an opportunity to wash his face in a muddy puddle, in company with Private Bushe, a hospital defender whose face was covered with blood from a wound in the nose caused by the bullet which had passed through and killed Private Cole as he fled.

The battered garrison used the lull and uncertainty to repair their defences. They strengthened and raised the walls, then contemplated removing the thatch from the roof of the commissariat store to prevent another fire should the Zulus return to renew their attack. Not being totally sure what the Zulus were doing, Chard initiated further patrols around the mission station perimeter to collect the arms and ammunition from the dead Zulus.

The defeated Zulus steadily made their way to the drift and, after quenching their thirst, they assembled on the far bank of the Buffalo river. It was at this stage that they first noticed the distant but approaching column led by Lord Chelmsford. The column was retracing the route it had taken a few days earlier and was approaching the drift from the direction of Sihayo's stronghold. Not wishing to engage the British, the Zulus turned right and followed the river bank, presumably so as to avoid conflict. It is uncertain whether the Zulus knew that Chelmsford and a portion of his force had survived; local myth suggests the Zulus genuinely believed that they had all died at Isandlwana. Some historians have suggested that the Zulus thought they were seeing the ghosts of vanquished British soldiers as the column approached the drift and avoided them on superstitious grounds. It is probable that Chelmsford's direct approach surprised the retreating Zulus but there is no evidence to support the ghost theory. In any event the two groups passed each other at a distance of 400 yards; Chelmsford's men had but twenty rounds of ammunition per man and the Zulus were exhausted: neither side had any enthusiasm for a fresh fight.

CHAPTER 7

The Aftermath of Battle

The dead Zulus lay in piles, in some places as high as the top
of the parapet.

COMMANDANT HAMILTON-BROWNE

Shortly after dawn on 23 January, the British defenders at Rorke's Drift realized that the Zulus had withdrawn en masse to a knoll well out of range of the outpost. With instructions from Chard to exercise extreme caution, inspection patrols were deployed around the smouldering and battered mission station. The cautious soldiers found dead and dying Zulus scattered all round the outpost perimeter; most were in piles, sometimes five deep. Those Zulu bodies crushed against the front wall outside the hospital almost reached the top of the barricade. Dying and wounded Zulus were calmly given the coup de grâce by bayonet to put them out of their misery – there was initially no malice on the part of the soldiers; in any event, taking prisoners had never been British Army policy in South Africa, so for the soldiers given the grim task, there was simply no alternative. Once the immediate area around the outpost had been secured, and with some 120 Zulu firearms and 300 spears brought into the outpost out of harm's way, the soldiers then spent some time examining their night's handiwork. Quietly, almost as though they were paying their respects, they wandered round the perimeter of the outpost; most were drawn to examine the dead foe. They noticed that many of the close-range dead bodies were locked in curious positions by rigor mortis and grotesquely disfigured by Martini-Henry bullet wounds. Initially no effort was made to remove the numerous dead from around the outpost; the soldiers were simply too exhausted or occupied with caring for their own wounded. Apart from the relief of still being alive, the survivors were all suffering the effects of firing their Martini-Henry rifles for hours on end; there were bruised chins and shoulders, burnt fingers, hands and blackened faces to attend to before any consideration would be given to the Zulu bodies.

Within the outpost the scene was equally disturbing; pools of congealed and smeared blood bore witness to the death throes of both British and Zulu warriors; the area was littered with spears, empty ammunition boxes, torn cartridge packets and clusters of spent ammunition cases. The remnants of discarded red army jackets lay in the dust; they had been torn apart by the soldiers as binding for the red-hot rifle barrels in the desperate attempt to save their hands from burns as they fired. The whole inner area was covered in trampled maize that had poured from the damaged sacks along the walls, walls that had successfully born the brunt of the Zulu attacks. The heat from the burnt-out hospital gradually abated and, not deterred by the smell of cooked human flesh, the defenders found the charred bodies of Sergeant Maxfield and the other patients who had died within its walls. As there were many more charred bodies than the defenders had expected, they naturally presumed that these were Zulus, killed either by the defenders or by the hospital fire. The heavily stabbed body of Joseph Williams was found just outside the room he had defended; the fourteen dead Zulus immediately in front of his position showed that he had fought bravely to the end.

While the defenders were taking stock of their situation, Colour Sergeant Bourne was reminded of the cask of rum that had been so carefully guarded throughout the battle; he relented and began issuing the spirit among the defenders. He was surprised by Private Hook, the last defender to leave the hospital building and a known teetotaller, who presented himself for the issue with a battered tin mug. He reacted to Bourne's surprise with the comment 'I feel I want something after all that'. He then returned to his campfire where he was attempting to make tea. At about 7 a.m. the Zulus slowly moved off towards the river and the defenders were wearily able to congratulate themselves on being alive. Some were so exhausted that they curled up in quiet corners or on the damaged maize sacks and simply fell asleep. Chard deployed several guards at the four corners of the outpost and it was one of these reluctant lookouts who first noticed Chelmsford's surviving half of the original column approaching through the early morning mist along the far side of the river. The word quickly spread but the soldiers were uncertain whether the advancing body was the remains of Chelmsford's column or the main Zulu army returning 'for the kill'. After conferring with Chard, Bourne shouted out the order 'stand to' and the exhausted men again scrambled back to their posts. Chelmsford's column had a great many native troops attached to it and it was not possible at a distance of over 2 miles to make out a significant number of redcoats. Chard knew only too well that his men had fired most of their rounds and less than fifty rounds per man remained. Thankfully, their frantic waving with an improvised white flag was answered from the column and some ten minutes later the first troop of mounted men, commanded by Major Cecil Russell and Lieutenant Walsh, crossed the drift and galloped up to the battered remains of the mission station. Russell and Walsh were relieved to find the outpost still in British hands as, having crossed the river, they had seen the rising smoke from other burning homesteads and farms far over the surrounding countryside. Lord Chelmsford, complete with his full complement of staff officers, arrived in due course.

After the mission station was relieved by Chelmsford's force, those defenders who had displayed exceptional bravery were interviewed, a few by Chelmsford himself. Private Hook was still engaged with his tea making when a sergeant called out to him that he was wanted by Lieutenant Bromhead, to which he replied 'Wait till I get a coat on'. The order was repeated with the words 'come as you are' and in Hook's own words he 'went into the midst of the officers and Lord Chelmsford asked me all about the defence of the hospital as I was the last to leave the building. An officer took down all our names and wrote down what we had done'. Chelmsford then made a short speech to the assembled defenders in which he thanked them for their endeavours. Gunner Howard recalled some of Chelmsford's words when he wrote home, 'The general said we were a brave little garrison, and this showed what a few men could do if they only had pluck'.[1] The garrison at Rorke's Drift had now increased dramatically to over 700 men, bolstered by the remnants of Chelmsford's once proud Centre Column; the arrivals included the surviving companies of the 2/24th and sixteen companies of the NNC. The mounted troops and the Royal Artillery horses under the command of Colonel Harness were ordered to move onto the high plateau at Helpmekaar where the air was deemed to be healthier for the horses; the Royal Artillery guns and men remained at Rorke's Drift.[2]

It was only then that any thought was given to the horrendous task of clearing the hundreds of Zulu bodies from the site. Even though the survivors were exhausted, the Commissariat officers had begun checking their stores and with a fresh supply of natives from Chelmsford's column, the mission station was prepared to withstand any further Zulu attacks that might materialize. Blocks of stone from the burnt-out hospital and the nearby garden wall were removed and used as a makeshift barrier to the front of the outpost while the remaining stores were searched so that hot food and tea could be prepared for the ravenous column. There can be little doubt that as Chelmsford and his staff rode out of Rorke's Drift, leaving a very subdued Colonel Glyn of the 24th Regiment in command, they departed with mixed emotions; Chelmsford now faced the task of reporting to the world how he and his senior staff officers had lost the battle of Isandlwana and with it a famous British regiment – and to report a magnificent victory at Rorke's Drift led by two lowly and humble lieutenants. Meanwhile, in the wreckage of one of the wagons, an undamaged bottle of beer was discovered. It was given to Chard and Bromhead who shared it, no doubt in celebration of their victory although at this stage neither had any idea of the impact their actions would have from that point in time.

It gradually dawned on the survivors that most of their jackets had been destroyed in the attempt to bind their red-hot Martini-Henry rifles during the heavy fighting of the night and there were certainly no replacement uniforms in the remaining piles of stores. Once the soldiers were fed they turned their attention to finding replacement clothes, and within the hour soldiers had used their scavenging initiative to manufacture jackets from the heavy and abundant mealie sacks that were littering the ground; they simply cut holes in the empty sacks for their heads and arms and the one size fitted all. It was to be several weeks before replacement uniforms reached the men, and even then it took a question in Parliament before one flannel shirt and a pair of trousers, but not jackets, could be issued to the defenders 'cost free' as compensation for uniforms damaged during the fighting. The *Referee*, an English newspaper, published the following verse to make its readers aware of the soldiers' plight.

RORKE'S DRIFT

There was an old soldier named Dan'el
He fought till his clothes were in rags,
So the Government gave him a flannel,
And also a new pair of bags.

And the news it went over the Channel,
Through Europe it's chaff for the wags,
That we honour our heroes in flannel,
And clothe their achievements in bags.

'Tis a blot on our glorious annals,
Oh, who were the elderly hags,
Who suggested those charity flannels
And ordered those beggarly bags?

When the public its jury empanels,
'Twill suggest, ere the interest flags,
That the Tories for skirts take the flannels,
And they might put their heads in the bags.

Within a matter of hours of the engagement at Rorke's Drift, and in true British Army fashion, an inventory was drawn up to account for the remaining ammunition; when redistributed, there were now seventy rounds per man. Donald Morris stated that 20,000 rounds of Martini-Henry ammunition had been fired in the space of twelve hours by the 104 British combatants.[3] This roughly equates with twenty-five rounds per man per hour – yet Zulu casualties from the battle amounted to not more than 500 at the highest estimate. This implies that it took roughly forty rounds to kill one Zulu in a battle that was fought at very close range. Were the British poor marksmen, was the figure of 20,000 rounds incorrect or were there other factors? This question becomes even more interesting in view of the lack of archaeological evidence concerning the few finds of empty ammunition cases or of fired rounds on the battlefield.[4] Commandant Hamilton-Browne, commander of the Natal Native Contingent, wrote of the aftermath of the battle:

> The dead Zulus lay in piles, in some places as high as the top of the parapet. Some killed by bullets and the wounds, at that short range, were ghastly but very many were killed by the bayonet.

If the figure of 20,000 rounds is correct, Hamilton-Browne's statement certainly appears to raise a question about the efficacy of the Martini-Henry rifle especially as so many of the Zulus had died of bayonet wounds. There were certainly many occasions during the night when the British defenders relied on their bayonets to drive the Zulus back from the defensive positions. It is possible the defenders were short of ammunition before the battle commenced – certainly the actual defenders in the hospital either were not well supplied with ammunition or had 'blazed away' in the opening stages and then found themselves short. In any event no medical examination was conducted to establish the individual causes of death among the Zulu attackers before they were buried and so the reason for the apparent ineffectiveness of the Martini-Henry rifle at Rorke's Drift remains unclear – other than to acknowledge that much of the fighting took place in darkness, only illuminated by the fire of the hospital thatch.

In December 1936 the BBC conducted a radio interview with Colour Sergeant Bourne about the battle of Rorke's Drift. In the programme he was asked about the rifles used by the Zulus; Bourne was adamant that the Zulus attacking the outpost had used British Martini-Henry rifles captured earlier in the day at Isandlwana. He stated:

The Zulus had collected the rifles from the men they had killed at Isandlwana, and had captured the ammunition from the mules which had stampeded and threw their loads; so our own arms were used against us. In fact, this was the cause of every one of our casualties, killed and wounded, and we should have suffered many more if the enemy had known how to use a rifle. There was hardly a man even wounded by an assegai – their principal weapon.[5]

Of all the Rorke's Drift defenders, Colour Sergeant Bourne was possibly the most experienced soldier present, both on army firing ranges and in battle; he would certainly have recognized the distinctive report of a Martini-Henry rifle being fired compared with the reports from antiquated Zulu muskets. Most historians have claimed the Zulus did not possess Martini-Henry rifles and have accordingly dismissed Bourne's report. It is historically accepted that the Zulus who attacked Rorke's Drift had earlier formed the reserve at Isandlwana and had not taken part in the destruction of the British camp; throughout the battle they were deployed at a distance between 1 and 2 miles from the action. Historians support their hypothesis by relying on two fundamental points: there were no weak links in the Zulu attack at Isandlwana and the Zulus who attacked Rorke's Drift had not taken part in the battle of Isandlwana. So, they argue, if the Zulus did have Martini-Henry rifles at Rorke's Drift, where did they obtain them?

Bourne was probably correct: they came from Isandlwana, although not from the main battle but from two comparatively minor encounters when the 4,000 Zulus detailed for the reserve at Isandlwana swept behind the mountain and overran two isolated groups of British soldiers before successfully blocking the British escape route back to Rorke's Drift. (See Appendix F for full details.)

Commandant Hamilton-Browne, the commander of the NNC who had accompanied Chelmsford during the previous two days, was ordered to remain at Rorke's Drift with his black troops. He later recalled some of the events that then occurred when he wrote:

Well we went into the laager. No one seemed to know what to do and certainly no one tried to do anything. I spoke to several of the seniors and suggested that the thatch should be taken off the store and more loopholes made, also that the stacks of forage should be removed, but until I came to Colonel Harness, R.A., no one would pay the least attention. He at once saw things in the same light as I did and said, "I will send my gunners to remove the thatch if you will get the forage away." This we did and in a short time the place was secure from fire.

No sooner had I seen my part of this work done than I began to feel as if I was rather hollow and I rejoined Lonsdale and Harford. Rations had been served out and we had bully beef, biscuit, tea and sugar in plenty but no cups, plates, knives, forks or spoons – not even a pot or kettle to boil water in. However we made shift to eat the bully and biscuits with our fingers, then boiled water in the empty bully tins, added tea and sugar and drank it with gusto.

Well Lonsdale and myself went round to the front and there saw what a tremendous effort must have been made by both sides.

The dead Zulus lay in piles, in some places as high as the top of the parapet. Some killed by bullets and the wounds, at that short range, were ghastly but very many were killed by the bayonet. The attack must have been well pushed home and both sides deserve the greatest credit. The hospital was still smouldering and the stench from the burning flesh of the dead inside was very bad; it was much worse however when we came to clear the debris away two days afterwards. Some of our sick and wounded had been burned inside of the hospital and a number of Zulus had been also killed inside of the building itself.

In front of the hospital lay a large number of Zulus also a few of our men, who had been patients, and who when the hospital had been set on fire had, in trying to escape, rushed out among the enemy and had been killed, their bodies being also ripped and much mutilated.

A few dead horses lay about, either killed by the assegai or by the bullets of the defenders, and I wondered why they had not been driven away before the fighting began.

One thing I noticed and that was the extraordinary way in which the majority of the Zulus lay. I had been over a good many battlefields and seen very many men who had been killed in action but I had never seen men lie in this position. They seemed to have dropped on their elbows and knees and remained like that with their knees drawn up to their chins.

One huge fellow who must have been, in life, quite 7 feet high lay on his back with his heels on the top of the parapet and his head nearly touching the ground, the rest of his body supported by a heap of his dead comrades.

The following days were undoubtedly difficult for the Rorke's Drift garrison, every member of which was either a survivor of the battle of Rorke's Drift or from Chelmsford's fatigued column; all were exhausted, hungry and undoubtedly anxious lest the Zulus should return in force. There was little order or control and it was commonly known that ammunition reserves were insufficient to enable the men to withstand a further sustained Zulu attack; there were few useful supplies and the men's uniforms were in tatters. Hamilton-Browne summed up what many felt on the first evening:

The evening grew on and Lonsdale went into the laager for orders. He returned and told us that the white troops were to hold the laager and that we were to remain outside. This was as absurd as it was shameful; not only were our white officers and non-coms to meet, unprotected by the laager, the first rush of the Zulus, in case of an attack, but we should have been swept away by the fire of our own friends inside it.

We were also to find the outlying pickets and the advanced sentries. Our natives, with the exception of the Zulus, were quite useless for this service. In fact they had all taken refuge in the caves and among the rocks of the mountain, and sternly refused to come out. And now there was a row. Of course the roster was lost and I regret to say that the officers and the non-coms, furious at what they considered their unfair treatment, refused to turn out. Lonsdale, Cooper and myself talked it over with them and at last we said we would take the outlying picket ourselves. Harford at once chipped in, so three commandants and a staff officer formed the most dangerous picket that night.

Quin, my servant, swore that I should not go on picket while he was to the fore and Captains Duncombe, Develin and Hayes volunteered for the other picket. Of course when we were moving off everyone wanted to come and the cuss words and recriminations flew like hail. We quieted them down. We took one picket, Captain Duncombe and three other officers formed the other; there was not much choice between them. In-lying pickets were told off and as soon as it was dark we took our posts, extending the Zulus in a chain between them. The night was very dark but passed off quietly although there was a false alarm at the laager, and most of our white men who had remained there got inside. I don't blame them. What was the use of staying outside to be shot down by their own friends?

The troops that had previously formed Chelmsford's Centre Column were now left at the mission station, many without orders or officers to organize them. There was no definite news and rumours of a renewed Zulu attack were rife; the command structure under Glyn appeared to be numb with indecision: little more is heard of Chard and Bromhead and the overall level of morale throughout the garrison began to sink at an alarming rate. Reserves of ammunition were critically low, as the scheduled ammunition supplies for Rorke's Drift had been hurriedly buried near Helpmekaar when the officer in charge of the supply wagon heard the news from Isandlwana; he ordered it all buried to prevent the Zulus getting possession of it in case he was overpowered during the night. After reaching Helpmekaar in safety, a party was sent to recover it but the incessant rain had removed all traces of the cache and although lines of soldiers were formed who advanced prodding the ground with their cleaning rods, no ammunition was ever found.

The awful sickly smell of burnt and bloated bodies, now crawling with flies, hung over the immediate area and finally, late in the day, the British reluctantly set about burying the putrefying Zulu dead. They had not reckoned on the refusal of their own black troops to handle the bodies due to their fear of *umnyama*, the belief that the spirits of the dead would attach themselves to anyone touching the bodies without due rituals having been completed. They were, however, prepared to dig the long deep pits and the British regulars of the 24th Regiment were then given the gruesome task of collecting the Zulu bodies; this they did by dragging the bodies with makeshift ropes and then dumping them in the freshly dug pits. The NNC were further ordered to collect brushwood and to cut down trees from the nearby orchards to provide the basis of a funeral pyre. When the resulting blaze subsided, the remains of the 371 Zulu bodies collected from the hospital and from around the perimeter wall were covered with the spoil previously dug from the pits; the whole macabre process took several days to complete.

The total number of Zulu dead from Rorke's Drift, it must be said, will never be known. Many wounded Zulus were helped away by their able-bodied colleagues only to die well away from the outpost or to drown during the river crossing; the river remained in full flood for three days after the battle. Even several years later, skeletons were still to be found near the Zulus' route back into Zululand.

Lieutenant Archibald Milne, the Royal Navy staff officer to Lord Chelmsford, mentioned in a report that when he arrived at Rorke's Drift at about 9.30 a.m. on the 23rd, 'the occupants received the General with three cheers. Then was seen the gallant defence made by the small garrison of 80 men'. The dead Zulus were lying about in scores, close up to the parapet. There was to be no mercy for captured or wounded Zulus and firing was still going on to bring down wounded men trying to escape. Evidently the grisly 'clearing up' operation to search out and kill the scores of wounded Zulus was just beginning when Chelmsford arrived.

During the early evening of the same day, a rumour began circulating around the Rorke's Drift garrison that several hundred Zulus, either wounded or in hiding, had been found and killed by British soldiers at two separate but nearby locations, one behind the Oskarsberg and the other in a maize field less than a mile from the outpost. To conserve their depleted ammunition supply, the British patrols that discovered the hiding Zulus had killed them all with bayonets or the Zulus' own spears. Commandant Hamilton-Browne wrote of one incident that occurred that same day:

> During the afternoon it was discovered that a large number of wounded and worn-out Zulus had taken refuge or hidden in the mealie fields near the laager. My two companies of Zulus with some of my non-coms and a few of the 24th quickly drew these fields and killed them with bayonet, butt and assegai. It was beastly but there was nothing else to do. War is war and

savage war is the worst of the lot. Moreover our men were worked up to a pitch of fury by the sights they had seen in the morning and the mutilated bodies of the poor fellows laying in front of the burned hospital.

Lieutenant Horace Smith-Dorrien, who had escaped from Isandlwana to Helpmekaar, later wrote concerning two gallows he had constructed at Rorke's Drift prior to the battle. These gallows were originally intended to stretch leather *riems* for the ox wagons. Smith-Dorrien wrote:

> The next day (23rd January) I rode down to Rorke's Drift, some twelve miles, to resume charge of my depot. There was the improvised little fort, built up mostly of mealy-sacks and biscuit-boxes and other stores which had so gallantly been defended by Chard, Bromhead, and their men, and Parson Smith, and all around lay dead Zulus, between three and four hundred; and there was my wagon, some 200 yards away, riddled and looted; and there was the riems gallows I had erected the previous morning. Dead animals and cattle everywhere – such a scene of devastation! To my young mind it was impossible that order could ever be restored, but I set to work, and next day, whilst sitting in my wagon, I saw two Zulus hanging on my gallows and was accused by the Brigade Major, Clery (afterwards General Sir Francis Clery) of having given the order. I was exonerated, however, when it was found that it was a case of lynch law performed by incensed men, who were bitter at the loss of their comrades. Other incidents of the same sort occurred in the next few days before law and order were re-established.

Later that same day, Lieutenant Curling RA returned to Rorke's Drift and that night he wrote:

> The farmhouse at Rorke's Drift was a sad sight. There were dead bodies of Zulus all round it, in some places so thick that you could hardly walk without treading on them. The roof had been taken off the house as it was liable to be burnt and the wounded were lying out in the open. A spy was hanging on one of the trees in the garden and the whole place was one mass of men. Nothing will now be done until strong reinforcements arrive and we shall have much bloodshed before it is all over.[6]

One Zulu warrior found alive and uninjured was taken prisoner by

Private Ashton of B Company. That evening Bromhead sent for Ashton to enquire after the prisoner only to find that the Zulu had been hanged by mistake. Apparently Ashton had asked Bromhead what to do with the prisoner and had been told 'to get the hell out of here with him'. Ashton had misinterpreted the oath as an instruction and executed the hapless Zulu.[7]

The necessity of killing seriously injured Zulus on the field of battle was generally if reluctantly accepted by the British soldiers, and so the British systematically killed the Zulu wounded at Rorke's Drift in the same way that the Zulus killed British soldiers wounded after Isandlwana; the fate of abandoned casualties was well understood by both sides. Regrettably, the fate of fleeing Zulus or those who had gone into hiding well away from the outpost was to be more disturbing, even in the climate of such total warfare; any comment on the Zulus' fate was deliberately omitted from official reports to prevent details of the events being published. This extraordinary and merciless mopping-up operation was nevertheless seen as a success and was thereafter repeated as a matter of military policy after each of the remaining battles of the Zulu War, especially after the British victories at Gingindlovu, Kambula and Ulundi. The indiscriminate and wholesale killing of Zulu survivors, those either in hiding or fleeing from the battlefield was, in later battles of the Zulu War, to cause the military authorities much embarrassment.[8]

On a daily basis, mounted troops from Rorke's Drift ranged far and wide to wreak havoc on distant Zulu villages. Hamilton-Browne wrote: 'by this time myself and my boys had made ourselves decidedly unpopular on the other side of the river. No decent kraal could retire at rest and be sure they would awake in the morning to find themselves alive in their huts and cattle intact'.[9] During the clearing-up operations in the week following the battle, only five Zulus were taken prisoner and brought back to the outpost; four were later released unharmed. The fate of the fifth Zulu was sealed when he was brought to Hamilton-Browne's position for questioning. In his memoirs Hamilton-Browne tells another version of the story of the hapless Zulu, claiming that he, and not Bromhead, had accidentally ordered his execution:

He [Glyn] ordered me to return to the prisoner, question him and then to report anything I might find out. This I did but of course could get nothing out of him, though he owned up readily he was a spy and that he wore the piece of red stuff round his head as a disguise. I was turning round to return to the O.C. when I struck my shin, which I had badly bruised a few days before, against the boom of the wagon. The pain was atrocious and I had just let go my first blessing when the Sergeant-Major, a huge Irishman, not seeing my accident, asked, "What will we do with the spoy, sor?" "Oh, hang the bally spy," I tripped out and limped away, rubbing my injured shin and blessing spies, wagons and everything that came in my way. On my reporting to the O.C. that I could get no information, but that the man owned up to being a spy, he ordered the Camp Adjutant to summon a drumhead courts-martial to try him. Paper, pens and ink were found with difficulty; true, there was no drum but a rum keg did as well.

The officers, warned, assembled and the Sergeant Major being sent for was ordered to march up the prisoner.

He stared open-mouthed for a few seconds, then blurted out, "Plaze, sor, I can't shure he's hung, sor." "Hung!" exclaimed the O.C., who was standing within earshot. "Who ordered him to be hung?" "Commandant Browne, sor," replied the Sergeant Major. "I ordered him to be hung?" I ejaculated. "What do you mean?" "Sure, sor, when I asked you at the guard wagon what was to be done with the spoy did you not say, sor, 'Oh, hang the spoy,' and there he is," pointing to the slaughter poles, and sure enough there he was. There was no help for it. It was clear enough the prisoner could not be tried after he was hung, so the court was dismissed and there was no one to blame but my poor shin.

Chard later wrote, albeit cautiously, of events at Rorke's Drift on the 23rd:

On the day following, we buried 351 bodies of the enemy in graves not far from the Commissariat Buildings – many bodies were since discovered and buried, and when I was sick at Ladysmith one of our Sergeants, who came down there invalided from Rorke's Drift, where he had been employed in the construction of Fort Melvill, told me that many Zulu bodies were found in the caves and among the rocks, a long distance from the Mission house,

when getting stone for that fort. As, in my report, I underestimated the
number we killed, so I believe I also underestimated the number of the
enemy that attacked us, and from what I have since learnt I believe the
Zulus must have numbered at least 4,000.

The killing of the Zulu wounded brought the most likely figure of Zulu
casualties at Rorke's Drift up to about 600 with probably another 300 being
accounted for during the subsequent securing of the immediate surrounding
area. British casualties of fifteen men killed and one officer and nine men
wounded (two mortally) were comparatively light. The daughter of the
Bishop of Natal, Frances Colenso, was an ardent campaigner for fair play.
Following representations made to her by sources she never revealed, she
strongly expressed her views on matters at Rorke's Drift. Although this and
other reports were later given limited publicity, no official denials of her
allegations were made. She wrote:

The general and his staff hurried on to Pietermaritzberg via Helpmekaar
while the garrison at Rorke's Drift was left in utter confusion. – as testified by
many present at the time. No one appeared responsible for anything that
might happen, and the result was one disgraceful to our English name, and
to all concerned. A few Zulu prisoners had been taken by our troops – some
the day before, others previous to the disaster at Isandlwana, and these
prisoners were put to death in cold blood at Rorke's Drift. It was intended to
set them free, and they were told to run for their lives, but they were shot
down and killed, within sight and sound of the whole force. An eye witness,
an officer, described the affair to the present writer, saying that the men he
saw killed numbered 'not more than seven nor less than five'. He said he was
standing, with others, in the camp, and hearing shots close behind him, he
turned, and saw the prisoners in question in the act of falling beneath the
shots and stabs of a party of our own men. The latter, were, indeed, men
belonging to the Natal Contingent, but they were supposed to be under
white control, and should not have been able to obtain possession of the
prisoners under any circumstances.

Bulwer, the Lieutenant Governor of Natal, also expressed his views
against cross-border raids. He believed that the indiscriminate burning of

empty kraals would be counterproductive and wrote, 'this action could hardly be attended with much advantage to us, it would invite retaliation'. The border Police commander, Major Dartnell, was also concerned to the point that he cautioned against further cross-border raiding on the grounds that it was provocative; he also forbade his men to cross the river unless they were part of a large raiding party sanctioned by the military authorities.

The deteriorating conditions at Rorke's Drift did nothing to improve morale or discipline. Major Clery commented on the conditions when he wrote home on 4 February:

> We have lost simply everything we had, except what we stood in – tent, clothing, cooking things, everything in fact – so that when we got anything to eat, we had nothing to cook it in, and when we got something to drink we had nothing to drink it out of.
>
> My present abode consists of a tarpaulin held up by some sticks and this I share with Col. Glyn and the other staff officers. We have a little straw to lie on, but as this is the rainy season and as the rain here comes down in torrents, our straw gets very soaky at times. The ground is too hard for lying on, so one wakes in the morning very tender about ones bones.
>
> At first it was very hard on the men for they used to get wet through and had no change; indeed, for that matter there is very little in the way of change for any of us yet, but fortunately the Buffalo River lies close by, so by spending some time every day therein, and utilizing the powerful rays of this tropical sun for the things we hang out to dry, we are holding on till we get some things from Pietermaritzberg.

Glyn and his staff officers could not believe that matters could get worse; then the largest force of men, the black troops of the NNC, collectively mutinied. There can be little doubt that the overall treatment received by the black troops left much to be desired. When they accompanied Chelmsford during the Zulus' successful decoy of the 22nd, they had been left without food for two days and the events of that day had severely dented their morale and their faith in Chelmsford's ability to defeat the Zulus. As they returned through Isandlwana they witnessed the awful consequences of the

Zulu victory and many recognized friends, now dead. At Rorke's Drift, too, they constantly expected a Zulu attack. They then witnessed the departure of Chelmsford and his staff and as darkness fell, they were abandoned outside the defences. Many believed their families would be massacred if the Zulus attacked Natal, and it was a collection of too many frightening circumstances that led to their mutiny. Perhaps wisely, Glyn allowed them to depart once they had been disarmed.

Hamilton-Browne also pondered the situation; they were, after all, his men. He called for the induna of his friendly Zulus, named Umvubie, and through him addressed the NNC. He told them that they were not cowards like the other NNC and he requested them to stay. Umvubie had a better idea; he and his men were quite ready to attack the 1,200 non-Zulu blacks to prevent them leaving. Hamilton-Browne dissuaded them from this course of action and, after further discussion with his white officers, it was agreed that all the black troops should be disbanded. Hamilton-Browne wrote,

> Umvubie paused for a minute to beg my permission to be allowed to kill only a few of the Natal Kafirs, who he was sure had annoyed me very much. Alas! I could not grant his modest request. The other natives had fallen in and gathered round me in a ring. I told them in a few plain words what I thought of them. I told them that the Great White Queen would send them women's aprons when she heard of their cowardice and that they had better go home and dig in the fields with their wives. This is the greatest insult you can offer a warrior and they hung their heads in shame.
>
> But when I told them to go, and advised them to go to a country even hotter than Natal, they waited not for pay or rations but those who had guns threw them down and the whole of them breaking ranks bolted each man for his own home. The Zulus (friendlies) forming themselves into solid rings, marched past our group of officers, raising their shields in the air, in salute, and rattled their assegais against them; then breaking into a war-song marched proudly away, every one of them a man and a warrior. So exited the rank and file of the 3rd NNC.

Glyn sent a pitiful note to Chelmsford, which read:

3.45 p.m.

January 24, 1879

My Dear General,

The whole of the native contingent walked off this morning. Their rifles were taken from them; all the hospital bearers then went, and now the native pioneers are going. I am now left without any natives. What is to be done with Lonsdale and his Europeans? I shall, of course, keep them until I hear from you.

I have &c

R. Glyn, Colonel

Lord Chelmsford then immediately wrote to Sir Henry Bartle Frere:

January 27, 1879

My dear Sir Henry,

I have just received this letter through Major Grenfell.

Unless these men are at once ordered back to their regiments, or punished for refusing to go, the most serious consequences will ensue. I myself by speaking to Major Bengough's battalion have, I hear, prevented them deserting.

I have &c

Chelmsford

The Resident Magistrate at Estcourt was tasked with conducting an enquiry into events and his detailed report, efficiently submitted on 4 February, was based on his examination of the NNC indunas. He reported:

Some of the men examined say that they understood they would be wanted again in two months, others say they did not hear anything about their being called out again.

No officers accompanied them out of the camp. The men complain:-
First. Of the insufficiency of food, they say that only a quarter of a beast was issued daily for 100 men, and a small pannikin of meal each, and that

instead of the insides of the cattle killed for them being given to them, the butchers sold them on their own account.

Secondly. That when they captured cattle and asked for some to kill and eat, according to their custom, they were refused and had no food given them, and when they surprised the enemy's people cooking and captured their food, they were not allowed to eat it, but it was restored to the enemy.

Thirdly. That they had no food at all for three days at the time of the General's advance against Matyane and the capture of the head-quarters camp.

Fourthly. That very many of their men were flogged for making water within certain forbidden bounds and for washing themselves in certain streams, although they never heard any orders that they were not to do so; the floggings ranging from 6 to 20 lashes.

Fifthly. That they could not understand their officers, many of them could not speak any native language, and the others only the Amapondo dialect, and if they (the men) spoke when they received any order they did not understand, their officers said they were impatient.

Sixthly. That they were drilled continually, and that the old men were tired and incapable of understanding the drill, and if they made mistakes their officers struck them.

Seventhly. That when out in the field their men were always divided into small companies and scattered in various directions, and could at any time have been destroyed by the enemy, being thus divided and dispersed.

Eighthly. That their system of fighting was ignored, and whatever they said regarding the Zulu movements in warfare were disregarded, and they were told to shut their mouths.

Ninthly. That the Zulus would fire at them as long as their ammunition lasted and then hide, and the Contingent men, were ordered not to kill them, but take them alive, and when men in caves fired at them they were not allowed to go in and kill them, but were ordered to make prisoners of them.

Tenthly. That whilst the Zulus spared no one, they were not allowed to kill different tribes.

The foregoing is the substance of the statement made to me by the indunas of the different tribes.

The Chiefs and indunas are unanimous in expressing their very strong desire to be allowed to fight tribally and in their own way and under their own indunas, with white leaders whom they know and who can speak their language.

If the natives are to be employed again in military service, I would strongly urge a favourable consideration of the foregoing wish of the native tribes to be allowed to fight in their own fashion; employed thus, under white leaders who understand them, they will doubtless render valuable service; if again called out and placed under the late organisation, they will be discontented, and may become insubordinate and a source of danger rather than of strength.

(Signed) PIETER PATERSON

Resident Magistrate, Weenen County.

Resident Magistrate's Office, Estcourt,

February 4, 1879.

Lord Chelmsford read the report and promptly wrote to Sir Bartle Frere:

February 22, 1879

The complaints made by the natives lately belonging to the contingent attached to No. 3 Column, and the reasons given for their dispersing and going to their homes, have no doubt a sub-structure of truth, but I do not believe that there was any serious cause for dissatisfaction up to the day of the Isandula misfortune, except that the natives were not supplied with food on the 21st, consequent upon their not returning to camp as originally intended.

There were, I believe, in every company officers or non-commissioned officers who were capable of making themselves understood. The men were arranged by companies tribally, and had their own indunas; several Chiefs also accompany them.

There was so much hesitation and delay on the part of the Natal Government in calling out or even in giving permission for the calling out of the 6,000 natives asked for, that it was impossible to make as good arrange-ment for their organisation as I should have wished. Natal could not supply the requisite number of Europeans, and I was obliged therefore to indent upon the Cape Colony.

Whilst fully recognising the necessity of having an interpreter in each company, capable of explaining the orders of the commander or the wishes of the men, I entirely dissent from the axiom which it is apparently the endeavour to lay down, that those officers who cannot speak the Zulu language are not only of no use with natives but absolutely an encumbrance.

If all the qualities required for a company leader are to be found in addition to that of speaking Zulu, there can be no question that he is the right man, but if an officer is selected purely for his linguistic knowledge, without reference to the other necessary qualities, then he can only turn out a failure.

Colonel Evelyn Wood has just had to get rid of men of the latter stamp, and has substituted British officers in their place (who are quite innocent of Zulu), with the most satisfactory results.

As the High Commissioner points out, natives when brought together under whatever conditions must have some recognised and workable organisation, and must be subdivided into recognised units corresponding to regiments or companies.

(Signed) CHELMSFORD

Lieutenant Governor

And there that particular matter rested. Meanwhile, life for the British soldiers still encamped at Rorke's Drift remained tough and harrowing, but it was not without the occasional glimmer of humour. Commandant Hamilton-Browne recalled an incident that became one of the classic stories of the Zulu War and confirmed the nickname of a young British officer, Lieutenant Harford, as 'the beetle collector'. Harford had already amused his fellow officers by the incident while he was leading the advance against Sihayo's homestead, when at one critical point in the attack he was seen on his knees – not wounded but placing a rare beetle into a matchbox. Hamilton-Browne wrote:

The 24th had a small amount of reserve mess stores at Rorke's Drift, we had nothing, and although there was plenty of Natal rum I could not face the filth; vile stuff it was and hot enough to burn the inside out of a graven image. This being so the 24th, like the rattling good fellows they were, always asked me over to their corner whenever they opened a bottle and I had my tot.

Well just about this time a Natal man rushed through a wagon load of stores and asked leave to sell them. I happened to have about £2 in my pocket at the time of the disaster and after buying two night-caps and some spoons and forks for Harford and myself, I asked the man if he had any liquor. He said he had a big square rigger of gin for his own use but not for trade. I offered all the money I had left and an equal-sized bottle of Natal rum for it and we traded. Well now there was corn in Egypt and I could, in a small way, return the hospitality of the 24th so I at once sent round to my friends to come to my corner, that evening after inspection, and partake of the plunder. They had run out of spirits and the news was joyful.

I handed the bottle over to my servant Quin and told him to guard it with his life, and he swore he would do so. I was called away and I left Quin on sentry go over that precious bottle; he placed it carefully between two sacks and sat down on it so I thought it safe and attended to my duty. That afternoon we had our usual rainstorm and when it was over Harford came to me and asked me if he could have some gin. I was very busy at the time and said "Certainly, ask Quin for some."

Now it struck me it was strange that Harford should ask for it as he never touched spirits, but I thought he might feel chill after the rain and want a tot to warm himself.

Well the retreat was blown, the men manned the parapet, the O.C. inspected, and the men fell away. In a few minutes round came my friends, anxious for the tot they fondly expected to be in store for them.

"Hoots, Maori, where's the drappie?" said Black. I turned to Quin, who was standing stiffly at attention, and at once saw the worthy man was disgusted, sulky, almost mutinous. "Give me the bottle, Quin," I said. "Better ask Mr Harford for it, sir," he answered, with a grin on his expressive mug like an over-tortured fiend. "Harford," said I, "where is the gin?" and at once my heart darkened with apprehensions. "Oh, Commandant," quoth he, "I have caught such a lot of beauties," and he produced two large bottles filled with scorpions, snakes and other foul creeping beasts and reptiles. "Do look at them.""But the gin, Harford?" I murmured, so full of consternation that I could hardly articulate. "I've preserved these with it," said he, utterly oblivious to his horrid crime. "What!" yelled I. "Oh yes," said he, "this is a very rare and poisonous reptile indeed" – pointing to a loathsome beast and beginning to expatiate on its hideousness and reel off long Latin names. "I don't care if it is a sucking devil," groaned I, "but where is the gin?" "In these bottles," said he, and so it was, every drop of it. Ye Gods! The only bottle of gin or any other drop of decent drink within 100 miles of us had gone to preserve his infernal microbes, and a dozen disgusted officers, who were just beginning to grasp the awful situation, were cursing him and lamenting sadly, oh, so sadly, his pursuit of Natural History, while dear old Black had to be supported back to his angle making remarks in Gaelic. He was such a good fellow he was soon forgiven, but I do not think the dear fellow ever quite understood what an awful sin he had committed or realized what a wicked waste of liquor he had perpetrated.

Much of the chaos and many of the problems following the battle of Rorke's Drift can be attributed to the lack of control by the commanding officer of the 1/24th Regiment, Colonel Richard Thomas Glyn, and his senior officers who were ultimately in command of the garrison. All the officers were undoubtedly shocked by the magnitude of the Zulu victory at Isandlwana and of those who suffered, none felt greater anguish than Glyn. In a complete state of shock at the loss of his regiment, fellow officers and men, he was left in the midst of chaos and despondency to repair the outpost and re-establish a fortified camp.

Although there were no armed Zulus within 10 miles of Rorke's Drift, Glyn feared that the Zulu Army would attack at any time; he had the perimeter around the camp rebuilt and made everyone move inside during the hours of darkness. Conditions were terrible and to make matters worse the rain was unremitting; the interior of the fort became such a quagmire from the trampling of so many feet that fatigue parties were employed for the best part of the day in carrying liquid mud away and emptying the slush outside. It was the repair and reconstruction of the defences around the mission station and the construction of the outpost cemetery that gradually brought discipline and order back to the garrison. On 25 January all the able-bodied were put to work repairing the storeroom and stones were collected from the nearby rock terraces in order to build a stronger fortification around the outpost's perimeter. This work continued until 29 January when the 5th Company of Royal Engineers commanded by Lieutenant Porter arrived and thereafter supervised the work; they swiftly constructed a loopholed barricade round the entire outpost. The new construction was formally renamed Fort Bromhead and boasted a 7 pound gun at each corner; these were the same guns that had accompanied Chelmsford to Mangeni and which had shelled Isandlwana camp on their return.

Such was the administrative chaos that no regimental orders were issued at Rorke's Drift until 28 January; even by 2 February, orders for the garrison clearly indicate that a Zulu attack was still expected.[10]

No tents were available but in recognition of B Company's bravery, the gallant defenders of Rorke's Drift were permitted to have sole use of a tarpaulin and the rafter section in the ruins of Witt's wrecked house. It was a meagre covering but it gave this select group of men some shelter from the rain; it was a sufficient honour in the eyes of the remaining garrison who slept out in the open with nothing more than a blanket or greatcoat, usually wet through, for their protection. The remaining garrison was crammed into the small walled area between sunset and sunrise, which was churned into a revolting, foul-smelling quagmire. Without tents, blankets or change of clothing and cold steady rain falling, the men began to suffer badly. Rotting stores and poor sanitation together with a monotonous diet contributed further to the low morale that afflicted everyone. Within two weeks disease broke out among the garrison, the patients soon including Lieutenant Chard; and as all medical supplies had been destroyed when the Zulus set fire to the hospital, there was little that could be done for the sick.

The grieving Colonel Glyn withdrew even further into his shell of despondency and took little interest in the misery around him. Without doubt, he was displaying all the symptoms of a breakdown. Not only did he feel bereaved by the loss of his regiment; he also expressed the feeling that he should have been with his men at Isandlwana as they fought for their lives, a common enough emotion amongst survivors who have lost friends. Captain Walter Parke Jones of the Royal Engineers, however, was not at all sympathetic and expressed what many felt: 'Col. Glyn (our chief) does nothing and is effete'.[11]

Morale throughout the garrison suddenly improved when, on 4 February, a patrol led by Major Wilsone Black discovered the bodies of Coghill and Melvill on the Natal bank of the Buffalo river just 5 miles from Rorke's Drift. A further search found the Queen's Colour in the river some half a mile downstream. A cairn of stones was piled on the bodies and the Colour was taken back to Rorke's Drift. Glyn was moved to tears when he received the Colour and learned of the fate of his favourite young officers.

When the companies of the 1st Battalion accompanied No. 3 Column of Lord Chelmsford's army, they had with them the Queen's Colour of the battalion, the Regimental Colour having been left with the detachment remaining at Helpmekaar. The rather melodramatic *Records of the 24th Regiment* clearly describe the drama concerning the Colour:

On the fatal 22nd January, 1879, when it was evident that all was lost in Isandhlwana camp, Lieutenant and Adjutant Melvill, 1st battalion 24th, received special orders from Lieutenant-Colonel Pulleine, to endeavour to save the colour. "You, as senior subaltern," that officer is reported to have said, "will take the colour, and make your way from here." Accompanied by Lieutenant A. J. A. Coghill, 1st battalion 24th, who was orderly officer to Colonel Glyn, but had remained in camp on account of a severe injury to his knee, Melvill rode off with the colour, taking the same direction as the other fugitives. Both officers reached the Buffalo, although, owing to the badness of the track, the Zulus kept up with them and continued throwing their spears at them. The river was in flood, and at any other time would have been considered impassable. They plunged their horses in, but whilst Coghill got across and reached the opposite bank, Melvill, encumbered by the colour, got separated from his horse and was washed against a large rock in mid-stream, to which Lieutenant Higginson, of the Native contingent, who afterwards escaped, was clinging. Melvill called to him to lay hold of the colour, which Higginson did, but so strong was the current that both men were washed away. Coghill, still on his horse and in comparative safety, at once rode back into the stream to their aid. The Zulus by this time had gathered thick on the bank of the river and opened fire, making a special target of Melvill, who wore his red patrol jacket. Coghill's horse was killed and his rider cast adrift in the stream. Notwithstanding the exertions made to save it, the colour had to be abandoned and the two officers themselves only succeeded in reaching the opposite bank with great difficulty, and in a most exhausted state. Those who knew the precipitous character of the Natal side at the spot can fully realize how great must have been the sufferings of both in climbing it, especially of Coghill with his wounded knee. They appear to have kept together, and to have got to within twenty yards of the summit when they were overtaken by the foes and fell.[12]

Glyn wrote a moving letter to one of his daughters following the discovery of the Colour:

Helpmekaar 16th April 1879

My own Bess,

Yesterday I went down to where poor Melvill and Coghill's remains were lying to erect the cross Sir Bartle Frere and staff sent. I had two strong coffins made and exhumed the bodies, rolled them up in blankets, put them into the coffins and buried them just under the rock on which the cross is placed. Henry D [Degacher] took a sketch which he is going to finish off at once and have photographed. I got from Melvill's pockets a white silk pocket handkerchief, ten shillings and six pence in silver, a little dog whistle and his gold watch and chain which I shall carefully keep until I hear from Mrs Melvill what she wishes done with them. The water when he was in the river has got into the watch – and discoloured the face – it stopped at ten minutes past two p.m. which must have been about the time they crossed the Buffalo – I am so glad you liked your presents and especially the locket.

Immediately after Isandlwana the two strategically important positions of Rorke's Drift and Helpmekaar were placed in a more secure state of defence, and revetments were built with locally collected stone. By the middle of February both locations were gripped by fever and – because of overcrowding, fatigue, exposure to the cold, rain and want of sleep – the morale of both officers and men sank to a new low. At Rorke's Drift Europeans and natives were now crowded together without tents or shelter, as at Help-mekaar; there were over 1,000 men exposed to cold and rain, some sleeping on wet mealie bags, others on the waterlogged ground saturated with the overflow from the latrines; even at night there was no respite from the constant alarms. When bilious, remittent, or enteric disease struck, it was the young and weakly men who first went down with fever, diarrhoea and dysentery.

At the end of February conditions had become so bad that a new fort, initially named 'Fort Revenge' but renamed Fort Melvill on Chelmsford's order (he thought the original name too provocative), was built 800 yards away on an adjacent hillock overlooking the pont river crossing. The defences at Rorke's Drift were abandoned and the stone walls of the outpost were demolished and used in the construction of Fort Melvill, an oblong fort, flanked with towers, a broad ditch surrounding the walls and built partly of masonry and partly of dry wall. *The Illustrated London News* commented:

> Fort Melvill, named after the late Lt. Melvill, is an oblong fort with flanking towers, built partly in masonry, partly with dry wall, loopholed throughout, and surrounded by a ditch, with an obstacle formed of aloes planted on the glacis. It is constructed on a height 150 yards from, and overlooking and commanding, the ponts by which the invading army crossed on January 11th last. Lieutenant da Costa Porter, RE, has superintended its erection; and manned with 200 Europeans, it may be considered impregnable against any number of Zulus. A large stone store, roofed with galvanised iron, has been built inside, to hold commissariat supplies.

Meanwhile, little could be done to alleviate the grim conditions. Even in the new fort the men continued to be tightly confined at night, allowing sickness and disease to spread unchecked. During the day it was possible, with the aid of a telescope, to observe the battlefield of Isandlwana where vultures wheeled overhead for weeks on end and the ground became white with bleaching bones. Disease and sickness continued to take its toll among the soldiers and during the short period of occupancy of Fort Melvill no fewer than twelve men died. This number excludes Second Lieutenant

Franklin of the 24th who, while seriously ill, was moved to Helpmekaar on 22 February. He died shortly after arriving and is buried in the Helpmekaar cemetery. Initially the soldiers' bodies were buried in the Rorke's Drift cemetery alongside those who had died in the fighting; when the total reached twenty-five, the remainder were buried in a small cemetery which lay across the river from the fort and which, over the years, became totally overgrown and forgotten. It was even omitted from military maps of the area, possibly due to the fact that it contained the bodies of fever cases rather than those killed in battle. During 2001 the cemetery was restored and repaired.

Those who died at Fort Melvill are as follows – gaps denote information unknown;

Regiment or Corps	Brigade or Battalion	Regimental No.	Rank and Name	Age	Date of death	Cause of death
24	2		Private J. Williams		5/2/79	Dysentery
24	2		Private G. Evans		23/2/79	Fever
24	2	1407	Private Farr		4/3/79	Fever
24	2	1320	Private C. Foster		6/3/79	Fever
24	2		Private P. Murphy		8/3/79	Fever
24	2	1146	Private T. Jones	25	10/3/79	Fever
24	2	1067	Sergeant D. Jones	21	10/3/79	Fever
24	2	1605	L-Corporal C. Frower	19	12/3/79	Fever
RE			Sapper J. Russell		20/2/79	Fever
Newcastle Rifles			Trooper Dixon		12/1/79	Drowned
24	2	605	Colour-Sergeant W. Cuthbert	23	12/3/79	Fever
24	2	1046	L-Corporal J. Haslam		18/3/79	Fever

At the beginning of April half of the battalion, under Lieutenant Colonel Degacher, moved to Dundee; four companies, under Brevet Major Black, remained at Rorke's Drift. On the advance of the northern column from Landman's Drift, two companies (G and H) 2/24th, under Brevet Major C.J. Bromhead, were brought down from Dundee to that post; but it having been decided to construct a strong fort at Koppie Alleen, Captain Harvey moved up with H company, and Major C.J. Bromhead joined with F company, under Lieutenant H. Mainwaring. The two companies speedily converted the small earthwork they had found on arrival into a substantial closed redoubt. On 3 June 1879 this detachment had the melancholy duty of furnishing a guard of honour and escort to the mortal remains of the Prince Imperial of France, whose body was escorted by the battalion from Koppie Alleen to Landman's Drift and Dundee on its way to Pietermaritzburg. Captain Harvey, with H company and a party of Native pioneers, was also employed in constructing another fort on the Itelezi ridge, which Major General Marshall, commanding the lines of communication in Zululand – who was much pleased with the work – named Fort Warwick, in honour of the regiment. To replace H Company, B Company, under Major Bromhead, which had been sent up from Rorke's Drift to a post near Conference Hill for woodcutting, was moved to Koppie Alleen. Detachments of the 24th remained at Rorke's Drift until after the battle of Ulundi on 4 July 1879, when a redistribution of companies took place. It was a monotonous posting; during the day the men could pass the time by sifting through wagonloads of military debris that had been collected at Isandlwana by the various burial parties and brought back to Fort Melvill. This was sorted through and all irrelevant material was dumped in one of the several fort rubbish pits.

After the second division was broken up on 28 July 1879, Sir Garnet, now Lord Wolseley, who had arrived to supersede Lord Chelmsford, took F and H companies, 2/24th, under Major C.J. Bromhead, as his special escort. They accompanied him to Ulundi and in all his movements until the conclusion of peace. These companies then fell back on Isandlwana, completing the burial of the dead there, and afterwards marching to Pietermaritzburg, where they arrived on 6 October, to await the battalion headquarters. Sir Garnet Wolseley had selected the 2/24th for an expedition against Sekukuni; he bivouacked at Rorke's Drift from 2 to 5 August and whilst there he presented Private Henry Hook with his Victoria Cross. On his arrival at Utrecht, on 9 September 1879, he gave the battalion the news that it was ordered to Gibraltar. Sir Garnet took the opportunity of presenting Victoria Crosses to Brevet Major Gonville Bromhead and Privates Robert Jones and Samuel Wassall.

In August the 24th were withdrawn from Rorke's Drift and were temporarily replaced by a company of the 99th regiment (Duke of Edinburgh's) who remained there until withdrawn in October. The final items of military property were sold off on 23 October. A Mr Craft (or Croft) occupied Fort Melvill and converted part of the building into a house, sharing it with the Revd Witt who was in the process of rebuilding the mission station.[13]

British Forces engaged in the defence of the mission station at Rorke's Drift

Unit	Officers	Wounded	ORs	Sick	Killed	Wounded	Remarks
In Command	Lt. Chard						
Staff			1				
Royal Artillery			4	3			
Royal Engineers			1				
2nd-3rd Regiment(Buffs)			1				
1/24th Regiment			11	5	3	2	1 died of of wounds
2/24th Regiment	Lt. Bromhead		98	17	8	5	1 died of wounds
Commissariat Department	Mr Dalton, Mr Byrne Mr Dunne	1	1		1		
Army Med. Department	Surgeon Reynolds		3				
Chaplains Department	George Smith						Civilian
90th Regiment			1	1			
Natal Mounted Police			3	3	1		
Natal Native Contingent	Lt. Adendorff		6	6	2	2	
Ferryman			1				Civilian Daniels
Totals	8	1	131	35	15	9	

Curiously, on 19 May 1879 the Natal newspaper *The Natal Colonist* reported the death of Chard from fever. The *Natal Witness* followed the story with a disclaimer:

> The Colonist on Saturday stated it was sorry to hear, on good authority, that Major Chard, one of the heroes of Rorke's Drift, was dead. The report, we are glad to say, was quite unfounded, and was brought to us on Friday. We found however, on enquiry at the proper quarters, that there was no foundation in it. Major Chard is in hospital, and is, we are glad to hear, recovering from the attack of fever, from which he has recently been suffering.

CHAPTER 8

Helpmekaar

Like the bottom of the sea with grass on it.

MAJOR HARNESS ON ARRIVING AT HELPMEKAAR

At its best Helpmekaar is a high, open, windswept and desolate location on the edge of the Biggarsberg range of hills. In 1879 it was described by Colonel Harness RA as being like the bottom of the sea with grass on it; it has changed but little over the years. It was never a popular place with British soldiers and its reputation was about to get much worse, especially for the sick and wounded.

When the bedraggled and exhausted survivors from Isandlwana reached Helpmekaar, the sight that greeted them offered little comfort. The bustling depot they had left just a fortnight earlier had been reduced to an unfortified windswept and sodden area consisting of three corrugated store sheds and a few battered tents belonging to a section of infantry that had been left behind as guards. As the senior officer now present, Captain Essex took command and organized its defence with the few tools that he had at his disposal. He made a small laager by surrounding the main zinc shed with the three wagons that were left and infilling the gaps with sacks of mealies. At this time there were forty-eight people, including volunteers, camp followers and three farmers with their families who had come in for protection. For several anxious hours, there were just twenty-eight rifles to defend Helpmekaar from the attack that was fully expected.

The fatigued volunteers had little enthusiasm left to fight and began to take their horses and drift away. When Essex realized that his force was melting away he threatened to shoot all the horses to stop further desertions, which lowered morale still further. Two of the men who had already ridden away were to become figures of controversy. Lieutenant Higginson of the NNC had been with both Melvill and Coghill as they had clung to the rock in the Buffalo river. On reaching the bank he had promised to fetch horses for the other two. Instead, once he had found a mount, he had ridden off to safety. At the same time Captain Stephenson of the NNC had deserted from Rorke's Drift as the Zulus were about to attack; he had paused at Helpmekaar before riding off, only to be later arrested, court-martialled and dismissed the service.[1]

Lieutenant Curling RA who had, alone, survived the front line at Isandlwana and escaped to Helpmekaar wrote to his mother on 30 January, mentioning that life at Helpmekaar was grim. 'We have 30 sick and wounded men inside and several typhoid patients who however are left in a tent outside where of course they will at once be killed if we are attacked'. In the aftermath of Isandlwana, there was a climate of suspicion and paranoia about any native caught near either Rorke's Drift or Helpmekaar. On a visit to Rorke's Drift Curling had seen a Zulu hanging from a tree and several natives met a similar fate at Helpmekaar, even though they were probably entirely innocent. On 2 February Curling wrote:

> What is going to happen to us, no one knows. We have made a strong entrenchment and are pretty safe even should we be attacked. The only thing we are afraid of is sickness. There are 50 sick and wounded already who are jammed up at night in the fort. The smell is terrible, 800 men cooped up in so small a place. Food, fortunately, is plentiful and we have a three months supply. All spys [sic] taken now are shot: we have disposed of three or four already. Formally [i.e. formerly], they were allowed anywhere and our disaster is a great extent due to their accurate information of the General's movements. What excitement this will cause in England and what indignation.

The suggestion that a Zulu spy network was the cause of Chelmsford's defeat was ludicrous and indicative of the wild theories and rumours circulating around the British camps. Curling was right, though, about the shock and outrage with which the news of the disaster was received in Britain.

Following the British defeat at Isandlwana, Lord Chelmsford paused at Helpmekaar long enough to convene a Court of Enquiry. It consisted of those senior officers then at Helpmekaar and commenced its deliberations five days later on 27 January 1879. The court president was Colonel F.C. Hassard with Lieutenant Colonel Law RA and Lieutenant Colonel Harness RA as court members. The nature of the enquiry was extraordinary when compared with standard military procedures; their brief was merely to 'enquire into the loss of the camp' at Isandlwana. Although a number of officers and men had been required to make statements after their escape from Isandlwana, the court recorded only the evidence of Majors Clery and Crealock, Captains Essex, Gardner and Cochrane, Lieutenants Curling and Smith-Dorrien and NNC Captain Nourse. It was subsequently argued, within the army and the press, both in the United Kingdom and South Africa, that insufficient evidence was heard, in order to divert the blame away from Chelmsford. Harness was later to defend himself by stating, 'it seemed to me useless to record statements hardly bearing on the loss of the camp but giving doubtful particulars of small incidents more or less ghastly in their nature'. The final line of his report indicated his defensive attitude. 'The duty of the Court was to sift the evidence and record what was of value: if it was simply to take down a mass of statements the court might as well have been composed of three subalterns or three clerks'.

As author Ian Knight wrote, 'Of course, the modern historian is left to ponder by what criteria Harness decided which statements were unreliable and worthless.' A moot point indeed.[2]

It was a transparent exercise and, at best, Harness saw the Court of Enquiry as a means of obtaining information about the defeat for Chelmsford. However, it served no real purpose apart from giving Chelmsford time to prepare his explanatory speech before he returned to England to present his case before the awaiting press and Parliament. The initial observations of the court certainly enabled the blame for the British defeat to be squarely laid upon the NNC and Colonel Durnford. At the enquiry, Colonel Crealock deliberately gave false evidence stating that he had ordered Durnford, on behalf of Chelmsford, to take command of the camp; this persuasive evidence totally exonerated Chelmsford in the eyes of the enquiry. Durnford was convenient as a scapegoat: he was dead; furthermore, he was not from a respected infantry regiment of the line. In addition, and it would become the subject of much subsequent debate, he was the senior officer present. The finding of the court conveniently accepted, on Crealock's false evidence, that Durnford had been in charge, that there had been a defeat, and accordingly highlighted Durnford's various deficiencies to the point that the deputy adjutant general, Colonel Bellairs, forwarded the court's findings to Lord Chelmsford with the following observation:

> From the statements made to the Court, it may be gathered that the cause of the reverse suffered at Isandhlwana was that Col. Durnford, as senior officer, overruled the orders which Lt. Col. Pulleine had received to defend the camp, and directed that the troops should be moved into the open, in support of the Native Contingent which he had brought up and which was engaging the enemy.

Not content with blaming Durnford, Chelmsford's staff then began focusing their attention onto Colonel Glyn, Chelmsford's second in command, now isolated from any news at Rorke's Drift. While the alienated Glyn was suffering both mentally and physically, Lord Chelmsford and his followers were attempting to play down their personal roles in the disaster. In a subtle piece of responsibility shifting, Chelmsford stated that 'Colonel Glyn was solely responsible' and, 'that Colonel Glyn fully and explicitly accepted this responsibility cannot, however, affect the ultimate responsibility of the General-in-Command'. This attempt to share the blame with Glyn rang hollow, as it was generally known that Glyn had little say in matters where Chelmsford gave the orders. Chelmsford's staff contributed to the growing controversy by saying that it was Glyn's failure to entrench the camp that caused it to be overrun. They deemed that, as he was commander of the Centre Column, the blame should be firmly laid at his door. Glyn was sent a number of official memoranda requiring him to account for his interpretation of orders relating to the camp at Isandlwana. Glyn recognized the possible entrapment and returned the memoranda, unanswered but with the comment, 'Odd the general asking me to tell him what he knows more than I do'. Glyn finally accepted all responsibility for details, but declined to admit any responsibility for the movement of any portion of troops in or out of camp. The acrimony continued with Chelmsford even suggesting that it was Glyn's duty to protest at any decisions with which he did not agree. Glyn maintained his position by stating that it was his duty to obey his commander's orders. Little was said beyond this point; with considerable dignity, Glyn remained silent and loyal to his general but Mrs Glyn robustly defended her husband in the coming months.

There was no defence for the NNC and initially there was no defence for Durnford. Chelmsford finally damned Durnford's reputation in his speech to the House of Lords on 19 August 1880. Chelmsford stated that 'in the final analysis, it was Durnford's disregard of orders that had brought about its [the camp's] destruction'. It was thereafter widely believed that Durnford had failed to assume command of the camp from the subordinate Pulleine and had then irresponsibly taken his men off to chase some Zulus.[3]

With regard to the departure from Rorke's Drift by Major Spalding, little that was sympathetic was ever said.[4] Many believed that he would automatically have been awarded the Victoria Cross as the commanding officer, if only he had remained at his post. After all, there was no valid reason for him personally to ride to Helpmekaar especially as Chard had already informed him that the Zulus were possibly approaching the position; and there were several underemployed officers who could easily have undertaken the task. It was also generally believed that, on his return, having reached a point less than 3 miles from the beleaguered mission station, Spalding and the two companies of the 24th could easily have pressed on to relieve Rorke's Drift. Perhaps it was to save him from embarrassment that no official questions were asked although Major Clery came straight to the point in one of his letters home. He wrote from Helpmekaar on 13 April: 'Spalding is utterly worthless, so that the General was – as regards an opinion on any subject – practically without an adjutant or quarter-master'. As well as being the officer commanding Rorke's Drift, Spalding was also the deputy assistant adjutant and quartermaster general. Spalding nevertheless submitted a full report detailing his actions on the day. He wrote:

1   At 2 p.m. on the 22nd instant I left Rorke's Drift for Helpmakaar, leaving a second horse at Varmaaks. My intention was to bring up Captain Rainforth's company, 1st Battalion 24th Regiment, to protect the ponts. Lieutenant Chard, R.E., on returning from the camp, Isandula, had observed Zulus on the neighbouring heights. I thought they might make a dash for the ponts during the night.

2   Between Varmaaks and Helpmakaar, where I arrived 3.45 p.m., I met two companies 1st Battalion 24th Regiment under Major Upcher; on returning from Helpmakaar, I met Major Upcher, who informed me of the disaster at Isandula.

3   We advanced as far as Varmaaks with the troops. I then pushed on to the foot of the Berg, accompanied by Mr. Dickson, of the Buffalo Border Guard. The road was covered with fugitives, chiefly Basutos and people in civilians' clothes, but there were one or two mounted infantry. Several of these I ordered to accompany me, but all except two, slipped away when my back was turned. My object was to ascertain whether the post at Rorke's Drift still held out. In this case I should have sent word to Major Upcher to advance and endeavour to throw myself into it.

4   But every single white fugitive asserted that the mission house was captured; and at about three miles from the same I came across a body of Zulus in extended order across the road. They were 50 yards off; a deep donga was behind them, capable of concealing a large force. They threw out flankers as if to surround the party.

5   On reaching the summit of a hill from which the mission house is visible it was observed to be in flames; this confirmed the statement of the fugitives, that the post had been captured. This being the case it was determined to save, if possible, Helpmakaar and its depot of stores.

6   It was growing dusk; the oxen had already had a long trek; the hill had to be re-ascended, and the heights were said to be lined with Zulus. I examined them with my glass, but could not observe the enemy. There may have

been a few detached parties, however, as these were observed by competent witnesses. No attack was made by them, and the column reached Helpmakaar by 9 p.m., when waggon laager was formed around the commissariat stores. Colonel Hassard, R.E., met us half-way up the Berg, and took over command from me.

7   The following morning a dense fog prevailed. About 9 a.m. a note arrived from Lieutenant Chard, R.E., stating that Rorke's Drift still held out, and begging for assistance. It was considered imprudent to risk the safety of Helpmakaar by denuding it of its garrison, and probable that Rorke's Drift had already been relieved by the column under the General. It was determined to push down to the drift some mounted men to gather intelligence. I was in command. A short distance from Helpmakaar Mr. Fynn was met, who communicated the fact that the General's Column had relieved Rorke's Drift. At the top of the Berg I met Lieutenant-Colonel Russell, who confirmed the news. At about noon I reached Rorke's Drift and reported myself to the General.

(Signed) H. S. SPALDING,

Major, D.A.A.G.

While Chelmsford pondered the political implications of events, the sick and wounded apparently received scant consideration from their general. On their arrival at Helpmekaar, the more seriously wounded from Rorke's Drift were accommodated in the end of a corrugated zinc shed. This was one of several, filled with commissariat stores, chiefly bags of maize that had been repeatedly soaked by heavy rains during their transportation from Pietermaritzburg. These many tons of damp bagged maize were then stored; they were now decomposing and giving off the most offensive smell. For the seriously sick and wounded, the only bedding consisted of long square biscuit boxes that were arranged along the inside of the building that then had empty sacks laid over them. This was all the bedding that was obtainable for more than a fortnight, during which time replacement stores were slowly making their way from the base of operations at Pietermaritzburg. The station's medical stores were non-existent, as all such stores had been allocated to the column's hospital at Rorke's Drift where all equipment and medicines had been destroyed in the fire.

Fortunately the doctor at Helpmekaar, Surgeon Blair-Brown, had one small personal medical kit that contained a mixture of pills, powders, bandages and a tourniquet; unfortunately, the labels of the pills and medication had been washed off in a storm and the doctor relied on his intuition and luck when dispensing to the patients. Surgeon Blair-Brown wisely took control of a crate containing bottles of brandy and port wine; this form of medication proved very popular and efficacious in treating most conditions. With the decline in morale and general health, the doctor was kept very busy: 646 soldiers reported sick or sought treatment during their first week at Helpmekaar. A week later about 600 more men from the 4th Regiment augmented the Helpmekaar force. The treatment list during the first weeks was as follows:

	Officers	Men
Royal Artillery	4	66
1st 13th Regiment	1	73
1st 24th Regiment	7	110
2nd 24th Regiment	0	45
Medical Department	2	3
Commissariat Department	1	6
Veterinary Department	1	0
Mounted Infantry	4	95
Mounted Police	3	84
Natal Mounted Volunteers	4	49
Royal Engineers	2	2
Mounted Basutos	4	80
TOTALS	33	613

When the shocked survivors from Chelmsford's column re-entered the camp at Helpmekaar, one of the greatest fears was of a Zulu night attack, even though the Zulus rarely – if ever – attacked at night. Consequently Captain Walter Parke Jones, R.E., and his able subordinate Lieutenant R. da Costa Porter commenced the construction of a substantial entrenchment; Porter subsequently wrote a prize-winning dissertation on military fortifications. Jones described the fort's location as 'vile'; its position having been determined by Lord Chelmsford who insisted that its construction must defend the existing iron storehouses. Jones thought the position unsuitable as it was prone to become waterlogged whenever it rained. Indeed, after one particularly heavy downpour, the ditch was filled with water to a depth of 6ft.

Chelmsford and his staff remained at Helpmekaar just long enough to give instructions for the Court of Enquiry; Colonel F.C. Hassard was left in charge. Hassard proved to be a weak commander and he occupied himself with strengthening the fort and then resolutely remaining within the defences. One week later, command at Helpmekaar was given to Colonel E.W. Bray who did what he could to improve the appalling conditions around the fort. Chelmsford's staff officer, Major Clery, once commented that the original store site been so located 'with regard to nothing but the convenience of the contractor erecting them'. On the positive side, the construction of the Helpmekaar fort was comparatively easy as the soil was soft but firm; an earthen parapet and deep ditch were soon constructed, the whole being surrounded by strong earthworks. A drawbridge made from bundles of brushwood was constructed to make a bulletproof barrier across the entrance at night. For added protection, the guns of Harness's RA detachment were brought from Rorke's Drift and positioned at three corners.

And then it rained; and when it rained, the fort quickly became waterlogged and a virtual swamp. Immediately following Isandlwana, there were few stores or tents and the men slept packed together within the fort; when supplies arrived from Pietermaritzburg tents were erected outside the fortifications but due to the close proximity of fit and sick men, the tents were moved on 31 March to a new location 500 yards away, and a wagon laager was built to house the hospital tents.

Due to the fear of Zulu night attacks, the whole garrison was confined within the fort between sunset and sunrise with uniform and boots worn at all times; the men were then released in groups and always under a police escort. Much discomfort arose from the total loss of personal possessions looted from Isandlwana and, with few stores, no comforts and constant driving rain, life at Helpmekaar was physically and mentally exhausting.

Washing facilities were limited to one bathe per week in a nearby stream and men and officers had to let their beards grow. Improvisation and invention flourished and rubbish heaps were scoured for empty tins that could be used to fashion knives and forks, and numerous items such as combs and brushes were created from pieces of wood.

The Natal Mounted Police shared these miserable conditions. At first the whole garrison was shut in every night and marched out an hour before daybreak under a police escort. As clothing and bedding were scarce, the people of Ladysmith sent a wagonload of useful articles for the police, who by the middle of February were more comfortably encamped. Then in early February the Natal press were informed of the plight of the Colonial volunteers:

TO THE EDITOR OF THE NATAL MERCURY.

Sir, – The following notice appears on the Government notice board, in an 'extra' published in the *Times*:

"Notice. – The Carbineers having suffered the loss of all their clothing, it is urgently requested that they be supplied with the following articles, each: – 2 shirts, 2 pair socks, 1 pair breeches, 1 blanket, 1 pair boots. Contributions for procuring above, either in money or kind, may be sent to Holliday's Mart. – J D Holliday, Volunteer Agent, Pietermaritzburg."

Does this mean that the Imperial authorities have taken no measure to supply these men with clothing in place of that burnt at the camp, and that unless contributions come in, the poor fellows are to be without these actual necessaries? What notice has been issued, signed by authority, that parents or wives are required to provide such articles to send to the front? Should it be left to a private individual to suggest and make provision for such necessities?

The Imperial Government, for Imperial policy, called these young fellows out, and now, through some unexplained blunder, they have been deprived of everything but what they stand in. The Imperial authorities seem so paralysed that they cannot even issue an order that an outfit similar to that lost shall be issued, but leave it to private subscription to send; and if private subscription fail, the poor fellows are to be left in the field destitute.

Why do not the Government authorities provide the things necessary, without delay, as they would be obliged to do for regulars in the same position? Should subscriptions be raised, there will be difficulty in expending the money for the good of those at the front.

When news of the appalling conditions reached the people of Pietermaritzburg, they collected and dispatched food, clothing and washing equipment for the Colonial troops, most of whom came from the town; there was little comfort for the Imperial troops who would have to wait until March before they were re-supplied. The only personal equipment to be purchased was that previously belonging to the officers and men killed at Isandlwana, including the possessions of Major Stuart Smith, which fetched high prices.

The garrison troops had no option but to wear their clothes and boots at night, and slept under wagons and tarpaulins, often being disturbed by false alarms. But even worse was to follow; annoyance and frustration were soon overtaken by sickness. By the beginning of February many of the Helpmekaar force succumbed and most became stricken with enteric fever or typhoid. The medical officers were mystified by the speed with which diseases spread and it was believed, mistakenly, that the sodden and rotting mealie bags were responsible. Captain Walter Parke Jones wrote: 'I cannot account for it all as the place used to be so healthy. Of course being crowded together in a fort with rotten meal and other stores and difficulties about sanitary arrangements has something to do with the question.' When fever broke out at Helpmekaar during February, the news quickly reached the War Office. Although it was usual for more men to die through sickness when campaigning than to be killed fighting, the rate of sickness was so severe that the Army Intelligence Branch at the War Office voiced its own opinion as to the cause:

Immediately after Isandhlwana this important place strategically was secured for defence by extemporizing with sacks of mealies to build revetments. The garrison of 1,000 Europeans and Natives were crowded together without tents or shelter except for a few tarpaulins, exposed to cold and rain. Some slept on wet mealie bags, others on the damp ground, disturbed by frequent alarms and subjected to noxious exhalation. The military authorities were informed of the danger from decomposing grain and mealies, and of the unsanitary conditions, but failed to take action, because it was considered vital for the military position. Thus men soon succumbed to the malaise, lost their appetite and the young men especially were attacked by fever, diarrhoea and dysentery.[5]

Psychological disturbances, largely bred by the disaster of Isandlwana, began to proliferate through all ranks, a condition made worse by inactivity, boredom and ill-founded rumours. All those associated with Isandlwana were haunted by it, and continually harked back to 22 January. Some of the officers began to display an unnatural lack of interest in their duties while the men became lethargic and sullen, no doubt due to the disaster and general malaise that followed. At Rorke's Drift, Glyn was dysfunctional due to the depression brought on by the loss of his regiment at Isandlwana. At Helpmekaar Colonel Harness, his friend Colonel Cecil Russell and Lieutenant Curling had all lost interest in their commands, though Curling could blame fever for his bout of apathy. The collapse of Russell could have had more serious consequences, as he was responsible for mounted patrols, which were sporadic and ill planned. His inertia was criticized by Clery, who realized that the absence of mounted forays, which Russell should have commanded, allowed the Zulus to roam at will. Among the troops, speculation on the progress of the war and possible future tactics occupied much time at Helpmekaar. It took several weeks, an improvement in the weather and the news of a new military commander before morale began to improve.[6] Even then conditions remained far from satisfactory. A letter dated March 5, from an unnamed Colonial soldier to his family, was reported in the *Natal Witness*. It reads:

Here we are, Foot, Artillery, Engineers, Police, and Carbineers (about 500 strong), living in tents during the day, and turning into the fort at night. With the exception of a stink of rotten mealies, and the rain continually swilling through and through, the fort is not so bad, being so strong and well built that the men here now could hold it against the whole of the Zulu army. It is not healthy though, for the hospitals are always full, and we have had eight or ten deaths here. Hay of the Carbineers died last night; one of the N.M.P. shot himself last week, and several Engineers have died. What with guards, videttes, &c., the duties are very heavy.

By the beginning of March Chelmsford's preparations for the second invasion of Zululand were well under way and the previous invasion route through Rorke's Drift was changed for the easier passage to the north. In any event, Chelmsford did not intend marching his rejuvenated army past Isandlwana which was still strewn with the debris of the wrecked camp and, worse, the unburied bodies of the 24th Regiment. This change of plan accordingly reduced the strategic importance of the Helpmekaar garrison whose role was transferred to Dundee, 20 miles to the north. By the middle of April only two companies of the 1/24th remained at Helpmekaar before they also joined the new advance into Zululand. Helpmekaar then became a shell with a small guard to watch over several sheds of unwanted supplies; these were eventually sold off at a public auction on 25 October when the garrison closed. Helpmekaar was again used as a military garrison during both the Boer War and the Zulu uprising of 1906.

CHAPTER 9

Explanations

The defeat of the Zulus at this post, and the very heavy loss suffered by them, has, to a great extent, neutralised the effect of the disaster at Isandhlwana, and no doubt saved Natal from a serious invasion.

LORD CHELMSFORD, 8 FEBRUARY 1879

Immediately following the battle at Rorke's Drift, Colonel Glyn and his team of staff officers arrived back at the mission station and, in theory, resumed command of the battered garrison. This relegated Chard and Bromhead back to their normal regimental duties and there is no record or account of Chard or Bromhead having any further impact on the scene thereafter; they had performed their duties bravely and admirably. Chelmsford had thanked the assembled defenders and in the minds of the two officers and all the soldiers involved, that was that. The newly combined garrison of the Rorke's Drift defenders and Chelmsford's recently arrived force was now in a state of chaos, shock, exhaustion and confusion; every man had either fought in the defence of Rorke's Drift or had been part of Lord Chelmsford's force that had, in intense heat, marched 50 miles in the previous forty-eight hours and witnessed the results of the slaughter of their colleagues at Isandlwana. There were no tents to accommodate the troops and the fierce heat of the previous two days had given way to torrential rainstorms. The garrison was without vital supplies and the troops were terrifyingly low on ammunition; most of the day-to-day stores and essentials had been lost or damaged in the battle and those stores that had been dispatched to Isandlwana were beyond reach, either destroyed or looted by the Zulus. In the midst of this distressingly desperate situation there was so much to be done; there were the British dead to be buried and hundreds of Zulu bodies to be cremated, the sick and injured required urgent medical treatment and the remaining stores had to be sorted and unpacked in the attempt to find food for the 700 men. It was to be several days before good military discipline and order was finally restored; meanwhile, the Zulu army, its location unknown, was still expected to descend upon the mission station at any time.

As and when the soldiers had any spare time, some sought to write letters home but all available paper had been burnt in the fire or destroyed during the fighting. When Commandant Hamilton-Browne sought to arrange a field court martial for a captured Zulu spy he had great difficulty finding paper or pens to record the proceedings. All of a sudden, paper had become a very rare commodity; one soldier, Private Robert Head, was so desperate to write a letter to his brother with the news that he was still alive that he paid one shilling, a day's pay, for a scrap of scorched paper. This morsel of a letter survived – but the true identity of the soldier remains unknown as there was no Private Robert Head recorded either in the 24th Regimental records or on the list of Rorke's Drift defenders.[1] Presumably he wrote home using his correct name but at the time of his enlistment had used a false name. Of greater significance is the statement by Lieutenant George Stanhope Banister of the 2/24th who, having accompanied Chelmsford during the previous four days, found himself appointed as assistant garrison adjutant at Rorke's Drift after the action there. In a brief note to his father dated 27 January 1879, Banister wrote, 'No paper or pens or in fact any single thing. I have managed to get some foolscap in my extra capacity as Garrison Adjutant.' Likewise, without paper, no camp orders could be issued until 28 January, six days after the battle, when a limited official supply arrived from Helpmekaar. The soldiers had to continue to make do with scraps; one soldier, Private John Bainbridge, even sent a note to his family in England with a request for writing paper – on the grounds that there was 'none to be had within 200 miles of here'.

Lieutenant Curling, who was a compulsive letter writer, couldn't find any writing paper; he bemoaned his plight but was thankful to have been the sole survivor from the British front line. He eventually managed to write home and stated:

One ought not to think of anything after having had such a wonderful escape. As to clothing, blankets etc., there have been sales of all the kits belonging to the officers who were killed and I have been able to get the most necessary things one requires. This paper I am writing on belonged to one of the poor fellows in the 24th.

Remarkably, amidst the incessant heavy downpours of rain, the mire and chaos, and within two days of the battle, Chard ostensibly managed to obtain a sufficient supply of clean undamaged paper in order to prepare and submit a perfectly sequential report of the battle that was carefully composed, neatly written and complete in extraordinary detail.[2] The report, apparently written in secret, included accurate timings, precise locations and the names of the thirteen different units represented as well as listing the names and units of those who were killed, injured or who might receive acknowledgement for their outstanding courage during the battle. Yet there is no known record of any participant in the battle having assisted Chard with his report, neither is it known how Chard was able accurately to recall the names of all the participants, or draw accurate pictures of the hospital building after it had been destroyed by fire. Bromhead was subsequently requested to write an account but he repeatedly avoided the issue until 15 February when a report was written outlining the bravery of certain participants in the battle. Likewise there is no evidence that any of the NCOs present during the battle assisted Chard or Bromhead in the preparation of their reports. Colour Sergeant Bourne left no contemporary account.[3]

For an officer with a reputation for slothfulness, and given the extraordinarily difficult circumstances under which Chard's report was written, the result is a truly masterful and perceptive account of the battle. Curiously, if Chard made any notes in the preparation of the report they have never been seen; when, over twelve months later, he was asked to rewrite the account for Queen Victoria, he reported that he had lost his original notes.[4]

Although Chelmsford had not remained at Rorke's Drift for more than a few hours, he had given specific instructions for a formal enquiry to be conducted into the Isandlwana defeat; it is also probable that he ordered a report concerning the victory at Rorke's Drift. It is now known from recently discovered letters that Chelmsford knew that an account was being prepared; his own correspondence reveals that he was most anxious to receive the account although it is not known who ordered the report or who was to write it. As early as 28 January Chelmsford wrote to Glyn:

> I hope you are sending me in a report of the defence of Rorke's Drift post and also the names etc of the killed during that gallant fight.

On 31 January Glyn received a further request from Chelmsford's staff officer. This request is ambiguous as it relates to the word 'reports', indicating that Chelmsford was expecting at least two reports, presumably concerning Isandlwana and Rorke's Drift. He wrote:

> Your immediate attention is called to the fact that no reports have been received from you regarding the entrenchment of your column or of the occurrences of the 22nd instant; neither has any return of casualties been made.

On 3 February Glyn received a further curt note from Chelmsford marked 'Private' reminding him that Chelmsford was still waiting for the Rorke's Drift report; not only was Glyn suffering depression from the loss of his regiment and friends, he was also aware of rumours that he was to be a scapegoat for Isandlwana – Glyn ignored the communication. His suspicions were soon confirmed when he received a formal request from Chelmsford's staff for information relating to Isandlwana. It was to this request that Glyn made the abrupt reply, 'Odd the general asking me to tell him what he knows more than I do'. Meanwhile Chard's report reached Chelmsford who immediately forwarded it to the Secretary of State for War. It would have been in Chelmsford's interest to have a dramatic report of the victory at Rorke's Drift – which he could then promulgate; he knew the spectacular victory at Rorke's Drift would deflect those who would soon seek to humiliate him for the appalling loss of men and the longer-term implications of a highly trained British force being defeated by a native army. Chelmsford's advisers would also have been aware that, especially in the minds of the British public, an inglorious defeat could be offset by a glorious victory. And so it was. Furthermore, before Parliament could act to censure Chelmsford for his unauthorized invasion of Zululand, Queen Victoria pre-empted any criticism by ordering a congratulatory message to be sent to Chelmsford via the Secretary of State for War:

> The Queen has graciously desired me to say she sympathises most sincerely with you in the dreadful loss which has deprived her of so many gallant officers and men and that Her Majesty places entire confidence in you and in her troops to maintain our honour and our good name.

This was followed by a further message from the Field Marshal His Royal Highness the Duke of Cambridge, Commander-in-Chief of the British Army. His telegram reads:

> Have heard, by telegraph, of events occurred. Grieved for 24th and others who have fallen victims. Fullest confidence in regiment, and am satisfied that you have done and will continue to do everything that is right. Strong reinforcements of all arms ordered to embark at once, February 13th.

The 'Chard Report' concerning Rorke's Drift was initially hailed throughout the British and Colonial press as evidence of Britain's strength in adversity while both Chard and Bromhead were fêted in the newspapers and popular weekly journals as heroes – as indeed they were. Amongst their fellow officers there was a certain amount of growing resentment and incredulity for their unexpected status as popular heroes; Curling and others were soon annoyed by the intensity of fame being attached to the two officers. Curling, the only officer to survive the front line at Isandlwana, wrote:

> It is very amusing to read the accounts of Chard and Bromhead. They are about the most common-place men in the British Army. Chard is a most

insignificant man in appearance and is only about 5 feet 2 or 3 in height. Bromhead is a stupid old fellow, as deaf as a post. Is it not curious how some men are forced into notoriety? [5]

On 15 February a report was written concerning the bravery of certain soldiers of the 24th during the battle at the mission station. Subsequently known as the 'Bromhead Report', it was signed by Bromhead and submitted to Glyn, the regiment's commanding officer, who relayed it without any comment to Chelmsford. It is not known who wrote the report although Bromhead signed it in his capacity as the commander of B Company. Strangely, and highly irregularly, Chelmsford personally added the names of Chard and Bromhead to the report without further comment. Why Chelmsford did not discuss with Glyn the matter of awards for the two officers is not known; Glyn had not seen fit to recommend them and in accordance with established military protocol, any recommendation should have come from Glyn as the commanding officer of Rorke's Drift. [6]

Apart from the 'Bromhead Report' and his note warning those at Helpmekaar, only two other letters are known to have been written by Bromhead. The first was written to Captain Goodwin-Austen of the 2/24th on 19 February; Goodwin-Austen had been with Chelmsford on the 22–23 January. It can be clearly seen that the style and syntax in the official Bromhead Report differs considerably from that used in the two letters – which indicates that Bromhead was not the author of the official report. [7]

It is possible that Bromhead suffered considerable anguish from the trauma of the battle as his ongoing lethargy subsequently irritated certain senior officers. Curling was not alone in disparaging Chard and Bromhead. Major Clery was one of Chelmsford's staff officers at Isandlwana and had remained at Rorke's Drift after Chelmsford's departure; he wrote on the subject:

Reputations are being made and lost here in an almost comical fashion, from the highest downwards. At the risk of being looked on as very ill-natured and scandalous, I will have a little gossip with you on the subject.

Well, Chard and Bromhead to begin with; both are almost typical in their separate corps of what would be termed the very dull class. Bromhead is a great favourite in his regiment and a capital fellow at everything except soldiering. So little was he held to be qualified in this way from unconquerable indolence that he had to be reported confidentially as hopeless. This is confidential as I was told it by his CO [Lt Col. H.J. Degacher 2/24th]. I was about a month with him at Rorke's Drift, and the height of his enjoyment seemed to be to sit all day on a stone on the ground smoking a most uninviting looking pipe. The only thing that seemed equal to moving him in any way was any allusion to the defence of Rorke's Drift. This used to have a sort of electrical effect on him, for up he would jump and off he would go, and not a word could be got out of him. When I told him he should send me an official report on the affair it seemed to have a most distressing effect on him. I used to find him hiding away in corners with a friend helping him to complete this account, and the only thing that afterwards helped to lessen the compassion I felt for all this, was my own labour when perusing this composition – to understand what it was all about. So you can fancy that there was not one who knew him who envied him his distinction, for his modesty about himself was, and is, excessive.

Of Chard there is very little to say about except that he too is a very good fellow – but very uninteresting. The fact is that until the accounts came out from England, nobody had thought of the Rorke's Drift affair except as one in which the private soldiers of the 24th behaved so well. For as a matter of fact they all stayed there to defend the place for there was nowhere else to go, and in it they fought most determinedly.[8]

Chard's company commander, Captain Walter Parke Jones, who had fortified Helpmekaar, was so irritated by Chard's lack of ambition that he wrote:

Chard makes me angry, with such a start as he got, he stuck to the company doing nothing. In his place, I should have gone up and asked Lord Chelmsford for an appointment, he must have got one, and if not he could have gone home soon after Rorke's Drift, at the height of his popularity at home. I advised him, but he placidly smokes his pipe and does nothing. Few men get such opportunities.

Chard was later attached to Colonel Wood's column where he avoided both work and any interpersonal contact. Both Wood and Buller were puzzled that such a brilliant and stubborn defence had apparently been orchestrated by such a mediocrity as Chard. Wood described him as 'A dull, heavy man, scarcely ever able to do his regular work.' Sir Garnet Wolseley, who succeeded Lord Chelmsford, and who presented both Chard and Bromhead with their Victoria Crosses, was also critical. He found Chard '...a hopelessly dull and stupid fellow, and Bromhead not much better'. Glyn had discussed Bromhead's future with Lieutenant George Banister who was the acting adjutant for the 24th Regiment at Rorke's Drift; Banister referred to the conversation in a letter to his father – Surgeon General Banister:

> The Colonel took me aside and said '*I promised you the Inspector of Musketry and it is still yours as I never go back on my word, but I should like to do something for Bromhead, and it is about the only thing he is fit for, so would you let him have it and instead take the Adjutancy?*' I told him I did not care for the Adjutancy and had always looked forward to the other thing, but that under the circumstances I would not for worlds stand in Bromhead's light. At first he would not hear of it, but eventually agreed if I would take up the Adjutant work.[9]

Despite the widespread scepticism on the part of their fellow officers, Queen Victoria favoured both Chard and Bromhead. With their fame and royal patronage, it is remarkable that both men's careers failed to prosper further and both died before they were 50. In the final analysis, it is probably Major Clery's observation above that lets the cat out of the bag; nobody in the invasion force had thought of the Rorke's Drift affair except as one in which the private soldiers of the 24th behaved so well. It is, after all, most likely that Chelmsford's staff took the initiative in ensuring that both Bromhead and Chard signed suitably impressive reports to offset the disastrous news and serious repercussions about to be unleashed following the unimaginable losses at Isandlwana. An examination of both reports reveals that they were not written by Bromhead and Chard, although the two officers signed and dated the documents.

One of Chelmsford's senior staff officers, Major Clery, had remained behind at Rorke's Drift after Chelmsford and his staff departed on 24 January. It is possible, therefore, that Clery was either the author or the instigator of these two important 'Chard' and 'Bromhead' reports. Clery was a confidant of Chelmsford and an experienced report writer; he would also have had access to an official scribe who could have written the reports – although there is no direct evidence of such a person having been at Rorke's Drift. Clery had been with Chelmsford while the Zulus sacked Isandlwana; he had also been culpable in the unfortunate decision-making process that led to the defeat and, of all people, he would have realized that a dramatic report from Rorke's Drift might deflect the criticism that would undoubtedly be unleashed upon Chelmsford and his staff once the news of Isandlwana reached home. Indeed, the timing of 'Chard's' report being written and publicized coincides exactly with the parallel deception that was being orchestrated by Chelmsford's staff following the defeat at Isandlwana. In that instance, Chelmsford's orders to Colonels Pulleine and Durnford, having been 'lost', were then suitably rewritten so as to imply that the two officers had disobeyed Chelmsford's orders relating to Isandlwana. Both Pulleine and Durnford, conveniently killed by the Zulus at Isandlwana, were then publicly and officially blamed for the disaster.[10]

As the former column commander, Glyn was also, unbeknown to him, cast in the role of scapegoat. Even though he was severely distraught by the loss of his regiment, Chelmsford deliberately isolated him at Rorke's Drift where he was unable to defend his reputation. It was not until 21 February that Glyn was able to write his highly emotive report;[11] by then he had access to writing paper and had carefully considered the sequence of events since the fateful 22 January. As the camp commander at Rorke's Drift, Glyn would have been able to call upon a scribe's services – had there been one. Because Glyn personally wrote his own report, it is most unlikely that Chard and Bromhead had the use of a scribe, unless surreptitiously and unbeknown to Glyn; the identity of the author of their reports therefore remains a mystery.

Later that year, and now safely back in England, Chard was required to submit a further report at the request of Queen Victoria. Nothing is known of the preparation or research that went into this second report, other than the fact that apologies for the delay were given to Queen Victoria as Chard claimed to have lost his notes.[12]

There are a number of other 'original' Chard reports in existence but none carries Chard's actual signature. Perhaps the most famous of these is owned by the Trustees of the Kimberley Public Library in South Africa. This particular 'Chard Report' came to light in 1929 when it was published by the *Natal Mercury* as part of the 50th Anniversary of the battle at Rorke's Drift. There are minor discrepancies in the report and a casual examination of the writing, and especially the signature, clearly reveal that it was not written or signed by Chard.

CHAPTER 10

Pulling the Strings –
Awards and Campaign Medals

One of the things that no fellow can understand.[1]

LIEUTENANT COLONEL PICKARD

OF THE ROYAL HOUSEHOLD

The glowing reports concerning the battle and victory at Rorke's Drift quickly and effectively steered public attention away from the disaster at Isandlwana, while the heroic accounts of outstanding bravery restored the reputation of the army and satisfied the British politicians, press and public alike. Now came the recognition and awards for that bravery. At first the matter was clear-cut; Victoria Crosses[2] were to be awarded to the six soldiers named in the Bromhead Report – and also to Lieutenants Bromhead and Chard, but only after Lord Chelmsford secretly added the officers' names to the list. This was an unprecedented breach of military protocol, which was further disregarded by the War Office as neither of the two officers responsible for these medal recommendations were ever consulted, namely Chard, as the senior officer during the battle, nor Glyn as the overall commander of those involved. A member of the Royal Household, Lieutenant Colonel Pickard, mentioned this in a letter to Sir Evelyn Wood (commander of the Northern Column in Zululand) after Chard had been to Balmoral to meet Queen Victoria. Pickard wrote:

It seemed odd to me that he [Chard] was not consulted on the distribution of the VCs. But it is only one of the things that 'no fellow can understand'. He is not a genius, and not quick, but a quiet plodding, dogged sort of fellow who will hold his own in most situations in which, as an English officer, his lot may be cast.

Was the award of so many medals due more to the perceived propaganda value of the victory than a measure of the enormous bravery of those involved? There can be little doubt that, as author Ian Knight wrote, 'by elevating Rorke's Drift to the level of a major strategic victory the more damaging significance of Isandlwana was obscured'.[3] This view was first aired publicly by Lieutenant General Garnet Wolseley, the new Commander-in-Chief and General Officer Commanding South Africa; he stated that it was 'monstrous making heroes of those who saved or attempted to save their lives by bolting or of those who, shut up in buildings at Rorke's Drift, could not bolt, and fought like rats for their lives which they could not otherwise save'.[4] Although Wolseley voiced his criticism of the awards, he had been personally obliged to escort the Victoria Cross medals all the way from London. The timing of the awards was also significant; it coincided exactly with the second invasion of Zululand when morale throughout the new invasion force was not high, especially among the many troops fresh from England. These recently arrived and inexperienced soldiers were, after all, in some trepidation at the reputation and prospect of meeting the hitherto victorious Zulu army and the widespread publicity of the award of an unprecedented number of Victoria Crosses would certainly have boosted the troops' morale.

The awards were also extremely popular with the British press and, quick to recognize the mood of the people, the War Office soon considered making further awards. This was just as well for by March, questions were being asked in Parliament as to why the ordinary soldiers at Rorke's Drift had not been nominated or considered for their acknowledged acts of bravery. It was also realized by the press that the only known nominations to date were for members of the 24th Regiment. In the House of Commons a number of difficult questions were asked; some boldly challenged the involvement of Queen Victoria and her uncle, HRH The

Duke of Cambridge, in his capacity as Commander-in-Chief of the British Army. On 27 March 1879 an MP, Mr Osborn Morgan, asked Colonel Stanley as Secretary of State for War why no awards had been conferred upon NCOs and private soldiers. The reply given was that such awards took a considerable time to process – but that the matter was under consideration. Another MP, Doctor Ward, asked on 8 May why Surgeon Reynolds had been overlooked for an award. The Secretary of State for War gave a defensive reply by stating that it was premature for him to consider what awards or honours should be given, and added that Surgeon Reynolds had already been promoted fourteen months in advance of his seniority and had passed over the heads of sixty-four other medical officers. Nevertheless, the first to benefit from such serious lobbying was Surgeon Reynolds; although his promotion to surgeon major was backdated to the date of the battle, his name was subsequently added to the medal list on 17 June 1879.

Other members of Parliament kept the pressure on Colonel Stanley when, on 16 June, Mr Stacpoole asked whether it was true that, in recognition of the gallantry of the NCOs and privates at Rorke's Drift, they had been awarded one free flannel shirt and one pair of trousers? Colonel Stanley, clearly stung by the innuendo, replied that such an order had been given to compensate the soldiers for damage to their uniforms and added, 'whether regard was had for gallantry or not I cannot say'.

Other reports began to circulate in England and South Africa about Dalton's role at Rorke's Drift. The belief grew that it was Dalton who was mainly responsible for the successful defence, especially when rumours were confirmed that he had previously gained a military qualification in field fortifications. Questions about Dalton's role were asked both in Parliament and by the Duke of Cambridge so the matter was referred on to Sir Garnet Wolseley, the new Commander-in-Chief and General Officer Commanding South Africa. Wolseley had already written about his unease:

> I presented Major Chard RE with his Victoria Cross: a more uninteresting or more stupid looking fellow I never saw. Wood tells me he is a most useless officer, fit for nothing. I hear in the camp also that the man who worked

hardest at Rorke's Drift Post was the Commissariat Officer who has not been rewarded at all.[5]

Clarification of the matter was finally sought from Major Chard who was asked to comment on the actions of both Dalton and Dunne but, rather surprisingly, though he acknowledged their actions his reply was less than supportive. Undaunted, Dunne's and Dalton's commissary general, Sir Edward Strickland, was convinced that the actions of his officers in the defence of Rorke's Drift had deliberately not been recognized; he wrote to Chelmsford in his new capacity as Military Secretary at the War Office and within a week the correspondence concerning the matter was placed before the Duke of Cambridge. His decision on 18 October was short, final and, worse, unfair.

> We are giving the VC very freely I think, but probably Mr Dalton had as good a claim as the others who have got the Cross for Rorke's Drift Defence. I don't think there is a case for Mr. Dunne.

Dalton was awarded the Victoria Cross in January 1880, and it was presented by Major General H.H. Clifford on a parade at Fort Napier. Rather perversely, Dunne received nothing other than the knowledge that he had been recommended for the VC. Nevertheless, Dunne fared pretty well. He was involved in the first Boer War in 1880–81 and was present at the battle of Tel-el-Kebir, when the British defeated the Egyptian Army. He transferred to the newly formed Army Service Corps as a Lieutenant Colonel, was awarded a CB and retired as a full colonel.

Another body of men, the Colonial forces, had originally been omitted from the medal list. When this was realized the reports were re-examined and on 29 November, Corporal Schiess NNC was gazetted as a recipient of the Victoria Cross for his actions during the battle. When he received his medal from Sir Garnet Wolseley on 3 February 1880, Wolseley expressed the wish that Schiess might live long to wear the decoration. Sadly he was to die a pauper only three years later.

The allocation of Victoria Crosses for Rorke's Drift was so disjointed that the time span of awards extended to more than one year and apart from the intense background politicking and intrigue, each award was given the highest level of publicity by the press, for which the government was equally grateful. Even so, there were dissenters. *The Broad Arrow* of 23 August 1879 wrote:

> It must be confessed that the military authorities in Pall Mall have shown lavish prodigality in the distribution of the Victoria Cross, which would probably startle their contemporaries in Berlin [a reference to the profusion of Iron Cross awards]. We say there is a chance of the Victoria Cross being cheapened by a too friendly eagerness in Pall Mall to recognise acts of equivocal valour.[6]

It is a myth that the Reverend George Smith was offered the choice of a Victoria Cross or an army chaplaincy; he received the chaplaincy but there is no evidence or recommendation to substantiate the story that he ever had a choice.

> "AN OFFICER" writes to *Punch* –
>
> "In your Cartoon, of March 22, you, as worthy head of the Army, thank Lieutenants Chard and Bromhead for their heroic defence of Rorke's Drift. In the background are seen some men of the 24th Regiment, and scattered about are quantities of Commissariat Supplies. Cannot you find some corner for a memorial to the only officer who was killed that night while gallantly doing his duty, Assistant-Commissary Byrne? Should you ignore the only officer 'severely wounded,' to whom all were indebted for his advice and skill in turning his supplies of flour and biscuits into parapets – Assistant-Commissary Dalton? Or the young officer who gained the admiration of all by erecting the last defence under a heavy fire, Assistant-Commissary Dunne? Or Surgeon Reynolds, who only laid on one side his rifle to attend to the wounded?"

Punch replied:

> *Punch* only wishes his Cartoon was as large as his gratitude, in which case he would certainly have found room not only for these gallant officers – combatant or non-combatant, who assisted in the defence of Rorke's Drift – but for every man who piled a biscuit-box, fisted a mealie-bag, levelled a rifle, or plied a bayonet on that memorable night. But pages have their limits, though gratitude has none, and so *Punch* and his artist have been fain

to lump under the names and presentments of the most prominent leaders of that noble defence all the officers and men who contributed to it, in their several ranks and capacities. He rejoices that "An Officer's" letter, in mentioning many of these names, secures a record of them in his immortal pages.[7]

The Victoria Cross (VC)

The Victoria Cross – the ultimate accolade – is Britain's highest honour for bravery in battle; it is a medal that has an awesome mystique. There is something brooding about the dark bronze of the medal with its dull crimson ribbon that sets it apart from the glittering silver and colourful ribbons of other awards.

Victoria Crosses were awarded for acts performed in terrifying and bloody circumstances: the tunnel vision of spontaneous bravery in saving a helpless comrade; the calculated act because there was no alternative or because the risk is worth taking.

After the hero was fêted by a grateful nation, the Victoria Cross could bring its own problems for, all too often, the qualities that made a man a hero in battle could elude him in times of peace. Of the 1,354 men who have won the VC, nineteen committed suicide, a far higher proportion than the national average today (although most recipients were Victorian). About the same number have died in suspicious circumstances. Others fell on hard times and died in abject poverty, having sold their hard-earned Cross for a pittance. In contrast, most officer recipients prospered, as did many other ranks who were held in high esteem by their neighbours. The VC changed some men's lives for the better while others could not come to terms with its constant reminder of nightmarish events. Along with the Charge of the Light Brigade, the most celebrated feat of arms during Victoria's reign was the Anglo-Zulu War of 1879 and in particular, the battle of Rorke's Drift.

Gonville Bromhead received his Victoria Cross from the new commander, General Sir Garnet Wolseley, a man who let it be known that he thought the awards for the defence of Rorke's Drift were 'monstrous'. When Bromhead returned to England, he was invited with Chard to dine with the queen at Balmoral. Rather typical of his luck, he had already gone fishing in

Ireland and did not receive his invitation until the date had passed. Despite sending his apologies, he was never invited again. Bromhead was promoted to captain and served in the East Indies and in the Burma Campaign of 1886. He attained the rank of major and was serving with the battalion in India when he was struck down by typhoid and died on 9 February 1891. Bromhead's medal is currently owned by his descendants.

John Chard received a hero's welcome when he arrived at Portsmouth. The Duke of Cambridge, who brought the invitation to dine with the queen, personally greeted him. In contrast to some of his critical superiors, Victoria was taken by Chard's unassuming manner and the modest way he related events. She was most impressed by the battle, asking for photo portraits of the Victoria Cross recipients and commissioning Lady Butler to paint a picture of Rorke's Drift.

Chard continued to enjoy the royal favour and rose in rank to colonel. He was posted abroad several times but never saw action again. In 1896 he was diagnosed as having cancer of the tongue and he was forced to retire. Queen Victoria was kept informed of his condition, which deteriorated and led to his death in November 1897.

An interesting postscript concerning Chard's Victoria Cross occurred in 1999. Stanley Baker, who played Chard in the celebrated film *ZULU*, acquired Chard's pair of medals in auction in 1972. Although the campaign medal was genuine, the Victoria Cross was catalogued as a copy and, as a consequence, Baker paid the comparatively modest sum of £2,700 for the pair. On Stanley Baker's death, the Cross changed hands three times until it ended up, lodged for safety, with Spinks medal dealers who decided to check the nature of Chard's 'copy' medal; its metallic characteristics were tested by the Royal Armouries. The test results were compared with those of the bronze ingot, kept at the Central Ordnance Depot, from which all Victoria Crosses are cast. The tests revealed that the 'copy' had come from this same block and there was no doubt that it was the genuine article. No price can be put on this authenticated VC awarded to such a famous recipient.

With the exception of Robert Jones's medal, all the VCs belonging to the men of the 24th are now on display at the Regimental Museum at Brecon.

Award of Rorke's Drift Victoria Crosses

Gazetted	Name	Date awarded	Where awarded	By whom
2 May 1879	Chard	16 July 1879	St Paul's, Zululand	Lt Gen. Wolseley
17 June 1879	Reynolds	16 July 1879	St Paul's, Zululand	Lt Gen. Wolseley
2 May 1879	Hook	3 August 1879	Rorke's Drift	Lt Gen. Wolseley
2 May 1879	Hitch	12 August 1879	Netley Military Hospital	Queen Victoria
2 May 1879	Bromhead	11 September 1879	Utrecht	Lt Gen. Wolseley
2 May 1879	Jones, R.	11 September 1879	Utrecht	Lt Gen. Wolseley
2 May 1879	Allen	9 December 1879	Windsor Castle	Queen Victoria
2 May 1879	Jones, W.	13 January 1880	Windsor Castle	Queen Victoria
17 November 1879	Dalton	16 January 1880	Fort Napier	Maj. Gen. Clifford
29 November 1879	Schiess	3 February 1880	Pietermaritzburg	Lt Gen. Wolseley
2 May 1879	Williams	1 March 1880	Gibraltar	Maj. Gen. Anderson

A full account concerning the gallantry and medal citations for Rorke's Drift appears in Chapter 15.

The Distinguished Conduct Medal (DCM)

The alternative gallantry award was the Distinguished Conduct Medal, which was instituted in December 1854 for other ranks only. Before this date there had been no way of rewarding outstanding acts of bravery by ordinary soldiers and, in the rush of jingoism that accompanied the outbreak of the Crimean War, the press and the public demanded some form of recognition for their heroes. Moving with unusual speed, the Horse Guards produced the DCM, which carried with it a gratuity of £15 for sergeants, £10 for corporals and £5 for privates. Many of these medals, such as the Crimean War medal, were issued to men actually serving at the front, and were worn by them in the trenches before Sebastopol.

Like most medals of this period, it was designed by William Wyon, Royal Academician. The obverse showed a trophy of arms, while the reverse had the inscription FOR DISTINGUISHED CONDUCT IN THE FIELD.

The medal was made of silver with a scrolled silver suspender that hung from a ribbon of red with a dark blue centre stripe. The result was aesthetically pleasing and generally well received.

The awarding of this medal, however, has a history of inconsistencies. For instance 800 were awarded during the Crimean War but only seventeen for the Indian Mutiny, while 2,090 were issued for the Boer War but just eighty-seven for the Sudan.

The Zulu War saw as many as twenty-three Victoria Crosses awarded compared with just sixteen DCMs. One wonders why only five DCMs were awarded for the defence of Rorke's Drift when there were so many acts of gallantry displayed. Indeed, one could argue that some of the Victoria Crosses awarded for this action probably merited the DCM instead. But then other motives were at work to lessen the impact of Isandlwana on the British public. The Rorke's Drift recipients of the 'Silver Medal', as it is sometimes known, were Corporal Francis Attwood, Army Service Corps, Gunner John Cantwell, Royal Artillery, the celebrated Colour Sergeant Frank Bourne 2/24th and Private William Roy 1/24th who was one of the defenders of the hospital. Private Roy left the army but could not settle; he emigrated to Australia where his health deteriorated. In 1887 a military concert was held in Sydney for his benefit as he was 'almost blind and helpless'. He lived out the remainder of his life in an institution. The fifth recipient was Corporal Michael McMahon, Army Hospital Corps who subsequently had his award taken away for theft and desertion.

Following the awards of the Victoria Cross, the press speculated about awards for the other participants. Comment from *The Times* was typical, even though nothing came of the suggestion:

> It is probable that the medal for Distinguished Service in the field will be given to the whole of the garrison at Rorke's Drift and that B Company, 2nd Battalion 24th Foot in commemoration of the gallant stand it made on the 22nd January 1879. This will be a lasting honour to the Company and the Regiment. It is satisfactory to note that the non-combatant officers have also received a step of rank. Surgeon Major Reynolds and Messrs. Dalton and Dunne have richly earned their promotion.

The South Africa Medal

The South Africa Medal, to give the Zulu War Medal its correct title, was given to all who were involved in the war effort and covered the period from 25 September 1877 to 2 December 1879. The original design was by William Wyon and was the same as the 1853 medal issued to participants of the 'Kaffir Wars' or, as they have been politically corrected, the Frontier Wars, for three separate campaigns during the years 1834–5, 1846–7 and 1850–53. The medal is a silver disc measuring 35.5mm (1.4in) diameter. The authority for the medal came from a royal warrant dated January 1880 which was followed by a further two royal warrants. This was followed by a general order (G.O.) No. 103 published in August 1880. Due to its ambiguous drafting, a further clarifying G.O., No. 134 was issued in October 1880. The medal obverse shows the diademed head of a young Queen Victoria with the legend VICTORIA REGINA. The 'young queen' design first appeared on medals as early as 1842 and was still used nearly forty years later on the 1879 medal. One might wonder why this should be when the other campaign medals of the 1870–80 period show a matronly head of the queen. The probable explanation is cost. Some 36,600 medals, all struck by the Royal Mint, were issued and as there was already a die for the South African War Medal, it was a fairly simple matter to mint a further quantity.

The reverse was designed by L.C. Wyon, (a son of William Wyon). Beneath the words SOUTH AFRICA is the graceful illustration of the lion which symbolizes Africa and is usually wrongly described as stooping to drink from a pool in front of a protea bush. In fact the artistic effect should convey submission. One under secretary hoped that 'the lion doing penance will not be taken for the *British Lion*'. In the exergue (the space below), the date '1853' was substituted with a Zulu shield and four crossed assegais. The recipient's name and unit were stamped or engraved on the rim in capital letters. After months of deliberation, Queen Victoria finally approved the ribbon of watered pale orange with two wide and two narrow dark blue stripes, which symbolized South Africa's parched terrain and many watercourses.

Also issued for fitting to the medal was a date bar or clasp. Of all the medals ever issued, that to the Zulu War presents a bewildering number of permutations. Date bars for 1877, 1877–8 and 1877–9 were issued to members of the Colonial forces who fought against the Gcalekas. There was a separate 1878 bar for operations against the Griquas. There were also bars for 1877–8–9 and 1878–9 and the Imperial regiments like the 3rd, 13th, 24th, 80th, 88th and 90th were also entitled to fix these to their medals, as were N Battery 5th Brigade Royal Artillery, the principle being that the year(s) on the clasp convey all the operations in which the recipient may have engaged. The 1879 bar was issued to all who took part in operations in Zululand. For those who remained in Natal, 5,600 medals without a bar were issued, with the largest number in this category being awarded to the sailors of HM ships *Euphrates*, *Boadicea*, *Himalaya*, *Orontes* and *Tamar*.[8]

Curiously, those members of B Company who fought at Rorke's Drift but did not cross the border into Zululand nevertheless received bars to their medals, whether by mistake or design is not known. General Order 103 dated 1 August 1880 specifically excluded the award of clasps to those who did not cross into Zululand.

Of all the campaign medals from Victoria's small wars, medal collectors today find the Zulu War Medal the most collectable. Prices vary according to the recipient, regiment and action. Rorke's Drift recipients command the highest price. A survivor of Isandlwana would be equally valued. Medals to soldiers of the 24th are more sought after than those of other regiments. An exception is for medals of the 80th who were at Ntombe Drift.

Colonial forces medals are naturally more sought after in South Africa, with Hlobane participants the most desirable. Because of their scarcity and mystique, Zulu War gallantry medals command very high prices and rarely appear on the market. Although it can be an expensive hobby, medal collecting offers the enthusiast the spur to research and learn more about the individuals involved in this most fascinating of colonial wars.

Miscellaneous medal awards relating to Rorke's Drift

Gold Medal of the British Medical Association
Besides his VC, Surgeon Major Reynolds also received the Gold Medal of the British Medical Association in July 1879.

Royal Red Cross
At the age of 19 years, nurse Janet Wells took part in the Russo-Balkan War of 1878. She was then sent to South Africa with the second Zululand invasion force where she supervised the military hospital at Utrecht and then moved to Rorke's Drift. After the battle of Ulundi she spent several weeks at Rorke's Drift. She returned to England while still only 20 years of age and resumed her career in nursing. Nurse Wells received the Zulu War campaign medal and in 1883 she was presented to Queen Victoria who awarded her the rare Royal Red Cross for her nursing services during the Zulu War. She was also awarded the Russian Red Cross for her services during the Russo-Balkan War.

CHAPTER 11

War's End

A gallant monarch defending his country.

A DESCRIPTION OF KING CETSHWAYO IN PARLIAMENT.

It was obvious to Lord Chelmsford that the war was turning in his favour, but both he and Sir Bartle Frere still needed a decisive victory in the field to erase the stain of Isandlwana. Moreover, throughout March and April, a steady stream of reinforcements had arrived in Durban and Chelmsford now had far more troops at his disposal than he had hoped for at the beginning of the campaign. With the Zulu capacity to mount an offensive broken, he was now in a position to initiate a fresh invasion of Zululand. As before, King Cetshwayo's principal homestead at Ulundi, in the heart of Zululand, remained Chelmsford's target.

Chelmsford had learned much from the disastrous first invasion of January. Whereas his original columns were weak and failed to take proper precautions on the march, he planned his new columns to be juggernauts. They would be much stronger than the original columns, and would not only protect their halts with improvised laagers each night, but would also establish a chain of fortified posts in their wake to guard their lines of communication.

For the second invasion of Zululand, Chelmsford planned on making two main thrusts. The first would follow the coastline northwards into Zululand using troops from Pearson's old Coastal Column. This force was designated the First Division under the command of Major General Henry Crealock, one of several major generals who had been sent to South Africa as reinforcements. Crealock was an experienced officer whose younger brother, John North Crealock, was Chelmsford's military secretary. Chelmsford planned that his second main thrust would come from the north-west, following roughly the line of the old Centre Column. However, as Chelmsford wished to spare his men the sight of the battlefield of Isandlwana, where the British dead still lay unburied, he planned a new line of communication through the village of Dundee, crossing the Mzinyathi (Buffalo) and Ntombe rivers upstream from Rorke's Drift. This column would pass Isandlwana to rejoin the old planned line of advance near Babanango mountain. It would be called the Second Division and was composed of troops fresh out from England. Although Chelmsford himself accompanied this column, it was commanded by another new arrival, Major General Edward Newdigate, who, like Glyn before him, found himself with little real opportunity to exercise his authority. A new cavalry division, consisting of the 1st (King's) Dragoon Guards and 17th Lancers commanded by Major General Frederick Marshall, was to be attached to the Second Division. Evelyn Wood's column was re-designated the Flying Column. Its orders were to affect a junction with the Second Division and advance in tandem with it to Ulundi.

Chelmsford was greatly concerned by the lack of wagons while the accumulation of reinforcements created further transport demands. The Natal authorities were becoming more and more reluctant to co-operate with Chelmsford's requests; they were increasingly worried that the ordinary commercial economy of the colony would grind to a halt as transport drivers abandoned their regular work for the easy pickings offered by the army. Many of the wagons accumulated by the old Centre Column were still abandoned on the field of Isandlwana so Chelmsford decided to recover any serviceable wagons from the battlefield. On 21 May he dispatched General Marshall to bury the dead and recover any undamaged wagons. A force of 2,490 men were dispatched including the 17th Lancers, the King's Dragoon Guards and four companies of the 24th. They were accompanied by a sizeable force of natives with 150 army horses to bring back the wagons. The complete force assembled at Rorke's Drift and set off at daybreak. A force of Lancers made a detour to Sihayo's kraal to clear the area and, unopposed, met up with the main force at Isandlwana. Major Bengough's natives were deployed in skirmishing formation to search the slopes of the Nqutu plateau while the main force, led by the marching 24th, approached the devastated campsite. Once General Marshall was satisfied the area was free of Zulus, the solemn but ghastly task of burying the dead commenced. The whole area was strewn with human bones and skeletons, some covered with parchment-like skin; the depredation was worsened by the ravages of vultures and predatory animals which included the formidable pack of soldiers' dogs, which had reverted to the wild. Most of the bodies were unrecognizable; others had desiccated in the hot African sun leaving their features shockingly recognizable. Captain Shepstone pointed out that of Colonel Durnford who was buried where he fell.

Forty-five wagons were recovered along with a large supply of stores that had been ignored by the victorious Zulus. With the dead now buried, the force departed the battlefield with the same precautions with which they had moved onto the scene.

From the first, Crealock's Coastal Column suffered from a serious lack of transport facilities and was dubbed 'Crealock's Crawlers' by the rest of the army. The health of Crealock's troops also deteriorated rapidly which seriously slowed his progress. Outbreaks of enteric fever, typhoid and dysentery soon hospitalized a worryingly high proportion of his men. Nevertheless, Crealock achieved some of his objectives when he destroyed two large Zulu homesteads containing over 900 huts. The Zulus made no attempt to distract the British from burning these two important complexes, which suggests their capacity to resist was suffering. King Cetshwayo now realized the grim truth: that though many Zulus remained loyal to him, with so many of their young men now dead they stood little chance of resisting the huge British columns which were steadily occupying their country.

Chelmsford's advance commenced on 31 May and was very different in character to that of Crealock's coastal division. Almost immediately further tragedy struck. It was not another great defeat at the hands of the Zulus but the death of the young exiled heir to the throne of France, Prince

Louis Napoleon. The Zulus had deployed a large number of scouting parties to observe the British progress; the main British advance would therefore be accomplished in the face of almost constant skirmishing. On 1 June a small patrol including Lieutenant Jaheel Brenton Carey of the 98th Regiment and the exiled Prince Imperial of France set out from the Second Division to select a suitable camping ground for Chelmsford's force. Despite the fact that the area had already been swept for Zulus and the Flying Column was only a few miles away, the patrol was ambushed at a deserted homestead and the prince was killed. Although his death was a minor incident in the history of the war, at home it created a greater scandal than the defeat at Isandlwana and resulted in a story that was set to run and run. The ingredients were potent. Brave young descendant of the century's outstanding leader forced into exile while serving with his adopted country in a far-off place; a violent death and cowardice by the British officer who abandoned him, a grieving widowed mother, Queen Victoria's involvement and the end of a dynasty. The public thoroughly enjoyed the *Schadenfreude*, not least because it had happened to a Frenchman.

By this time Chelmsford had become increasingly ruthless in his determination to bring the war to a conclusion by any means possible. British soldiers burned any Zulu homestead they came across, whether it had any military connection or not, and confiscated whatever cattle they could find.

At the end of June Chelmsford established camp on the banks of the White Mfolozi river overlooking King Cetshwayo's capital. A flurry of last-minute diplomatic activity by the Zulu king took place. Chelmsford was not concerned with Cetshwayo's diplomatic overtures so much as with his own urgent need to bring the war to a close. His replacement, Sir Garnet Wolseley, was already in South Africa and both wanted the glory of the final battle. Wolseley sent Chelmsford several desperate telegrams attempting to halt the British advance; Chelmsford ignored them.

At first light on 4 July 1879, Chelmsford led the fighting men of the Second Division and Flying Column across the river to bring the second invasion of Zululand to its dreadful and inevitable conclusion. They engaged with and defeated the Zulu army at Ulundi in a brief one-sided battle dominated by the Gatling gun. By this stage the marching troops were unrecognizable as such: they were weather-beaten, their uniforms were in tatters, many of their red jackets had disintegrated and long hair and beards were common.

King Cetshwayo escaped but was finally captured by a patrol on 28 August. While much of Zululand had not been affected by the war, vast swathes had either been destroyed by the British or were denuded of population because of the consequences of British action. Most Zulu men were still mobilized with the Zulu army or in hiding. The second invasion saw the worst excesses of destruction, when Imperial troops returned to the Nqutu area of Zululand, including Isandlwana and Sihayo's homestead: the British carried out further intensive attacks, burning villages and confiscating cattle. The district's women, children and surviving cattle had also disappeared; they had moved into caves and thickly forested areas for safety. On 10 May the invading column commander, General Newdigate, ordered the advancing mounted troops to burn all the homesteads they encountered; Major Bengough described the destructive action and burning villages as 'a perfect line of fire'. When W.E. Montague rode through the area towards the end of the second invasion, he wrote that 'there was no sign of life, except for the rising smoke from burning kraals, no labourers in the fields, just dead silence'.[1] When he returned in October 1879 nothing had changed; the retreating victorious British army continued their policy of destruction, possibly to deter any Zulu retaliation. Although the Colonial Office memorandum acknowledged that the Zulu War had been declared 'against Cetshwayo and not against the Zulu nation', it was the Zulu people that largely suffered the long-term consequences of widespread destruction and death.[2]

The British forces then marched out of Zululand and left its destitute people to their fate. Starved of good news and needing a lift, the British nation cheered; the public welcomed home the worn-out regiments that had suffered greatly during the mismanaged campaign. There were plenty of heroes to fête and their names became known in every household. Queen Victoria, after years of refusing to involve herself in the nation's affairs, was pleased to pin decorations and orders on the fresh tunics of her brave soldiers. For several weeks the country enjoyed being proud of its army until memories faded and fresh news succeeded old. Sir Bartle Frere was recalled, his credibility ruined. He defended his position to the end; on his deathbed his last words were: 'Oh, if only they would read "The Further Correspondence": they must understand'.[3] Lord Chelmsford survived the wrath of the press and, being a favourite of Queen Victoria, still more honours came his way, though Disraeli refused to receive him. In 1906 Chelmsford died of a heart attack while playing billiards at his club.

King Cetshwayo was exiled to Cape Town from where he frequently petitioned Queen Victoria to grant him an audience. He was described in Parliament as, 'a gallant Monarch defending his country and his people against one of the most wanton and wicked invasions that ever could be made upon an independent people'.[4]

He finally arrived in England in July 1882 and was presented to Queen Victoria at Osborne House on the Isle of Wight. As a result of the meeting Cetshwayo was escorted back to Zululand and reinstated as King of the Zulus. During Cetshwayo's three-year absence Wolseley had independently restructured Zululand into thirteen chiefdoms, a classic case of 'divide and rule'. It was never in the newly appointed chiefs' interest to accept King Cetshwayo in his former role and in 1883 his homestead was attacked by rival Zulus causing him to flee. He took refuge under the protection of the British resident at Eshowe but died on 8 February 1884; it is believed his own people poisoned him.

Meanwhile the debacle of the Zulu War convinced the Boers that the British Army was not invincible. Encouraged by widespread discontent throughout the Transvaal, the Boer community made preparations to resist further British influence. Within a few months of the battle of Ulundi they commenced limited military action against the British; it was a conflict that quickly developed into the first of a series of Boer Wars. Zululand remained in turmoil until 1906 when parts of the country erupted in a ferocious uprising, from which it never recovered.

After the Zulu War a steady stream of visitors made their way to the battlefields of Rorke's Drift and Isandlwana; the battlefield of Isandlwana was still littered with battle debris – smashed boxes, derelict wagons, rotting clothing and, most distressing, scattered bleached human bones. Following

a number of protests from visitors, the Governor General of Natal instructed Alfred Boast to organize the cleaning of the site. The task took one month
and was completed on 9 March 1883. Boast listed no fewer than 298 cairns
marking graves, each containing upwards of four bodies. He even removed
the skeletons of the artillery horses killed in the ravine during the flight
along the fugitives' trail. The bodies of Captain Anstey and Durnford were
re-buried by their families, Anstey at Woking and Durnford at Pietermaritzburg. Over the years a number of regimental and family memorial stones
were erected at Isandlwana; in March 1914 a memorial to the 24th Regiment
was erected by the regiment.

Of the survivors from the war, Horace Smith-Dorrien rose to the rank
of general when he commanded the II Corps during their First World War
retreat from Mons; he died in a car crash near Bath in 1930. John Crealock
rose to command his regiment, the 95th; he saw battle during the Boer War
and retired in 1900. Edward Essex had several narrow escapes during the
Boer War, earning himself the nickname 'lucky Essex'; he then became an
instructor at Sandhurst before commanding the Gordon Highlanders. Sir
Henry Evelyn Wood VC died a field marshal in 1918 aged 81. Colonel
Richard Glyn never recovered from losing his regiment at Isandlwana;
when the 1/24th was reconstituted, Major Dunbar (who had resigned his
commission at Isandlwana) was promoted to command the regiment. Glyn
became Colonel of the Regiment; he died in 1900 at the age of 69.

PART TWO

CHAPTER 12

Medical Treatment of the Wounded

*Without medicines, lint, bandages, or any of the usual equipment at
Helpmakaar, I had to make use of what I could find.*

SURGEON BLAIR-BROWN

The experiences and reports of the medical officers, Rorke's Drift defender
Surgeon James Henry Reynolds and the Helpmekaar hospital Surgeon David
Blair-Brown FRCS, make interesting reading as both were involved with the
Rorke's Drift casualties. Their reports clearly illustrate the nature of the
wounds and treatments rendered to the casualties. Because they had fought
behind walls and barricades their wounds were all in the upper parts of the
body, and those who died had been hit in the head. If Zulu fire had been
better aimed, there is no doubt that the British casualty rate would have
been much higher. It is also uncertain whether Surgeon Reynolds examined
the British fatalities before their burial, as he left no report detailing the causes of their deaths. Had such an examination taken place, it is possible that
Reynolds could have differentiated between soldiers killed by Zulu rifle fire
from Martini-Henry rounds and those killed by an assortment of elderly
Zulu muskets. Certainly all the gunshot wounded survivors had been hit by
rounds from the older style of Zulu muskets; many of these casualties suffered
horrendous injuries, but lived to tell the tale. It is known that some of the
British gunshot fatalities were killed instantly; the question therefore has to
be asked, could Martini-Henry rounds have caused these instantaneous
deaths? Indeed, it is unlikely that the slow velocity rounds from Zulu muskets

fired from a range of 300 yards could have produced the instantaneous death of Byrne and the clean bullet wound that passed straight through the body of Scammell: this question will probably never be answered.

After the battle, Chard wrote that some of the bullet wounds suffered by the Zulus were 'very curious':

> One man's head was split open, exactly as if done with an axe. Another had been hit just between the eyes, the bullet carrying away the whole of the back of his head, leaving his face perfect, as though it were a mask, only disfigured by the small hole made by the bullet passing through. One of the wretches we found, one hand grasping a bench that had been dragged from the Hospital, and sustained thus in the position we found him in, while in the other hand he still clutched the knife with which he had mutilated one of our poor fellows, over whom he was still leaning.

Surgeon Reynolds had little time to examine the piles of dead Zulus apart from ordering their collection and burial; understandably he concentrated his attention on the wounded and dying British soldiers before having the worst cases moved to Helpmekaar where he, mistakenly, thought there would be better medical facilities.

Casualties at Rorke's Drift

1/24th Casualties

Number	Rank	Name	Born/Home	
135	Pte	BECKETT William	Manchester	Dangerously wounded in hospital – assegai penetrating abdomen. DIED on 23/1/79.
568	Pte	DESMOND Patrick	Hubberstone	In hospital. Slightly wounded – gunshot through fleshy part of thumb.
1861	Pte	HORRIGAN William	Manchester	KILLED in hospital.
841	Pte	JENKINS James	Monmouth	KILLED in hospital.
625	Pte	NICHOLAS Edward	Newport	KILLED in hospital – gunshot through head.
447	Pte	WATERS John	Lichfield	Severely wounded – gunshot through arm and shoulder.

/24th Casualties

Number	Rank	Name	Born /Home	
23	Sgt	MAXFIELD Robert	Newport	KILLED in hospital – assegaied to death.
328	L/Sgt	WILLIAMS Thomas	Brecon	Dangerously wounded – gun shot left side of chest fracturing ribs. Ball not lodged. DIED on 25/1/79.
240	Cpl	ALLEN William (VC)	York	Severely wounded – gunshot through arm and shoulder.
112	Cpl	LYONS John	Ireland	Dangerously wounded – gunshot through neck fracturing spine. Ball lodged – later removed.
87	Pte	ADAMS Robert	Middlesex	KILLED.
350	Pte	BUSHE James	Dublin	Slightly wounded – struck on nose by ball which had previously killed Pte Thomas Cole.
335	Pte	CHICK James	Unknown	KILLED.
301	Pte	COLE Thomas	Chatham	KILLED in hospital – gunshot through head.
69	Pte	FAGAN John	London	KILLED.
769	Pte	HAYDEN Garret	Dublin	KILLED in hospital – stabbed in 16 places, abdomen cut open in 2 places and part of cheek cut off.
362	Pte	HITCH Frederick (VC)	London	Dangerously wounded – gunshot through shoulder joint.
373	Pte	HOOK Alfred H. (VC)	Churcham	Slightly wounded – assegai contusion of forehead.
716	Pte	JONES Robert (VC)	Raglan	Slightly wounded – assegai contusion of abdomen.
1051	Pte	SCANLON John	Birmingham	KILLED.
1005	Pte	SMITH John	Wigan	Slightly wounded – assegai slash of abdomen.
812	Pte	TASKER William	Birmingham	Slightly wounded – gunshot, splinter of ball breaking skin of forehead.
398	Pte	WILLIAMS Joseph	Monmouth	KILLED in hospital – body mutilated and dismembered.

Other Casualties

Commissariat Department. James Dalton VC – wounded; Byrne – killed.
NNC and NMP. Corporal C. Schiess – wounded; Trooper R.S. Green – wounded; Trooper Hunter – killed; Corporal Scammell – wounded; Corporal W. Anderson – killed (shot by own side, in the act of deserting).

Throughout the Zulu War, close combat fighting such as occurred at Rorke's Drift resulted in the heads and shoulders of British troops being chiefly exposed to the attacking Zulus. Consequently most of the severely wounded under those conditions received penetrating injuries to the head, neck and shoulders, some of which ended fatally. The medical records of Surgeon Blair-Brown FRCS who examined the Rorke's Drift casualties at Helpmekaar confirm the injuries and the appalling lack of medical facilities:

Corporal 1112 John Lyons of the 2/24th regiment, when engaged in the defence of Rorke's Drift, received a bullet in his neck, near the posterior margin of the sterno-mastoid on the left side, about the upper portion of the middle third of its length. Only one wound, that of entrance, was present. He complained of great pain in the neck on the slightest movement. When in bed, the pillow caused an increase of this. He had lost almost all use of his arms and hands, especially the right one, which he described as "quite dead." Painful "twitchings" were experienced in the arms. Whenever he wished to move his head from the bed, some one had to support it between their hands before he could do so. At Rorke's Drift several surgeons tried to find the bullet, but were unsuccessful. In the above condition, he came under my care at Helpmakaar on the 26th January, 1879, four days after the injury. Next day I put him under chloroform and made a prolonged attempt to find the bullet. The course I found it had taken was in a direct line with the spinal cord. I made a free opening in the middle line as far down the course as possible, and again attempted to reach the bullet. I found, by digital examination now, that the processes of two adjacent vertebrae were smashed. I could also feel the spinal cord itself. Pressure, thereon, instantly caused the patient to turn pale and the pulse to be almost imperceptible, and necessitated the immediate withdrawal of the chloroform and the adoption of artificial respiration. I took away several pieces of the vertebrae processes which were lying loose, but had to give up attempting to reach the bullet. The case continued much as described for some time. He was sent to the base hospital at Ladysmith, and on taking over the medical charge of that hospital a month later, I found my old patient much in the same condition. He was suffering greatly from the pain in his arms, and wished "to have them both off to relieve him from it." On examination, I found a distinct hard substance beneath the ligamentum nuchae, which was not present on former occasions. On consultation with the Surgeon-General of the forces, who happened to be on a tour of inspection at the time, I cut down upon it and enucleated an ordinary round bullet with a rather long rough process extending from its smooth surface. This wound healed rapidly, but the original one continued to discharge slightly for a long time. In a few days the pain entirely disappeared from his arms, and their use nearly returned. He was shortly after this sent home to England.

The following cases relate to gunshot injuries which occurred at Rorke's Drift and which were dealt with by Blair-Brown. The following cases are also taken from his original notes.

Private Frederick Hitch of the 2nd 24th Regiment was hit in the right shoulder. The bullet entered near the base of the scapula, having been fired from the hills opposite to which he was fighting. The bullet made its exit over the bicipital groove in the humerus. There was great swelling of the whole shoulder when seen by me on the 26th of January 1879, and   ecchymosis. The tract of the wound was sloughing. Poultices and cold water sufficed to allay this, and the case did well.

Corporal Carl Scammell of the Natal Native Contingent was wounded at Rorke's Drift. The bullet hit the back of the head, at the posterior margin of the left sternomastoid at its origin, and took a course towards the middle of the scapular base, where the bullet lodged subcutaneously, from which position it had been removed when I took charge of him on the 26th

January. Here also, the whole shoulder was greatly swollen and painful, requiring poultices. This case, after the usual slough came away, got well.

Corporal William Allen of the 2nd 24th Regiment was hit in the right shoulder. The bullet entered near the insertion of the deltoid muscle to the humerus, and made its exit at the upper and inner angle of the scapula. The bullet appears to have passed under the scapula, no bone or joint being touched. This wound sloughed and then very rapidly healed up.

Acting Assistant-Commissary James Dalton was hit in the right shoulder when busily engaged forming the 'laager' which he had originally commenced, and to which was due the safety of the place. The bullet entered about half an inch above the middle of the clavicle, and made its escape posteriorly at the lowest border of the trapezius muscle. The course taken was curious, regularly running round the shoulder and down the back, escaping all the important structures. The wounds, like all those received at Rorke's Drift, were wide and open and sloughing when seen by me on the 26th January. After the slough came away the usual tenax was applied. The whole of the field medical equipment having been captured by the enemy at Isandhlwana, I had no antiseptic to use. I thought of quinine, which I knew was a wonderful preserver of animal tissues, and used a solution of that, experimenting in this case. It seemed to answer, as the wounds got well after being injected several times with it. My subsequent experience, however, is that the wound would have done as well without it.

Private John Waters of the 1st 24th Regiment. This man had been left behind by his regiment (the one annihilated at Isandhlwana), as he was fulfilling the duties at Rorke's Drift of a hospital orderly. During the fight, he was hit in the right shoulder. The bullet entered the deltoid muscle about its lower third anteriorly, and lodged opposite the surgical neck of the humerus posteriorly, where it had been cut out. On probing this wound, no bone was felt, and after the usual sloughing, it healed. In every case the projectile found was an ordinary round one, and the nature of the injuries tend to show that they were all produced by similar bullets.

Surgeon Blair-Brown continues:

In every instance the wounds when seen by me on Jan 26th were in a sloughy condition. Large masses of purulent matter could be withdrawn with a little pulling by dressing forceps. The wounds were unmistakably made by ordinary round bullets fired from smooth-bored guns. The ease with which most of the bullets were turned aside from their straight course after penetrating can, I think, be accounted for by the fact that they were fired, from such weapons, at considerable range, and the charges of powder must have been limited, as the enemy individually carry but one bullock's horn, transformed into a powder-flask; this is usually all they have. Their fire is described to be very poor, blazing away and only occasionally hitting. It is with the assegai, however, they can do their deadliest work; but this necessitates very close quarters, what is scarcely likely to occur again. The assegais – a lance-shaped piece of steel or iron, on a comparatively thin but well-balanced round stick as a handle – are of two kinds; the 'throwing' assegais are longer and broader in the blade than the 'stabbing' kind. The handles of both also differ; that of the first kind is exceedingly well-balanced, to allow of its flight through the air, which it traverses like an arrow, the broad blade acting the part the feathers do in the other, only at opposite ends of the instruments. The Zulus hold them in their right hand, their fingers clenched round the handle not far from the blade, and bending their forearm at right angles to their arms, with a backward and forward movement they direct with a sudden jerk the instrument upwards into the air, where it is seen coursing like an arrow, and descending in a similar manner. At thirty yards many of them are very accurate in hitting their object. The 'stabbing' assegai has a short and stouter handle, has a much smaller and narrower blade, and is attached to the handle by a continuation of the blade in the form of a steel shaft for about half a foot, and there securely fastened. In stabbing they keep the edge very low, making numerous cuts, stabs, and dashes therewith as they approach; suddenly raising the point, they make a direct stab, and, without withdrawing, a rip. It appears to be a thoroughly methodical operation, requiring considerable skill to acquire. It is an error often made to think that, on nearing an enemy, they all, at a certain signal, bend the handles of their long assegais on their knees, and break them short. I am told this does not take place except when they have no 'stabbing' and all 'throwing' instruments with them – a circumstance which rarely occurs, as they always keep close to one of the latter as their chief defence.

The wounds, therefore, received from these different proceedings must also differ in character. My late *confrère* and friend, Surgeon-Major Shepherd, was killed by a thrown assegai just as he was starting from the side of a wounded Natal Carabineer whom he was examining. Trooper Muirhead, of the Carabineers, who was with him at the time, informs me that he saw it coming, bent his head down on his horse's neck, and escaped it. Shepherd was close to him, and received it in his back. He at once fell from his horse with a loud exclamation, and was surrounded by Zulus and finished. The depth a thrown assegai will penetrate is great. In stabbing the abdomen appears to be the target they aim at, if possible. Assegai wounds of the extremities I have met with none – except the case already recorded – of any interest, no important vessel having been injured. One officer of the Contingent received one through the calf of his leg, 'pinning him to his saddle'; this healed at once, and he hopped about all the time. I simply kept a bandage upon it.

It will therefore, be readily conceived that severe and numerous cases of gunshot injuries are not likely to occur in Zulu warfare as far as we are concerned.

If we have to retreat rapidly, then a wounded man means a dead one, as the enemy converts the one into the other at once. Assegai wounds of regions not immediately fatal generally require but the simplest treatment.

Without medicines, lint, bandages, or any of the usual equipment at Helpmakaar, I had to make use of what I could find. A considerable amount of well-tarred tow was found in a box where some wine bottles were packed. This I used as the dressing for all the wounds, and no case did badly. Water or watery lotions were not used, except the former to wash the skin in the neighbourhood of the injuries. A few fibres of the tow were used as drains in the wounds, and appeared to serve the purpose as well as anything else.

Private J.H. Mayer of the 1st Battalion 3rd Regiment Native Contingent had sustained an assegai wound to his leg during the assault on Sihayo's stronghold and was a patient at Rorke's Drift during the battle. While there several outbursts of severe haemorrhage occurred from the wound, and though the bleeding points were searched for by the surgeons at the camp it could not be permanently stopped, breaking out again after a day or more, or whenever the local means of arrest were withdrawn. On 26 January he was sent to Helpmekaar for treatment by Surgeon Blair-Brown. The surgeon wrote:

I found a wound of a regular punctured nature in the lower end of the left ham, a little above the popliteal space. As there was no bleeding, I simply ordered the limb to be kept as quiet as possible. Next day, however, haemorrhage – which was found by two civil surgeons who attended, to be almost impossible to control – took place. When I arrived, he had fainted, and his pulse could only just be felt. No further bleeding took place for two days, when it burst forth again. Assisted by Surgeon M'Gann and others, the patient being put under chloroform, I enlarged the wound to look for the bleeding vessels. Having made the incisions, I found a large cavity filled with coagulated blood extending up the limb and amongst the muscles; compression over the femoral during this procedure was maintained. On relaxing this, after the clot was cleared out, numerous points of bleeding were seen, none of which could be seized for torsion or ligature. The patient was again almost pulseless and his face very pale. Raising the limb, prolonged digital and instrumental pressure all failing, it was agreed that ligature of the femoral was the only remedy left to us. I proceeded at once to do that. On reaching the sheath of the vessel, the profunda was found to have a longer course than usual, and to be lying very close to the superficial femoral, both vessels being plainly felt pulsating. On applying pressure with the point of one finger on the profunda branch, I found not a drop of blood escaped at the wound after the withdrawal of the tourniquet from the groin. I therefore adopted the lesser operation, and tied the profunda. The wound healed rapidly, and after the first two days, when he complained of slight uneasiness in the limb, there was nothing else to note. On the 15th of

February he left Helpmakaar for the base hospital. He afterwards returned to duty and joined "Buller's Horse," with which famous body he went through all the reconnaissances and battles, including Ulundi, without any inconvenience. This patient was one of those in the hospital at Rorke's Drift on the memorable 22nd January, and managed, under fire, to hop out from one building to the other.

He therefore had four marvellous escapes within a few days – first, that of the stab at Sihayo's Kraal; secondly, the escape under fire from the hospital at Rorke's Drift; thirdly, the frequent profuse haemorrhages; and fourthly, the operation.

CHAPTER 13

Personalities and Defenders
at Rorke's Drift

Lord Chelmsford: Second Baron, Commander-in-Chief

There are two categories that matter for a military leader; successful and unsuccessful. Wellington, Campbell, Wolseley, Roberts and Wood can be counted as belonging to the former. Cornwallis, Raglan, Colley and Lord Chelmsford can reasonably be argued as belonging to the latter. Although both categories of leaders shared setbacks at some time, only the second group actually presided over military disasters: Cornwallis at Yorktown, Raglan with the loss of the Light Brigade, Colley at Majuba and Chelmsford at Isandlwana. Lieutenant General Frederic Augustus Thesiger, or Lord Chelmsford as he became following his father's death, lost his reputation when his inadequately defended camp at Isandlwana was overrun and laid waste by Cetshwayo's army. Despite his eventual success in defeating the Zulus and the strenuous efforts of his friends in high places to absolve him of blame, Chelmsford is generally regarded as an unsuccessful commander.

Chelmsford was born in 1827 to parents of German origin; his father became Lord High Chancellor and was raised to the peerage as Baron Chelmsford, Essex in 1858. His background, despite lacking much wealth, was conventional for a Victorian gentleman. His education at Eton was followed by the purchase of a commission, initially into the Rifle Brigade

Note for this chapter: Long Service and Good Conduct Medal is abbreviated to LSGC Medal and India General Service Medal is abbreviated to IGS Medal.

and then into the Grenadier Guards. He was a conscientious and diligent officer at a time when most officers did not take much interest in their military duties. He was subsequently promoted to the rank of captain and appointed aide-de-camp (ADC) to the commander of forces in Ireland. In 1855 he joined his regiment in the Crimea and thus missed the battle of Inkerman, in which the Guards played so crucial a role. He was designated to a succession of staff duties and ended his posting to the Crimea as deputy assistant quartermaster general.

A further promotion brought him the lieutenant colonelcy of the 95th (2nd Bn Sherwood Foresters) and it was with his new regiment that he sailed for India in 1858. By the time they arrived, the Indian Mutiny had all but been suppressed, but the regiment was involved in mopping-up operations in Central India during 1859.

Chelmsford's reputation as a competent staff officer resulted in his appointment as deputy adjutant general. It was in this capacity that he was a bit player in a cause célèbre which tested the army establishment. His younger brother, Captain Charles Weymess Thesiger, was serving with the 6th Dragoon Guards and became embroiled in a notorious scandal known as the Crawley affair. This issue stemmed from a bitter personality clash between the newly appointed commanding officer, Henry Crawley, and most of his officers, who objected to his autocratic behaviour. In his paranoia, Crawley saw plotting against him from every quarter, even from his most senior NCO, Regimental Sergeant Major Lilley. What made the case sensational was the close arrest of RSM Lilley who, with his dying wife, was confined in an ill-ventilated room at the height of the Indian summer. The RSM died through heatstroke. Chelmsford sided with the 'Establishment' and, despite two trials, justice was not seen to be done as Crawley was acquitted. It is of interest that one of the officers serving with the 6th at that time was Frederick Weatherley, who later commanded the ill-fated Border Horse at Hlobane during the Zulu War.

When General Sir Robert Napier was ordered to mount an expedition against King Theodore of Abyssinia in 1868, he chose Chelmsford to be his deputy adjutant general. In a well-organized and successful expedition, the Anglo-Indian force suffered few casualties despite the potential for disaster. Chelmsford emerged from the campaign with much credit, being mentioned in dispatches and made Companion of the Bath for his tireless staff work. He was also appointed ADC to the Queen and made Adjutant General of India. This period of his life was to be his happiest and most successful, for he also married the daughter of an Indian Army general who eventually bore him four sons. It was also at this time that he became friendly with the Governor of Bombay, Sir Henry Bartle Frere, a man who would have considerable influence on his life. After sixteen years service in India, Chelmsford was recalled home. With little in the way of family wealth, for Chelmsford had married for love and not for money, the prospect of expensive entertaining befitting an officer of his rank was a constant source of worry to him.

When he was offered the post of deputy adjutant general at Horse Guards, he felt obliged to decline and made known his wish to take a command again in India, where the cost of living was much lower. Instead, he was promoted to brigadier general commanding the 1st Infantry Division at Aldershot pending a suitable overseas posting. It was fate that the vacancy he accepted occurred in South Africa and was, coincidentally, his first independent active service command in thirty-four years. He was able to renew his association with Sir Bartle Frere, now the High Commissioner for South Africa, and to share Frere's vision of a confederation of southern African states under British control.

When Chelmsford arrived at the Cape in February 1878, the fighting against the Xhosa rebels was entering its final stages. His subsequent experiences against a foe that relied on hit-and-run tactics, rather than becoming involved in a full-scale battle, coloured his opinion of the fighting capabilities of South African natives. Chelmsford did, however, show himself to be a commander who did not shirk hard work, often riding great distances over rugged country in an effort to break any remaining resistance. He was a commanding figure with his tall, spare frame, his pleasant features usually hidden by a black beard and bushy eyebrows. The Frontier Wars finally petered out in May and Chelmsford felt that he had acquitted himself well. His handling of troops had been exemplary and he even earned the grudging respect of the generally ill-disciplined Colonial volunteers.

For such an experienced staff officer, he displayed a curious personal weakness that did not help the British cause in the coming confrontation with the Zulus. He virtually disposed of his personal staff, surrounding himself instead with just a few trusted colleagues. Chelmsford thereafter found himself heavily embroiled in petty matters that should never have involved an army commander. This reluctance to delegate put enormous pressure on him, affecting his judgement and causing vacillation and an apparent lack of leadership. He was not helped by his choice of military secretary in Major John Crealock, a colleague from the 95th Regiment. Crealock's abrasive and sarcastic manner antagonized anyone approaching the commander; this trait, together with his habit of vetting everything reported to his chief, produced circumstances that conspired to make Chelmsford a rather remote figure.

Despite this Chelmsford was considered a true gentleman who, at the beginning of the invasion at least, was regarded warmly even if he did not inspire. His letters reveal his tireless capacity for work and his commitment to trivia. They also show him to be solicitous as to the health and welfare of his colleagues, particularly his friends Evelyn Wood and Sir Bartle Frere. He displayed particular warmth to the former. His writing is not without irony and humour, though these are more in evidence before the invasion of Zululand began. In writing to Wood, he explained:

> All the other transport officers have been told off to their respective stations – I could send you up Lt. Col. Law to do the work, but it is questionable whether you would care to have him. He could do the work well enough if he chose, but he is not over-fond of work and his present idle life suits him down to the ground.

He was critical of many of the officers and officials and openly wished they could all be like Wood and Buller. Significantly he was irritated by Lieutenant Colonel Anthony Durnford's role on the Boundary Commission once it found in favour of the Zulus and he was to find further fault with Durnford's actions in the days leading up to the Invasion. In one particularly stinging rebuke Chelmsford actually threatened to remove Durnford from his command. One can see that in the aftermath of Isandlwana

Chelmsford would have had little compunction in laying the blame for his defeat on a despised, and now conveniently dead, subordinate officer. During this period before the Invasion, those who came into contact with Chelmsford found him unfailingly courteous but not outgoing. He kept his emotions firmly under control, until the enormity of the events at Isandlwana nearly crushed him, for he had no confidant to whom he could unburden his feelings. He wrote to his wife but her support and sympathy took many weeks to reach him. Chelmsford's letters to Wood reveal much about his state of mind: seeming to suffer from bipolar depression, Chelmsford fluctuated between confidence and despair. Six days after the disaster he appears to have partially recovered, and wrote:

> If we establish ourselves in good positions at different points in that part of the country and make good use of the mounted men for reconnoitring and raids, we ought to be able to bring the Zulus down upon us again when thoroughly prepared to meet them.

He then followed this with a despairing letter:

> The situation of affairs does not seem to improve, and I am fairly puzzled when I contemplate our future operations. I wish I saw my way with honour out of this beastly country, and you as my travelling companion. Best love to Buller – You two will have to pull me out of the mire.

He and Frere obviously discussed the option of resigning and Chelmsford accordingly wrote both to the Duke of Cambridge and to Colonel Frederick Stanley, the Secretary of State for War. In his letter to the latter, he reveals that he had contemplated being replaced as far back as June 1878. He wrote '...the strain of prolonged anxiety & exertion, physical & mental, was even then telling on me – What I felt then, I feel still more now.' He suggested that '...an officer of the rank of Major General should be sent out to South Africa without delay.' Furthermore ... 'H E Sir Bartle Frere concurs in this representation, & pointed out to me that the officer selected, should be fitted to succeed him in his position of High Commissioner.' The result was the appointment in May of Lieutenant General Sir Garnet Wolseley as both High Commissioner for South Eastern Africa and

Commander-in-Chief of the Forces in South Africa. It is of interest that several other senior officers suffered physical and mental breakdowns during the closing stages of this campaign. Such suffering also affected many of the soldiers, some of whom went insane on campaign.[1]

Adding to Chelmsford's woes were the relentless personal attacks on him by the newspapers, which blamed him for the loss of the camp, despite the exoneration given him by the Court of Enquiry, which he convened solely to report back to him. Affecting disdain for the newspapers and in particular the ever-present war correspondents, Chelmsford was deeply hurt and shaken by the vitriolic attacks on his reputation, attacks which further eroded his confidence. His friends advised him to retire on health grounds but, with Wood's decisive victory at Khambula and the arrival of several regiments of Imperial troops, Chelmsford seemed to sufficiently recover his determination to defeat the Zulus.

He personally chose to lead the column to relieve Colonel Pearson's besieged force at Eshowe. Moving cautiously and laagering at night, Chelmsford put into practice the painful lesson he learned from Isandlwana. Within sight of Eshowe, his well-entrenched men fought off a large Zulu impi at Gingindlovu and, in the following pursuit, inflicted many fatalities on the fleeing Zulus. Within the entrenchment, Chelmsford and his staff displayed the Victorian officers' disdain of enemy fire by remaining standing to encourage the troops, many of whom were newly arrived raw recruits. The result of such foolhardy exposure was that, although Chelmsford was not hit, Crealock was slightly wounded in the arm and lost his horse while Captain Molyneux had two horses killed. As they constituted the high command, it seems an unnecessary risk to have taken.

With Eshowe relieved, the ever-present spectre of the unburied remains at Isandlwana was the next priority. Besides soothing his conscience, Chelmsford had a much more practical reason for sending a large burial party; their role was to recover the precious wagons of the slaughtered Centre Column which he urgently needed for the re-invasion of Zululand. Chelmsford had a long-running feud with civilian authorities in Natal and both parties bombarded an increasingly despairing British government with dispatches that revealed the lack of firm leadership or determination to end the conflict. Chelmsford displayed all the signs of being demoralized and bereft of inspiration. However, as his forces and supplies built up so his confidence appeared to return. Once the invasion was under way he moved cautiously, laagering his camp every night, building forts to protect his lines of communication and scouting well ahead. Nevertheless, it was on one of these map-making reconnaissances that another misfortune befell the luckless commander.

The young Prince Louis Napoleon of France, exiled to England with his mother, had badgered both the Horse Guards and Queen Victoria to allow him to serve in Zululand in the furtherance of his military career. He succeeded and arrived in Zululand to work in a junior staff capacity under Chelmsford. It was during a routine reconnaissance by a small patrol which included the prince that a party of Zulus silently approached through long grass. At point-blank range the Zulus opened fire on the party and, in the scramble to safety, the prince and two troopers were caught and slain. When the news broke in the British newspapers, the shock was even greater than that of the Isandlwana massacre. Chelmsford could not reasonably be blamed for the prince's death but, following all the previous disasters, his culpability was implied. As with Isandlwana, a scapegoat was required and Captain Carey, the patrol leader who escaped uninjured, was the obvious candidate to face a court martial.

Chelmsford also received the news that he was to be replaced by General Sir Garnet Wolseley, both a blow to his ego and a spur to his intention of personally defeating the Zulus in a final showdown. In the event, it was a close run thing. Wolseley arrived just too late to prevent Chelmsford disobeying Wolseley's previous direct order not to attack Cetshwayo. Chelmsford proceeded to inflict a crushing defeat on the Zulus at Ulundi, which allowed him to hand over his command on a high note. It is interesting that no real attempt was made by the British force to capture Cetshwayo. Did Chelmsford leave the Zulu king at large in order to confound and occupy Wolseley while he reaped the glory on his progression back home?

In any event, and wishing to return home as soon as possible, Chelmsford journeyed to Cape Town, where he received an enthusiastic reception by a population for whom Ulundi had eradicated the memories of earlier disasters. He sailed home on the RMS *German* in the company of Wood and Buller, his most effective and reliable commanders. Both were friends of Wolseley, who would have liked them to remain with him in South Africa, but both were suffering from the effects of the campaign. Buller, in particular, had physically deteriorated so much that he required a lengthy convalescence before returning to duty. Before sailing, they confided in Wolseley that 'Chelmsford is not fit to be a Corporal', but they still found him an extremely likeable person.

Opinion at home had polarized. Disraeli refused to receive the commander who had cost the country so much and brought discredit to the government. Some newspapers continued to pillory Chelmsford and popular songs mocked him; even some of his fellow peers were critical. But it was those who really mattered, the Horse Guards and Queen Victoria, who rallied to his support. Chelmsford was showered with honours. His rank of lieutenant general was confirmed, the queen bestowed the Knight Grand Cross on him and used her influence to have him appointed Lieutenant of the Tower. He later became a full general and colonel of the Sherwood Foresters and then of the 2nd Life Guards.

Even with such protection, he was frequently drawn into defending his conduct during the Zulu War in general and Isandlwana in particular. Although some 1,400 men were lost at Isandlwana, it was not the worst military disaster of the period. In America, the loss of Custer's Seventh Cavalry at the Little Big Horn in 1876 troubled that nation's conscience for decades.[2]

After his retirement, honours still came Chelmsford's way. Queen Victoria appointed him Gold Stick at Court, an honour that was carried over when her son Edward succeeded her. He also made the ageing general a GCVO. Many soldiers who had achieved success in the field were rewarded with less.

Chelmsford lived out his last years in London enjoying his family and the companionship of long-time colleagues. His eldest son was rising in the Colonial Office and eventually became Viceroy of India and First Lord of the Admiralty. On 9 April 1905 and at the age of 78, Lord Chelmsford had a seizure and died while playing billiards at the United Service Club. So died a man with many admirable attributes but who was thrust into a position for which he was not intellectually equipped. Instead of being a long-forgotten Victorian general, his name is still remembered as the man ultimately responsible for the Victorian Army's greatest military defeat.

Colonel Richard Thomas Glyn: Column Commander and 24th Regiment
The Anglo-Zulu War was a brief conflict that enhanced few reputations but damaged many. Colonels Evelyn Wood and Redvers Buller emerged with credit while others like Lord Chelmsford and Colonel Hugh Rowland lost their former standing through their questionable competence and actions.

Other participants were badly affected by what they experienced, both physically and mentally. In an age when mental trauma was misunderstood, there was little sympathy or understanding for those who broke under the strain of witnessing the savagery of fighting Zulus. In an institution like the army it was expected that emotions should be kept on a tight rein, especially amongst the senior officers; the 'stiff upper lip' syndrome prevailed. It is well documented that Chelmsford underwent a period of severe depression in the aftermath of Isandlwana. Colonel Hassard, Officer Commanding Royal Engineers, had such a severe nervous breakdown that he was replaced. Colonel Pearson, the defender of Eshowe, was invalided home suffering from mental and physical exhaustion. Of all the senior officers who suffered in such a way, none felt greater anguish than the commanding officer of the 1st 24th Regiment, Colonel Richard Thomas Glyn.

Born 23 December 1831 in Meerut, India, he was the only son of R.C. Glyn Esquire, an officer in the Honourable East India Company. On his return to England, a conventional country upbringing produced an expert horseman and a fanatical huntsman. Despite his short stature (he was just 5ft 2in) Glyn was physically strong and keen to pursue a military career. When he was 19, his father purchased him a commission into the 82nd (Prince of Wales Volunteers) Regiment, later the 2nd South Lancashires.

After several years of duty in Ireland, Glyn and his regiment were sent to the Crimea and arrived on 2 September 1855, just six days before the fall of Sebastopol, thus missing any fighting and becoming part of the army of occupation until 1856. It was in this year that he married Anne Clements, the daughter of the former Colonel of the Royal Canadian Rifles. Their honeymoon period was cut short when Glyn's regiment was rushed to India to become part of Sir Colin Campbell's force that relieved the besieged force at Lucknow in mid November 1857. Just a few days later the 82nd received a drubbing at Cawnpore from rebel forces and sustained many casualties. Glyn was then promoted to captain and soon gained much experience in the hard and brutal suppression of the Indian Mutiny.

Like many officers, Glyn found post-Mutiny India an agreeable place to serve, particularly enjoying the opportunities to indulge his passion for hunting. Anne joined him and they set about producing a family, the result of which was four daughters. He advanced up the promotion ladder by purchasing his majority in 1861. In 1867 he purchased the lieutenant colonel-cy of the 1/24th Regiment, then stationed at Malta. In 1872 the regiment was transferred to Gibraltar, where Glyn was promoted to full colonel. Even here he was able to hunt into Spain, which was about the only excitement to be had in this peaceful outpost.

After three pleasant but uneventful years, the regiment was relieved to have a change of posting. At the end of November the Glyns and most of the 1/24th embarked on Her Majesty's Troopship *Simoon*, and thirty-five sailing days later the ship dropped anchor in Table Bay, Cape Town. Glyn's appearance at this time could be described as 'bristling' with his full wax-tipped moustache and short aggressive stature; he looked as if he was on the point of exploding with rage. This appearance, however, belied his true personality. He had a steady and unflappable temperament, though somewhat unimaginative and lethargic. He was fortunate to command some very able officers, including Henry Pulleine who could be relied upon to administer expertly the day-to-day running of the regiment.

By 1876 Southern Africa was a cauldron of small states and territories, of which the Cape Colony was the richest and largest. To the north lay the diamond-rich territory of Griqualand West, which was in a state of ferment and on the verge of rebellion. The Cape Government ordered Colonel Glyn to take his regiment and restore the appointed civil authorities. The march to Kimberley was long and arduous, crossing mountains and the dreary

ABOVE Lord Chelmsford *(Brian Best Collection)*

ABOVE RIGHT Colonel Richard Glyn *(24th Regimental Museum, Brecon)*

Ultimatum being read, 11 December 1878 *(Author's collection)*

OPPOSITE TOP B Company, the defenders of Rorke's Drift, post-battle
(*24th Regimental Museum, Brecon*)

OPPOSITE BELOW Rorke's Drift from the direction of Helpmekaar (*Author's collection*)

ABOVE Rorke's Drift homestead before the battle (*Killie Campbell Africana Library*)

Ponts over Rorke's Drift (*Killie Campbell Africana Library*)

ABOVE **John Chard**
(Ron Sheeley Collection)

Gonville Bromhead
(Ron Sheeley Collection)

ABOVE James Langley Dalton *(Illustrated London News)*

ABOVE RIGHT Major Spalding *(National Army Museum)*

Colour Sergeant Bourne and family *(24th Regimental Museum, Brecon)*

ABOVE Present day view of Rorke's Drift from Oskarsberg *(Author's collection)*

OPPOSITE Natal Native Contingent at Rorke's Drift *(Killie Campbell Africana Library)*

LEFT Contemporary engraving of the defence of Rorke's Drift *(London Graphic)*

ABOVE Contemporary impression of the battle of Rorke's Drift based on survivor's reports *(Author's collection)*

BELOW Painting of Rorke's Drift by Henri Duprey *(Ron Sheeley Collection)*

The relief of Rorke's Drift *(Illustrated London News)*

ABOVE Helpmekaar *(Killie Campbell Africana Library)*

BELOW Modern representation of the battle of Rorke's Drift *(Jason Askew)*

RIGHT The morning after *(London Graphic)*

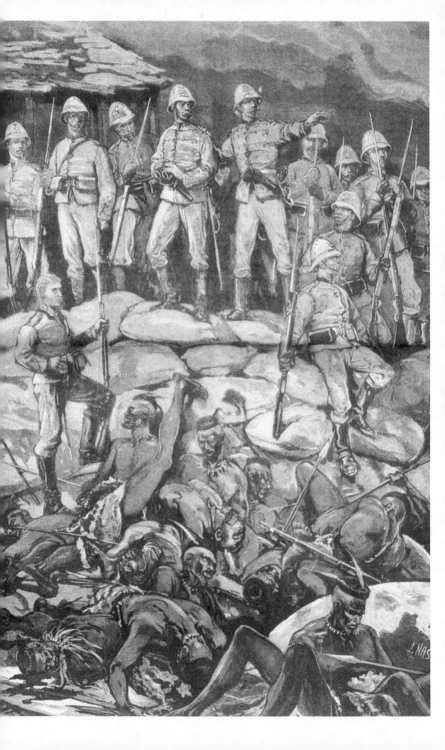

ABOVE King Cetshwayo *(Mary Evans Picture Library)*

OPPOSITE TOP The Mission Station today *(Author's collection)*

RIGHT Modern church built on the site of the old store room *(Author's collection)*

Excavations at Rorke's Drift (courtesy Dr Lita Webley)

dry Great Karoo plain. Keeping up a steady pace through the heat of the African days, the 1/24th took two months to cover the 700 miles. When they arrived they found that their presence alone was enough to stifle the rebellion and there was little more to do than march all the way back to the Cape. One positive aspect of the long march was that the regiment was now physically hardened and ready for the tough campaign that was looming to the north-east.

In the meantime there was more than enough time for recreation in the form of hunting. As the fox does not exist in southern Africa, the nearest equivalent quarry was the black-backed Cape Jackal. Colonel Glyn, as Master of the Hunt, kept a full pack of hounds and three hunters. He appointed his three Irish subalterns, Daly, Hodson and Coghill as whips. His officers viewed Glyn with affection and Coghill wrote, 'The Colonel is good a little man as ever breathed has what amounts to monomania, 'untin' being 'is 'obby'. They exercised the pack three times a week and sometimes went hunting for up to ten days at a time. Besides hunting, Glyn and his officers organized small game and partridge shoots. While it was undeniably true that Glyn enjoyed his hunting, it was common knowledge that he craved male companionship as an escape from his all-female household. His wife Anne had become that most formidable of women, 'The Colonel's Wife', and she gave her easy-going husband little peace.

The Glyns regarded the regimental officers as part of their own family. Neville Coghill was a particular favourite and it is not inconceivable that he was looked upon as the son Glyn never had. When he had arrived in Cape Town, he had been taken into their home until his own quarters were ready. Full of charm, he not only rode well but he was also a good dancer and particularly popular with the Glyn women. He was even asked by Mrs Glyn to organize a quadrille for a ball given by the Governor General's wife, Lady Barkly.

The pleasant round of socializing came to an end with problems in the Transkei, east of Cape Colony. Sir Bartle Frere ordered the 1/24th to this trouble spot and appointed Colonel Glyn as commander in the Transkei, with the rank of colonel of the staff and brevet brigadier general. In a frustrating campaign that involved three columns sweeping the country, the

Xhosa foe was seldom persuaded to stand and be shot at. They finally made a determined stand at a stream called Nyumaga where, on 14 January, Glyn's men routed them. Another fight took place at Centana in February where the Xhosa were again beaten by the superior firepower of the British. By keeping the Xhosas on the move, the British wore down their will to resist. Despite this successful campaign, General Cunynghame was removed from overall command and Lieutenant General Frederick Augustus Thesiger was appointed in his place. There was little for the new commander to do except to keep the Xhosa on the move until they submitted in the summer of 1878.

The 24th Regiment had performed well and duly received the thanks of the Governor. Colonel Glyn received high praise from both the Duke of Cambridge and Sir Bartle Frere and, in a more tangible form of gratitude, he was made a Companion of the Bath. Under Glyn's command the 1/24th had gained a reputation for good behaviour in the towns where they were stationed. They were also highly experienced at campaigning in South Africa and were already designated to be the army's backbone in the next step in Frere's expansionist plan. The feeling amongst the Governor and the military was that the subjugation of the Xhosa was little more than a prelude to a confrontation with the far more formidable Zulus.

Glyn and his regiment were ordered to Pietermaritzburg in Natal where the regimental headquarters were established. Sir Bartle Frere also left Cape Town and took up residence at the nearby Government House where he could more effectively connive with General Thesiger and keep at bay his opponents in the Natal government. As war with the Zulus became inevitable, Coghill asked Glyn to find him a place on his staff as soon as Sir Bartle Frere would release him.

It was on 30 November that Colonel Glyn bade farewell to his wife and daughters and, to the accompaniment of the band, led his regiment out of Pietermaritzburg towards the distant and desolate post at Helpmekaar. Glyn had been given command of Number 3 column, which became known as the Centre Column. Enduring constant heavy rain and deep mud, the column took a week to cover the 100 miles to the Biggarsberg plateau overlooking the Buffalo river valley and the frontier with Zululand.

Glyn was experienced in campaigning and relished the coming invasion. It therefore came as a great blow to him when Chelmsford and his staff, instead of establishing an independent force headquarters, attached themselves to Glyn's column. Chelmsford, ever the considerate gentleman he was, sought to assure Glyn that he would not interfere in the running of the column. In practice this did not work. With two staffs, each jealous of the other and, in Chelmsford's case, high-handed and arrogant, there was considerable friction. Major Clery and Chelmsford's military secretary, Lieutenant Colonel John Crealock, both lacked diplomacy and possessed vitriolic tongues which further strained relationships between the two camps. Crealock dismissed Glyn by saying, 'do not expect anything. [of him]. He is a purely regimental officer with no ideas beyond it.'

Glyn and his staff were effectively relegated to mere figureheads. Clery caustically remarked that 'Colonel Glyn and his staff were allowed to work the details – posting the guards, etc., and all the interesting work of that kind'. This usurping of his command caused Glyn to become disinterested and withdrawn for it was not in his nature to object or challenge any orders. He may well have felt intimidated both by Chelmsford's status and his height. (The tall lanky general towered over his diminutive column commander). Clery again: 'he [Glyn] was scarcely ever seen or heard of, the more so as he got anything but encouragement to interest himself in what was going on'.

The tone in Chelmsford's dealings with Glyn is one of impatience and some antipathy. Glyn had wanted to fortify both Helpmekaar and Rorke's Drift in accordance with Chelmsford's instructions, but he was overruled. Upon arrival at Isandlwana, Glyn gave instructions for the layout of the camp and, in normal circumstances, would have followed the instructions as laid down in the manual for field operations. He would have had trenches dug or stone walls constructed and a wagon laager formed. As it was, Chelmsford felt that it would take a week to entrench the camp and some of the wagons were scheduled to return to Rorke's Drift for further supplies. Chelmsford also considered that the position of the camp possessed such a commanding view into Zululand that the Zulus could not possibly take the British unawares.

After Chelmsford's defeat at the battle of Isandlwana, Glyn was in a complete state of shock at the loss of his regiment. He was left at Rorke's Drift to clear up the mess and, in the following weeks, establish a fortified camp on an adjacent hillock.

Fearing that the Zulus would attack at any time, Glyn had a strong perimeter built around the destroyed mission station and made everyone move inside at night. No tents were allowed except for the Rorke's Drift survivors who were provided with the only large groundsheet for protection; the remaining garrison was crammed into the small defended area, which was soon churned into a foul quagmire. The grieving Glyn withdrew into his shell of despondency and took little interest in the misery around him. Without doubt, he was displaying all the symptoms of a breakdown. Not only did he feel bereaved by the loss of his regiment; he also expressed the feeling that he should have been with his men as they fought for their lives, a common enough emotion amongst survivors. Captain Walter Parke Jones of the Royal Engineers, however, was not at all sympathetic and wrote what many felt, 'Col. Glyn (our chief) does nothing and is effete'.

It was not until 4 February that a patrol led by Major Wilsone Black discovered the bodies of Coghill and Melvill on the Natal bank of the Buffalo river. A further search found the Queen's Colour in the river some half a mile downstream. A cairn of stones was piled on the bodies and the colour was taken back to Rorke's Drift. Glyn was moved to tears when he received the Colour and learned of the fate of his favourite young officers. While the isolated Glyn was suffering both mentally and physically at Rorke's Drift, Lord Chelmsford and his followers were attempting to play down their role in the disaster. In a subtle piece of responsibility shifting, Chelmsford stated that, 'Colonel Glyn was solely responsible' and, 'that Colonel Glyn fully and explicitly accepted this responsibility cannot, however, affect the ultimate responsibility of the General-in-Command'. This attempt to share the blame with Glyn rang hollow, as it was generally known that Glyn had little say in matters. Chelmsford's staff contributed to the growing controversy by saying that it was Glyn's failure to entrench the camp that caused it to be overrun. As he was commander of the Centre Column, the blame should be firmly laid at his door.

Anne Glyn, recovering from the terrible news, was incensed at the attempts to blame her husband and was outspoken in her criticism of Chelmsford. Glyn himself seemed too numb to do more than briefly give the facts, without comment, to the Board of Enquiry. Chelmsford then turned to Colonel Durnford as the conveniently dead scapegoat.

When, eventually, a cavalry burial party went to Isandlwana in May, Glyn accompanied them. He made a rather unusual request that the remains of his regiment should be left to be buried by the regiment. This emotional request was allowed but it was not until the end of June, six months after the event, that the remains of the 1/24th at Isandlwana were interred under three large cairns.

As the months passed, so reinforcements began to reach South Africa and Chelmsford could put his new invasion plans into effect. Chelmsford wrote to Evelyn Wood from the assembly point at Dundee, 'I am forced to make Glyn a Brigadier with Newdigate, as there is absolutely no one who is better!'

After several delays, the Second Invasion finally got under way on 31 May when Glyn led his brigade across the border and back into Zululand. Within a day, Chelmsford was further devastated by the news that Louis Napoleon, the Prince Imperial, had been killed while on a patrol led by Captain J.B. Carey. A Field Court Martial was convened and Glyn was appointed president. The court listened to the evidence regarding the culpability of Carey and found him guilty but did not publish its findings, preferring to refer the matter to Horse Guards in London. Carey was sent home to face the music but was exonerated.

The advance into Zululand towards the capital of Ulundi continued at a snail's pace. Eventually, they arrived within sight of Ulundi. Much to the disappointment of the 1/24th, they were ordered to remain guarding the camp by the White Mfolozi river, while the rest of the brigade advanced on Ulundi. Glyn did take with him eight officers of the old 1/24th and they were with him in the huge square against which Cetshwayo's army was finally destroyed.

For the 24th, the war was over and they began the long march back to Pietermaritzburg, where the Glyns were reunited. Then they travelled to the encampment at Pinetown, where Colonel Glyn had the pleasant duty of presenting the Victoria Cross to Lieutenant Edward Browne 1/24th for his bravery at Hlobane and Khambula.

Finally the 24th embarked on the troopship *Egypt* and set sail for England on 27 August. Because of mechanical problems the journey took four weeks to complete. During that time the redoubtable Anne Glyn used her needlework skills to repair the tattered Queen's Colour. In May 1880 Glyn relinquished his command of the 1/24th and took charge of the brigade depot at Brecon. The following year the regiment was given the new title of 'The South Wales Borderers'.

In 1882 Richard Glyn was promoted to major general and appointed a KCB. He eventually retired as a lieutenant general and lived at Mortimer in Berkshire. A sad and stooped little man, Glyn's remaining years were overshadowed by the memory of his lost regiment on the rocky slopes of Isandlwana. In 1898 he was honoured with the title of Colonel of the South Wales Borderers. It was in this capacity that he saw off his old regiment as they went off to South Africa again, this time to fight the Boers. He died on 22 November 1900, within a few months of their departure, and was buried in the family grave at Ewell, Surrey.

Lieutenant Colonel John Rouse Merriott Chard VC, Royal Engineers (Lieutenant during the action)

John Chard was born on 21 December 1847 at Boxhill, near Plymouth. He was the son of William and Jane Chard and he had two brothers and four sisters. His older brother, Wheaton Chard, became Colonel of the 7th Royal Fusiliers and his younger brother, Charles, joined the Church. Chard attended school in Plymouth and was a pupil at the town grammar school. Following a lengthy period of private tuition, he entered the Royal Military Academy at Woolwich – which he struggled to pass; he was mainly remembered for his ability to arrive late for meals. In any event, he was commissioned on 14 July 1868 and after two further years of training with the Royal Engineers at Chatham he was posted to Bermuda in October 1870. He returned to England in 1874 in order to attend his father's funeral and was then posted to Malta where he was engaged in the construction of the island's sea defences. In 1876 he was posted back to England where he held a number of minor positions before being posted to the 5th Company Royal Engineers at Aldershot. On 2 December 1878 Chard and the unit sailed from Gravesend for South Africa, arriving at Durban on 5 January 1879. He was then detailed to take a small party of men to assist with the river crossing at Rorke's Drift, where he arrived on the evening of the 19th January, three days before the Zulu attack.

Chard remained at Rorke's Drift after the battle and for several weeks he assisted with the collection of stone and the construction of more permanent stone walls around the fort. Due to the atrocious weather conditions (it was the rainy season) and the unsanitary cramped living inside the fort, Chard and many of the men succumbed to fever during early February and incorrect reports of Chard's death appeared in Natal newspapers. He was sent to Ladysmith to recover, staying with a Dr Hyde and his wife and, in spite of several newspaper reports to the contrary, he did recover sufficiently to rejoin 5th Company for the re-invasion of Zululand where he was present in the British square for the final battle against the Zulus at Ulundi on 4 July.

Chard resumed duty at Devonport at the end of January 1880, before proceeding to Cyprus in December 1881 and returning home in March 1887. During this time the brevet majority he had gained at Rorke's Drift was substantiated with effect from 17 July 1886. In England he was posted to Preston in April 1887, remaining there until being ordered to Singapore in December 1892. His promotion to lieutenant colonel followed a month later. He returned to England in January 1896 and in September of that year he assumed his final post, that of Chief Royal Engineer (CRE), at Perth, Scotland.

It was whilst serving as the CRE Scottish Command that he was found to have cancer of the mouth. In November 1896 Chard underwent an operation in Edinburgh. Whilst recuperating from this, he received his promotion to colonel on 8 January 1897. His doctors realized that a second operation was necessary. In March 1897 surgeons removed Chard's tongue; it is reputed that despite having this operation he was able to converse to a remarkable degree. He made a third visit to Edinburgh in August 1897, and the doctors' prognosis was dire – the cancer was terminal. John Chard returned to the rectory at Hatch Beauchamp, Taunton, Somerset, the home of his younger brother, the Revd Charles E. Chard. Chard bravely accepted the fact that all hope of recovery was gone. Whilst at Hatch Beauchamp he was attended by Dr Brown of Taunton and Dr Hatherall of Hatch Beauchamp. Despite terrible suffering and great distress over the last fortnight of his life, borne it must be added with remarkable fortitude and great strength of character, Colonel John Rouse Merriott Chard VC, hero of Rorke's Drift, died peacefully in his sleep shortly after 9.30 p.m. on Monday 1 November 1897.

Chard's death brought an immediate response from all over the country and his passing was widely reported in the press. Many telegrams of condolence arrived at Hatch Beauchamp. Her Majesty Queen Victoria had asked for and received reports of his condition. In July 1897 she had dispatched her Diamond Jubilee Medal to Chard, and an exceedingly kind letter accompanied it from General Sir Fleetwood Edwards. It was as recently as 30 October 1897 that Her Majesty had sent a message to the Revd Chard asking for a report on his brother's progress and expressing her sympathy for his suffering.

Other messages of sympathy were received by the Revd Chard including one from HRH the Duke of Connaught who had attended the Royal Military Academy, Woolwich with Chard; and Lord Chelmsford, the military commander of the Anglo-Zulu War.

The funeral service and burial took place on 5 November 1897, at his brother's church, the Parish Church of St John the Baptist at Hatch Beauchamp. The grave had been prepared on the south-east side of the church, close to the wall of the transept vestry. It was lined with moss and creeper and studded with white chrysanthemums, white geraniums and violets. At the head was a large cross of white chrysanthemums.

There were a great number of wreaths delivered to the graveside, which produced a magnificent floral display. Her Majesty Queen Victoria sent a wreath of laurel leaves tied with long streamers of white satin. The tribute bore a card in Her Majesty's own handwriting:

> *A mark of admiration and regard for a brave soldier.*
> *From his Sovereign,*
> *Victoria R.I.*

It is worthy of note that Queen Victoria's wreath lay for many years beneath the Chard Memorial Window, which was installed in 1899 and located on the south side of the chancel, near to the altar.

Other principal wreaths were from the Deputy Adjutant General RE on behalf of the Corps of Royal Engineers, *In sorrow for the loss of their gallant brother officer*; from fellow Zulu War VC, Colonel E.S. Browne and the officers of the Depot, South Wales Borderers, 24th Regiment, *With deep sympathy*; from the officers of the Royal Engineers, Scottish District; from fellow Rorke's Drift defender Colonel Walter Dunne, Assistant Adjutant General York; The Countess of Camperdown, *With heartfelt sympathy*; Lady Frere, widow of Sir Henry Bartle Edward Frere, Governor of Cape Colony during the Zulu Campaign, *In memory of the heroic defender of Rorke's Drift*; and an anonymous wreath bore the legend, *In remembrance of Rorke's Drift, 22nd January 1879 – That day he did his duty.*

The tolling of the church bell at half-past two in the afternoon signalled the departure of the funeral cortege from the rectory, a little over half a mile from the church. The coffin had reposed in the hall of the rectory, with the Sovereign's wreath placed upon it; at either end were two other wreaths; one anonymous, the other from the rectory's servants. On the hall table lay Colonel Chard's dress cocked hat and sword; his Victoria Cross, together with his South Africa Medal with the bar 1879 and his Diamond Jubilee Medal. Beside these was a signed photograph of Queen Victoria, sent in commemoration of her Diamond Jubilee of 1897.

The coffin was of polished oak, with brass mountings. It had been made by James Mills of Hatch Beauchamp and bore the following inscription:

> John R.M. Chard
> Born 21st December 1847
> Died 1st November 1897

The coffin was borne on the North Curry bier and the procession was entirely on foot. Flanking the coffin marched an escort of Royal Engineers.

The Dean of St Andrew's conducted the service. The organist, Miss Alice Rich, played the aria 'O Rest in the Lord'. The Dean proceeded with the service and read the lesson. The hymn 'Days and Moments Quickly Flying' was sung, and as the procession left the church the organist played the 'Dead March' from *Saul*. The remainder of the service was completed at the graveside and closed with the Benediction and thanks on behalf of the Revd Chard to the assembled gathering, for all their kindness and the sympathy they had expressed by their presence.

In due course a headstone was placed on the grave. Some years later this headstone was replaced by the present one, which consists of a cross on a three-tiered plinth, surrounded by a rail and all in rose-coloured marble. The headstone is inscribed:

In Memoriam

Col. J.R.M. Chard, VC, RE.

The Hero of Rorke's Drift

Born 21st Dec. 1847. Died 1st Nov. 1897

Son of W.W. Chard of Pathe, Somerset

And Mount Tamar, Devon.

Major Gonville Bromhead, VC, B Company 2/24th (Warwickshire) Regiment (Lieutenant during the action)

Born on 29 August 1845 at Versailles, France, he was the third son of Edmund de Gonville Bromhead, 3rd Baronet, who had fought at Waterloo, and his wife Judith Christine Cahill, daughter of James Wood of Woodville, County Sligo. The family home was Thurlby Hall at Newark. He was educated at Magnus Grammar School, Newark and entered the 24th Foot as an ensign, by purchase, on 20 April 1867. On 28 October 1871 he was promoted by selection to lieutenant. In 1878 he was posted to South Africa and embarked at Plymouth on 2 February. Bromhead has unfairly been portrayed elsewhere as a 'duffer' with poor mental acuity and little enthusiasm for activity; in reality he was very popular with his men, being a champion boxer, wrestler and an accomplished top scoring regimental cricketer. He served in the Frontier War 1878 and the Zulu War 1879, and commanded B

Company 2/24th Foot at the defence of Rorke's Drift, being mentioned in dispatches and awarded the Victoria Cross for his conduct on that occasion. Lieutenant Chard also mentioned him in his letter to Queen Victoria. Lieutenant Bromhead received his Victoria Cross from Sir Garnet Wolseley at Utrecht on 11 September 1879, the citation (LG 2/5/79) reading: 'For gallant conduct at the defence of Rorke's Drift, 22nd and 23rd January 1879'. He was promoted captain and brevet major on 23 January 1879, and major on 4 April 1883. From South Africa he was posted to Gibraltar, where he served until August 1880, then to the East Indies until March 1881. On being posted home he attended the School of Musketry, Hythe, from 1 October to 5 December 1882, gaining a First Class Extra Certificate. On 2 January 1883 he embarked at Portsmouth in the *Serapis* to join the 2nd South Wales Borderers at Secunderabad, India. He served in Burma from 27 October 1886 to 24 May 1888 (IGS Medal with clasps 'Burma 1885–7' and 'Burma 1887–89'), returning to the East Indies. He died of enteric fever on 9 February 1891, aged 45 years, at Camp Dabhaura, Allahabad, India. He was unmarried.

Bromhead received an address and a revolver presented to him by the tenants of Thurlby Hall. (He must have treasured the revolver, for it remained with him for the next twelve years.) The people of Lincoln gave him a sword, and Queen Victoria a photograph of herself. On 7 November 1891, in his will, originally drawn up at Taunton, Somerset, in 1869, he left these items, together with his Victoria Cross and a watch belonging to his late father, to his brother, Colonel Charles J. Bromhead. The residue of his estate went to his sisters Alice Margaret Bromhead and Elizabeth Frances Pocklington.

James Langley Dalton VC: Commissariat

James Dalton was born about 1833 – the exact year is unknown – and it was when working as a printer's apprentice that he enlisted into the 85th (Shropshire) Regiment at Victoria, London, on 20 November 1849, giving his age as 17 years and 11 months. Like many young recruits, he was underage and should have initially joined as a 'boy'. Even so, many of his friends believed he was younger still, by possibly as much as two years. Military records reveal that the recruiting party who attested him received 2s. 6d. as their bounty while Dalton received the handsome amount of £3 to join the

85th Regiment at Waterford in Ireland. After six months the regiment returned to Preston and he stayed with the regiment during subsequent postings to Hull and Portsmouth and when in 1853 the regiment sailed in the *Marion* to Mauritius. By 1855 he had reached the rank of sergeant and three years later he sailed with his regiment to the Cape of Good Hope where he was engaged in a number of frontier disputes.

In March 1862 he returned to England and transferred into the Commissariat Corps. While stationed at Aldershot he was promoted to colour sergeant on 1 June 1863. From 1868 to 1871 he served in Canada and on the reorganization of the Commissariat Corps he was transferred to the Army Service Corps in 1870 with promotion to staff sergeant. He received his discharge from the army in London on 20 November 1871 after nearly twenty-two years' service, being awarded the LSGC Medal.

Then, as a civilian, Dalton sailed for South Africa. Exactly where he went and what he did is uncertain although on the outbreak of the Ninth Cape Frontier War in 1877, he was employed on commissariat duties. Commissary Furze, who had signed Dalton's discharge six years before and knew him as a very experienced man, was a senior officer in the area where Dalton was working and, knowing his reputation, he appointed Dalton as an acting assistant commissary on 13 December 1877. It was in this role that he met Colonel Glyn of the 24th Regiment. Dalton's skill at successfully supplying the British columns did not go unnoticed and at the end of the campaign Dalton was the only civilian to be mentioned in dispatches.

With the preparations for the invasion of Zululand during 1878 came the requirement for experienced commissariat officers. Dalton moved to Natal and along with Acting Storekeeper Louis Byrne, he arrived at Rorke's Drift on New Year's Day 1879. There can be little doubt that Dalton's appointment was due to Glyn's influence. The senior Commissariat officer with Glyn's No. 3 Column was Assistant Commissary Walter Dunne, who had also served in the Ninth Cape Frontier War with Glyn's columns.

Dalton was severely wounded in the action at Rorke's Drift and spent the following six months on sick leave before being appointed as the senior commissariat officer at Fort Napier, Pietermaritzburg, for the remainder of the Zulu War campaign. It was while Dalton was recuperating from his injuries at Pietermaritzburg that, on 16 October, the 24th Regiment marched into town on their way back to Durban. When B Company saw Dalton in the crowd they gave him a spontaneous cheer. Dalton was promoted assistant commissary on 13 December 1879 and was placed on half pay, sailing to England in February 1880, whereupon he passed into obscurity. Little is known of his remaining years other than the fact that he returned to South Africa and worked in, and was a part owner of, the Little Bess gold mine. He was taken ill and died on 7 January 1887 while staying with his friend ex-sergeant John Williams, who paid for his funeral and memorial. He is buried in Russell Road Catholic Cemetery, Port Elizabeth. On 26 September 1986, Dalton's medals were auctioned at Spink and Son in London. The Royal Corps of Transport purchased them for £62,000.

1st Battalion 24th Regiment present at the Defence of Rorke's Drift [3]

The individuals named in the following list are those referred to in the rolls originally prepared by:

Chard 'C'

Bourne 'B'

Bourne's amended roll 'Ba'

Dunbar 'D'

56 Sergeant WILSON Edward

Born at Peshawar, India; trade – labourer. Religion: C/E. Attested at Kingston on 28/1/74, aged 18 years 4 months. Previously served in 3rd Surrey Militia. Description: 5ft 6in tall, fresh complexion, hazel eyes, brown hair. Married Mary Ann Evans at Gosport on 13/5/80. Children: Irene Mary (b. not recorded), Francis George (B. 16/5/81), Thomas Gilbert John (b. 22/2/82). Promoted Corporal 5/7/75, appointed Lance Sergeant 16/5/77, promoted Sergeant 12/1/78. (Followed by several demotions and promotions.) Final rank: Sergeant on 18/1/89. Served in South Africa from 25/11/74 to 2/10/79.

Engaged for South Wales Borderers at Brecon on 22/1/86, as permanent staff – 3rd Battalion. Died of hypotrophy of heart on 19/9/91. Medal for South Africa with clasp '1877–8–9'. (Ref. 'C' and 'Ba' rolls.)

135 Private BECKETT William

Attested at Manchester on 14/4/74, aged 18 years 3 months. Posted to 2/24th on 17/6/74, transferred to 1/24th on 25/11/74. Served in South Africa and sent with reinforcement to Komgha in 1877. He was a patient in the hospital at Rorke's Drift and during the battle was dangerously wounded by an assegai penetrating his abdomen. Died of wound on 23/1/79. Mentioned in Lieutenant Chard's letter to Queen Victoria, also in a letter by Private Waters. Effects claimed by his relatives. He is buried in the cemetery at Rorke's Drift and his name appears on the monument. Medal for South Africa with clasp '1877–8–9'. (Ref. 'B' and 'C' rolls, the latter gives his number incorrectly as '129' and names him as 'R. Beckett'.)

568 Private DESMOND Patrick

Attested at Fort Hubberstone on 27/3/75, aged 18 years. Posted to 2/24th on 15/4/75, transferred to 1/24th on 15/7/76. Received eighteen fines for drunkenness between July and October 1878, also imprisoned by Civil Power. Wounded in action at Rorke's Drift. Discharged on 15/11/80 as a 'worthless character'. Medal for South Africa with clasp '1877–8–9'. Medal forfeited on 19/6/06 (68/24/623), however there is no trace of the medal having been returned. (Ref. 'C' and 'Ba' rolls.)

1861 Private HORRIGAN William

Attested on 12/11/63, aged 14 years 7 months. Re-engaged at Gibraltar on 16/12/73. Served in South Africa and was at East London in August–September 1877. He was a patient in the hospital at Rorke's Drift and assisted in the defence of the building. Killed in action. (Appendix A.) Effects claimed by next of kin. Mentioned in Lieutenant Chard's letter to Queen Victoria, also in accounts by Privates Hook and Waters. Mentioned in the citations for the award of the Victoria Cross to Privates Hook and Williams. He is buried in the cemetery at Rorke's Drift and his name appears on the monument.

Medal for South Africa with clasp '1877–9'. (Ref. 'C' roll but incorrectly named as 'Harrigan' on 'B' roll.)

841 Private JENKINS James

Attested at Monmouth on 18/7/76, aged 22 years 4 months. Sent with a draft to join battalion on 2/8/77. He was a patient in the hospital at Rorke's Drift and assisted in the defence. Killed in action. Effects claimed by his father. Mentioned in Lieutenant Chard's letter to Queen Victoria. He is buried in the cemetery at Rorke's drift and his name appears on the monument. Medal for South Africa with clasp '1879'. (Ref. 'C' roll which also incorrectly list 1083 Pte Jenkins as surviving the action; 'B' roll gives 1083 Pte M. Jenkins as killed but omits 841 Pte James Jenkins. In fact 1083 Matthew (real name Watkin) Jenkins was killed at Isandlwana.)

625 Private NICHOLAS Edward

Attested at Newport on 30/7/75, aged 18 years. Sent with a draft to join battalion on 2/8/77. He was a patient in the hospital at Rorke's Drift and assisted in the defence. Killed in action. Effects claimed by next of kin. Mentioned in an account by Private Hitch. He is buried in the cemetery at Rorke's Drift and his name appears on the monument. Medal for South Africa with clasp '1877–8–9'. (Ref. 'C' roll gives his name as E. Nicholls, this error being repeated in the Regimental History where he is shown as a casualty twice, once under 'Nicholls' and again under 'Nicholas'. 'B' roll names him as W. Nicholas. The error regarding his name is reflected throughout the regimental documents; one pay roll gives him as 'Nicholls', this latter being amended to his correct name 'Nicholas'.)

372 Private PAYTON Thomas

Attested at Manchester on 13/7/74, aged 21 years. Posted to 1/24th on 11/10/74. Served in South Africa and was at East London during August–September 1877. Discharged at Gosport on 2/1/80; to Army Reserve, AGL 103. Intended place of residence 7 Planet St., off Cross St, Stafford. Medal for South Africa with clasp '1877–8–9'. (Ref. 'C' and 'Ba' roll in both instances show name as 'Paton'.)

1542 Private ROY William DCM

Born at Edinburgh, Midlothian; trade – baker. Attested for 32nd Light Infantry at Edinburgh Castle on 8/8/70, aged 17 years. Transferred to 1/24th Foot on 4/12/77. Description: 5ft 5½in tall, fresh complexion, brown eyes, red hair. Served in Mauritius and South Africa. He contracted malaria and was frequently admitted to hospital as a result of this. Present at the defence of Rorke's Drift, mentioned in dispatches and awarded the DCM. Appointed lance corporal on 22/8/79, corporal 24/11/79. A specific disease, acquired at King William's Town in January 1876, seriously affected his vision. Following a medical examination at Haslar, Gosport, on 2/10/79, he was found unfit for further service and was discharged on 7/12/80, having served for 8 years, 303 days. Intended place of residence, Post Office, Gosport. Medal for South Africa with clasp '1877–8–9'. (Ref. 'C' gives incorrect number '1522' and name 'R. Joy'. Details correct on 'B' roll.)

104 Private TURNER Henry

Born at Ball Bridge, Dublin, also given as Bassbridge and Killeatty, Wexford; trade – bricklayer. Attested at Aldershot on 27/3/74, aged 23 years. Religion: C/E. Description: 6ft 1in tall, fresh complexion, light hazel eyes, and brown hair. Posted to 2/24th on 31/3/74, transferred to 1/24th on 26/11/74. He was struck over the left ear by a black bottle when on picket duty in 1876, the wound scar being evident. From that time he suffered epilepsy, the first attack being at Simm's Town, Cape Colony, in 1876. He was examined by a medical board at Pietermaritzburg on 9/9/79 and found to be unfit for further service. On arrival in England he was sent to Netley, having suffered two further epileptic attacks, one of which was on the ship bringing him home. Medical opinion considered his disability to be permanent and that he 'may not be able to struggle for a precarious livelihood'. Discharged as unfit for further service on 9/2/80. Medal for South Africa with clasp '1877–8–9'. (Ref. 'C' and 'Ba' rolls.)

447 Private WATERS John

Born at Lichfield, Staffordshire; trade – clerk. Attested at Westminster on 8/3/58, aged 18 years 2 months. Re-engaged at Malta on 9/9/67. Description:

5ft 5in tall, fresh complexion, hazel eyes, brown hair. Served in the Mediterranean and in South Africa. Promoted corporal 10/1/71. Reduced to private 2/3/75. Served as special orderly at the hospital at Rorke's Drift, where he was wounded in action. Mentioned in Lieutenant Chard's letter to Queen Victoria. Due to the severity of the shoulder wound, there is no mention of a knee wound; Waters was examined by a medical board at Pietermaritzburg on 14/7/79. The wound was described as having been caused by a 'bullet entering outer side of arm, six inches from joint of shoulder, and lodging'. 'It was cut out behind shoulder 12 hours after – distance travelled through fleshy part of arm – 4 inches'. 'The joint not injured – bone uninjured'. 'He has fair power of motion of the injured arm in all directions, but complains of pain in the track of the wound and shoulder when exerting himself'. 'From length of service and wound, his capacity to earn a living will be considerably impaired'. Waters was found unfit for further service and discharged on 27/10/79. Intended place of residence: 12 Courtfield Gardens, Kensington, London. Medal for South Africa with clasp '1877–8–9'. The medal roll originally gave his initial as 'G' and entitlement to the clasp with dates '1877–8–9'. This was later corrected under 68/124/211 and the medal with the initial J and the clasp dated '1877–8–9' was handed to him on 15/10/80. (Ref. 'C' and 'Ba' rolls.)

2nd Battalion 24th Regiment
present at the Defence of Rorke's Drift

Defining the home or members of the two battalions of the 24th Regiment actually present at the battle of Rorke's Drift is very difficult. Army records are often incomplete, missing or inaccurate. Many of the places listed include the place of attestation for service – and this is hardly ever the same as their home address or where they were born. This confusion has been complicated since the release of the film *ZULU* in 1964. The film frequently referred to the regiment as a 'Welsh regiment'. It clearly was not Welsh, as the full title of the regiment indicates; it was the 24th (The 2nd Warwickshire) Regiment of Foot. The few Welshmen who did find their way into the regiment did so having left Wales to find work in and around Birmingham;[4]

unsuccessful in their quest, they probably joined the army as a desperate measure to avoid poverty, hunger or their civil responsibilities and for a variety of reasons many a recruit chose to enlist under a false name.

The individuals named in the following list are those referred to in the rolls originally prepared by:

Chard 'C'

Bourne 'B'

Bourne's amended roll 'Ba'

Dunbar 'D'

2459 Lieutenant Colonel Frank BOURNE DCM
(Colour Sergeant during the action)

Born on 27 April 1854 at Balcombe, Cuckfield, Sussex; no trade. Being the youngest of a farmer's eight sons, he must have felt there was little chance of his inheriting the farm; and the prospect of spending the rest of his life at the bottom of the pecking order and within the narrow environs of a rural community probably did not appeal to this intelligent and active youth. Despite his father's attempts to prevent his son leaving the farm to join the army, with all the stigma that such service implied, young Bourne travelled to the nearest recruiting centre at Brighton and volunteered on 17 December 1872. He was just 18. Attested at Reigate on 18/12/72, aged 18 years 8 months. Finally approved at Chatham on 24/12/72. (His father again attempted to prevent him from enlisting, but was prevailed upon not to do so.) Description: 5ft 3in tall, dark complexion, grey eyes, brown hair; he was painfully thin and hardly an imposing figure. In fact he was like many of the recruits of that time, short and underweight. In January 1873 he was posted to the 2nd Battalion 24th (2nd Warwickshire) Regiment. Bourne thought that the sergeant major must have had a sense of humour when he was put in A Company, traditionally the Grenadier Company and manned by the tallest soldiers. The 2/24th had served in India and Burma since 1860 and were due for a spell of home service and it was during this period that Private Bourne learned his new trade. He was keen, abstemious and, rare for that period, literate; then aged almost 21, he was rewarded with promotion to corporal on the 11/4/75. Appointed Colour Sergeant 27/4/78. Served in South Africa, Mediterranean, India and Burma (IGS medal and clasp 'Burma 1887–89'). Served in B Company at the defence of Rorke's Drift. Mentioned in Lieutenant Chard's report of the action. Wrote and broadcast his own account of the battle. Awarded the Silver Medal for Distinguished Conduct in the Field, with a £10 annuity. He was also offered a commission but had to refuse, as he could not afford the expense involved as an officer. Although hostilities had all but ceased, the men of B Company, led by Lieutenant Gonville Bromhead, were involved in the fighting around Mount Kempt and remained in the African bush for several weeks until a general amnesty was proclaimed at the end of June. His wife, Eliza Mary, was included on the married roll on 27/9/82. Promoted quarter master sergeant to his battalion, he transferred to the South Wales Borderers (SWB 1141) on 26/3/84. He was promoted honorary lieutenant and quartermaster on 21/5/90. On 15/11/93 he was appointed adjutant at the School of Musketry, Hythe, where Mary Frances, the youngest of his five children, was born. He continued in this post for 14 years until his retirement under the age limit in 1907. For some years he assisted Lord Roberts in the work of the Society of Miniature Rifle Clubs in London. On the outbreak of the Great War he again offered his services and was appointed adjutant to the School of Musketry, Dublin, a position that he held for over four years. Promoted lieutenant colonel and awarded the OBE in recognition of his services.

Bourne then retired to live in a modest house in the centre of Dorking. Although there was no veteran's association, he was persuaded to attend the Northern Command Military Tattoo at Gateshead in 1934. To a tumultuous ovation, he appeared in the arena with the only other living Rorke's Drift survivors, Alfred Saxty, William Cooper, John Jobbins and Caleb Woods. In December 1936 he broadcast on radio in the 'I Was There' programme and as a result received over 350 letters, to which he replied personally in every instance.

In response to an unknown 'Special Request' he compiled a roll of the defenders of Rorke's Drift, which is dated 4/7/10. Lieutenant Colonel Bourne was an extremely modest man who, when asked about the defence of Rorke's Drift, invariably replied that he considered himself 'lucky to have been there'. The anniversary of the battle was always commemorated by a family dinner held at his home. He died on 8 May 1945 (within sight of the ending of the Second World War), aged 91 years, and is buried at Elmers End, Kent; it is believed that he was the last surviving member of the Rorke's Drift garrison. Medal for South Africa with clasp '1877–8–9'. (Ref. 'C' and 'B' rolls, also 'D' list.) Thus ended the life of a remarkable and modest man, a true hero. See also Appendix E.

81 Sergeant GALLAGHER Henry

Born at Killendale, Thurles, Tipperary; trade – clerk. Attested at Liverpool on 13/3/74, aged 19 years. Religion: R/C. Description: 5ft 6¼in tall, fresh complexion, amber eyes, and dark brown hair. Promoted corporal 11/3/75. Appointed lance-sergeant 17/1/77. Promoted sergeant 9/10/77. Served in South Africa, Gibraltar, India and Burma (IGS medal and Clasp 'Burma 1887–89'). Served in B Company at the defence of Rorke's Drift. Married Caroline Maria Stanley at Dover on 7/4/77. Children: Caroline Lillian Gertrude (b. 4/9/81 at Brecon), Henry Edward (b. 8/7/83 at Secunderabad), William Alfred (b. 11/11/85 at Madras), Violet Elizabeth (b. 19/2/88 at Toungov), Daisy Dorothea (b. 9/3/90 at Raniket), Lawrence Stanley (b. 10/7/95 at Cosham). Service extended on 27/4/80 to complete 12 years with the colours. Appointed colour sergeant on 26/1/81. Re-engaged for the South Wales Borderers (SWB/1590) at Madras on 28/7/85. Promoted to warrant officer as sergeant major on 9/1/89. Permitted to continue in the service beyond 21 years, by authority dated 28/2/95. Appointed to army staff as garrison sergeant major on 10/8/95. Discharged from South Wales Borderers (Staff) on 10/5/97. In addition to his pension, he also received, for a limited period, a pension for services as Barrack Warden. Payment of his pension appears to have ceased in 1929. He died at Drayton, Hants and was buried at Christchurch, Portsdown Hill, Hants. Medal for South Africa with clasp '1877–8–9'. (Ref. 'C' and 'B' rolls, also 'D' list.)

623 Sergeant MAXFIELD Robert

Attested at Newport on 30/7/75, aged 18 years 3 months. (He allegedly came from Cinderhill Street, Newport.) Posted to 2/24th on 18/8/75. Appointed lance corporal 25/5/76, promoted corporal 11/11/76, sergeant 1/2/78. Awarded a 'Good Shooting' prize in 1878. He served in G Company and was a patient in the hospital at Rorke's Drift. Killed in the hospital when the Zulus broke into the building. Effects claimed by his mother, brothers and sisters. Mentioned in Lieutenant Chard's letter to Queen Victoria, and also in accounts by Privates Hook and Jobbins. He is buried in the cemetery at Rorke's Drift and his name appears on the monument. Medal for South Africa with clasp '1877–8–9' issued on 29/3/82, AGL 105. (Ref. 'C' and 'B' rolls.)

1387 Sergeant SMITH George

Born at Islington, London; trade – labourer. Attested at Finsbury on 29/5/60, aged 18 years. Previously served for six weeks in Royal London Militia. Description 5ft 4in tall, sallow complexion, grey eyes, brown hair. Served in Mauritius, East Indies, South Africa and Gibraltar. Re-engaged at Rangoon on 10/1/68. Promoted corporal 4/8/71. Appointed lance-sergeant 1/4/76. Promoted sergeant 1/2/78. Married Fanny Martin at the Wesleyan Chapel, Brecon, on 30/6/77. Served in B Company at the defence of Rorke's Drift. Transferred from B to A Company, in rank of sergeant, on 4/2/79. Permitted to continue in the service beyond 21 years, by authority dated 22/8/81. Transferred to permanent staff – 3rd South Wales Borderers – on 28/12/81. Discharged on 31/7/83 – not passed to reserve. Medal for South Africa with clasp '1877–8–9'. (Ref. 'B' and 'B' rolls, also 'D' list.)

735 Sergeant WINDRIDGE Joseph

Born at Birmingham, Warwickshire; trade – carpenter. Attested at Birmingham on 26/1/59, aged 18 years 4 months. Description: 5ft 10½in tall, fresh complexion, hazel eyes, brown hair. Served in Mauritius, East Indies, South Africa and Gibraltar. Promoted corporal 6/5/61, sergeant 2/3/62, quartermaster sergeant 21/12/63. He was demoted and promoted several times and again achieved the rank of sergeant on 27/4/77. Re-engaged at

Rangoon on 3/9/68 to complete 21 years service. Married Helena Catherine Rawlinson at Holy Trinity, Dover, on 14/6/77. Served in B Company at the defence of Rorke's Drift. Mentioned in Lieutenant Chard's report of the action and also in his letter to Queen Victoria. Windridge suffered from dyspepsia. He was reduced to private on 20/11/79. Appointed lance corporal 3/9/80. Promoted corporal 6/10/80, transferring to the South Wales Borderers in that rank on 1/7/81. Promoted sergeant 31/3/82. Discharged at Gosport on 7/8/83, having completed his service. Medal for South Africa with clasp '1877–8–9'. (Ref. 'C' and 'B' rolls, also on 'D' list.)

82 Lance Sergeant TAYLOR James

Born at Meltham, Halifax, Yorkshire; trade – clerk. Attested on 13/3/74 at Manchester, aged 19 years. Religion: C/E. Description: 5ft 8½in tall, fresh complexion, blue eyes, and brown hair. Served in South Africa, Mediterranean, India and Burma (IGS Medal with clasp 'Burma 1887–89'). Promoted corporal 3/3/75. Reduced to private 27/5/75. Appointed lance corporal 10/1/76. Promoted corporal 4/8/76. Appointed lance sergeant 26/10/77. Reverted to corporal 25/11/77. Appointed lance sergeant 11/7/78. Served in E Company at the defence of Rorke's drift. Promoted sergeant on 23/1/79, in E Company. Reduced to private 20/3/80. Extended his army service on 27/4/80. Promoted corporal 16/9/83. Appointed lance sergeant 3/9/84. Re-engaged in the South Wales Borderers (SWB 1682) at Madras on 23/11/85. Again promoted, eventually becoming orderly room sergeant on 5/6/91. Presumably discharged after 8/3/94. Next-of-kin: mother – Mrs S. Taylor, 33 Parkfield Road, Rusholme, Manchester. Medal for South Africa with clasp '1877–8–9'. (Ref. 'C' roll, 'B' roll gives his rank incorrectly as Corporal, also on 'D' list.)

1328 Lance Sergeant WILLIAMS Thomas

Attested at Brecon on 6/3/77. Posted to 2/24th on 13/12/77. Appointed lance corporal 8/1/78. Promoted corporal 1/2/78. Date of appointment to lance sergeant not recorded and it is possible that this may have been a local appointment. Served in B Company at the defence of Rorke's Drift. Wounded in action and died of wound on 23/1/79. Mentioned in

Lieutenant Chard's report and also in his letter to Queen Victoria. He is buried in the cemetery at Rorke's Drift and his name appears on the monument. Medal for South Africa with clasp '1877–8–9'. The medal roll gives his initial incorrectly as 'J'. (Ref. 'C' and 'B' rolls.)

1240 Corporal ALLEN William Wilson VC

Born in 1844. Attested at York on 27/10/59, aged 15 years 8 months. Description: 5ft 4in tall. Joined the regiment at Aldershot on 31/10/59. He is known to have served in Mauritius and South Africa. During his early service career he was confined in cells Oct.–Nov. 1860, July–Sept. 1861, Jan.–March 1861, July, Aug., Sept. 1864, Oct.–Nov. 1864. Re-engaged in 1873. Posted to regimental depot on 21/4/74. Appointed lance corporal 18/5/76. Promoted corporal 6/7/77. Appointed assistant schoolmaster whilst at the depot, receiving an additional 6d. per day. Returned to 2/24th on 26/1/78. Appointed lance sergeant 22/5/78. Reverted to corporal on 21/10/78. Awarded Good Shooting and judging distance prize in 1878. His wife, Sarah Ann, who appears on the married roll at Brecon in 1879, received from him a monthly allowance of £3. Children born circa May 1877, July 1878, August 1880, April 1882 (twins). The twins seem to have died about 1883. Served in B Company and wounded in action at Rorke's Drift. Mentioned in Lieutenant Chard's report on the action, and also in his letter to Queen Victoria. Corporal Allen was awarded the Victoria Cross for his gallant conduct at Rorke's Drift and received his decoration from Queen Victoria at Windsor Castle on 9/12/79. Following the action at Rorke's Drift, he was sent to Pietermaritzburg and from there to England on 26/8/79. He was serving with the 3rd South Wales Borderers Militia at Brecon by 8/11/79 and later served with the Provisional battalion at Colchester. Appointed sergeant instructor of musketry (date not traced). Died on 12/3/90 aged 46 years at 85 Monnow Street, Monmouth, and was buried at Monmouth. Medal for South Africa with clasp '1877–8–9'. (Ref. 'C' and 'B' rolls, also on 'D' list.)

582 Corporal FRENCH George

Born at Kensington, London; trade – groom. Attested at Westminster on 16/12/59, aged 18 years. Description: 5ft 4in tall, fair complexion, blue eyes, brown hair. Promoted corporal 8/11/60. (Followed by several demotions and promotions.) He gained extra pay as a fencing and gymnastics instructor. Promoted corporal 16/7/71. His wife, Mary, appears on the married roll in 1873; by 1877 they had two children. Served in B Company at the defence of Rorke's Drift. Promoted sergeant in B Company 23/1/79. Later transferred to 'G' Company and reduced to private on 28/6/79. Promoted corporal 9/2/81. Reduced to private 3/8/81. Discharged on 3/1/82 on completion of his service (22 years 11 days). Intended place of residence: 8 Hillaire Street, London. Medal for South Africa with clasp '1877–8–9'. (Ref. 'C' and 'B' rolls, also on 'D' list.)

2389 Corporal KEY John

Attested on 28/8/71 at Secunderabad, India. Appointed drummer in 1873. Reduced to private 25/9/77. Appointed lance corporal 3/5/78. Promoted corporal 13/7/78. Served in B Company at the defence of Rorke's Drift. Appointed lance sergeant 31/3/79 in 'H' Company. Promoted sergeant 20/3/80. To unattached list 1/3/84, while at Secunderabad, which suggests he settled at the same place as he enlisted. Medal for South Africa with clasp '1877–8–9'. (Ref. 'B' roll where his rank is incorrectly given as lance corporal.)

1112 Corporal LYONS John

Attested on 28/1/77. Posted to 1/24th, transferred to 2/24th on 22/2/77. Appointed lance corporal 13/1/77. Promoted corporal 26/11/77. Served in B Company at the defence of Rorke's Drift, where he was wounded in action (see p. 208). Mentioned in Lieutenant Chard's letter to Queen Victoria (see p. 375), and also wrote an account of the battle. He was sent to the depot at Pietermaritzburg on 1/3/79. Date of discharge not traced. Died on 1/5/03. The bullet that had caused his wound was extracted and given to him as a memento. Lyons had the bullet mounted on a silver watch chain, which he evidently wore on his person. The bullet and chain are on display in the regimental museum at Brecon. Medal for South Africa with clasp '1877–8–9' issued on 5/9/81. (Ref. 'C' and 'Ba' rolls, neither of which lists him as wounded, also on 'D' list.)

849 Corporal SAXTY Alfred

Born at Buckland Dinham, Somerset; trade – labourer. Attested at Newport on 18/9/76, aged 19 years. Religion: R/C. Description: 5ft 7¹/₂in tall, fresh complexion, blue eyes, and light brown hair. Served in South Africa, Mediterranean, India and Burma (IGS Medal and clasp 'Burma 1885–7'). Appointed lance corporal 24/4/77. Promoted corporal 23/8/77. Appointed lance sergeant 1/2/78. Reverted to corporal 11/7/78. Served in B Company at the defence of Rorke's Drift. Promoted sergeant 23/1/79. Reduced to private 18/5/81. (Followed by several promotions and demotions.) Married Mary Copeland at Madras on 30/12/85. Children: Albert (b. 20/5/87 at Wellington). Following the death of his first wife, he married Mary Cole at Wellington, Madras. Children: Wilfred (b. 2/11/90 at Secunderabad), Leo (b. 20/12/94 at Rangoon). He re-engaged at Wellington, Madras on 1/1/88 into the 2nd Battalion, Bedfordshire Regiment, to complete 21 years service. On 30/11/91 he transferred to the 2nd Royal Inniskilling Fusiliers in the rank of sergeant. Discharged at his own request at Thayetmyo, Burma, on 28/2/95 as a corporal with 18 years 170 days service. Admitted as an In-Pensioner at the Royal Military Hospital, Chelsea, on 12/6/1930. Died on 11/7/36, of myocarditis and senility, at Woolaston House Infirmary, Newport. Medal for South Africa with clasp '1877–8–9'. Two replacement medals (for South Africa and Burma) issued under 68/GEN/5160. (Ref. 'C' and 'B' rolls, the latter giving his rank incorrectly as sergeant, also on 'D' list.)

1287 Lance Corporal BESSELL William

Born at Bethnal Green, London; trade – porter. Attested at Bow Street, London, on 26/2/77, aged 20 years 11 months. Religion: C/E. Description: fresh complexion, hazel eyes, and brown hair. Served in South Africa, Gibraltar and India. Served in B Company at the defence of Rorke's Drift. Appointed lance corporal 26/11/78. Promoted corporal 23/1/79, in B Company, vice

Jones. Reduced to private 25/11/79. Transferred to army reserve on 28/6/83. Discharged 26/2/89. Medal for South Africa with clasp '1877–8–9'. (Ref. 'C' roll and 'B' roll which shows his name incorrectly as Bissell, also on 'D' list.)

1282 Lance Corporal HALLEY William

Attested on 3/3/77. Posted to 1/24th, transferred to 2/24th on 13/12/77. Served in South Africa, India and Burma. Appointed lance corporal 17/7/78. Served in B Company at the defence of Rorke's Drift. Promoted corporal 23/1/79 in B Company vice French. Reduced to private 2/8/79. Appointed lance corporal 21/2/80. Reduced to private 10/1/82. Died on 30/4/87 at Thayetmyo, Burma. Medal for South Africa with clasp '1877–8–9'. Medal returned to mint on 23/11/97. (Ref. 'C' and 'B' rolls, also on 'D' list.)

1713 Drummer GALGEY Patrick

Attested at Cork on 12/3/65, aged 14 years. Description: 4ft 7½in tall. Appointed drummer 1/2/66. Joined the regiment in India on 5/4/69. Reduced to private 1/7/70. Appointed drummer 23/2/72. Served in D Company at the defence of Rorke's Drift. Reduced to private 1/2/80. Discharged (date not known) under AGL 89. Medal for South Africa with clasp '1877–8–9' issued on 17/6/81. (Ref. 'C' and 'Ba' rolls, also 'D' list.)

2067 Drummer HAYES Patrick

Born at Newmarket, Co. Clare: trade – labourer. Attested at Ennis on 8/9/68, aged 14 years. Description: 4ft 8¼in tall, fresh complexion, grey eyes, light brown hair. Appointed drummer (boy) on 8/12/69. Reverted to boy 8/11/70. Appointed private 9/9/71. Appointed drummer 1/4/73. Served in India, South Africa, Mediterranean and Burma. Served in B Company at the defence of Rorke's Drift. Re-engaged on 22/11/79. Appointed lance corporal 28/4/84. Promoted corporal 22/9/85. Reverted to private 10/9/87. Appointed bandsman 7/10/87. Permitted to continue in the service beyond 21 years by authority dated 19/10/89. Discharged on 30/11/92. Following his discharge he became a civilian workman at the barracks at Brecon, remaining in this capacity until well past 60 years of age. On retirement he lived at a house in Riverhall Street, Wandsworth Road, London. Medal for South Africa with clasp '1877–8–9'. (Ref. 'C' and 'B' rolls, also 'D' list.)

2381 Drummer KEEFE James

Born at St Andrew's, London; trade – none. Religion: C/E. Attested at Marlborough Police Court on 3/3/71, aged 14 years 10 months. Description: 4ft 7½in tall, fresh complexion, grey eyes, brown hair. private 4/3/73. Appointed drummer 21/8/74. Served in South Africa, Mediterranean, India and Burma. Served in B Company at the defence of Rorke's Drift. Re-engaged at Secunderabad on 18/12/79, to complete 21 years service. Reverted to private 6/4/83. (Followed by several promotions and demotions.) Transferred to South Wales Borderers (SWB 2311), as a private, on 10/10/87. Sent to depot and promoted corporal 28/11/89. Married Margaret Ellis at Brecon Registry Office on 17/4/89. (His son, also named James, served in the South Wales Borderers.) Transferred to 3rd Battalion, South Wales Borderers, as permanent staff on 16/4/90, having been promoted sergeant on 15/4/90. To 3rd Volunteer Battalion – permanent staff – on 22/9/91. Permitted to continue in the service beyond 21 years, by authority dated 10/3/92. Appointed lance sergeant 4/3/92. Died on 18/9/93. Medal for South Africa with clasp '1877–8–9'. (Ref. 'C' and 'B' rolls, also 'D' list.)

Drummer MEEHAN John

Date of attestation not traced. He appears on the muster roll for 1/1/73, at Warley, as a 'Private from the depot'. Appointed drummer 7/8/78. Awarded 42 days hard labour, of which 11 days were remitted, in June 1877 – yet still retained his rank. He was awarded a 'Good Shooting' prize in 1878. Served in A Company at the defence of Rorke's Drift. Posted from India to England, for discharge, on 29/1/83. Medal for South Africa with clasp '1877–8–9'. (Ref. 'C' roll, which names him incorrectly as Pat Meeham, and 'Ba' roll which appears to name him as T. Meechan, also on 'D' list.)

987 Private ADAMS Robert

Attested on 21/12/76. Previously served in East Middlesex Militia. Posted to 2/24th on 22/1/77. Sent to general depot on 1/11/78, returning on 21/12/78.

He served in D Company and was a patient in the hospital at Rorke's Drift. Killed in action. Effects claimed under E/78649/4 AGL 77. He is buried in the cemetery at Rorke's Drift and his name appears on the monument. Medal for South Africa with clasp '1877–8–9'. (Ref. 'C' and 'B' rolls.)

913 Private ASHTON James

Born at St Mary's, Liverpool; trade – groom. Religion: C/E. Attested at Cork on 3/3/59, aged 17 years 9 months. Description: 5ft 5½in tall, fresh complexion, hazel eyes, dark brown hair. Served in Mauritius, East Indies and South Africa. Served in B Company at the defence of Rorke's Drift. There is a report that on 23 January, after the Zulus had been repulsed at Rorke's Drift, Private Ashton appeared with a Zulu prisoner. No one in authority had time to spare for either the soldier or his prisoner, and he was told to dispose of the captive. It was later discovered that Ashton had taken this in a literal sense and had hanged the Zulu. Colour Sergeant Bourne stated that Ashton had told him: 'I took him [the Zulu] to Lieutenant Bromhead and he told me to get the hell out of here with him – and I did.' Similar confirmation is provided by Lieutenant Smith-Dorrien who had ridden to Rorke's Drift on the day following the battle and was shocked to discover two Zulus hanging from the gallows he had erected to stretch hides. Private Ashton was discharged on 29/3/81, on completion of his service (21 years 110 days). Medal for South Africa with clasp '1877–8–9'. (Ref. 'C' and 'B' rolls, with the latter giving his number incorrectly as 912, also on 'D' list.)

1381 Private BARRY Thomas

Attested at Newport on 6/4/77. Posted to 2/24th on 11/5/77. Served in South Africa and India. Served in B Company at the defence of Rorke's Drift. Returned to England from India on 26/4/83. Medal for South Africa with clasp '1877–8–9'. (Ref. 'B' roll only.)

918 Private BENNETT William

Attested at Brecon on 22/11/76. Posted to 2/24th on 15/12/76. Confined in cells from 29/10/78 to 5/11/78. Served in B Company at the defence of

Rorke's Drift. Sent to Netley on 1/2/80, and from there discharged to army reserve (AGL 149). Medal for South Africa with clasp '1877–8–9'. (Ref. 'B' roll only.)

1427 Private BLY John

Date of attestation not known. Posted to 2/24th on 1/1/73. Served in B Company at the defence of Rorke's Drift. Sent to Netley on 1/2/80, and from there discharged to army reserve (AGL 149). Medal for South Africa with clasp '1877–8–9'. (Ref. 'B' roll only.)

1524 Private BROMWICH Joseph

Born at St Mary's, Warwick; trade – porter. Religion: C/E. attested for the 6th Regiment, 28 Brigade (18B/1028), at Warwick on 27/8/77, aged 18 years. (His attestation papers originally gave his name as 'Bromage', this later being amended in all instances to his correct name. See note below re 'B' roll.) Description: 5ft 5½in tall, fair complexion, brown eyes, dark brown hair. Next of kin: mother, Mrs M. Bromwich, 12 Brook Street, Warwick. Transferred as a private to 2/24th Regiment on 24/1/78. Served in South Africa, India and Mauritius. Served in B Company at the defence of Rorke's Drift. Transferred from B Company to A Company on 29/1/79. Transferred to South Wales Borderers on 1/7/81. As a result of his military service and the climate, he developed chronic hepatitis resulting in an irreparably damaged liver. Following a medical examination at Netley on 1/7/82, his disability was found to be permanent and 'Will for some 12 months impair his power of earning a living.' He was invalided from the service on 25/7/82. Medal for South Africa with clasp '1877–8–9'. (Ref. 'C' roll and 'Ba' roll, which show him as Bromatch, also on 'D' list.)

1184 Private BUCKLEY Thomas

Attested on 15/2/77. Posted to 2/24th on 23/2/77. Served in South Africa, India and Burma (IGS Medal with clasps 'Burma 1885–7' and 'Burma 1887–89'). Served in B Company at the defence of Rorke's Drift. Served in the South Wales Borderers, but did not transfer to the regiment. Appointed lance corporal 2/10/82. Promoted corporal 1/8/83. Reduced to private on 6/10/83.

Returned to England on 12/1/89. He is known to have been alive in 1932. Medal for South Africa with clasp '1877–8–9'. Two replacement medals (for South Africa and Burma) were issued to him on 5/7/24, under AG10/19689 and IV475/AG10 respectively. (Ref. 'C' and 'B' rolls, on 'D' list.)

1220 Private BURKE Thomas

Born at Liverpool, Lancashire; trade – labourer. Religion: R/C. attested at Liverpool on 14/2/77, aged 18 years. Previously served in 2nd Royal Lancashire Militia. Description: 5ft 4in tall, fresh complexion, blue eyes, brown hair. Served in South Africa, Mediterranean, India and Burma (IGS Medal with clasp 'Burma 1885–7'). Served in B Company at the defence of Rorke's Drift. Appointed lance corporal 24/11/80. Promoted corporal 1/11/81. Served in South Wales Borderers, but did not transfer to the regiment. To army reserve on 21/6/83. Rejoined in 1st Liverpool Regiment on 19/10/84. Re-engaged at Fuzabad on 20/8/88, to complete 21 years service. (Followed by several demotions and promotions.) Discharged at his own request on 15/10/97, as a sergeant, after 18 years service. Medal for South Africa with clasp '1877–8–9'. (Ref. 'B' roll only.)

2350 Private BUSHE James

Born at St John's, Dublin; trade – tailor. Religion: C/E. Attested at Dublin on 14/9/70, aged 18 years. Description: 5ft 5in tall, fresh complexion, grey eyes, black hair. Served in India, South Africa, Mediterranean and Burma (IGS Medal with clasp 'Burma 1887–89'). Promoted corporal 20/11/75. Reduced to private 17/5/77. Served in B Company at the defence of Rorke's Drift. Injured in action. Mentioned in Lieutenant Chard's letter to Queen Victoria. Appointed lance corporal 10/2/79 and transferred from B to F Company. Promoted corporal 28/11/79. Appointed lance sergeant 24/11/80. Served in South Wales Borderers, but did not transfer to the regiment. Re-engaged at Secunderabad on 2/12/80, to complete 21 years service. Reverted to private, at own request, on 2/11/81. Appointed lance corporal 1/6/83. Promoted corporal 27/4/87. Discharged on 10/10/91. Medal for South Africa with clasp '1877–8–9'. (Ref. 'C' and 'B' rolls, in both instances incorrectly shown as Bush, 'B' roll also gives his rank as corporal, on 'D' list.)

1181 Private CAMP William Henry

Born at Camberwell, Surrey; trade–clerk. Attested at Liverpool on 8/2/77, aged 23 years. Description: 5ft 8$\frac{1}{2}$in tall, sallow complexion, hazel eyes, dark brown hair. Served in B Company at the defence of Rorke's Drift. Embarked at Bombay, for England, in HM Troopship *Malabar* on 28/10/81. Following a medical examination at Netley on 25/11/81, he was found to be suffering from melancholia caused by an 'hereditary predisposition and aggravated by self-abuse'. His illness was found to be permanent and he would be unable to contribute to his own support. He was declared insane and discharged unfit for further service on 27/12/81. Intended place of residence: c/o Union Authorities, Camberwell, Surrey. Medal for South Africa with clasp '1877–8–9'. (Ref. 'C' and 'B' rolls, also 'D' list.)

1241 Private CHESTER Thomas

Born at Calthorpe, Leicester; trade – labourer. Religion: C/E. Attested at Bow Street Police Court on 19/2/77, aged 24 years 7 months. Description: 5ft 10$\frac{1}{4}$in tall, fair complexion, blue eyes, brown hair. Served in South Africa, Mediterranean and India. Appointed lance corporal 16/2/78. Reverted to private 25/6/78. Served in B Company at the defence of Rorke's Drift. Returned to England, from India, on 28/5/83. Married Ellen Cave at Cheltenham on 9/12/83. Served in South Wales Borderers but did not transfer to the regiment. Discharged to army reserve on 21/6/83, having served 6 years 121 days. Medal for South Africa with clasp '1877–8–9'. (Ref. 'C' and 'B' rolls, also 'D' list.)

1335 Private CHICK James

Attested on 8/3/77. Posted to 2/24th on 11/5/77. Acted as assistant schoolmaster during 1877. He served in D Company, and despite being a patient in the hospital at Rorke's Drift, he assisted in the defence. Killed in action. (Appendix A.) Mentioned in Lieutenant Chard's official report on the action. He is buried in the cemetery at Rorke's Drift and his name appears on the monument. Medal for South Africa with clasp '1877–8–9'. (Ref. 'C' and 'B' rolls.)

755 Private CLAYTON Thomas

Born at Leominster, Herefordshire; trade – labourer. Attested at Monmouth on 9/2/76, aged 20 years 8 months. Posted to 2/24th on 10/3/76. Served in B Company at the defence of Rorke's Drift. Died of disease at Helpmekaar on 5/4/79. (He left the sum of £10 18s. 3d.) Medal for South Africa with clasp '1877–8–9'. (Ref. 'C' and 'B' rolls, the latter gives his initial incorrectly as 'F').

1459 Private COLE Robert

Born at Chatham, Kent; trade – gun maker. Religion: C/E. Attested at Brecon on 29/10/77, aged 19 years. Description: 5ft 6in tall, fresh complexion, grey eyes, brown hair. Posted to 2/24th on 13/12/77. Served in South Africa, Gibraltar and India. He served in F Company and was, presumably, a patient in the hospital at Rorke's Drift. (Corporal Michael McMahon, Army Hospital Corps, was awarded the Distinguished Conduct Medal for rescuing Private Cole from the Zulus at Rorke's Drift.) Posted from India to England on 1/12/83. Married Elizabeth Gibelin at St Bartholomew's Church, Birmingham, on 20/4/84. To South Wales Borderers on 1/7/81, but did not transfer to the regiment. Discharged to Army Reserve at Brecon on 8/12/83. Medal for South Africa with clasp '1877–8–9'. (Ref. 'C' and 'Ba' rolls, also 'D' list.)

801 Private COLE Thomas

Attested at Monmouth on 23/3/76, aged 20 years 10 months. Posted to 2/24th on 20/6/76. Served in B Company at the defence of Rorke's Drift. Killed in action. Mentioned in Lieutenant Chard's official report on the action, also in letters by Private Hook and Corporal Lyons. He is buried in the cemetery at Rorke's Drift and his name appears on the monument. Medal for South Africa with clasp '1877–8–9'. (Ref. 'C' and 'B' rolls.)

1396 Private COLLINS Thomas

Born at Camrose, Haverfordwest, Pembroke; trade – labourer. Religion: C/E. Attested at Monmouth on 22/5/77, aged 22 years. Previously served in the Monmouth Militia. Description: 5ft 6½in tall, fresh complexion, grey eyes, light brown hair. Served in South Africa, Mediterranean, India and Burma (IGS Medal with clasps 'Burma 1885–7' and 'Burma 1887–89'). Served in B Company at the defence of Rorke's Drift. Re-engaged for the South Wales Borderers (SWB 28) at Ranikhet, Bengal, on 19/8/89. As a result of his service and the climate, he suffered from rheumatism, and following a medical examination at Netley he was invalided as 'unfit for further service' on 16/6/91. Medal for South Africa with clasp '1877–8–9'. (Ref. 'C' and 'B' rolls, also 'D' list.)

906 Private CONNOLLY John

Born at Trevethin, Monmouth; trade – labourer. Religion: R/C. Attested at Newport on 20/11/76, aged 20 years 8 months. Description: 5ft 6½in tall, fresh complexion, blue eyes, light brown hair. Previously served in Monmouth Militia. Posted to 2/24th on 25/11/76. He served in C Company and was a patient in the hospital at Rorke's Drift. Wrongly named as Conley and injury incorrectly described as a 'broken leg'. In actual fact, Connolly was suffering from synovitis due to a partial dislocation of the left knee, caused whilst loading a wagon at the Lower Tugela river. He was brought before an Invaliding Board in Natal on 11/3/79, and recommended for return to this country. Following an examination by a medical board at Netley he was found unfit for further service and invalided from the army on 25/8/79. Medal for South Africa clasp '1877–8–9'. (Ref. 'C' roll which gives his number as '106', and 'Ba' roll, also 'D' list.)

2310 Private CONNORS Anthony

Date of attestation not traced. He arrived in India to join the 2/24th on 28/12/71. In July 1873 he was sentenced to 168 days hard labour at Millbank Prison. Served in B Company at the defence of Rorke's Drift. Sent to Netley on 18/7/80. No trace of date of discharge. Medal for South Africa with clasp '1877–8–9'. (Ref. 'C' roll, which gives his name incorrectly as 'Arthur', also on 'B' roll with wrong initial 'H' amended to 'A' on 'Ba' roll, also on 'D' list.)

1323 Private CONNORS Timothy

Born at Killeaty, Co. Cork; trade – labourer. Attested at Bandon on 15/3/60. Description: 5ft 4³/₄in tall, fair complexion, blue eyes, dark brown hair. Served in India, Mauritius, South Africa and Gibraltar. Served in B Company at the defence of Rorke's Drift. Re-enlisted at Rangoon on 26/7/67. He was discharged at Colchester on 2/5/82, having served 21 years 7 months (LSGC Medal). Intended place of residence: Lough, near Bandon, Co. Cork. Medal for South Africa with clasp '1877–8–9'. (Ref. 'C' and 'Ba' rolls, also 'D' list.)

2453 Private COOPER William

Date of attestation not traced. Posted to 2/24th in January 1873 when stationed at Warley. Served in 'F' Company at the defence of Rorke's Drift. Sent to Netley on 1/2/80 and subsequently discharged to the army reserve. Medal for South Africa with clasp '1877–8–9' issued on 17/6/81. (Ref. 'C' and 'Ba' rolls, also 'D' list.). Attended Military Tattoo at Gateshead with Frank Bourne in 1934. Committed suicide in 1942 while suffering from depression, probably as a result of long-term tuberculosis and pleurisy.

470 Private DAVIES George

Attested at Wrexham on 15/10/74, aged 21 years. Posted to 2/24th on 4/12/74. Served in B Company at the defence of Rorke's Drift. There is no trace of his name in the regimental records after 4/3/81, and it is presumed that he was discharged on or about this date. Medal for South Africa with clasp '1877–8–9'. (Ref. 'B' roll only.)

1363 Private DAVIS William Henry

Born at St Bartholomew's, London; trade – porter. Religion: C/E. Attested at Bow Street Police Court on 26/2/77, aged 24 years. Description: 5ft 4¹/₂in tall, dark complexion, hazel eyes, dark brown hair. Served in South Africa, Mediterranean and India. Served in B Company in the defence of Rorke's Drift. Transferred to army reserve on 21/1/83. Discharged on 10/8/89. Medal for South Africa with clasp '1877–8–9'. (Ref. 'B' roll only.)

1178 Private DAW Thomas

Born at Merriott, Somerset; trade – labourer. Religion: C/E. Attested at Crewkerne on 5/2/77, aged 18 years 6 months. Description: 5ft 4¹/₂in tall, florid complexion, grey eyes, brown hair. Served in South Africa, India and Mediterranean. Served in B Company at the defence of Rorke's Drift. Served in South Wales Borderers from 1/8/81 but did not transfer to regiment. Discharged to army reserve on 31/5/83. Medal for South Africa with clasp '1877–8–9'. (Ref. 'B' roll only.)

1467 Private DEACON George

Born at Bank; trade – clerk. Attested at Chatham on 10/11/77, aged 19 years. Confined in cells from 12 to 18 March 1878. Served in B Company at the defence of Rorke's Drift. Confined in cells from 11 to 24 February 1879 for 'Failing to obey an order'. Deserted at Pietermaritzburg on 9/9/79. Medal for South Africa with clasp '1877–8–9'. Medal rolls searched on 6/1/20 under 19/Inf/239 and 2177. (Ref. 'C' and 'B' rolls.)

1357 Private DEANE Michael

Attested on 10/3/77. Posted to 2/24th on 26/1/78. Served in B Company at the defence of Rorke's Drift. Deserted at Gibraltar on 22/7/80. Did not, therefore, receive his campaign medal for South Africa with clasp '1877–8–9'. (Ref. 'C' and 'B' rolls, the latter giving his initial incorrectly as W, also on 'D' list.)

1697 Private DICK James

Born at Island Magee, Co. Antrim; trade – labourer. Attested at Belfast on 3/2/65, aged 18 years. Description: 5ft 7in tall, fresh complexion, grey eyes, curly brown hair. Served in India, South Africa and Mediterranean. May have served in B Company at the defence of Rorke's Drift. Re-engaged at Secunderabad on 18/11/71. Discharged at his own request on 20/2/89, having completed 24 years 15 days service. (LSGC Medal.) Medal for South Africa with clasp '1877–8–9'. Incorrectly named on medal as W. Dicks (see next entry). (Ref. 'B' roll only named as 1697 W. Dicks.) In view of the confusion regarding this man and 1634 Pte William Dicks, it is impossible to determine whether either or both were present at the defence of Rorke's Drift. James Dick was illiterate and therefore may not have been aware of the confusion regarding his true name.

1634 Private DICKS William

Born at Islington, London; trade – labourer. Attested at Westminster Police Court on 26/11/64, aged 17 years. Description 5ft 6in tall, fresh complexion, brown eyes, brown hair. Transferred tom 1/24th to 2/24th on 31/1/65. Served in India, South Africa and Mediterranean. Re-engaged at Secunderabad on 6/8/72. Appointed lance corporal 17/9/77. Promoted corporal 14/11/77. Appointed lance sergeant 3/5/78. Reduced to private on 19/9/78. May have served in B Company at the defence of Rorke's Drift. Served in South Wales Borderers from 1/7/81, but did not transfer to regiment. Next of kin: sister, Mrs A. Framplar, 42 Havelock Street, London. Discharged on 9/2/86, having completed 21 years 65 days service. Medal for South Africa with clasp '1877–8–9'. (Ref. 'C' roll only.) The official records frequently confuse him with James ('William') Dick (see previous entry). For example, his medical history sheet originally bore James Dick's number 1697, which was later amended to the correct number 1634, also on 'D' list.

971 Private DRISCOLL Thomas

Attested on 15/12/76. Posted to 2/24th on 22/1/77. Served in South Africa and India. Served in B Company at the defence of Rorke's Drift. Transferred from B to A Company on 29/1/79. Served in South Wales Borderers but did not transfer to regiment. Date of discharge not traced. Medal for South Africa with clasp '1877–8–9'. (Ref. 'C' and 'B' rolls, also on 'D' list.)

1421 Private DUNBAR James

Attested at Newport on 20/6/77. Posted to 2/24th on 13/12/77. Appointed lance corporal 1/2/78. Promoted corporal 15/3/78. Reduced to private and awarded 28 days hard labour on 22/7/78. Served in B Company at the defence of Rorke's Drift. Mentioned in Lieutenant Chard's letter to Queen Victoria. Served in India and returned to England on 11/4/83.

Discharged to army reserve on 9/10/83. Intended place of residence: Newport. Medal for South Africa with clasp '1877–8–9'. (Ref. 'C' and 'B' rolls, also on 'D' list.)

972 Private EDWARDS George (Real name George Edward Orchard)

Born at Charles Street, St James's, Bristol, in 1855. He worked as a shoemaker's apprentice and in the building trade before enlistment. Attested at Newport on 24/11/76, aged 21 years. To 2/24th on 15/12/76. Served in B Company at the defence of Rorke's Drift. Confined to cells for 10 days during June 1880. Served in India and returned to England on 29/1/83. Discharged in 1889. Intended place of residence: Withy Mill, Paulton, Somerset. Married (wife – Rena, Elizabeth), and had 10 children. Lived at New Pit, Paulton, Somerset, and worked in a boat factory. Died on 14/2/04 and is buried at Paulton Cemetery. Medal for South Africa with clasp '1877–8–9'. (Ref. 'C' and 'B' rolls, also on 'D' list.)

969 Private FAGAN John

Attested on 13/12/76. Posted to 2/24th on 22/1/77. Convicted by Civil Power to 5 days imprisonment on 7/11/78. Served in B Company at the defence of Rorke's Drift. Killed in action. Mentioned by Lieutenant Chard in his report of the action. He is buried in the cemetery at Rorke's Drift and his name appears on the monument. Medal for South Africa with clasp '1877–8–9'. (Ref. 'B' and 'B' rolls.)

2429 Private GEE Edward

Attested in November 1872. Transferred from 1/24th to 2/24th on 1/1/73. Served in B Company at the defence of Rorke's Drift. Sent to Netley on 1/2/80. Transferred to army reserve under AGL 120, date of transfer not recorded. Medal for South Africa with clasp '1877–8–9'. (Ref. 'C' and 'B' rolls, also on 'D' list.)

798 Private HAGAN James

Born at Neenagh, Co. Tipperary; trade – labourer. Religion: R/C. Attested at Monmouth on 23/3/76, aged 18 years 7 months. Previously served in

Royal Monmouth Militia. Description: 5ft 6¹/₂in tall, grey eyes, brown hair, fresh complexion. Next of kin, Mary Ann Martland, N.E. America. Served in South Africa, Gibraltar and India. Served in B Company at the defence of Rorke's Drift. To South Wales Borderers Depot on 25/11/81. Transferred to army reserve on 24/3/82. Recalled to army service at Salford, Lancashire, on 3/8/82. Re-transferred to army reserve on 8/2/83. Married Catherine Barry at Treforrest, Glamorgan, on 8/7/72. Discharged from army reserve on 23/3/88. Medal for South Africa with clasp '1877–8–9'. (Ref. 'C' roll only, also on 'D' list incorrectly named as 'Hogan'.)

1062 Private HARRIS John

Born at Crickhowell, Breconshire; trade – labourer. Religion: Wesleyan. Attested at Brecon on 15/1/77, aged 19 years. Previously served in the Royal South Wales Borderers Militia Rifles. Description: 5ft 6in tall, sallow complexion, grey eyes, light brown hair. Posted to 2/24th on 31/1/77. Served in India, South Africa and Gibraltar. Served in B Company at the defence of Rorke's Drift. (Confirmed by entries in his service documents, 'Present at Defence of Rorke's Drift' and 'Compensation – loss of kit at defence of Rorke's Drift'.) He was brought before a medical board at Gibraltar on 16/7/80 and invalided from the service as a result of chronic osteoarthritis. Sent to Netley on 24/7/80 and discharged as unfit for further service on 14/9/80. Intended place of residence: Wandsworth, Surrey. Medal for South Africa with clasp '1877–8–9'. (Ref. 'C' and 'Ba' rolls, also on 'D' list.)

1769 Private HAYDEN Garret

Attested at Dublin on 9/12/65, aged 18 years. Description: 5ft 5in tall, joined the battalion at Port Blair on 11/7/67. Appointed drummer on 1/10/68. Reduced to private on 10/9/76. He served in D Company and was a patient in the hospital at Rorke's Drift. He was killed and mutilated by the Zulus when they broke into the hospital. Mentioned in Lieutenant Chard's official report on the action. At the time of his death Hayden's home was in John Street, Brecon. Effects claimed by his father. He is buried in the cemetery at Rorke's Drift and his name appears on the monument. Medal for South Africa with clasp '1877–8–9'. (Ref. 'C and 'B' rolls.)

1362 Private HITCH Frederick VC

Born at Edmonton, London, on 28/11/56. Religion: C/E. Attested at Westminster Police Court on 7/3/77; trade – bricklayer's labourer. Age given as 20 years 3 months. (He was illiterate at the time of his enlistment.) Description: 5ft 8¾in tall, fresh complexion, hazel eyes, brown hair. Posted to 2/24th on 11/5/77. Served in B Company and wounded in action at Rorke's Drift. Mentioned in Lieutenant Chard's report on the action, also in his letter to Queen Victoria. Hitch wrote an account of his part in the battle, and he is also mentioned in a narrative by Private Hook. Private Hitch was awarded the Victoria Cross for his gallant conduct at Rorke's Drift, and received his decoration from Queen Victoria at Netley on 12/8/79. Hitch was sent to Netley on 10/6/79, and following examination by a medical board on 28/7/79 he was invalided from the service on 25/8/79. Intended place of residence: Southgate, Middlesex. He obtained employment as a commissionaire at the Royal United Services Institute, Whitehall, and whilst there his VC was stolen from his coat. A replacement VC was ordered by King Edward VII and this was presented to him in 1908. In later years Hitch became a cab driver in London, and resided at 62 Cranbrook Road, Chiswick. He died on 7/1/13, and was buried at Chiswick cemetery on 11/1/13. Medal for South Africa with clasp '1877–8–9', issued on 23/5/81. (Ref. 'C' and 'B' rolls, also on 'D' list.)

1373 Private HOOK Alfred Henry VC

Born at Churcham, Gloucestershire in May 1850. Attested at Monmouth on 13/3/77; trade – farm labourer. Previously served in the Monmouth Militia for a period of 5 years. (He was a married man and enlisted in the regular army as the result of a foreclosure on a mortgage.) Posted to 2/24th on 11/5/77. Served in B Company and slightly wounded whilst defending the hospital at Rorke's Drift. Mentioned in Lieutenant Chard's report on the action and also in his letter to Queen Victoria. Transferred from B to G Company on 29/1/79, and appointed servant to Major Black. Private Hook was awarded the Victoria Cross and received his decoration from Sir Garnet Wolseley at Rorke's Drift on 3/8/79. Hook purchased his discharge for £18 on 25/6/80. On returning to his home at Churcham he discovered his property had been sold and his wife, who believed he had been killed, had remarried. He moved to Sydenham Hill, London, and on 26/12/81 he commenced employment as a labourer at the British Museum, later becoming a cloakroom attendant in the reading room. He married Ada Taylor at Islington on 10/4/97. Hook suffered from ill health, but despite this he served for many years as a Sergeant in the 1st Vol. Battalion, Royal Fusiliers. His health continued to deteriorate and he was advised to retire, which he did on 31/12/04. Harry (as he preferred to be called) Hook returned to Gloucester and died of pulmonary tuberculosis on 12/3/05 at 2 Osborn Villas, Roseberry Avenue, Gloucester. He was buried in the churchyard at Churcham. Medal for South Africa with clasp '1877–8–9'. (Ref. 'C' and 'B' rolls, also on 'D' list.)

1061 Private JOBBINS John

Attested at Pontypool on 12/1/76. Previously served in Monmouth Militia. Posted to 2/24th on 31/1/77. Served in B Company at the defence of Rorke's Drift. Described the battle in a letter to his father who was then working at the Crown Hotel, Pontypool. Returned to England from India on 29/1/83. Discharge not traced. Died at Pontnewenydd, Monmouthshire, in December 1934, aged 79 years. Medal for South Africa with clasp '1877–8–9'. (Ref. 'C' and 'B' roll, also on 'D' list.)

1428 Private JONES Evan

Born at Ebbw Vale, Monmouthshire; trade – labourer. Attested at Brecon on 20/7/77, aged 18 years 4 months. Previously served in Royal Monmouth Engineers. Description: 5ft 4½in tall, fresh complexion, grey eyes, light brown hair. Religion: R/C. Posted to 2/24th on 26/1/78. Served in South Africa, Mediterranean, India and Burma (IGS Medal with clasp 'Burma 1887–89'). Served in B Company at the defence of Rorke's Drift. Appointed drummer 8/8/80. Reverted to private 31/10/84. Appointed drummer 17/12/87. Served in South Wales Borderers from 21/7/89, but did not transfer to the regiment. Re-engaged at Ranikhet on 24/8/89. Transferred to Gloucester Regiment 30/9/89, to then unattached list on 10/10/89. Transferred to South Wales Borderers (SWB 2835) on 31/12/92. Reverted to private on 16/12/93. Appointed lance corporal 13/7/94. Appointed drummer

25/9/95. To South Wales Borderers at Brecon on 27/5/96 as permanent staff – 4th Battalion. Allowed to continue in the service beyond 21 years. Claimed discharge on 17/10/99. Married Alice Evans (widow) at Welshpool Registry Office on 15/10/98. Attested at Welshpool on 17/3/00 for Royal Northern Reserve Battalion (1226); trade – musician. Discharged on 16/3/01. Served in Montgomery Yeomanry, dates of service not traced. (Territorial Long Service Medal.) Attested at Aberystwyth on 15/4/15 for 2/7th Royal Welch Fusiliers (291067). Appointed drummer 9/5/15. Appointed lance corporal 29/8/15, acting corporal 24/8/16, acting lance sergeant 7/8/17. Discharged on 15/2/19. Attested at Wrexham on 12/8/19 as a private in the Northumberland Fusiliers (99052). Discharged on 10/2/20. Intended place of residence: 18 Union Street, Welshpool. At the time of his discharge he had served for 43 years. Died in 1931 aged 72 years and was buried at Welshpool. Medal for South Africa with clasp '1877–8–9'. (Ref. 'C' roll which shows him incorrectly as Evan Jordes, and 'B' roll which names him correctly, also on 'D' list.)

970 Private JONES John
Attested on 13/12/76. Posted to 2/24th on 22/1/77. Served in B Company at the defence of Rorke's Drift. Served in South Wales Borderers but did not transfer to the regiment. Returned to England from India on 29/1/83. Date of discharge not traced. Medal for South Africa with clasp '1877–8–9'. (Ref. 'C' and 'B' rolls, also on 'D' list.)

1179 Private JONES John
Born at Merthyr, Glamorgan; trade – labourer. Attested at Tredegar on 2/2/77, aged 24 years. Previously served in Cardiff Militia. Description: 5ft 5¹⁄₂in tall, dark complexion, blue eyes, brown hair. Religion: C/E. Posted to 2/24th on 23/2/77. Served in South Africa, Gibraltar and India. Served in B Company at the defence of Rorke's Drift. To South Wales Borderers on 1/7/81, but did not transfer to regiment. Next of kin: cousin, D. Morgan, High Street, Merthyr Tydfil. Transferred to army reserve on 28/6/83. Discharged on 6/2/89. Medal for South Africa with clasp '1877–8–9'. (Ref. 'C' and 'B' rolls, on 'D' list.)

716 Private JONES Robert VC

Born at Penrose, Raglan, Monmouth; trade – labourer. Attested at Monmouth on 10/1/76, aged 18 years 5 months. Description: 5ft 7½in tall, fresh complexion, grey eyes, brown hair. Religion: C/E. Posted to 2/24th on 28/1/76. Served in South Africa, Gibraltar and India. Served in B Company and slightly wounded whilst defending the hospital at Rorke's Drift. Mentioned in Lieutenant Chard's report on the action and also in his letter to Queen Victoria. Private Jones was awarded the Victoria Cross for his gallant conduct at Rorke's Drift, and received his decoration from Sir Garnet Wolseley at Utrecht on 11/9/79. To South Wales Borderers but did not transfer to regiment. Served at the depot from 1/7/81 to 26/1/82, then to army reserve. Recalled on 2/8/82 and re-transferred to reserve on 7/2/83. Discharged on 26/1/88. Married Elizabeth Hopkins at Llantilio on 7/1/85. Committed suicide on 6/9/98 and is buried at Peterchurch, Hereford. Medal for South Africa with clasp '1877–8–9'. (Ref. 'C' and 'B' rolls, on 'D' list.)

593 Private JONES William VC

Born at Evesham, Worcester; trade – shoemaker. Attested at Birmingham on 21/12/58, aged 19 years. Description: 5ft 5in tall, sallow complexion, brown eyes, brown hair. Served in Mauritius, East Indies and South Africa. Promoted corporal 1/9/59. Reduced to private 4/9/60. Re-engaged at Rangoon on 10/1/68, to complete 21 years service. An unconfirmed story published in the *Natal Mercury* on Wednesday 18 June 1879 states: 'When he [Jones] came here with his regiment his wife came with him, but after he had been at the front some time she became dangerously ill, and he obtained leave of absence to come down to attend to her. Jones took a little room in a house facing the St George's hotel Tap, and there, by working night and day repairing boots and shoes, he managed to earn many comforts for his then dying wife. He was a steady, plodding fellow, but his wife was beyond recovery and he remained with her until she died. The next day he buried her remains, and at once started off to join his regiment...' Served in B Company and assisted in the defence of the hospital at Rorke's Drift. Mentioned in Lieutenant Chard's report on the action, and also in his letter to Queen Victoria. Jones was awarded the Victoria Cross and received his decoration from the Queen at Windsor Castle on 13/1/80. Jones was examined by a medical board at Pietermaritzburg on 3/9/79 and was found to be suffering from chronic rheumatism. Invalided to England, he was sent to Netley and discharged on 2/2/80 as 'unfit for further service due to chronic rheumatism of the joints'. Intended place of residence, 174 Lupin Street, Birmingham. Jones, having remarried, later moved to Rutland Street, Chorlton, Manchester. In 1912 he was found wandering the streets, and although able to identify himself, he could give no address. He was taken to Bridge St Workhouse, where, later having been identified by his wife, he was returned to his home. Jones was found to be ill and in an impoverished state. He had been forced to sell his VC some twenty years previously when out of work and unable to provide for his family. He died at 6 Brampton Street, Ardwick, Manchester, on 15/4/13. He was buried on 21/4/13 in a public grave at Phillip Park Cemetery (Bradford Ward), Manchester. Medal for South Africa with clasp '1877–8–9' issued on 5/9/81. (Ref. 'C' and 'B' rolls, also on 'D' list.)

2437 Private JUDGE Peter

Date of attestation not traced. Posted to 2/24th in January 1873. Awarded a 'Good Shooting' prize in 1878. Served in B Company at the defence of Rorke's Drift. Returned to England from India on 29/1/83. Discharged to army reserve (AGL 105), date not traced. Medal for South Africa with clasp '1877–8–9' issued on 28/3/82. (The medal roll gives his initial incorrectly as 'T'.) (Ref. 'C' and 'B' rolls, also 'D' list.)

972 Private KEARS Patrick

Born at Liverpool, Lancashire; trade – labourer. Attested at Liverpool on 6/12/76, aged 19 years. Previously served in 2nd Royal Lancashire Militia. Description: 5ft 4³/₄in tall, fresh complexion, blue eyes, brown hair. Religion: R/C. Served in South Africa from 1/2/78 to 1/10/79. Served in B Company at the defence of Rorke's Drift. (Confirmed by an entry in his service documents 'Took part in the Defence of Rorke's Drift'.) Examined by a medical board at Pietermaritzburg on 23/7/79 as a result of debility and recommended for a 'change of climate'. Sent to Netley on 3/10/79 and then to depot at Brecon on 17/10/79 and married Annie Lewis at Brecon on 16/11/80. Transferred to army reserve on 1/2/83 and discharged on 8/12/88. Medal for South Africa with clasp '1877–8–9'. (Ref. 'C' and 'B' rolls, also 'D' list.)

1386 Private KILEY Michael

Attested at Brecon on 24/4/77. Posted to 2/24th on 11/5/77. Confined by Civil Power on 7/10/78 and sentenced to 5 days hard labour. Served in B Company at the defence of Rorke's Drift. Confined on 11/3/79, tried by Court Martial for insubordination on 17/3/79, sentenced to receive 50 lashes and to be fined £1. Again confined by Civil Power on 26/9/79. On release he was sent to the general depot on 1/1/80 and appears to have been struck off the strength. He made remittances to Helen Kiley and Mary Sullivan. Transferred from B to G Company on 29/1/79. Medal for South Africa with clasp '1877–8–9'. (Ref. 'C' roll which names him incorrectly as Riley. Correctly named on 'B' list, also 'D' list.)

963 Private LEWIS David

Attested at Brecon on 9/12/76. Posted to 2/24th on 22/1/77. Served in B Company at the defence of Rorke's Drift. No trace of his further service or date of discharge found. He made a pay allowance to Miss Emma Owens. Medal for South Africa with clasp '1877–8–9'. A search of the medal roll (for the Royal Hospital, Chelsea) was made on 7/5/28 under 68/L/261. (Ref. 'B' roll only.)

1528 Private LINES Henry

Attested at Birmingham on 11/10/64, aged 18 years. Description: 5ft 5in tall. Served in Mauritius, South Africa and India. Promoted corporal 4/7/68, sergeant 12/8/69. Reduced to private 14/1/70. Attended a course at the School of Musketry, Hythe, in 1874. Served in B Company at the defence of Rorke's Drift. Appointed lance corporal 2/11/81. Promoted corporal 31/1/82. Reduced to private on 6/3/83. Returned to England from India in October 1883. Date of discharge not traced. He died at Horden, near West Hartlepool, in 1922 at the age of 76 years. Medal for South Africa with clasp '1877–8–9'. (Ref. 'C' and 'Ba' rolls, also 'D' list.)

1409 Private LLOYD David

Born at Dowlais, Merthyr, Glamorgan; trade – collier. Attested at Brecon on 5/6/77, aged 19 years 1 month. Previously served in Royal South Wales Borderers. Description: 5ft 4½in tall, fresh complexion, grey eyes, brown hair. Religion: C/E. posted to 2/24th on 3/8/77. Served in South Africa, Mediterranean and India. Served in B Company at the defence of Rorke's Drift. Returned to England from India on 30/11/83. Transferred to army reserve on 13/12/83. Discharged on 5/6/89. Married Mary Price at Merthyr Tydfil on 21/1/85. Medal for South Africa with clasp '1877–8–9'. (Ref. 'C' and 'B' rolls, also 'D' list.)

1176 Private LOCKHART Thomas

Born at St Michael's, Manchester; trade – fitter. Attested at Derby on 6/2/77, aged 19 years. Description: 5ft 9¼in tall, fresh complexion, dark grey eyes, brown hair. Religion: C/E. Posted to 2/24th on 23/2/77. Served in South Africa and Gibraltar. Served in B Company at the defence of Rorke's Drift. He returned to England from Gibraltar on 11/8/80. In September 1881, whilst at Colchester, he was attacked by other soldiers and received a blow on the head, which caused him to suffer from epilepsy. Following an examination by an invaliding board at Colchester on 30/1/82 his epilepsy was found to be of a 'permanent nature', being 'induced by an injury to the head received at the hands of soldiers of the Colchester Garrison who waylaid and maliciously ill-treated him without provocation and notice – causing a fracture of the orbit and displacement of certain other bones'. It was considered that his disability would 'very seriously interfere with his powers of supporting himself'. He was found unfit for further service and discharged on 6/2/82. Intended place of residence: 41 Butler Street, Manchester. Medal for South Africa with clasp '1877–8–9'. (Ref. 'C' and 'Ba' rolls, also 'D' list.)

1304 Private LODGE Joshua

Attested on 4/3/77. Posted to 2/24th on 16/1/78. Served in B Company at the defence of Rorke's Drift. Appointed lance corporal 1/11/81. Promoted corporal 1/1/82. Reduced to private on 21/7/82. Served in South Wales

Borderers but did not transfer to regiment. Returned to England from India on 1/5/83. Date of discharge not traced. Medal for South Africa with clasp '1877–8–9'. (Ref. 'C' and 'B' rolls, also 'D' list.)

942 Private LYNCH Thomas Michael

Born at Limerick, Co. Limerick; trade – letter sorter. Attested at London on 10/11/76, aged 18 years 2 months. Description: 5ft 4¼in tall, fresh complexion, blue eyes, brown hair. Religion: R/C. Served in South Africa, India and Gibraltar. Served in B Company at the defence of Rorke's Drift. Appointed drummer 1/6/82. Transferred to army reserve on 30/3/83. Rejoined the Colours on 16/10/84 and posted to the Cameron Highlanders. Transferred to permanent staff, as a drummer, 4th Battalion, Argyll and Sutherland Highlanders, on 14/1/85. Convicted of 'Felony' by Civil Power on 9/3/88 and in consequence discharged from the service on 17/4/88, at Stirling. Next of kin: mother – Covent Garden, London. Medal for South Africa with clasp '1877–8–9'. (Ref. 'B' roll only.)

1441 Private LYONS John

Born in Killaloe, O'Brien's Bridge, Co. Clare; trade – labourer. Attested for the 87th Foot at Ennis on 31/3/59, aged 22 years. Description: 5ft 7¾in tall, fresh complexion, grey eyes, red hair. Transferred to 2/24th Foot 1/7/61. Served in Mauritius, East Indies and South Africa. Served in A Company and was a patient in the hospital at Rorke's Drift at the time of the Zulu attack. Awarded LSGC Medal with gratuity of £5. Sent from South Africa to England and admitted to Netley on 10/6/79. Examined by a medical board at Netley on 16/7/79 and found to be suffering from 'General debility at the Cape 1879. Treated for supposed Bright's Disease referable to exposure to wet and cold – after 10 days treatment at Rorke's Drift was transferred to other hospitals. A very clear and honest case of a worn–out old soldier – scarcely able to earn anything for his family'. Discharged as unfit for further service on 4/8/79. Intended place of residence: Manchester. Medal for South Africa with clasp '1877–8–9'. (Ref. 'C' and 'Ba' rolls, on 'D' list.)

1731 Private MANLEY John

Attested at Cork on 17/4/65, aged 15 years 3 months. Description: 5ft 1in tall. Appointed drummer on 1/12/66. Served at the depot until posted to 2/24th about December 1868. Reduced to private on 14/7/68. Appointed drummer 1/1/69. Reduced to private 7/8/76. Served in A Company and was a patient in the hospital at Rorke's Drift at the time of the Zulu attack. Sent to Netley on 1/2/80. Date of discharge not traced. Medal for South Africa with clasp '1877–8–9' issued on 17/6/81. (Ref. 'C' and 'Ba' rolls, on 'D' list wrongly named as Momley.) In 1885 he was convicted of a minor assault and after the authorities heard that Manley was one of the defenders of Rorke's Drift, he was sentenced to 18 months imprisonment with hard labour.

964 Private MARSHALL James

Born at Hitchin, Hertfordshire; trade – chimney sweep. Attested at London on 4/12/76, aged 20 years 9 months. Description: 5ft 6in tall, fresh complexion, hazel eyes, brown hair. Religion: C/E. Served in South Africa, India and Gibraltar. Confined on 1/8/77, tried and convicted of 'Fraudulent enlistment' on 3/9/77, released on 25/11/77. Re-convicted on 22/10/78, released on 11/11/78. Served in B Company at the defence of Rorke's Drift. Served in South Wales Borderers but did not transfer to regiment. Transferred to army reserve on 28/6/83. Discharged at Brecon on 4/12/88. Medal for South Africa with clasp '1877–8–9'. (Ref. 'C' roll only, also on 'D' list.)

756 Private MARTIN Henry

Born at Binegar, Somerset; trade – quarryman. Attested at Newport on 10/2/76, aged 19 years. Posted to 2/24th on 10/3/76. Served in B Company at the defence of Rorke's Drift. Returned to England from India on 28/10/81. Date of discharge not traced. Married (Wife – Polly), no children. Died in 1937 and was buried at Binegar Parish Church. A memorial was erected in 1965. Medal for South Africa with clasp '1877–8–9'. (Ref. 'C' and 'B' rolls, also on 'D' list.)

1284 Private MASON Charles

Born at Aldersgate, London; trade – solder maker. Attested at London on 26/2/77, aged 22 years 5 months. Description: 5ft 6¼in tall, fresh complexion, hazel eyes, brown hair. Religion: C/E. Served in South Africa, Gibraltar and India. Served in B Company at the defence of Rorke's Drift. Transferred to army reserve on 28/6/83. Recalled to 1st South Wales Borderers on 30/10/84. Discharged on 26/2/89. Medal for South Africa with clasp '1877–8–9'. (Ref. 'C' and 'B' rolls, also on 'D' list.)

1527 Private MINEHAN Michael

Born at Castlehaven, Co. Cork; trade – groom. Attested at Bandon on 14/10/64, aged 19 years. Description: 5ft 9¾in tall, fair complexion, blue eyes, brown hair. Found to have joined West Coast Artillery Militia on 9/5/64. Allowed to continue in 2/24th Foot. Served in India, South Africa and Mediterranean. Re-engaged at Secunderabad on 7/10/71. Served in B Company at the defence of Rorke's Drift. Penn Symons wrote: 'Minehan was a great pal of mine; he was right-hand man, front rank of "B" Company, who knew his drill well and had often kept me straight.' At one stage of the battle at Rorke's Drift, Minehan had been posted in the kraal. The day after the fight he was unable to speak as a result of exhaustion, but had taken Penn Symons to the corner of the kraal at which he had been stationed. By means of gesticulation he indicated the body of a Zulu, partly hidden under the straw. It appeared that during the battle the Zulu had crawled under the straw and grabbed Minehan by the leg. Minehan had 'prodded' the straw with his bayonet and one such thrust had penetrated the Zulu's body, killing him instantly. Private Minehan was again posted to India on 12/8/80 and whilst there contracted cholera on 15/4/84. He was invalided to England on 30/4/84, and following his examination by a medical board at Netley on 29/6/84 he was found unfit for further service and discharged on 2/9/84. Next of kin: sister, M. Regan, Castletown, Co. Cork. Minehan was apparently highly regarded by his officers and received a testimonial from Lieutenant Bromhead on 24/3/84. Medal for South Africa with clasp '1877–8–9'. He is named incorrectly in the medal roll as 'Minshaw'. (Ref. 'C' roll which gives his name incorrectly as 'Michan', and 'B' roll which names him correctly, also on 'D' list.)

968 Private MOFFATT Thomas

Attested on 13/12/76. Posted to 2/24th on 22/1/77. Served in B Company at the defence of Rorke's Drift. Transferred from B to G Company on 29/1/79. Served in India and returned to England on 27/1/83. Date of discharge not recorded. Died at Runcorn, Cheshire, aged 80 years. Medal for South Africa with clasp '1877–8–9'. (Ref. 'C' and 'B' rolls, on 'D' list.)

1342 Private MORRIS Augustus

Born at Dublin, Co. Dublin; trade – labourer. Attested at Liverpool on 3/3/77, aged 20 years. Description: 5ft 7in tall, fresh complexion, grey eyes, red hair. Religion: R/C. Served in South Africa, Gibraltar, India and Burma (IGS Medal with clasp 'Burma 1885–7'). Served in B Company at the defence of Rorke's Drift. Appointed lance corporal on 5/2/79. Reverted to private on 21/10/79. Served in South Wales Borderers but did not transfer to regiment. Appointed lance corporal 12/6/86. Transferred to army reserve on 18/12/87. Discharged on 5/3/89. Next of kin: sister – Mrs Hughes, 46 Oliver Street, Bootle, Liverpool. Medal for South Africa with clasp '1877–8–9'. (Ref. 'C' and 'B' rolls, on 'D' list.)

525 Private MORRIS Frederick

Attested at Liverpool on 4/12/74, aged 19 years. Posted to 2/24th on 13/12/76. Served in B Company at the defence of Rorke's Drift. Posted to India and died of disease at Secunderabad on 26/9/83. Medal for South Africa with clasp '1877–8–9'. (Ref. 'C' and 'B' rolls, on 'D' list.)

1371 Private MORRISON Thomas

Attested on 8/3/77. Posted to 2/24th on 11/5/77. Served in B Company at the defence of Rorke's Drift. Served in India and returned to England on 26/4/83. Date of discharge not recorded. Medal for South Africa with clasp '1877–8–9'. (Ref. 'C' and 'B' rolls, on 'D' list.)

662 Private MURPHY John

Attested at Tredegar on 22/11/75, aged 19 years. Posted to 2/24th on 6/1/76. Name amended from John to James in various documents. Confined on

11/2/78 and sentenced to receive 25 lashes. Served in B Company at the defence of Rorke's Drift. Returned to England from India on 28/10/83. Date of discharge not recorded. Medal for South Africa with clasp '1877–8–9'. (Ref. 'C' roll where his name is given as James, and 'Ba' roll, on list.)

1279 Private NEVILLE William

Born at Wigan, Lancashire; trade – collier. Attested at Liverpool on 23/2/77, aged 19 years. Description: 5ft 5¼in tall, fresh complexion, hazel eyes, brown hair. Religion: C/E. Served in South Africa, Gibraltar and India. Served in B Company at the defence of Rorke's Drift. Transferred to army reserve on 21/6/83. Married Sarah Elizabeth Graham at Ince-in-Makerfield on 1/6/80. Confined by Civil Power on 30/11/85, tried and convicted of assault and sentenced to 12 months imprisonment with hard labour. Released from prison on 18/5/87, he then completed his service in the army reserve and was discharged on 25/2/89. (He signed his service documents 'William Nevil' which may be the correct spelling of his surname). Medal for South Africa with clasp '1877–8–9'. (Ref. 'C' and 'Ba' rolls, on 'D' list.)

1257 Private NORRIS Robert

Born at Liverpool, Lancashire; trade – labourer. Attested at Liverpool on 22/2/77, aged 19 years 2 months. Description: 5ft 7¼in tall, fresh complexion, grey eyes, brown hair. Religion: C/E. Served in South Africa, India and Mediterranean. Served in B Company at the defence of Rorke's Drift. Transferred to army reserve on 28/6/83. Rejoined for army service in the Royal Sussex Regiment (1922) on 5/5/85. Appointed lance corporal 18/8/86. Promoted corporal 17/12/86. Reverted to private on 27/7/87. Re-engaged on 29/2/88. Transferred to Corps of Military Foot Police (301) on 1/8/88. He was admitted to hospital at the Curragh on 14/9/89 suffering from the effects of a specific disease he had acquired in India in 1882. Following examination by a medical board at the Curragh Camp, Ireland, on 13/6/89, it was found that the disease had affected his heart. He was declared unfit for further service and invalided from the army on 17/7/89. Next of kin:

uncle, J. Norris, 15 Hind Street, Edge Hill, Liverpool. Medal for South Africa with clasp '1877–8–9'. (Ref. 'B' roll only.)

1480 Private OSBORNE William

Attested at Pontypool on 28/11/77. Posted to 2/24th on 26/1/78. Served in B Company at the defence of Rorke's Drift. Posted to India and returned to England in October 1883. Date of discharge not recorded. Medal for South Africa with clasp '1877–8–9'. (Ref. 'C' and 'B' rolls, on 'D' list.)

1399 Private PARRY Samuel

Born at Sirhowy, Tredegar; trade – labourer. Attested at Monmouth on 23/5/77, aged 20 years. Previously served in Monmouthshire Militia. Description: 5ft 5½in tall, fresh complexion, grey eyes, light hair. Religion: C/E. Served in South Africa. Served in B Company at the defence of Rorke's Drift. Following an attack of fever in January 1879 he was examined by a medical board at Pinetown on 29/1/80 and recommended for return to England. On arrival at Netley he was again examined by a medical board and found to be suffering from chronic rheumatism, which had originally been manifested at Rorke's Drift in 1879. The cause of his disability was attributed to the climate and military service as 'His regiment underwent exposure'. He was found unfit for further service and invalided from the army on 25/5/80. Medal for South Africa with clasp '1877–8–9'. (Ref. 'B' roll.)

1410 Private PARTRIDGE William

Born at St Paul's, Ross, Hereford; trade – labourer. Attested at Newport on 5/6/77, aged 20 years. Previously served in Monmouthshire Militia. Description: 5ft 6¼in tall, fresh complexion, grey eyes, brown hair. Religion: C/E. Served in South Africa and Gibraltar. Served in G Company at the defence of Rorke's Drift. In his letter Bourne, then Colour Sergeant of B Company in 1878, mentions that his batman was named Partridge. William Partridge may possibly have been this man, having been transferred to G Company prior to the action at Rorke's Drift; however, it is strange that Bourne failed to include him in his original 'Roll of Defenders'. He served in the South Wales Borderers but did not transfer to the regiment. Married to Mary Letitia at Brecon on 15/11/80. Discharged at Davenport on 11/11/81, as unfit for further service, and awarded a 12 months conditional pension of 7d. per diem. Medal for South Africa with clasp '1877–8–9'. (Ref. 'C' and 'Ba' rolls, also on 'D' list.)

1186 Private PITTS Samuel

Attested on 14/2/77. Posted to 2/24th on 22/2/77. Served in B Company at the defence of Rorke's Drift. Posted to India and returned to England on 26/4/83. Date of discharge not traced. Medal for South Africa with clasp '1877–8–9'. (Ref. 'C' roll and 'D' list, incorrectly named as Pitt in both.)

1286 Private ROBINSON Thomas

Born at St Patrick's, Dublin, Co. Dublin; trade – none. Attested at Bow Street Police Court, London, on 23/2/77, aged 24 years. Description: 5ft 9in tall, fresh complexion, grey eyes, brown hair. Served in South Africa, Gibraltar and India. Confined on 24/4/78, convicted of disgraceful conduct 'In losing a pair of boots' and imprisoned on 27/4/78. Released on 29/7/78. Served in B Company at the defence of Rorke's Drift. Served in South Wales Borderers from 1/7/81 but did not transfer to regiment. Transferred to army reserve on 21/6/83, discharged on 25/2/89. Medal for South Africa with clasp '1877–8–9'. (Ref. 'C' and 'B' rolls, also on 'D' list.)

1065 Private RUCK James

Attested on 18/1/77. Posted to 2/24th on 31/1/77. Promoted corporal 12/1/78. Reduced to private 17/7/78. Served in South Africa and India. Served in B Company at the defence of Rorke's Drift. Appointed lance corporal 23/1/79. Transferred to G Company on 14/3/79. Promoted corporal 30/4/79. Reduced to private on 13/10/79. Promoted corporal 15/5/81. Reduced to private 14/3/82. Placed on unattached list on 28/11/86 whilst serving at Madras, India. Medal for South Africa with clasp '1877–8–9'. (Ref. 'B' roll only.)

1185 Private SAVAGE Edward

Born at St Woolas, Newport, Monmouth; trade – labourer. Attested at Cardiff on 8/2/77, aged 19 years. Previously served in Monmouthshire Militia. Description: 5ft 4³/₄in tall, fresh complexion, blue eyes, light brown hair. Religion: R/C. Served in South Africa only. Served in B Company at the defence of Rorke's Drift. Transferred from B to G Company on 29/1/79. Served in South Wales Borderers from 1/7/81 but did not transfer to regiment. Married Joanna McCarthy on 26/3/83. Transferred to Army Reserve on 11/2/83. Whilst serving at Gosport in 1880 he acquired a specific disease that eventually rendered him unfit for further service. He was discharged from the army reserve on 20/6/92, having been admitted to Glamorgan County Asylum. A medical certificate dated 6/6/92 was provided by the institution and sent to the Regimental Headquarters at Brecon, together with a letter written at 137 Wellington Street, Canton, Cardiff. The letter is signed 'Mary Savage, Wife' and it can only be presumed he had remarried. Medal for South Africa with clasp '1877–8–9'. (Ref. 'C' roll and 'D' list.)

1051 Private SCANLON John

Attested on 16/1/77. Posted to 2/24th on 31/1/77. He served in A Company and was a patient in the hospital at Rorke's Drift. Killed in action. Effects claimed by his mother. Mentioned in Lieutenant Chard's official report on the action. He is buried in the cemetery at Rorke's Drift and his name appears on the monument. Medal for South Africa with clasp '1877–8–9'. (Ref. 'C' and 'B' rolls.)

2404 Private SEARS Arthur

Born at Sunbury, Kingston, Middlesex; trade – labourer. Attested at Little Warley on 14/2/73, aged 19 years. Description: 5ft 9in tall, fresh complexion, grey eyes, light brown hair. Religion: C/E. Served in South Africa, Mediterranean, India and Burma. Was at Kneller Hall School of Military Music in 1874–5. Appointed bandsman 4/2/78. Served in A Company and was presumably a patient in the hospital at the defence of Rorke's Drift. Transferred to South Wales Borderers (SWB 1404) on 1/7/81. Promoted corporal 6/3/83, sergeant 1/4/84. Served in Burma (IGS Medal and clasp 'Burma 1887–89'). Re-engaged at Madras on 30/1/85. Married Emma Patrick at Secunderabad on 14/8/82. Children: Mildred Clara (b. 14/9/83), Arthur John (b. 12/9/85), Alice Emma (b. 4/1/89). Awarded LSGC Medal on 4/10/92. Discharged on 14/2/94. Medal for South Africa with clasp '1877–8–9'. (Ref. 'C' roll incorrectly shows as Pears, given correctly on 'Ba' roll and on 'D' list.)

1618 Private SHEARMAN George

Born at Hayes, Middlesex; trade – labourer. Attested at Westminster on 4/11/64, aged 17 years. Description: 5ft 5½in tall, fresh complexion, grey eyes, brown hair. Served in India, South Africa, Mediterranean and Burma. Re-engaged at Secunderabad on 6/7/72. Promoted corporal 2/6/74. Reduced to private 11/7/74. Served in B Company at the defence of Rorke's Drift. Appointed lance corporal 5/2/79. Reduced to private on 18/11/79. (Followed by several promotions and demotions.) Served in South Wales Borderers but did not transfer to regiment. Discharged at Gosport on 14/12/86. Medal for South Africa with clasp '1877–8–9'. (Ref. 'C' roll only, incorrectly named as Sherman, as he is in medal roll, also on 'D' list.)

914 Private SHERGOLD John

Born at St George's, London; trade – labourer. Attested at Coventry on 1/3/59, aged 18 years 3 months. Description: 5ft 5¾in tall, fresh complexion, hazel eyes, light brown hair. Served in Mauritius, India and South Africa. Re-engaged at Rangoon on 26/3/68. Served in B Company at the defence of Rorke's Drift. (He claimed compensation for his field kit, 'lost at Isandlwana'.) Examined by a medical board at Pinetown on 15/11/79 and recommended for return to England. On arrival at Netley he was found to be suffering from debility and rheumatism and was declared to be 'weakly and worn out'. Discharged as unfit for further service on 6/4/80. Intended residence: 43 East Road, Clapham. Medal for South Africa with clasp '1877–8–9'. (Incorrectly shown in medal roll as J. Shergo.) (Ref. 'B' roll only.)

1005 Private SMITH John

Born at Wigan, Lancashire; trade – labourer. Attested at Ashton 24/12/76, aged 25 years. Previously served in Royal Lancashire Militia. Description: 5ft 7½in tall, fresh complexion, blue eyes, brown hair. Religion: C/E. Served in B Company at the defence of Rorke's Drift where he was wounded in action. Examined by a medical board at Pietermaritzburg on 6/8/78 and recommended for return to England. Admitted to Netley on 20/9/79 and returned to duty on 10/10/79. To army reserve on 21/7/80. Rejoined 46 Brigade on 1/3/81 and posted to South Africa on 5/3/81. Injured by rupture on 10/5/81 on line of march in Natal. Returned to England 19/3/82 and transferred to Royal West Kent Regiment (46B/2333) on 1/7/81. Discharged at Dublin on 25/7/82 as unfit for further service. Intended place of residence: Bury, Lancashire. Medal for South Africa with clasp '1877–8–9'. (Ref. 'B' roll only.)

777 Private STEVENS Thomas

Born at Exeter, Devonshire; trade – bricklayer. Attested at Brecon on 9/3/76, aged 22 years. Description: 5ft 5½in tall, dark complexion, brown eyes, black hair. Religion: C/E. Next of kin: father – 'Robin Hood Inn', Dowlais, Glamorgan. Served in South Africa, Gibraltar and India. Appointed lance corporal 20/1/77. Promoted corporal 12/8/77. Confined on 13/1/78, tried and reduced to private on 19/1/78. Served in B Company at the defence of Rorke's Drift. Served in South Wales Borderers from 1/7/81 but did not transfer to regiment. Transferred to army reserve on 17/3/82 and recalled to army service on 2/8/82. Re-transferred to army reserve on 8/2/83. Married Ellen Calvert at Merthyr on 1/9/83. Discharged from army reserve on 16/3/88. Medal for South Africa with clasp '1877–8–9'. (Ref. 'C' roll which names him incorrectly as Stephens, named correctly on 'Ba' roll, also on 'D' list.)

1812 Private TASKER William

Born at St Martin's, Birmingham; trade – buffer. Attested at Sheffield on 20/9/66, aged 20 years 7 months. Description: 5ft 6¼in tall, fair complexion, grey eyes, fair hair. Next of kin: brother – J. Tasker, 68 Church

Street, Birmingham. Served in India, South Africa and Mediterranean. Re-engaged at Warley on 20/8/73. Deserted on 10/3/74, rejoined on 25/3/74. Confined, tried and imprisoned on 30/3/74, released on 10/5/74. Appointed lance corporal 13/8/75. Reverted to private and confined on 26/5/77, tried on 2/6/77 and sentenced to 28 days imprisonment with hard labour. Served in B Company at the defence of Rorke's Drift where he was wounded in action. Served in South Wales Borderers but did not transfer to regiment. Married Elizabeth Ridney at Brecon on 29/9/83. 'Prematurely discharged for the benefit of the public service' on 31/1/85. Medal for South Africa with clasp '1877–8–9'. (Ref. 'C' and 'B' rolls, also on 'D' list.)

973 Private TAYLOR Frederick

Attested at Newport on 9/12/76. Previously served in Royal Monmouth Militia. Posted to 2/24th on 22/1/77. Served in B Company at the defence of Rorke's Drift. Died of disease at Pinetown, Natal, on 30/11/79. Medal for South Africa with clasp '1877–8–9' issued on 29/8/81. (Ref. 'C' and 'B' rolls.)

889 Private TAYLOR Thomas

Attested 16/11/76. To 2/24th, 25/11/76. Served in B Company at the defence of Rorke's Drift. Returned to England 27/1/83. Date of discharge not recorded. Medal for South Africa with clasp '1877–8–9'. (Ref. 'C' and 'B' rolls, also 'D' list.)

1280 Private THOMAS John (Real name Peter Sawyer)

Born at Liverpool, Lancashire; trade – labourer. Attested at Liverpool on 23/2/77, aged 24 years. Description: 5ft 5¾in tall, sallow complexion, blue eyes, brown hair. Religion: R/C. Served in South Africa, Gibraltar and India. Served in B Company at the defence of Rorke's Drift. To South Wales Borderers on 1/7/81 but did not transfer to regiment. On 26/5/82, whilst stationed at Secunderabad, India, he signed (with his mark since he was illiterate) a declaration before the Cantonment Magistrate. The document states that he had enlisted under the assumed name of John Thomas and his true name was Peter Sawyer, as confirmed by his baptismal certificate. Married Annie Louisa Kelsey at Portsea, Hants, on 5/7/83. Discharge from army reserve on 25/2/89. Medal for South Africa with clasp '1877–8–9'. (Ref. 'C' roll only and 'D' list.)

1394 Private THOMPSON John
Attested at Brecon on 3/5/77. Posted to 2/24th on 26/1/78. Served in South Africa and India. Served in B Company at the defence of Rorke's Drift. Appointed lance corporal on 15/5/79. Reduced to private 6/12/79. Returned to England from India in October 1883. Date of discharge not recorded. Medal for South Africa with clasp '1877–8–9'. (Ref. 'C' roll only and 'D' list.)

879 Private TOBIN Michael
Born at Windgap, Co. Kilkenny; trade – labourer. Attested at Monmouth on 6/11/76, aged 20 years. Description: 5ft 9½in tall, fresh complexion, grey eyes, brown hair. Religion: R/C. Served in South Africa, Gibraltar and India. May have served in B Company at the defence of Rorke's Drift. Confined on 4/7/79, tried and sentenced to receive 50 lashes – sentence remitted. Served in South Wales Borderers from 1/7/81 but did not transfer to regiment. Transferred to army reserve on 28/3/83. Married Margaret Mohan at Windgap in February 1886. Discharged from army reserve on 10/11/92. Intended residence: Ninemile House, Tipperary. Medal for South Africa with clasp '1877–8–9'. (Ref. 'B' roll only – see next entry.)

641 Private TOBIN Patrick
Attested at Newport on 17/9/75, aged 18 years. Posted to 2/24th on 21/3/77. May have served in B Company at the defence of Rorke's Drift. Appointed lance corporal in 1880 (precise date not recorded), but wrongly shown as 'Michael Tobin'. Promoted corporal in April 1881, being again incorrectly named as 'John Tobin' – evidently he had been confused with 2698 Lance Corporal John Tobin who received the medal for South Africa without clasp. Returned to England on 28/10/81. Date of discharge not recorded. Medal for South Africa with clasp '1877–8–9'. (Ref. 'C' roll only and 'D' list.

In view of the confusion regarding this man and 879 Pte Michael Tobin, it is impossible to determine whether either or both were present at the defence of Rorke's Drift.)

1281 Private TODD William John

Attested on 2/3/77. Posted to 2/24th on 21/3/77. Served in South Africa and India. Served in B Company at the defence of Rorke's Drift. Returned to England from India on 26/4/83. Date of discharge not recorded. Medal for South Africa with clasp '1877–8–9'. (Ref. 'C' and 'B' rolls, the latter gives his initials incorrectly as W.G., also on 'D' list.)

1315 Private TONGUE Robert

Born at Ruddington, Nottingham; trade – frame knitter. Attested at Nottingham on 26/2/77, aged 19 years. Previously served in Nottinghamshire Militia. Description: 5ft 7in tall, fresh complexion, grey eyes, brown hair. Religion: Wesleyan. Served in South Africa, Gibraltar and India. Served in B Company at the defence of Rorke's Drift. Served in South Wales Borderers but did not transfer to regiment. Transferred to army reserve on 21/6/83. Married Mary Wright at Ruddington on 27/6/84. Discharged from army reserve on 28/2/89. Medal for South Africa with clasp '1877–8–9'. (Ref. 'C' and 'B' rolls, also on 'D' list.)

1497 Private WALL John

Born at St James's, Deptford, Kent; trade – labourer. Attested at Chatham on 1/12/77, aged 18 years. Previously served in West Kent Light Infantry (8100). Description: 5ft 5½in tall, fresh complexion, blue eyes, brown hair. Served in South Africa and India. Confined on 17/10/78, tried on 19/10/78 and sentenced to 21 days imprisonment with hard labour. Released on 8/11/78. Served in B Company at the defence of Rorke's Drift. Embarked at Bombay for England in HM Troopship *Malabar* on 28/11/81. Following a medical examination at Netley on 27/12/81 he was found to be insane 'as a result of intemperance'. He was declared insane and discharged from the service on 27/12/81. Intended residence: Lunatic Asylum, Barming Heath, Maidstone, Kent. Medal for South Africa with clasp '1877–8–9'. (The medal roll gives his initial incorrectly as 'F'.) Medal returned to the Mint on 7/11/82. (Ref. 'C' and 'B' rolls, also on 'D' list.)

977 Private WHETTON Alfred

Born at St Luke's, London; trade – labourer. Attested at Westminster, on 24/3/59, aged 17 years 10 months. Description: 5ft 5½in tall, fresh complexion, hazel eyes, brown hair. Served in Mauritius, East Indies, South Africa and Gibraltar. Re-engaged at Secunderabad, India, on 15/4/69. Served in B Company at the defence of Rorke's Drift. (Confirmed by an entry in his service documents, 'Present at the defence of Rorke's Drift'.) Awarded LSGC Medal with gratuity of £5. Discharged at Gibraltar on 27/5/80 on completion of his service. Intended residence: 5 Tower Hamlets Road, London, later amended to Shoreditch, London. Medal for South Africa with clasp '1877–8–9'. Medal sent to depot under 60/2-24/129. (Ref. 'C' roll incorrectly shown as 'Whatton', 'B' roll shown as 'Whitton', which, according to his own signature, was his correct name; also on 'D' list as 'Whetton'.)

1187 Private WILCOX William

Attested on 14/2/77. Posted to 2/24th on 23/2/77. Served in B Company at the defence of Rorke's Drift. Convicted of disgraceful conduct and confined to prison at Pinetown in January 1880. He was still in prison when the battalion was posted to Gibraltar. Medal for South Africa with clasp '1877–8–9'. Medal forfeited. (Ref. 'C' and 'B' rolls, also on 'D' list.)

1395 Private WILLIAMS John VC (Real name John Williams Fielding)

Born at Abergavenny, Monmouthshire, on 24/5/57 to Irish parents who had fled to Wales to escape poverty. Attested at Monmouth on 22/5/77; trade – labourer. (He ran away from home to enlist and used his second Christian name as a surname to avoid being traced.) Posted to 2/24th on 3/8/77. Served in South Africa and India. Served in B Company and assisted in the defence of the hospital at Rorke's Drift. Mentioned in Lieutenant Chard's report on the action, and also in his letter to Queen Victoria. Mentioned in Private Hook's accounts of the battle. Private Williams was awarded the Victoria Cross and received his decoration from Major General

Anderson at Gibraltar on 1/3/80. After serving in India, he returned to England in October 1883. Transferred to army reserve (date of transfer not recorded). Discharged from army reserve on 22/5/93. He was married and had three sons (the eldest was killed during the retreat from Mons in the First World War) and two daughters. For many years he was attached to the civilian staff at the regimental depot at Brecon, and retired from this post on 26/5/20. In 1932 he was taken ill whilst living at the home of his daughter in Cwmbran, his wife having died some years previously. He died at Cwmbran on 25/11/32 and was buried at St Michael's Churchyard, Llantarnam. Medal for South Africa with clasp '1877–8–9'. (Ref. 'C' and 'B' rolls, also on 'D' list.)

934 Private WILLIAMS John

Born at Barristown; trade – collier. Attested at Pontypool on 28/11/76. Previously served in Glamorgan Artillery. Posted to 2/24th on 15/12/76. Served in E Company at the defence of Rorke's Drift. Died of disease at Rorke's Drift on 5/2/79, leaving the sum of £8 4s. 6d. Medal for South Africa with clasp '1877–8–9' issued on 29/3/81, AGL 82. (Ref. 'C' and 'B' rolls, also on 'D' list.)

1398 Private WILLIAMS Joseph

Attested at Monmouth on 23/5/77. Posted to 2/24th on 3/8/77. Served in B Company and assisted in the defence of the hospital at Rorke's Drift. Killed in action. Effects claimed by his father. Mentioned in Lieutenant Chard's report on the action. Mentioned in the citations for the award of the Victoria Cross to Privates Hook and John Williams. (It is thought, and not without reason, that had Joseph Williams survived he also would have received the Victoria Cross for his exceptional gallantry.) He is buried in the cemetery at Rorke's Drift and his name appears on the monument. Medal for South Africa with clasp '1877–8–9' issued under 68/2-24/260. (Ref. 'C' and 'B' rolls.)

1316 Private WOOD Caleb

Attested on 6/3/77. Posted to 2/24th on 26/1/78. Served in South Africa and India. Served in B Company at the defence of Rorke's Drift. Transferred from B to G Company on 29/1/79. Appointed drummer on 1/2/81. Returned to England from India on 1/5/83. Served in South Wales Borderers but did not transfer to regiment. Date of discharge not recorded. Medal for South Africa with clasp '1877–8–9'. (Ref. 'C' and 'Ba' rolls, also on 'D' list.)

Others attached to B Company 2/24th

Royal Artillery

Bombardier Lewis T.

Gunner Cantwell J

1643 Gunner Evans A.

Gunner Howard A.

3rd Buffs

Sergeant Milne F.

Royal Engineers

Driver (RE) Robson E.

General Staff

Colour Sergeant Mabin G.

90th Light Infantry

Corporal Graham J.

Commissariat and Transport department

Assistant Commissary Dunne W.A.

Acting Assistant Commissary Dalton J.L.

Acting (volunteer) Storeman Byrne L.A.

Army Service Corps
Second Corporal Attwood F.

Army Medical Department
Mr Pearce
Surgeon James Henry Reynolds (see p.318)

Army Hospital Corps
Corporal Miller R.
Second Corporal McMahon M.
Private Luddington T.

Natal Mounted Police
Trooper Green R. S.
Trooper Hunter S.
Trooper Lugg H.

Civilian
Mr Daniells

Natal Native Contingent
Lieutenant Adendorff
Of all the participants at Rorke's Drift, it is Lieutenant Adendorff and his activities that are the most difficult to unravel. Adendorff brought news to the garrison of the defeat earlier that day, but whether he stayed on and participated in the defence of Rorke's Drift is still open to debate. If he did remain, why has he gone unrecognized? After all, he would have been the only man on the British side to be present at both Isandlwana and Rorke's Drift. Yet the suspicion lingers that he did not remain, and thus an air of disapproval continues to hang round his name, as if he 'let the side down', in a way that other survivors of Isandlwana somehow did not.

Any attempt to rehabilitate Adendorff is hampered by the fact that very little is known about him. Even his name is in some doubt – he appears variously as Adendorf – one 'f' – and Adendorff – two 'f's – and his initial is variously given as 'J' and 'T', though the former somehow seems more likely ('T' could in any case be a misprint for 'J' – though the reverse could equally be true). There is nothing unusual about Adendorff in this; most of the Volunteers and Irregulars who served with the Imperial forces in Zululand remain shadowy figures, who merit occasional mentions in official records for as long as their service lasted, and then they return to obscurity. This is particularly true of the officers and NCOs of the Natal Native Contingent, among whom Adendorff served, whose records are notoriously incomplete or lost.

The case against Adendorff largely rests on a comment by Donald R. Morris in his classic account of the war, *The Washing of the Spears*. Among the notes on his sources, Morris comments: 'My suspicion that Adendorff did not stay to aid the defence is based on analysis of all the sources listed for both battles. Space precludes a review of the evidence, which I hope to publish separately.' Morris never did publish that evidence, however, and it is probably fair to say that a good deal more evidence has been unearthed since the publication of his book, some of which suggests the opposite of his original conclusion.

There are two basic charges against Adendorff, which amount to a comprehensive accusation of cowardice. Since Chard was adamant that Adendorff appeared on the Zulu bank of Rorke's Drift while he, Chard, was still at his tent by the ponts, it is argued that Adendorff must have left the camp at Isandlwana rather earlier than he should, because the Zulu right horn, sweeping down the Manzimyama valley behind Isandlwana, had cut the road to Rorke's Drift long before the majority of the survivors got away. That being the case, those who did manage to escape did so by means of a hair-raising ride across country, crossing the Mzinyathi (Buffalo) several miles downstream from Rorke's Drift, at a rocky crossing known as Sothondose's Drift, subsequently known as Fugitives' Drift. Secondly, it is argued that since there are no references to Adendorff staying at Rorke's Drift, other than his name appearing on the 'Chard Roll', and since all the other fugitives from Isandlwana fled, Adendorff must have done the same.

Quite why Adendorff should be singled out for disapproval in this regard is not explained; no one suggests that there was anything shameful in the conduct of, say, Captains Gardner and Essex, or Lieutenants Curling, Cochrane and Smith-Dorrien, all of whom thought it wiser to head straight for Helpmekaar. This despite the fact that these officers were all professional soldiers, while Adendorff, as a lieutenant in the Native Contingent, was a volunteer. Indeed, given that the survivors from Isandlwana were all exhausted, shocked – even traumatized – and in some cases almost hysterical, it seems absurd that anyone would have thought badly of them for avoiding another fight (which under the circumstances must have seemed pretty hopeless). Nor did anyone; except possibly in the case of Adendorff.

It is interesting to note that Chard was initially sceptical of Adendorff's movements, but was clearly fully convinced by his explanations. This is only likely to have been the case if Adendorff were able to supply sufficient details of the fighting at Isandlwana to make his story credible. Moreover, Chard fixed the time of Adendorff's arrival at the Drift at 3.15 p.m, which is consistent with him having left Isandlwana between 1 p.m. and 1.30 p.m., when the British front line collapsed. In his official report, Chard said simply but emphatically: 'I was informed ... [by] Lieutenant Adendorff of Lonsdale's regiment (who later remained to assist in the defence), of the disaster at Isandlwana camp.' In his later, longer account, written at Queen Victoria's request, he expanded on this point:

> My attention was called to two horsemen galloping towards us from the direction of Isandlwana. From their gesticulations and their shouts, when they were near enough to be heard, we saw that something was the matter, and on taking them over the river, one of them, Lieut. Adendorff of Lonsdale's Regiment, Natal Native Contingent, asking if I was an officer, jumped off his horse, took me on one side, and told me the camp was in the hands of the Zulus and the army destroyed; that scarcely a man had got away to tell the tell, and that probably Lord Chelmsford and the rest of the column had shared the same fate. His companion, a Carbineer, confirmed his story – He was naturally very excited and I am afraid I did not, at first, quite believe him, and intimated that he probably had not remained to see

what did occur. I had the saddle put on my horse, and while I was talking to
Lieut. Adendorff, a messenger arrived from Lieut. Bromhead, who was with
his Company at his little camp near the Commissariat Stores, to ask me to
come up at once.

This last comment is significant because, of course, Bromhead had just
received the news from other survivors, who had reached the post via Fugitives' Drift at about the same time that Adendorff reached Rorke's Drift.
Chard even went on to supply details of Adendorff's role in the battle:

As far as I know, but one of the fugitives remained with us – Lieut.
Adendorff, whom I have before mentioned. He remained to assist in the
defence, and from a loophole in the store building, flanking the wall and
Hospital, his rifle did good service.

The mystery of Chard's misidentification is solved in the 'Chard Report'
of the Rorke's Drift survivors – presented to Queen Victoria. Corporal Francis Attwood of the Army Service Corps was one of five soldiers who received
the Distinguished Conduct Medal for bravery at Rorke's Drift. In Chard's
report of the defenders, he describes certain actions of Adendorff, but these
were well known by those present to have been performed by Attwood. It
was a straightforward case of mistaken identity by Chard; Attwood was
awarded his DCM at Pietermaritzburg on 15 November 1879. By then
Adendorff had disappeared into obscurity, although weeks later news
reached the garrison at Rorke's Drift that Adendorff had been arrested at
Pietermaritzburg for desertion. He was due to face a court martial but there
is no evidence this ever took place. Chard's report that Adendorff had
'stayed to fight' had already been submitted to higher authority and had
the trial taken place, Chard would certainly have been called to give
evidence, against his own report – and so the matter of Adendorff's court
martial appears to have been quietly dropped.

In the final analysis the evidence that Adendorff was present at the
defence of Rorke's Drift is inconclusive; even Chard was less confident
when he presented his second report – concerning Adendorff he used the
words 'As far as I know…' If he stayed then it is time he was rehabilitat-
ed, and his courage more widely accepted. To have endured the horror of

Isandlwana, and voluntarily stayed to risk a repetition at Rorke's Drift, when he might in all conscience have ridden off with the other survivors, shows remarkable strength of character. If evidence can be found that he stayed to fight, then Adendorff deserves to be remembered as one of the heroes of Rorke's Drift.

Captain Stephenson and the NNC

The action at Rorke's Drift on 22–23 January 1879 is certainly the most studied battle in the Anglo-Zulu War, and indeed arguably one of the most famous in British military history. Yet while the actions and identities of the regular British troops during the fight have been the subject of meticulous scrutiny, some mystery still surrounds the role of auxiliary troops, the Natal Native Contingent.

Several credible observers confirm that there were NNC troops present at Rorke's Drift before the battle. Lieutenant Chard himself mentioned the fact in both his apparent official report of the action, and his longer account to Queen Victoria; so, too, did Colour Sergeant Bourne, Private Hook, Chaplain Smith and others. Only Chard gives us the name of their officer, Captain Stephenson. Nevertheless, few of these accounts display any real knowledge of who they were, or what they were doing. Estimates of their strength vary wildly: Bourne put their number at 100, Smith thought there were 350, and Harry Lugg of the Natal Mounted Police believed there were 2,000. This ignorance is in many ways surprising, since the NNC had been camped near the mission station since 11 January; not only must the men have been conspicuous to the regular troops nearby, but some interaction between their officers, at least, must surely have occurred. Nevertheless it is typical of the reaction of the regular troops to auxiliary forces, whose professional pride and experience distanced themselves from both Colonial-born irregular troops and, in particular, black auxiliaries. The attitude of the British officer towards the latter is perhaps best summed up by a remark by Captain Edward Essex, 75th Regiment, who said simply of the NNC at Isandlwana, 'I did not notice the latter much, save that they blazed away at an absurd rate'.

The general order authorizing the raising of the Natal Native Contingent was published on 23 November 1878. Since the war began on 11 January 1879 just six weeks were allowed to raise, organize, officer, equip and train the Contingent. Yet the Contingent would be pitched into the war before the men had come to know, or learned to trust, their officers. Many, indeed, complained of being bullied by their NCOs, who issued incomprehensible orders, then used their fists to enforce them. They found European drill confusing, and only the most imaginative commanders made any attempt to harness their traditional military skills. So far from using African terms of respect when addressing their headmen, as they were urged to do, many officers and NCOs referred to them with utter contempt. Furthermore, early good intentions to encourage the morale of the corps by issuing uniforms and firearms were abandoned for reasons of economy. Only one in ten, usually the designated black NCOs, were issued with firearms, and the rest of the men carried their traditional weapons. Although some commandants attempted to procure old military uniforms from the government stores, most NNC were distinguished by nothing more than a red rag, worn around their heads. Under such circumstances, while the showing of the Contingent in the war was undoubtedly poor, it was perhaps better than the British deserved.

The 3rd Regiment, NNC, was appointed to the British Centre Column, which was to cross into Zululand at Rorke's Drift. The Contingent assembled at Sand Spruit, behind the Helpmekaar range, not far from the modern village of Pomeroy, where the groups from the various chiefdoms came together, and were issued with their equipment. The 3rd Regiment consisted mostly of men from the *abaThembu*, *amaChunu* and *amaBhele* chiefdoms, with a contingent of iziGqoza, all of whom were from Weenen County, which lay along the headwaters of the Thukela river. The iziGqoza were Zulu, exiled followers of King Cetshwayo's brothers who had opposed him in the civil war of 1856, and who had fled to Natal. One of Cetshwayo's brothers, Sikhotha kaMpande, actually accompanied the iziGqoza into the field in 1879, and for these men support for the British invasion was less important than the chance to settle old grievances. Nevertheless, there were not enough men from Weenen County to fill the 3rd Regiment, and several hundred were raised from Klip River County, around Ladysmith. These men did not join the Contingent until the war was about to begin.

On 11 January the Centre Column crossed into Zululand at Rorke's Drift and established a camp on the Zulu bank. On the 12th it saw its first taste of action when it attacked the followers of Chief Sihayo kaXongo, who lived in the Batshe valley, a few miles further along the track into Zululand. On the 20th the entire column moved up to Isandlwana.

Who then were the men left at Rorke's Drift? On the 14th a detachment of the NNC raised in Klip River County arrived to join the column, and a company was apparently left to guard the ponts at the Drift. These men were officially part of the 2nd Battalion, 3rd Regiment NNC, but it should be noted that they had not received any of the training given to the rest of the 3rd Regiment, nor had they had any time to develop a sense of belonging to their unit. Their numbers remain obscure – in theory a company consisted of nine white leaders (a captain, two lieutenants, and six NCOs) and 101 Africans (a black officer, ten NCOs and ninety privates) – but it seems probable that this company was over-strength, due to the casual way the Klip River levy had been deployed. Moreover they seem to have been lacking in white NCOs, probably as a result of their hasty formation. They were commanded by Captain William Stephenson, 'a gentleman from the Cape Colony [who] spoke the language perfectly', but seems to have had no lieutenants or sergeants present, and only three corporals. It is unlikely, therefore, that their morale and military effectiveness can have been up to much even before news broke mid afternoon on the 22nd that the Centre Column had been shattered at Isandlwana, and that the Zulu were approaching Rorke's Drift.

When the Contingent first heard the news, they reacted in traditional manner, singing war songs and probably attempting to complete the necessary ritual preparations. Chard asked them to help build the barricades, and Stephenson did 'good service in getting his men to work'. At about 3.30, however, a party of mounted auxiliaries rode up from the Drift. These were some of Colonel Durnford's command, which had survived Isandlwana; they were mostly followers of the Basuto chief, Hlubi, and they were under the command of a Lieutenant Henderson. While most of the mounted Native Contingent who had survived the disaster had crossed the Mzinyathi (Buffalo) river downstream, at the place now known as Fugitives' Drift, these seem to have cut through the Zulu cordon and reached Rorke's Drift. Henderson reported to Chard, who asked him to deploy his men beyond Shiyane hill, in the direction of the Zulu advance, to delay the Zulu attack as long as possible. They had been gone perhaps forty-five minutes when the garrison heard a smatter of shots, and they came into sight, riding off towards Helpmekaar.

Henderson had escaped in the company of a civilian meat contractor, R.J. 'Bob' Hall, who had been in the camp discussing business with the army. According to one of the garrison, Harry Lugg, it was Hall who shouted that the Zulu were approaching, as he described it, 'as black as hell and as thick as grass'. By Hall's account, he and Henderson lingered in the bush at the front of the post to fire a few shots at the Zulus as they swung into view of the mission station, before riding off to Helpmekaar. No one seems to have blamed them; even Chard commented that he saw the same men fight well later in the war, and he seems to have accepted that they were demoralized by Durnford's death. No action was later taken against Henderson.

But the sight of the mounted Contingent in full flight was too much for Stephenson's NNC, whose martial spirit promptly evaporated. The men threw down the mealie bags, biscuit boxes or weapons they had in their hands, and simply jumped over the barricades, heading for Helpmekaar. While the garrison had clearly not expected much from the rank and file, they were infuriated by the sight of the white NCOs in flight, and someone from B Company shot and killed one of the NNC's white NCOs. The dead man is generally accepted as being Corporal Anderson, the only man of the NNC who was killed in the battle whose death is not accounted for by other evidence.

Colour Sergeant Bourne perhaps summed up the reaction of the garrison to this desertion when he commented, 'the desertion of these detachments of 200 men appeared at first sight to be a great loss, with only a hundred of us left, but the feeling afterwards was that we could not have trusted them, and also that our defences were too small to accommodate them anyhow'. Whether he meant that the men could not be relied upon to stand and fight, or whether he suspected the Contingent might desert to the Zulu (which was highly unlikely), he does not say.

With their desertion the NNC pass out of the Rorke's Drift story, save for a few white NCOs, not from Stevenson's company, who were patients in the makeshift hospital, and who distinguished themselves in the fight.

Corporal Christian Ferdinand Scheiss (see p.319)

Corporal Dougherty M.

Corporal Mayer J.H.

Corporal Scammell C.

Corporal Wilson J.

Private Soldier – name unknown

Reverend Otto Witt

Witt purchased the Rorke's Drift farm on behalf of the Church of Sweden Mission in 1878 and, having sent his wife and children to friends near Umsinga, had stayed at the post when the British occupied it on the eve of the war. He was still there on 22 January, although he departed just before the battle began. His actions received a good deal of criticism at the time, and his reputation has suffered as a result, partly because he was publicly critical of the attitude of white settlers in Natal to the Africans, and partly because his claim to have been present at both Isandlwana and Rorke's Drift has been held up to ridicule.

Yet history has not treated Witt fairly. In fact, what he actually said was that he had seen something of the battle of Isandlwana from the top of the Oskarsberg hill, which overlooks Rorke's Drift, and that, as he was riding away from Rorke's Drift, he witnessed the first Zulu assault on the post.

Were these claims as ridiculous as they have sometimes seemed? Witt climbed the hill in the company of Chaplain Smith and Surgeon Reynolds shortly after noon, when the battle was just beginning at Isandlwana. By the time they reached the peak of the hill the battle would have been well under way. From the summit of the Oskarsberg there is a magnificent view of the entire theatre of operations of the Centre Column, from the crossing point at Rorke's Drift on the left towards Isandlwana, and the Isipezi mountain beyond. Only where the river enters the gorge above Fugitives' Drift is the view lost. Isandlwana itself blots out the plain in front of it, where much of the battle took place, but the spurs of the iNyoni ridge, where Mostyn and Cavaye's companies were deployed, are clearly visible. So, too, as the Manzimyama valley, where the Zulu right horn descended, and the near slope of the *nek* below Isandlwana itself, where many of the 24th stands were broken up and overwhelmed. Is there anything improbable, then, about Witt's account of what he actually saw that day? He wrote:

> My position was on a hill on the other side of the river from where the fight was raging. I watched the Zulus descend and draw themselves in long lines between the camp and the river. From where I stood I could see the English forces advancing to attack; but I could not see any hand-to-hand fighting. I observed that the Zulus were fighting heavily, and presently I saw that the English were surrounded in a kraal some little distance from the camp ... As the fight progressed, and I saw that the English were beaten ... I noticed that the Zulus were crossing the river.

In a long and admittedly rather confused account, Witt went on to add more details, all of them quite plausible. Once he realized he was in danger, he 'saw there was no time to be lost, and I dashed away on horseback as hard as I could go.' There was no reason for him to stay; as a civilian and a missionary, he had no duty to support the British troops, nor does anyone seem to have expected him to. He claimed that he was 'chased by the Zulus, who did their best to catch me, but failed'. His account of Rorke's Drift is clearly a mixture of his own observations, and reports published after the events. He probably paused to look back at the battle when he was a safe distance away; moreover, the site of the battle would have been visible for several miles as he rode towards Helpmekaar:

> Before I started I saw a Zulu alone at the barricade, kneeling and firing. The whole force drew nearer, and the battle drew on heavier. Soon the hospital was on fire. Our people found it impossible to defend themselves inside the barricade. They must retire within the walls, thus entering the commissariat

store. The sick people were brought here, except five who could not be removed, and who were stabbed by the Zulus and burnt. That the hospital was set on fire was certainly a great personal loss for me, as all my property was burnt; but it was of great importance for the whole colony, and especially for the people in the commissariat stores, as the flames of the burning house enabled them to aim properly on the Zulus and thus keep them at a fair distance. If the Zulus had known what they ought they should never have put fire to the house, and the heavy darkness of that dreadful night would have made our troops unable to defend themselves as they did.

There is nothing in this account to cause us to question Witt's veracity. It seems that his marginal role in the eyes of the successive generation of British commentators has caused his reputation to suffer unfairly – a situation perhaps not helped by his conducting (unsuccessfully) legal action for £600 compensation against the British government for the destruction of his mission station.

CHAPTER 14

An Examination of the Rolls
of Rorke's Drift Defenders

The defenders of Rorke's Drift were comparatively few in number; furthermore the garrison mainly consisted of soldiers belonging to B Company of the 2nd Battalion, the 24th (2nd Warwickshire) Regiment. On the basis of these facts the accurate identification of the individual men present during the action on 22 and 23 January 1879 would appear to be a relatively simple task; however, such is not the case.

During the years 1964–71, Zulu War historian Norman Holme researched various records in order to publish a definitive list of Rorke's Drift defenders, the results of which appeared in published form in 1971[1] and was based on two contemporary rolls of Rorke's Drift defenders, attributed to Lieutenant Chard and Colour Sergeant Bourne respectively. It was considered that these two documents represented the only authoritative sources of information, despite the fact that the lists failed to agree in a number of instances. In addition to the inaccuracies contained in both rolls, the fact that two such lists existed represented a puzzling anomaly. Neither roll was considered totally accurate, and in view of the conflicting information Holme undertook a complete re-investigation in respect of the Rorke's Drift defenders belonging to the 24th Regiment. Various documentary sources were used in this new work, with the result that several names have been amended and others excluded from the revised roll. The roll published earlier in this book is therefore an amended combination based upon the original lists accredited to Chard and Bourne.

The apparently original rolls of Rorke's Drift defenders were initially accepted, with reservations, in respect of a number of factors. Chard was a Royal Engineers officer and he had not spent any significant time at the mission station. He first arrived at Rorke's Drift late on 19 January and his acquaintance with Bromhead was therefore brief and informal; after all, it was Bromhead who was the officer commanding B Company, Chard merely had command of his handful of sappers who were based half a mile away at the river crossing into Zululand. Due to his seniority over Bromhead, Chard first assumed nominal responsibility for the mission station during the afternoon of 22 January to cover the temporary absence of the officer commanding, Major Spalding; this responsibility then became significant for the duration of the battle as Spalding had failed to return before the Zulus attacked.

Like many researchers and historians before him, Holme presumed that Chard had personally undertaken the compilation of the roll bearing his name; the fact that it was generally believed Chard had signed the document tended to impart a degree of authority to it. The roll is dated '3rd February 1879' and although this date may not be correct, it may be assumed that the document was compiled prior to the award of decorations for gallantry since the roll does not contain references to any of these awards. The general acceptance of the origin and authenticity of this roll is clearly not without justification, and had there been no other source of comparison, then the contents and authenticity would doubtless never have been disputed. A most important point relates to the fact that a large copy of the roll is mounted in a frame and displayed in the regimental museum of the South Wales Borderers (24th Foot). A facsimile of the roll is reproduced in *The South Wales Borderers 24th Foot 1689–1937* by Professor C.T. Atkinson (1937). Holme considered it unusual for Atkinson to have included the roll without making any reference to it in the text of his book. *Records of the 24th Regiment* by Paton, Glennie and Penn Symons, published in 1892, contains a list of casualties at Isandlwana, yet Chard's list of Rorke's Drift defenders is, curiously, neither included nor even mentioned. It seemed at the time impossible to account for the omission of this important roll, particularly in view of the fact that it had supposedly been in existence since 1879, and presumably would have been available to the authors of the book.

Similar problems exist in respect of the subsequent roll compiled by Frank Bourne. Bourne's document is dated 4 July 1910 and contains a reference to the effect:

> By Special Request, And In Order To Preserve A Record Of Those Who Took Part In The Defence, This Roll Was Prepared By Major F. Bourne (Late Colour-Sergeant 'B' Company) From The Regimental Pay List For January 1879, Kindly Placed At His Disposal By The Public Record Office.

As the former senior Non-Commissioned Officer of B Company, Bourne was eminently qualified to compile such a roll; he must necessarily have known many of the soldiers on a personal basis. In view of this, Holme considered it unusual that Bourne had not been called upon to provide information, at least in respect of his own company, for inclusion in Chard's roll. It is evident that Bourne cannot have been consulted in this matter; otherwise he would surely not have undertaken to compile a second list of defenders, as this would have represented a contradiction of information previously submitted by himself.

Bourne's knowledge of at least some of his men is confirmed by his reference to 1524 Private Joseph Bromwich as 'Bromatch'. This appears to have been the pronunciation used by the man himself when giving his name, as verified by his attestation document. Similarly Bourne was aware, when others were not, that 972 Private George Edwards had enlisted under an alias, his true name being Orchard. After a lapse of so many years it was thought unreasonable that Bourne would have remembered each and every man belonging to B Company. The pay list, which should have encompassed several months prior to January 1879, could have provided him with only slight assistance when preparing the roll as soldiers were frequently transferred on a temporary basis for other duties. Bourne's list of defenders is far less comprehensive than Chard's roll. This was thought to be the reason that Professor Atkinson included Chard's roll in his book. Obviously the roll compiled by Bourne could not have been included in

Historical Records of the 24th Regiment as this publication pre-dated the roll by some eighteen years. It has proved impossible to determine the source of the 'Special Request' that prompted Bourne to prepare his list, and it has been conjectured that the request may have been made as a result of dissatisfaction with Chard's roll.

Interestingly, a ledger *Records of the 2nd Battalion 24th Regiment* (Regimental Archive) states that: 'On the 14th October 1910, 4 copies of the Roll of B Company 2nd Battalion, who took part in the Defence of Rorke's Drift, were sent to the Officer i/c Records, Shrewsbury, for safe custody'. These copies were presumably copies of the newly compiled Roll by Major Bourne.

The above anomalies represented a series of interesting problems and Holme made only a brief mention of these factors in his original published work, since any elaboration would have provoked a number of questions for which Holme was unable to provide satisfactory answers. Having resolved to undertake further investigations in respect of these matters, Holme's preliminary investigations involved a re-examination of Chard's roll contained in the regimental museum at Brecon. First it was necessary to establish the date on which this document had come into the possession of the museum, and of equal importance, the provenance of the roll. The answer to these questions is contained in *The Journal of The South Wales Borderers* issue 7, dated 1935. The entry reads as follows:

> This roll [the 'Chard' roll] has been brought to light through the services of two gentlemen in South Africa, who have been indefatigable in their efforts to obtain it. The thanks of the Regiment are accorded to them for their trouble. The gentlemen in question are – Mr F. Avon of Malvern, Natal, and Colonel G. Molyneaux, CMG, DSO, of Natal.

Additional information concerning the roll was found in the museum accession book and this eventually yielded the following information in respect of the year 1935:

> Roll of all ranks, in manuscript, who were at Rorke's Drift (original and duplicate) from Mrs. Cantwell, 1935.

The hitherto unheard of duplicate was displayed in the officers' mess at Brecon. On examination it proved to be a photograph of the original roll and therefore was an exact duplicate of the one exhibited in the museum. The roll's wooden frame bore a silver plaque on which was inscribed:

> Copy of Lieutenant Chard's Roll of Officers, NCOs and Men Present at Rorke's Drift dated 3/2/1879. The original, which was presented to the Regiment by the Widow of Bombardier Cantwell, Royal Artillery through the Durban Light Infantry Comrades Association, is in the Regimental Museum at Brecon.

The fact that the documents had been presented in 1935, although no precise month was indicated, offered two possible solutions as to the reason why Professor Atkinson included the roll in his book, but failed to refer to it in the text. At that time the work must have been nearing completion, therefore it may have been difficult for Atkinson to insert retrospective comments appropriate to the roll. Alternatively, being aware of the source from which the roll came, Atkinson may have decided to refrain from an explanation of the matter.

It is an undeniable fact that Bombardier (Gunner) John Cantwell, RA, was present at the defence of Rorke's Drift, as he was awarded the Distinguished Conduct Medal for that action. He is noted in Chard's roll as 'Wounded' but there is no evidence whatsoever to support this statement. Cantwell's service documents reveal the following:

> John Cantwell was born at St James's, Dublin, Ireland; he was by trade a servant. He enlisted in the 9th Regiment of Foot on the 6th November 1868 and gave his age as twenty-three years 6 months. Cantwell transferred to the Royal Artillery on 1st April 1872 and joined N Battery, 5th Brigade on 1st July 1877. Having served at St. Helena, he arrived at the Cape of Good Hope on 9th January 1878, and subsequently took part in the advance into Zululand. Promoted Bombardier Wheeler on 29th July 1878, he reverted to Gunner on 21st January 1879. [Therefore, at the defence of Rorke's Drift his correct rank was that of Gunner.] Cantwell, his wife and daughter, returned to England on 31st March 1879

(P.E. Abbott 'N Bty, 5th Bde, RA, at Isandlwana', *Journal of the Society for Army Historical Research*, Vol. LVI.) Discharged at Woolwich on 19th July 1887 as medically unfit for further service. Intended place of residence: 8 Loop St. Pietermaritzburg, South Africa. Awarded the DCM for Rorke's Drift (Submitted to the Queen, 11/2/1880. RA Regimental Order No. 29, April 1880); South Africa Medal with clasp 1877–8–9; Long Service and Good Conduct Medal.

The Rorke's Drift roll of defenders, apparently authenticated by Chard's signature and correctly addressed to Colonel Glyn, was regarded by many as being an official document. The discovery that Cantwell, or to be more precise his widow, Caroline Margaret Cantwell, had been instrumental in providing the regimental museum with copies of the roll posed a question as to how the document had come into John Cantwell's possession. Consequently, in the belief that Chard's roll held by the regimental museum was a copy of an original official document, Holme commenced by endeavouring to establish the whereabouts of Chard's original roll. Though he was in possession of copies of the official correspondence relating to the Zulu War, Holme could find no written request for the submission of a list of names of those present at the defence of Rorke's Drift; Chelmsford had indeed made written requests, but these were not known to Holme at the time of his research.

Logic dictated that the Public Record Office (PRO) was the obvious repository for such a document. Accordingly Holme engaged three professional researchers (Mr Geoffrey Keay, Mrs Kay Twyman-Musgrave and Lieutenant Commander Michael Godfrey – the latter two were former members of staff at the Public Record Office), each working independently, to undertake the necessary work. After a lengthy interval of time, Holme received assurances that the roll was not to be found in the PRO. This fact having been established, further investigations were undertaken at the former Colonial Office, the regimental museum of the Royal Engineers, the War Office Library, the National Army Museum and the Royal Archives, but without success. A copy of the roll of Rorke's Drift defenders was finally located at the British Museum Library, but significantly this transpired to be Bourne's roll. Nothing was known of Chard's roll, therefore assistance was sought from the descendants of Lieutenant Chard. Lieutenant Colonel W.W.M. Chard and Mrs D. Phillips, who actually possessed living memories of John Rouse Merriott Chard, very kindly responded to Holme's request and searched through the papers formerly belonging to their forebear. There was neither trace nor mention of the Rorke's Drift roll.

As a result of these protracted investigations it was evident that the location of the original Chard roll was unknown. In consequence of this fact Holme again scrutinized the roll contained in the regimental museum. After some time he was able to formulate a number of conclusions regarding the document. To his untrained eye the manuscript appeared to consist of two distinctive styles of handwriting. The names of the garrison, with three notable exceptions, seemed to have been written in a conventional hand. A more ornate style was employed in the heading and sub-headings, and also in respect of the names of 'Lieutenant Chard (In Command),' 'Lieutenant Bromhead (Com'd B Comp)' and 'Bomb J. Cantwell.' These three names, and no others, were made more distinctive by being underlined.

It became increasingly evident to Holme that the roll and duplicate copy in the possession of the regimental museum represented the only known examples attributed to Chard. The number and significance of the various anomalies associated with the document aroused Holme's suspicions, regarding not only the authenticity but also the accuracy of the information on the roll. In view of the documents having originated from Cantwell's widow, it became a matter of necessity to confirm whether or not Chard had approved and signed the roll bearing his name. Mr Derek Davis, a well-known expert in forensic handwriting, most generously agreed to undertake an analysis of the roll. An authenticated sample of Chard's handwriting, including his signature, together with a photocopy of the Rorke's Drift roll was submitted. Holme considered the possibility that Lieutenant Bromhead may have been responsible for compiling the roll; accordingly, an authenticated sample of his handwriting was also submitted. Unfortunately Holme did not possess an example of Bombardier Cantwell's handwriting. Precise information and specific instructions regarding the work were submitted as follows:

Written instructions to examine photostat copies of historical documents relating to the defence of Rorke's Drift. To compare the handwriting on these documents and offer opinions as to authorship.

In due course Mr Davis produced a comprehensive report in which he stated:

The handwriting in each document was examined and notes made of the personal handwriting habits, tendencies and formation found. Examination of all notes allowed opinions to be formed as to specific authorship of the documents. In my considered opinion, one person wrote the whole of the Roll, including the headings and the signature of Lieutenant Chard. This includes the names that visually appear to be a different writing. The only clue that I can offer as to the production of the roll is that it is possible that a man from the 2/24th Regiment produced it – Due to the use of first names in that regiment. The only name that shows as carefully written is that of Private Michael Kiley, although this may be coincidence. The numbers of the men are mentioned in the 1st and 2/24th Regiment, but omitted from others.

As a result of the conclusions contained in the report, it is obvious that Chard did not sign the document; neither did Bromhead contribute to any part of the roll. Holme's attention was then given to the right-hand portion of the document that contains a return enumerating the strength and composition of the garrison, together with notes referring to those killed, wounded and died of wounds. This information, with the figures slightly amended, was contained in Chard's dispatch dated '25th Jan 1879' and correctly addressed to 'Colonel Glyn, CB.' It was evident that this was the only part of the roll of defenders that had been transmitted to higher authority. Assuming that Chard had ordered that the information be obtained for inclusion within his dispatch, then the person undertaking the task would presumably have first compiled a list of names, subdivided into regiments and corps etc. It would then have become a comparatively simple matter to extract the required information that could then have been presented in numerical form. The evidence for this is contained in the fact that each name appearing on the roll is numbered sequentially from '1' to '141' representing the figure given as the total strength of the garrison. It is a matter of conjecture as to the identity of the man who actually compiled the roll of Rorke's Drift defenders. Whoever this person was, he, for some unknown reason, provided Cantwell with a high degree of prominence in the roll, perhaps in the knowledge that once having been used for its intended purpose, the document would then become no longer of use. Further examination of the roll reveals it not to be a hastily scribbled note, rather is it a work bordering on draughtsmanship. The layout as a whole is neat, and the surrounding lining with its bastion shaped corners obviously took some time and care to execute. A difficult accomplishment given the acute shortage of writing paper and the conditions prevailing at Rorke's Drift during the seven days between the battle and the date attributed to the compilation of Chard's roll. Whatever the correct date for the compilation of the roll is, it pre-dates 29 April 1880, the date on which the DCM awarded to Cantwell was promulgated in Royal Artillery Regimental Orders.[2] Furthermore, the roll contains no mention of any of the other decorations awarded to certain members of the garrison.

During the course of Holme's research it was decided that the Rorke's Drift roll should be examined for traces of a watermark, thus establishing the date of manufacture of the paper on which it was written. Unfortunately, on Holme's pursuing the matter at the regimental museum, it was found that the roll was pasted to a cardboard backing and could not be removed. No doubt modern scientific methods could help establish the precise type and age of adhesive used, but the process in removing the roll could have resulted in damage to the document, therefore the matter had to be left in abeyance. In more recent times a professional paper restorer has examined the document. He concluded that the paper on which the roll is written was 'machine manufactured circa 1880', therefore it would be devoid of watermarks. In addition, the paper on which the original roll was written exhibited crease marks, thus indicating that the document had been subjected to folding. The crease marks were not visible on the photograph of the roll. It is impossible to determine the sources from which the roll was compiled. As previously stated, Colour Sergeant Bourne does not appear to have been involved in the compilation of the roll insofar as B company was concerned. It was Holme's personal opinion that the degree of authority attributed to Chard's roll of Rorke's Drift defenders is not supported by the evidence as described in the foregoing.

The list of defenders compiled by Major Bourne, as he then was, was totally unrelated to Chard's roll; therefore it represented an independent means of verifying a portion of the information contained in the latter document. Holme considered that the individuals named in both rolls were present at the action; however, the numerous instances of names appearing on one roll but not on the other constituted a series of anomalies. During the course of his investigations a fortunate coincidence revealed the whereabouts of Mrs Mary Frances Whitby, youngest daughter of Frank Bourne. Major Egerton of the regimental museum kindly provided the necessary assistance in communicating with Mrs Whitby, and as a result Holme was able to obtain from her a considerable amount of valuable and hitherto unknown information. The most important single aspect to emerge from this information was the fact that Frank Bourne had amended his personal copy of the roll previously compiled by himself. These amendments had been undertaken after the publication of Atkinson's book containing the 'Chard' roll. An examination of Bourne's amended roll revealed that the work was in Bourne's handwriting, as confirmed by Mrs Whitby, and each name had been examined and duly marked by Bourne, thus signifying his obvious agreement. Furthermore, Bourne had added most but not all the names previously omitted from his original roll. His failure to include certain individuals from Chard's roll disclosed his obvious lack of agreement regarding their presence at the action. Of equal significance was the fact that Bourne had not deleted one single name from his original roll, and there are indications that in part this may have been justified. For example, Chard's roll fails to include 1005 Private John Smith, who, according to his service papers, was undeniably present at the defence of Rorke's Drift. In view of the amendment undertaken by Bourne it was considered that there existed a closer relationship between his amended roll and Chard's roll. This provided a greater degree of confirmation in respect of the majority of individuals named in both documents. At least four men belonging to B Company were killed in action at Isandlwana. Two men who served in B Company at the defence of Rorke's Drift had items of equipment lost, and in one case later recovered, at Isandlwana. It is not unusual to discover items of field equipment at one camp whilst the owners of the material are elsewhere. This may indicate that the men concerned were by chance present at Rorke's Drift at the time of the Zulu attack. At the time in question B Company appears to have been a somewhat fragmented unit. It is possible that this factor, plus the passage of time in compiling the roll, contributed to the errors and omissions in Bourne's original roll. The importance of the amendments undertaken by Lieutenant Colonel Bourne is contained in the fact that Chard's roll had finally been examined by a known and extremely well qualified authority.

During the later stages of the investigation, F.W. David Jackson brought to Holme's attention the existence of yet another roll of Rorke's Drift defenders. This roll, signed by Lieutenant Colonel Dunbar, appeared in the *Natal Colonist* dated 15 January 1880. Having obtained a photocopy of the newspaper, Holme discovered that the roll had been specially prepared in connection with the 'Presentation of an Address by the Mayor of Durban', a copy of which was given to individual soldiers. This roll of defenders appeared to be based on Chard's roll and Holme concluded that the unknown compiler of the latter was likely to have been present with the battalion, or, alternatively, he had provided the information for Dunbar. Lieutenant Colonel Dunbar, who was then commanding the 2/24th, had signed the list of defenders that related exclusively to the survivors of B Company. No mention was made of the soldiers belonging to the 1/24th. Similarly the men who had served in other regiments and corps, both Imperial and Colonial, were likewise excluded. The honour conferred by the mayor and people of Durban was somewhat unfairly reserved for members of B Company.

After assessing the rolls of Rorke's Drift defenders, and taking into consideration not only the contents but also the evidence regarding the source of each document, Holme saw no reason to amend his former evaluation of those present at the action. As previously stated, this evaluation was based on a provisional acceptance of all the names appearing on the various rolls, research then being undertaken in each individual case. Very few soldiers' records of service refer specifically to the defence of Rorke's Drift, therefore alternative documentary sources have been utilized. In addition to the pay rolls, muster rolls, casualty lists and effects rolls, these included reports, official and otherwise, together with various reports, letters and narratives relating to the battle. The results of this work indicated that a number of individuals named in one or more of the original rolls were not present at the defence of Rorke's Drift, and in consequence their names have been omitted from Holme's roll. In certain instances, where entries in service documents have obviously been confused, there must remain an element of doubt and notes applicable to the cases have been included.

CHAPTER 15

The Rorke's Drift Medal Citations

With regard to the first awards of Zulu War Victoria Crosses, the *London Gazette* citations of 2 May 1879 read:

> The Queen has been graciously pleased to signify her intention to confer the decoration of the Victoria Cross on the under mentioned Officers and Soldiers of Her Majesty's Army, whose claims have been submitted for Her Majesty's approval, for their gallant conduct in the defence of Rorke's Drift, on the occasion of the attack by the Zulus, as recorded against their names.

LIEUTENANT JOHN ROUSE MERRIOTT CHARD,
5th Company Royal Engineers

LIEUTENANT GONVILLE BROMHEAD,
24th (2nd Warwickshire) Regiment

These two officers' names are forever linked together in one of the greatest feats of the British Army, the defence of Rorke's Drift.

The mission station by the west bank of the Buffalo river was taken over by the military as a commissariat stores and hospital and it was from there that Chelmsford's invasion force crossed into Zululand. On the morning of 22 January 1879, having been left behind at Rorke's Drift and without clear orders, Lieutenant Chard and his four sappers rode to the camp at Isandlwana to obtain clarification of their duties. Chard's personal orders were to return to Rorke's Drift and keep the ferry ponts in working order and to mount guard over them. As he left Isandlwana he noticed a large force of Zulus gathering in the distant hills. Chard was probably the last man to leave Isandlwana before the Zulus overwhelmed the camp.

On his return to Rorke's Drift Chard reported to Major Spalding, the commander, and related what he had seen at Isandlwana; furthermore, he expressed his concern that in the event of an attack he would be unable to defend the ponts until the replacement troops arrived. The company that had been detailed for this defence were several days overdue, so Spalding decided to ride to Helpmekaar to hurry things along. Before he rode off he gave command of the camp to Chard.

Less than two hours later the Zulus attacked the mission station with a force of 4,500 warriors. By comparison, Chard and Bromhead had just 100 fit and thirty-five sick soldiers with which to defend the position. The Zulus commenced their attack at about 4 p.m. on 22 January and sustained their attack until the following morning when Lord Chelmsford relieved the post. For saving the post from the Zulus the two officers were subsequently recommended for the award of the Victoria Cross. Curiously, their well-earned awards were both highly irregular; the original recommendation for the Rorke's Drift awards of the Victoria Crosses was in respect of Corporal Allen and Privates Hook, Hitch, Williams and the two Joneses and was submitted by Lieutenant Bromhead in his capacity as commander of B Company, through the correct military channels via Colonel Glyn, his commanding officer. Glyn forwarded these recommendations to Chelmsford on 15 February without further comment by Glyn. It was only when this report reached Chelmsford that he personally added the names of Chard and Bromhead, without the necessary recommendations or referring the matter back to Glyn. Both officers received their Victoria Crosses from General Wolseley while still serving in Zululand; Bromhead at Utrecht on 11 September 1879, Chard at St Paul's on 16 July 1879. Their joint citation, prepared in London and not by Chelmsford, reads:

> For their gallant conduct at the defence of Rorke's Drift, on the occasion of the attack by the Zulus on the 22nd and 23rd January, 1879.
>
> The Lieutenant General commanding the troops reports that, had it not

been for the fine example and behaviour of these two officers under the most trying circumstances, the defence of Rorke's Drift post would not have been conducted with that intelligence and tenacity which so essentially characterised it. The Lieutenant General adds, that its success must, to a great degree, be attributable to the two young Officers who exercised the chief Command on the occasion in question.

ACTING ASSISTANT COMMISSARY JAMES DALTON,
COMMISSARIAT AND TRANSPORT CORPS

The two men who managed to escape via Fugitives' Drift had brought a written message from Isandlwana warning the Rorke's Drift garrison of the Zulus' approach. Consulting together, Chard and Bromhead were persuaded by Dalton that it was too dangerous to attempt a retreat to Helpmekaar and risk being attacked in the open. They would not be able to move quickly as the sick from the hospital had to be evacuated and the considerable amount of ammunition and stores would have to be abandoned to the Zulus. The best option was to stay and fight from a good defensive position; something Commissary James Dalton had already set about constructing with piled sacks of corn, biscuit boxes and wagons.

When the Ninth Frontier War broke out in 1877, Dalton came out of retirement and was appointed to the rather cumbersome rank of acting assistant commissary, which gave him officer status.

At this time, Rorke's Drift was home to approximately eighty-four men of B Company 2/24th, thirty-six sick or injured men in the hospital, three Royal Engineers, three Commissariat, four medics and one detached man of the Buffs; in all, a total of about 140 men. In addition, there were between 200 and 300 African recruits of the Natal Native Contingent. With so many hands, the barricades were all but completed by the time the Zulus appeared. Meanwhile, there was a succession of exhausted and demoralized fugitives passing by who tried to persuade the defenders to run and save their lives. When a large body of Native Horse were seen to head up the road to Helpmekaar, it was too much for the NNC who, with their colonial officer and NCOs, deserted en masse. This defection meant that the perimeter was too large to defend so a second defensive line was hurriedly constructed, leaving the hospital out on a limb. Both Chard and Bromhead assisted Dalton to organize the men around the perimeter, making sure there would be a constant supply of ammunition. As the Zulus attacked, Dalton occupied himself around the barricades, encouraging the men and taking shots where necessary. Then, as he leaned over the parapet to take aim, he was hit by a bullet that passed through his right shoulder. Surgeon Reynolds rendered him first aid and after a short rest Dalton was back passing ammunition and offering advice to the hard-pressed defenders. After the war James Dalton was promoted to commissariat officer, but he was put on half pay and returned to England. South Africa was too much of a magnet for him and he returned a few years later and took an interest in a mining company. He was suddenly taken ill and died on 17 January 1887, aged only 54. The citation for Dalton's Victoria Cross was dated 17 November 1879 and reads:

> For his conspicuous gallantry during the attack on Rorke's Drift by the Zulus on the night of the 22nd January 1879, when he actively superintended the work of defence, and was amongst the foremost of those who received the first attack at the corner of the hospital, when the deadliness of his fire did great execution, and the mad rush of the Zulus met its first check, and where by his cool courage he saved the life of a man of the Army Hospital corps by shooting the Zulu, who, having seized the muzzle of the man's rifle, was in the act of assegaing him.
>
> This officer, to whose energy much of the defence of the place was due, was severely wounded during the contest, but still continued to give the same example of cool courage.

PRIVATE JOHN WILLIAMS, 2/24th
PRIVATE HENRY HOOK, 2/24th
PRIVATE WILLIAM JONES, 2/24th
PRIVATE ROBERT JONES, 2/24th
CORPORAL WILLIAM WILSON ALLEN, 2/24th
PRIVATE FREDERICK HITCH, 2/24th

The defence of the hospital was a battle within a battle. The defenders were mostly isolated from each other by walls and partitions so individual soldiers fought without so much as an NCO in command. At first their fire from the loopholes was effective but once the Zulus had managed to reach the outside walls, the defenders felt their isolation. The Zulus set fire to the roof thatch, which forced some of the defenders to retreat to other rooms. Privates Williams and Hook found themselves in the same room with the Zulus breaking down the door. Using a pickaxe Williams knocked a hole in the far wall, while Hook, using his bayonet, kept the Zulus from entering. As the last patient was dragged through the escape hole, Hook jumped through and joined them in the next room. With Hook defending this hole, Williams again picked a hole in the far wall and knocked through into a small room occupied by Privates William and Robert Jones. They had been defending this room for some time and had managed to get most of the patients out through the window, while taking turns in preventing the Zulus entering.

Well defended though they were, the soldiers around the perimeter were taking casualties, mostly from gunfire from the Oskarsberg. Corporal Allen was one of the sharpshooters who tried to dislodge the snipers from their rocky cover. In doing so, he exposed himself to fire over a considerable period of time even after he was hit in the right arm by a Zulu bullet.

By this time the rest of the defenders had retreated to the new perimeter, leaving defenders and patients with 30 yards of open ground to cross under heavy fire and the threat of being stabbed by the pressing Zulus. Their colleagues laid down covering fire while both Corporal Allen and Private Hitch crossed the yard to assist in bringing back the wounded and sick. It was a miracle that so many did escape, thanks in the main to the bravery and coolness of four humble privates.

Although wounded, both Hook and Robert Jones joined the rest of the company in continuing their desperate defence. With nightfall the fire from the hospital illuminated the dark and helped the defenders to see any approaching Zulus. Hitch was very prominent during the battle; he was stationed on the thatched roof of the hospital as a lookout and was the first to see the approaching Zulus. He was then sent to help man the weakest part of the defences, the veranda of the hospital. Although the ground sloped away quite steeply in front of the hospital, there had not been enough time to build up the barrier to more than waist height. Also, the warriors could creep up closely through the undergrowth before hurling themselves up the slope. The fixed bayonet soon proved just how effective a weapon it was in a tight defensive role. Most of the fighting here was hand to hand, the defenders having little time to reload as wave upon wave of Zulus charged them. Hitch recalled that one large warrior grabbed his rifle and struggled to disarm him. Managing to slip a cartridge into the breech, Hitch fired point-blank and dislodged his assailant.

The fighting had been going on for about an hour and a half and the mounting toll of casualties persuaded Chard to withdraw to the second line of defence, thus abandoning the area between the hospital and the storehouse. The Zulus could not occupy this open ground but could get to the barricades and put down deadly fire. At the most exposed part of the wall, Hitch and Bromhead fought alongside each other, while comrades fell dead or wounded. Finally Hitch, too, was hit in the shoulder, which shattered the bone. Despite this terrible wound, Hitch managed to remove his tunic and strap his wounded arm under his waist-belt. He borrowed Bromhead's revolver and, with Bromhead's assistance in loading it, carried on firing. He was also later seen delivering ammunition to his comrades.

By being forced to withdraw to the inner defence line, Chard had effectively left the occupants of the hospital to fend for themselves. It should be remembered, however, that the events within the hospital were taking place at the same time as those related above.

The attacks became more sporadic and the last serious attempt by the Zulu to rush the barricades was about 11 p.m. by which time the opposing sides were both physically and emotionally spent.

The soldiers had been firing almost continually for at least six hours. Their hearing was dulled; their heads were pounding, their shoulders were badly bruised from the notoriously heavy recoil of their Martini-Henry rifles and their hands were blistered by the overheated barrels. But still they could not relax their guard one moment during the long night. A flurry of shots were fired at them around 2 a.m., which they later discovered was the time the Zulus began to withdraw; and by dawn the Zulus had gone.

The citations for the above read:

PRIVATE JOHN WILLIAMS

Private John Williams was posted with private Joseph Williams and Private Horrigan, 1st Battalion 24th Regiment, in a distant room of the hospital, which they held for more than one hour, so long as they had a round of ammunition left: as communication was for the time cut off, the Zulus were enabled to advance and burst open the door; they dragged out Private Joseph Williams and two of the patients, and assagaied them. Whilst the Zulus were occupied with the slaughter of these men, a lull took place, during which Private John Williams, who, with two patients, were the only men left alive in this ward, succeeded in knocking a hole in the partition, and in taking the two patients into the next ward, where he found private Hook.

John Williams lived to be the last surviving Rorke's Drift VC. He served in India during the period 1880–83 and then in various volunteer battalions until discharged. Because of the events of 22 January, his hair turned prematurely white. This appears to have been the only effect the battle had on him. When the First World War broke out Williams volunteered for duty at the age of 57, and was taken on as recruiting sergeant, Brecon Barracks. Within a few weeks he had lost a son killed in action during the retreat from Mons. After the war, he was still associated with the regiment when he was kept on the civilian staff at Brecon. When he died on 25 November 1932 he was given a lavish military funeral in keeping with such an extraordinary record of service. He was buried in St Michael's Churchyard, Llantarnam, Wales.

PRIVATE HENRY HOOK

These two men together, one man working whilst the other man fought and held the enemy at bay with his bayonet, broke through three more partitions, and were thus enabled to bring eight patients through a small window into the inner line of defence.

Henry Hook uniquely received his Victoria Cross at the site of Rorke's

Drift from Sir Garnet Wolseley. He is said to have flinched when his medal was pinned to his tunic as the medal clasp also pierced his breast. The medal fastening at that time was a rather vicious-looking double prong designed so that the queen could dispense the award with one hand while on horseback. It was not till later that a safer brooch fastening was fitted. Along with most of the surviving defenders, Hook had to endure weeks of privation and hardship as they slept rough at Helpmekaar in cold and wet conditions. This, as much as the actual battle, probably prompted him to purchase his discharge and return to London. He joined the British Museum staff and was employed as a cloakroom attendant; in 1893 he again met Wolseley when he visited the museum. Hook remained at the museum until ill health forced his retirement in 1904. He returned to his native Churcham in Gloucestershire, where he died the following year.

PRIVATE WILLIAM JONES and PRIVATE ROBERT JONES

In another ward, facing the hill, Private William Jones and Private Robert Jones defended the post to the last, until six out of the seven patients had been removed. The seventh, Sergeant Maxfield, 2nd Battalion 24th Regiment, was delirious with fever. Although they had previously dressed him, they were unable to induce him to move. When Private Robert Jones returned to endeavour to carry him away, he found him being stabbed by the Zulus as he lay on his bed.

William Jones was invalided home suffering from chronic rheumatism, a condition that led to his discharge in 1880. He received his Victoria Cross from the queen. Unable to find regular work, he performed in theatres, reenacting the defence of Rorke's Drift. He even appeared with Buffalo Bill's Wild West Show when it toured Britain in the 1880s. Labouring jobs, when he could find work, followed. Poverty, however, forced him to pawn his Cross, which he was never able to redeem. By 1910 recurring nightmares of his ordeal were making him act irrationally. One night he took his small granddaughter from her bed in the belief that the Zulus were attacking and on another occasion he was found wandering the back streets of Manchester. He died confused and in great poverty. He was buried in Bradford

Cemetery, Manchester, on 21 April 1913.

Robert Jones, William's comrade in the hospital, also had a tragic end. Despite receiving four wounds, he soon recovered and went back on active duty. He received his Victoria Cross at the same time as Major Bromhead; he returned to the regiment and served in India 1880–81. After years in the army reserve, he was discharged and went to work as a labourer for Major de la Hay in Peterchuch, Herefordshire. Bouts of depression and headaches made Jones increasingly turn to drink for solace. During the summer of 1898 he suffered a fit, which was followed by a blinding headache. Borrowing his employer's gun, Jones said he was going to shoot crows. A shot was heard from the garden and a maid found his body. He had apparently committed suicide to end his terrible anguish, but suicides were generally excluded from burial in consecrated ground. The authorities partially relented: Robert Jones VC was buried in the churchyard of Peterchurch in Herefordshire, but to this day his headstone still faces away from the other graves to signify the nature of his death.

CORPORAL WILLIAM ALLEN and PRIVATE FREDERICK HITCH

It was chiefly due to the courageous conduct of these men that communication with the hospital was kept up at all. Holding together at all costs a most dangerous post, raked in reverse by the enemy's fire from the hill, they were both severely wounded, but their determined conduct enabled the patients to be withdrawn from the hospital, and when incapacitated by their wounds from fighting, they continued, as soon as their wounds had been dressed, to serve out ammunition to their comrades during the night.

William Allen was invalided home because of his wound, which never really healed. As a consequence he received his Victoria Cross from the queen at Windsor Castle. He served on as a sergeant-instructor of musketry in the 4th Volunteer Battalion of the South Wales Borderers. He died at Monnow Street, Monmouth on 12 March 1890, aged only 46 years, from influenza.

Frederick Hitch was also sent home with Allen. His wound was severe and some thirty-nine pieces of bone had to be removed. He, too, received his

Victoria Cross from the Sovereign at a ceremony held in the hospital. He was medically discharged and joined the Corps of Commissionaires. In 1901 his VC was snatched off his coat and a replacement was presented to him seven years later. He later became a London cab driver and died at home during a taxi strike in 1913. At his funeral, as well as family and military representatives, an estimated 1,500 cabbies paid their respects. His medals were purchased in June 1906 by Philip Wilkins, and they are now deposited at the regimental museum at Brecon.

SURGEON JAMES HENRY REYNOLDS,
Army Medical Department

This 35-year-old Irishman had served in the tropics for many years. He had come to South Africa with the 1/24th in 1875 and was experienced enough to treat some battle wounds but not on the scale or under conditions he was about to experience. It was about 4.30 p.m. that the first Zulus were seen approaching from the shoulder of the Oskarsberg hill which loomed over the mission station to the south. As the Zulus extended to surround the defenders, the soldiers opened fire at about 500 yards and battle commenced.

The Zulus had no plan and attacked in a headlong rush, probing for a weak point. The soldiers were heartened to see how many warriors they were killing, but such was their bravery and ferociousness, they kept coming on until they reached the barricades. It then became a primitive struggle of assegai and bayonet, knobkerrie and rifle butt; slashing, stabbing, clubbing and firing at point-blank range. The casualties were not carried to the hospital as portrayed in the film *ZULU*, but were treated in a makeshift redoubt in front of the storehouse by Surgeon Reynolds and his staff. When he was not tending the wounded, Reynolds delivered ammunition through the window of the hospital, which left him very exposed. In fact a bullet passed through his helmet. Dangerous and bloody though the fighting was on the perimeter, the events that unfolded in the hospital were even more dramatic.

For his conspicuous gallantry he was gazetted on 17 June 1879 to receive the Victoria Cross. He was also mentioned in dispatches and promoted to the rank of surgeon major with effect from 23 January 1879. After the battle he remained at Rorke's Drift and then joined the second invasion of Zululand. He took part in the battle of Ulundi and on 16 July 1879 at St Paul's in Zululand, Lord Wolseley presented him and the recently promoted Major Chard with their Victoria Crosses. Reynolds lived a long and prosperous life until his death in 1932, a month after his eighty-eighth birthday. He was buried at Kensal Green, London. His Victoria Cross is held by the Royal Army Medical Corps Museum near Guildford.

CORPORAL CHRISTIAN FERDINAND SCHIESS,
NATAL NATIVE CONTINGENT

One of the patients in the hospital was a 23-year-old Swiss who was laid up with either bad blisters, a gunshot wound or a spear wound in the foot (various accounts). An orphan, he was brought up at Bergdorf near Berne in Switzerland and had joined the French Army at the age of 15 and seen action in the Franco-Prussian War. Coming to South Africa, he had joined the 2nd Battalion, 3rd NNC as a corporal. Early in the battle Frederick, as he preferred to call himself, had limped out of the hospital to take up a position at the barricades.

Chard observed Schiess take careful aim on some of the enemy who were causing problems. Directly on the other side of the wall a Zulu fired almost point-blank and blew off his hat. Schiess immediately sprang up and bayoneted the Zulu, shot another and bayoneted a third. He then took a painful gunshot wound on his instep but fought on like a demon.

Frederick Schiess was the first man serving with a locally raised force to be awarded the Victoria Cross. The colonial authorities brought pressure to bear on the British government, who overcame the objections of the War Office, to break the British-only policy when awarding the Victoria Cross. After the war he worked at the telegraph office in Durban but by 1884 he was out of work and destitute. Sick through exposure, he took the offer of a free passage to England in the hope of better things. Sadly, he died off the coast of West Africa and was buried at sea aged only 28 years. No photograph exists of Schiess; his Victoria Cross can be seen on display at the National Army Museum.

The captain's log of HMS *Serapis* reads:

Sunday, 14th December, 1884

10.20 a.m. Departed this life Mr. F.C. Schiess, VC

5.10 p.m. Stopped. Committed to the Deep the remains of the late Mr. Schiess, VC

5.15 Proceeded

Ship's Noon observed Position: Lat S. 13.00: Long W. 7.24

PRIVATE SAMUEL WASSALL,
80th (SOUTH STAFFORDSHIRE REGIMENT)

Although not strictly a Rorke's Drift award, Wassall won his medal at exactly the same time and within sight of Rorke's Drift. His award was the only other Victoria Cross awarded at the time for 22 January 1879.

When Lord Chelmsford left his base camp at Isandlwana to reinforce the mounted patrols he had sent out the previous day, he left behind a large widely spread camp at the base of the mountain. Private Wassall, an excellent horseman, was one of the Imperial Mounted Infantry (Carrington's Horse), who had been left in the main camp by Chelmsford. Having no particular duty, he and his fellow Mounted Infantrymen were stood down and in camp when the Zulus struck. As the right flank gave way it became 'every man for himself'. Wassall, in shirtsleeves and without a weapon, caught a small Basuto pony and joined the ranks of those desperately trying to escape over the narrow pass to the safety of Helpmekaar via Rorke's Drift. Only a few were able to reach safety by this route before the Zulu right horn had reached this escape route and had advanced around the mountain to cut off all retreat. There was no alternative but to head off across rough country and face swimming the Buffalo river.

With the Zulus in close pursuit and due to the steep hills on either side, the escapees had little option but to follow a hazardous 5-mile route that led them to a spot known today as Fugitives' Drift. All along the route men were dying as the Zulus overtook and killed them but a number of mounted men did reach the river, including Private Wassall. What he found was a river in full spate and, in normal circumstances, unthinkable to attempt to cross. With Zulus opening fire and closing fast, Wassall urged his pony into the torrent. About halfway across he heard a cry and saw Private Westwood of his regiment being swept round in a raging whirlpool. Despite the approaching Zulus, Wassall turned his mount and returned to the bank, coolly tied his horse to a bush and waded in after Westwood. Reaching him, Wassall dragged the half-drowned man to the bank and hauled him onto his pony. Then, pursued by a hail of bullets and spears, pony and men plunged back into the river and managed to reach the far bank, scrambled up the steep sides of the gorge and staggered on to Helpmekaar. The next day Wassall was back in the saddle and was re-posted to the Northern Column where he saw further action at Hlobane and Khambula.

He received his Victoria Cross at Pietermaritzburg a few weeks later; he was, at the age of 23, the youngest recipient of the award. After he left the army he married, raised a family and lived out his life in Barrow-in-Furness until his death in 1927. He was the only survivor of Isandlwana to be awarded a VC.

LIEUTENANT TEIGNMOUTH MELVILL 1/24th
LIEUTENANT NEVILL JOSIAH COGHILL 1/24th

There were several double acts during the Zulu War that resulted in the Victoria Cross award (as with Chard and Bromhead). Although not strictly Rorke's Drift medals, the awards to Coghill and Melvill are probably the most celebrated and were the result of actions at exactly the same time and within sight of Rorke's Drift.

As the Zulus broke through on the British right flank at Isandlwana, Melvill took the Queen's Colour and carried it out of the camp to safety. The Colour was in a black leather case at the end of the long staff, a clumsy object for a rider to handle at the best of times, especially when harried by a determined and fast closing enemy.

Melvill left the camp on horseback in the company of Lieutenant Walter Higginson, 3rd Battalion Natal Native Contingent and they followed the cross-country trail of the other fugitives. Contrary to popular belief, Coghill did not accompany Melvill and each descended into the Buffalo river gorge by a different route; the first time they met that day was in the swirling river.

It was unfortunate for Coghill that he was left behind at Isandlwana; he was Colonel Glyn's orderly officer and would have accompanied Lord Chelmsford's column but for the effects of a previous accident. The question has subsequently been raised about Coghill's actions: as a serving officer of the 24th, should his first duty have been to remain with his regiment? Instead he joined the disorganized every-man-for-himself rabble that headed off across country and away from the battle. Nevertheless, his bravery in returning to save his drowning brother officer is unquestioned.

The fugitives had to run a gauntlet of Zulus, who were not only chasing from behind but also attacking from the flanks. The fugitives on foot were quickly overwhelmed and even those on horseback who could not manage more than a cautious trot over the rocky ground were run down and killed. Somehow the three officers variously and independently managed to reach the Buffalo river, closely pressed by the Zulus. Coghill plunged into the torrent ahead of Melvill and attained the Natal bank. While pausing for breath, he looked back and saw the other two in trouble. Higginson was unhorsed and clinging to a rock in midstream. Melvill, still holding on to the Colour that had unbalanced him, was floundering in the river and being swept towards the rock sheltering Higginson. Higginson tried to help Melvill but the current was too strong and both officers lost their grip on the rock and the Colour was lost.

Seeing their predicament and ignoring the Zulus who were firing from the far bank, Coghill turned to ride back into the river. Almost immediately his horse was shot and killed. Despite this setback he swam out to Melvill and Higginson and under heavy fire, all three managed to swim to the Natal bank. With Melvill exhausted and Coghill lame, Higginson set off to find some horses. Exhaustion, heavy wet clothing and Coghill's crippled leg meant that he and Melvill could only climb a short distance before they were caught by previously friendly local natives and forced to make their last stand, their backs against a large rock.

Some days later, a patrol found their bodies together with a number of dead natives, evidence that Melvill and Coghill had sold their lives dearly. Their attempts to save the Colour and the manner of their deaths made them national heroes but there was no provision in the warrant for posthumously awarding the Victoria Cross. On the contrary, there was some ill feeling that resulted in a sarcastic statement by General Wolseley when he visited their graves. He merely commented that it was 'unfortunate that they had not died on the battlefield'.

On 2 May 1879 two official memoranda appeared in the *London Gazette*. One read:

> On account of the gallant efforts made by Lt Melvill to save the Queen's Colour of his regiment, he would have been recommended to her Majesty for the Victoria Cross had he survived.

The item concerning Lieutenant Coghill read:

> On account of his heroic conduct in endeavouring to save his brother Officer's life, he would have been recommended to Her Majesty for the Victoria Cross had he survived.

It was not until the Boer War and the posthumous VC awarded to Lieutenant Frederick Roberts, the son of Field Marshal Lord Roberts, that the relatives of Melvill and Coghill lobbied for the retrospective award. It still took a direct petition by Melvill's widow to Edward VII before the awards were finally made on 15 January 1907, nearly twenty-eight years to the day of the anniversary of their sacrifice. (Incidentally, they were not the only Victoria Cross winners to perish at Isandlwana. Private William Griffiths 2/24th, who won his VC in the Andaman Islands in 1867, also died.)

CHAPTER 16

Origins and History
of the 24th Regiment

It is generally acknowledged that until the twentieth century regiments were raised in troubled times, and the birth of the 24th Foot was in accordance with this dictum. It was from 8 March 1689 that King William and Queen Mary, recently arrived from Holland, reigned uneasily over a Britain still recovering from James II's determined bid to retain the throne of England in the revolution of 1688. That revolution led to war with Louis XIV of France and for Britain to fight the war it was necessary to raise troops. King William signed the proclamation for the raising of ten 'Regiments of Foot' and Sir Edward Dering of Pluckley, a Kentish baronet, was given the task of raising one of these regiments from Kent, as recorded by the memorial stone in Pluckley church that commemorates the event. In 1703 this Kentish regiment began its collection of battle honours under the colonelcy of John Churchill, the Duke of Marlborough, with deeds such as Ramillies, Blenheim, Malplaquet and Oudenarde being recorded on the regiment's colour. In 1751 the regiment became known as the 24th Regiment of Foot. In those days there were few permanent training depots and most regiments recruited soldiers from their immediate locality. The events in Scotland (in the 1750s) and Ireland (in the 1830s) created the need for sufficient soldiers and the growth of the large cities provided the source of the majority of recruits for the British Army. Wales was sparsely populated until the expansion of the coal, iron and steel industries in the late nineteenth century; for example, until 1880, Brecon had a static population of only 5,000 people covering a wide rural area. In 1881 Brecon still had a population of only 5,033 (2,551 males of all ages) while the county of Brecknock had a total population of 54,131. The number of men of recruiting age was, therefore, very small.

After their return from the American War of Independence, the 24th Regiment of Foot was based in Warwickshire. On 31 August 1782 a royal warrant conferred county titles on all regiments not already possessed of special designations such as 'The Queen's' or 'The King's Own'. The 24th Regiment was accordingly given the title '2nd Warwickshire' and was ordered to send a recruiting party to Tamworth as it was intended that regiments should cultivate a recruiting connection with the counties whose names they took. No special link with the County Militia was established nor were any depots or permanent recruiting centres set up. At the same time the 6th Regiment of Foot, a separate regiment, was given the title '1st Warwickshire'. The 6th Regiment of Foot subsequently became the Royal Warwickshire Regiment (1892), the Royal Warwickshire Fusiliers (1963) and The Regiment of Fusiliers (1968). The 24th Regiment has never been part of the 6th Regiment of Foot.

The 24th Regimental depot was founded at Brecon in 1873 and had recruited in the counties of Brecknock, Cardigan and Radnor as well as the neighbouring English counties for the six years immediately prior to the Zulu War with most of the recruits going to the local 2nd Battalion. The 1st Battalion, though, had seen continuous service in various Mediterranean garrisons for the eight years prior to arriving in South Africa on 4 February 1875. At this point in time the 1st Battalion's link with Wales was, at the very best, tenuous; indeed, its regimental march was the 'Warwickshire Lads', composed for the Shakespearean Centenary Celebrations at Stratford-on-Avon in 1769.

Following the Zulu War the 1st Battalion returned to England. Queen Victoria expressed a wish to see the Isandlwana Colour, and with her own hands placed upon it a wreath of immortelles, directing that a silver replica should always be borne round the staff of the Queen's Colour of both battalions, to commemorate the devotion of Lieutenants Melvill and Coghill and the noble defence of Rorke's Drift by B Company of the 2nd Battalion. This silver wreath, with the sphinx won in Egypt, was adopted in 1898 as the cap badge of the regiment. It also appeared as the centre badge of the regimental colour, encircling the Roman numeral XXIV. This Queen's Colour was carried by the 1st Battalion until 1933, and now hangs in the regimental chapel in Brecon Cathedral. Beneath it, in an oaken case, is Queen Victoria's original wreath.

The regiment was honoured to carry the title 24th (The 2nd Warwickshire) Regiment of Foot until 1 July 1881 when measures were taken to give county names to infantry regiments of line. The 24th Regiment thus became the South Wales Borderers. This was originally the title of one of the militia battalions that since 1873 had been under the command of the officer commanding the brigade depot at Brecon.

In 1936 the Chillianwallah Colours of the 24th Regiment that were carried in the Second Sikh War of 1849 and which had been laid up in St Mary's Church, Warwick since 1868, were removed to the regimental chapel in Brecon Cathedral. The church council of St Mary's Church, understandably, was not inclined to part with the colours but the regiment applied for a faculty for their removal. The case was argued before the Chancellor of the Diocese of Coventry on 6 May 1936, and judgement was given in the regiment's favour. The decision was made on 26 July 1936 and the colours needed to be restored before 23 August, the date set for a regimental reunion. At a cost of 12 guineas, the Royal School of Needlework set to work restoring the colours. They met the deadline and, with full military ceremony, the colours were laid up at Brecon. If fate had taken another turn the 24th might have become an established regiment of Warwickshire. The spirit of the 24th Regiment is strongly maintained by the Royal Regiment of Wales (24th/41st Foot). It is one of the outstanding regiments of the British Army and one with a distinct Welsh flair. Its motto is proudly displayed on the regimental colour – 'Gwell Angau na Chywilydd' – Death rather than Dishonour.

At the time of the Zulu War, mention of Wales as an entity did not feature in any official or regimental documentation or reports. Following Isandlwana, a famous music hall song, 'The Gallant 24th' by Lee and Green, included the words:

In Zululand the Twenty-Fourth, a gallant little band
Of British soldiers bold and true, 'gainst legions made a stand.
Surrounded by their dusky foe, shut in both left and right,
'Gainst fearful odds they fought as none but Englishmen can fight.

The name they made will never fade
And all with pride will tell
How England's gallant 24th
As heroes fought and fell.

Private Robert Jones VC 2/24th, born at Monmouth, was awarded the Victoria Cross for his part in the defence of Rorke's Drift. When recounting his experiences he innocently wrote in the language of his time,

On the 22nd January 1879, the Zulus attacked us, we being only a small band of English soldiers. My thought was only to fight as an English soldier ought to for his most gracious Sovereign, Queen Victoria, and for the benefit of old England.

The emphasis on 'English' is understandable, simply because the language of the time emphasized the term 'Anglo' as meaning things 'British' and the term 'English' was similarly used in everyday parlance. In reference to the 24th Regiment, Lord Chelmsford's copious records always used the term 'English' as he did when referring to all matters relevant to the United Kingdom. In view of the subsequent change in designation of the 24th into the South Wales Borderers in 1881, it is worth considering the actual representation of Welshmen then serving in the two battalions at Isandlwana and Rorke's Drift. With regard to the 1/24th lost at Isandlwana, there was virtually no connection with Wales, as the battalion had neither served in the UK since 1867 or ever recruited from Wales. Indeed, when the news of the loss of the 1/24th reached Britain, the *Daily News* commented: 'Death had prematurely visited hundreds of peaceful and happy homes in England', which sadly ignored the high proportion of Irishmen serving in both battalions.

The 2/24th certainly had a small proportion of Welshmen serving in its ranks; but there were many more Irishmen while the greater number by far were English, a fact that is reflected by the composition of B Company 2/24th and the four soldiers of the 1/24th when they defended Rorke's Drift:

1st Battalion

England	1	Staffordshire
Scotland	1	Midlothian
Ireland	1	Dublin
Other	1	Peshawar, India (of British parents)
Total 4		

2nd Battalion

England: 47

1 each from Cheshire, Gloucestershire, Leicestershire, Nottinghamshire, Surrey, Sussex, Worcestershire and Yorkshire

2 each from Kent and Middlesex

3 each from Herefordshire and Warwickshire

4 from Somerset

9 from Lancashire

11 from London

5 from Monmouthshire

Ireland: 13

1 each from Antrim and Limerick

2 each from Clare, Cork, Kilkenny and Tipperary

3 from Dublin

Wales: 5

1 each from Breconshire and Pembrokeshire

3 from Glamorgan

Other: 1

(France – of British parents)

Re-formation of the 1st Battalion – Subsequent Services of both Battalions to the End of the War.

As soon as tidings of the disaster at Isandlwana reached England, volunteers were called for to re-form the 1st Battalion, and a draft of 520 non-commissioned officers and men, furnished by the following regiments: 1st Battalion 8th, 1st Battalion 11th, 1st Battalion 18th, 2nd Battalion 18th, 1st Battalion 23rd, 2nd Battalion 25th, 32nd, 37th, 38th, 45th, 50th, 55th, 60th, 86th, 87th, 103rd, 108th and 109th was collected at Aldershot, under the command of Lieutenant Colonel H.F. Davies, Grenadier Guards. The draft embarked at Woolwich, in the *Clyde*, on 1 March 1879; Captains Brander and Farquhar Glennie and Lieutenant T.J. Halliday, 24th regiment, and a number of special service officers proceeded with the draft.

The *Clyde* had an uneventful voyage until 4 April 1879, when she ran upon a reef 70 miles east of Simon's Bay, between Dyer's Island and the mainland. The sea was perfectly smooth at the time, and the troops were all got safely on shore by 11.30 a.m., except two companies which were left on board two hours longer to look after the baggage. These companies had not long landed when, with the rising of the tide, the ship slid off the reef and suddenly went down, all clothing, books etc. being lost in her. The chief officer of the *Clyde* had previously been dispatched to Simon's Bay, where he arrived at 10 p.m. the same night, and early on the morrow the *Tamar* arrived, took the draft on board, returned to Simon's Bay, and on 7 April started for Durban, arriving there on the 11th. The troops were at once landed and marched up country, reaching Pietermaritzburg on 18 April; Ladysmith, 29 April; and Dundee, 4 May.

At Dundee the 1st battalion was re-formed with D and G companies

1st Battalion 24th, which had remained at Helpmekaar, under command of Brevet Major Russell Upcher, since the first arrival of the battalion there (D becoming A Company.) B Company, which was still at St John's river (B became H company), and B, C, D, E and F new companies formed from the draft. The acting officers of the re-formed battalion were:

Major W.M. Dunbar, commanding.

Major J.M.G. Tongue, Acting Major Wm. Brander.

Captains Brevet Major Russell Upcher (A company), Rainforth (G company), A.A. Morshead (B company), L.H. Bennett (D company), Honourable G.A.V. Bertie, Coldstream Guards (E company).

Lieutenants W. Heaton (F company), C.R.W. Colville, Grenadier Guards (C company), R.A.P. Clements (Acting Quartermaster), – Weallens, W.W. Lloyd.

Sub Lieutenants W.A. Birch, J.D.W. Williams, W.C. Godfrey, M.E. Carthew Yorstoun, Robt. Scott-Kerr, R. Campbell, Honourable R.C.E. Carrington.

Captain C P H. Tynte, Glamorgan Militia, Lieutenant St Le Malet, Dorset Militia, Lieutenant E.P.H. Tynte, Glamorgan Militia, E.R. Rushbrook, Royal East Middlesex Militia, Second Lieutenant Lumsden, 2nd Royal Lanarkshire Militia.

On 13 April 1879, previous to the re-formation of the battalion, a re-organization of the forces under Lord Chelmsford was promulgated:

The 1st division, in two brigades, under Major General Hope Crealock, CB, was to operate from the Tugela. Wood's force was to remain independent, under the name of Brigadier General Wood's Flying Column.

The remainder of the troops in the Utrecht district, in which were both battalions 24th, were to constitute the second division under Major General Newdigate, and operate from Landman's Drift. The cavalry brigade was ordered to join the northern column.

On 13 May 1879 the new 1st Battalion 24th left at Dundee, under command of Colonel R.T. Glyn, CB, marched to join Major General Newdigate's division, and on 7 June was formed into a brigade with the 58th and

94th regiments, under Colonel Glyn. The brigade marched towards Ulundi, and on 27 June arrived within 10 miles of that place. Leaving two companies in laager at Entonganini, the remainder of the battalion advanced with its division, carrying ten days' rations and no tents, towards Umsenbarri, joined General Wood's column, and formed laager and built a stone fort on the banks of the Mfolozi. The whole of the mounted men, including the mounted infantry under Lieutenant and Local Captain E.S. Browne, 24th Regiment, crossed the river and reconnoitred as far as Ulundi. In the battle which followed there Colonel Glyn's brigade was present, with the exception of the 1st Battalion 24th, which with detachments of other corps was left in the entrenched camp on the Umvelosi [i.e. Mfolozi], under Colonel Bellairs, CB. On 4 July, the Zulu power being regarded as broken, the brigade retraced its steps to Entonganini, where it lay during the great storm of wind and cold of 6–8 July 1879. It subsequently returned to Landman's Drift.

On 26 July the battalion received orders to march to Durban, to embark for England. Moving by Dundee, Greytown, and Pietermaritzburg to Pine Town, it encamped, and there at a brigade parade, on 22 August 1879, the Victoria Cross was presented to Lieutenant E.S. Browne, H (late B) company, having rejoined from St John's River. The battalion, under command of Colonel Glyn, numbering twenty-four officers, forty-six sergeants, thirty-six corporals, eleven drummers and 767 privates, embarked in the transport *Egypt* on 27 August 1879, landed at Portsmouth on 2 October, and marched into quarters in the New Barracks, Gosport.

The 2nd battalion remained at Rorke's Drift from its arrival there on 23 January 1879 until the middle of April. The privations to which the officers and men were subject were at first very great. The battalion had nothing but what it stood in. There were no tents, no covering of any sort; all they had to shelter them from the cold sleet and rain that fell nightly, converting the enclosed space into a slough of mud, was their thin kersey frocks. The sick list increased alarmingly, and, to make matters worse, the medicines having been burnt with the hospital, all that remained at the disposal of the medical officers, then and for some time afterwards, was contained in the small field companions they carried with them. It speaks volumes for the healthiness of the Natal climate that during these three months the battalion only lost one officer (Lieutenant Reginald Franklin) and twelve men by death, and two officers and thirteen men invalided.

At the beginning of April half of the battalion, under Lieutenant Colonel Degacher, moved to Dundee; four companies, under Brevet Major Black, remaining at Rorke's Drift. On the advance of the northern column from Landman's Drift, two companies, (G and H) 2nd Battalion 24th, under Brevet Major C.J. Bromhead, were brought down from Dundee to that post; but it having been decided to construct a strong fort at Koppie Alleen, Captain Harvey moved up with H company, and Major C.J. Bromhead joining with F company, under Lieutenant H. Mainwaring, the two companies speedily converted the small earthwork they had found on arrival into a substantial closed redoubt. On 3 June 1879 this detachment had the melancholy duty of furnishing a guard of honour and escort to the mortal remains of the Prince Imperial of France, whose body was escorted by the battalion from Koppie Alleen to Landman's Drift and Dundee on its way to Pietermaritzburg. Captain Harvey, with H company and a party of Native pioneers, was also employed in constructing another fort on the Itelezi ridge, which Major General Marshall, commanding the lines of communication in Zululand – who was much pleased with the work – named Fort Warwick, in honour of the regiment. To replace H Company, B Company, under Brevet Major Bromhead, which had been sent up from Rorke's Drift to a post near Conference Hill for woodcutting, was moved to Koppie Alleen. The battalion remained in these positions until after the battle of Ulundi, 4 July 1879, when a redistribution of companies took place.

After the second division was broken up on 28 July 1879, Sir Garnet, now Lord, Wolseley, who had arrived to supersede Lord Chelmsford, took F and H companies, 2nd Battalion 24th, under Major C.J. Bromhead, as his special escort. They accompanied him to Ulundi and in all his movements until the conclusion of peace. These companies then fell back on Isandlwana, completing the burial of the dead there, and afterwards marching to Pietermaritzburg, where they arrived on 6 October, to await the battalion headquarters. Sir Garnet Wolseley had selected the 2nd Battalion 24th for an expedition against Sekhukune, but on his arrival at Utrecht on

9 September 1879 he brought the news that the battalion was ordered to Gibraltar. Sir Garnet took the opportunity of presenting their Victoria Crosses to Brevet Major Gonville Bromhead and Private Robert Jones. He had already given one to Private Henry Hook at Rorke's Drift. Two other Rorke's Drift men, Corporal Allen and Private Hitch, received their crosses from the hands of Her Majesty at Netley.

The march of 250 miles down country began on 29 September, and on 14 October the remaining companies entered Pietermaritzburg, where great demonstrations awaited 'the battalion that saved Natal'. The march was resumed on 21 October, and after some delay in camp at Pinetown, awaiting transport, the battalion embarked in the SS *Ontario*, reached Gibraltar on 12 February 1880, and went into quarters in the Casemate barracks.

CHAPTER 17

Archaeological Investigations
at the Battlefield

*Very few military items were recovered which support
the historical accounts.*

DR LITA WEBLEY

One individual in particular, Sir Bartle Frere, was particularly responsible for the original interest in archaeological research relating to the area of Rorke's Drift. It will be remembered that Frere was appointed Governor of the Cape Colony and British High Commissioner in South Africa in 1877, and it was Frere who was responsible for the British invasion of Zululand in 1879. Frere had wide ranging interests that included a passion for archaeology and anthropology. Before moving to South Africa he had been President of the Asiatic Society in 1872 and the following year he became President of the Royal Geographical Society. He was an avid collector of artefacts, especially from Natal and Zululand, and most items from his collection are now deposited with the British Museum in the Department of Ethnography.

During the Zulu War a number of British officers collected artefacts; many came from Rorke's Drift, others from along the Buffalo river, Isandlwana and Pietermaritzburg. One officer, Colonel Henry Fielden, not only collected artefacts but also subsequently established that Bushmen collected glass from soldiers' discarded soda water bottles to make arrowheads.

Fielden's Zulu War collection came from his line of march from Newcastle to Rorke's Drift; he wrote that he 'took advantage of every opportunity that arose for leaving the line of march and examining the "dongas" and denuded surfaces that lay contiguous to this route'.[1] Artefacts collected by Fielden are now held in the Sturge collection in the British Museum and Liverpool Museum. At first sight it appears strange that officers would take time from their official duties to study and collect artefacts; yet perusal of early collections reveals that army officers were initially responsible for many, ranging from the Anglo Zulu War and the Boer Wars through to the Bechuanaland Expedition of 1884; their endeavours were certainly responsible for spurring initial interest in archaeology in this area although little more happened until the period between 1983 and 1993.

During this later period, a serious archaeological excavation was undertaken at Rorke's Drift with the aim of further elucidating the course of events at the mission station during the Anglo-Zulu War of 1879. The foundations of the British Commissariat store as well as the hospital burnt down by the Zulu were located. Walling, which can probably be linked to Fort Bromhead, was uncovered and a preliminary survey with a metal detector provided new information on the Zulu side of the war. Surprisingly, very few items were recovered which could unequivocally be linked to the battle despite the scale of military operations at the site both during and after the conflict of 22 January 1879. Indeed, when Bertram Mitford visited the battlefields in 1882 he found the site at Isandlwana littered with battle debris:

> Strewn about are tent pegs, cartridge cases, broken glass, bits of rope, meat tins and sardine boxes pierced with assegai stabs, shrivelled pieces of shoe leather and rubbish of every description; bone of horses and oxen gleam white and ghastly and here and there in the grass one stumbles upon a half-buried skeleton.[2]

By contrast he found very little evidence of any conflict at Rorke's Drift:

> Few or no traces of the old fortifications remain, but a large house was in the course of construction. Outhouses stood around, hard by was the chapel, belonging to the Mission, but of the defences, not a trace.[3]

Background to the excavations

Before the Centre Column descended on Rorke's Drift, Assistant Commissary Chermside turned the church into a commissariat store and the missionary's 'eleven-roomed house' into a field hospital. Witt gave the dimensions of the store as 80ft by 20ft while the hospital was 60ft by 18ft in size.[4] Although the walls of the store are reported to have been of solid stone, photographs taken of this structure soon after the battle indicate a combination of stone and brick.

Most books written on the subject claim that British soldiers fired some 20,000 rounds of ammunition during the battle; their source appears to be the classic *The Washing of the Spears* by Morris. If this were so, the majority of these cartridge cases are likely to have fallen within the temporary barricades.[5] The British used the Martini-Henry breech-loading rifle and, while some of the Zulu are reported to have owned obsolete firearms, such as muzzle-loading flintlocks, these are considered to have had no significant effect on Zulu tactics.[6] The hospital was set alight during the battle and the ruins offered cover to the Zulus until the next morning; for this reason Chard ordered that the walls of the hospital be pulled down. The stones of the walls were brought across to the storehouse to strengthen the redoubt.

In March 1879 troops started with the construction of Fort Melvill overlooking the river in order both to protect the pont and to move the troops out of the old fort, which was very unhealthy. The majority of the troops moved out in April although some stayed on until the end of the war in July. It is not known when the walls of the old fort were finally dismantled although the defences of the area were finally abandoned in October 1879. Otto Witt returned and constructed a large house and church on the site after the war. There are no records indicating whether the new mission house was built on top of the foundations of the hospital or whether the church was built on the ruins of the store. It would appear, however, that the 8ft high stone walling of the old fort was demolished and the stone used in the construction of the new buildings.

Witt's house and church are still standing and while the latter structure continues to function in daily use the former has now been converted into a museum. The land on which the battlefield is located still belongs to the

Evangelical Lutheran Church but has been let to the Natal Provincial Administration on a ninety-nine year lease. The battlefield area was declared a
national monument in 1969.

Prior to the conversion of the mission house into a museum, an eminent
South African archaeologist, Dr Lita Webley, was requested to undertake
an archaeological research programme with the following aims:

1   To establish the original position of the hospital;
2   To establish the position of the commissariat store;
3   To determine whether there was any evidence to substantiate the
    present position of stones which have been placed to demarcate the
    original lines of the battle of 22–23 January 1879;
4   To try and find the foundations of Fort Bromhead which was
    constructed on the site immediately after the battle;
5   To determine whether any evidence could be found for the position
    of Zulu snipers who apparently fired at the British troops from caves
    in the hillside of Shiyane.

Excavations were also considered to be of a rescue nature as significant artefacts or *in situ* features had to be recovered before building
contractors destroyed them. Archaeological excavations commenced in
September 1988 with subsequent field trips in May 1989 and March, June
and August 1990. Members of the Evangelical Lutheran Community assisted with the excavations during the first three field trips.

1 The location of the hospital foundations

To avoid confusion regarding this structure, some of the above history is
briefly summarized. Rorke's house, subsequently occupied by Witt, became
the field hospital during the Anglo-Zulu War. It was burnt down by the
Zulus. It is believed that Lutheran missionaries returning to the site rebuilt
their mission house on the foundations of the hospital. It is this house which
has been converted into a museum.

Some 20 metres were excavated around the house but no trace of previous foundations was observed. The deposit around the house was nowhere
very deep. The deposit was not particularly rich anywhere except around the

kitchen area where fragments of ceramics, glass and bone were recovered.

A number of trenches were then excavated inside the building. A comparison of the original floor plan of the hospital drawn by Lieutenant John Chard (who was a Royal Engineer) with that of the plan submitted by Otto Witt when he rebuilt the mission house in 1882 indicates that the former was slightly smaller than the latter. Excavations inside the house in Room 7 uncovered several large quartzite stones that form a neat straight edge, as well as a more roughly constructed inner wall running at right angles. These features probably relate to the foundations of the hospital. The deposit around these stones was rich in charcoal and pieces of melted glass that testify to the blaze relating to the battle itself.

2 The location of the Commissariat store

In order to locate the position of the British Commissariat store a trench was excavated at right angles from the present church across the battlefield towards the rocky ledge for a distance of some 12 metres. As the aim of the excavation was to look for a specific feature, the trench was excavated to varying depths with pick and shovels and no sieving was undertaken. Close to the church the trench reached bedrock at about 1.2m while near the end of the trench it was reached at only 45cm. This is because there is a pronounced slope down from the church to the kraal and the position of the original redoubt.

However, while excavating the trench some dressed stone blocks were recovered 3 metres from the church. Stratigraphically these stones are assisted with a level of sandstone rubble and red brick some 50cm from the soil surface. Most of the historic artefactual remains such as Martini-Henry cartridge cases and gin bottle fragments were found close to these stones. The excavation strategy was then altered to determine whether these stones were in fact the foundations of the store. Two square metres were uncovered to the west of the trench. More dressed stones were uncovered at the same depth as the previous finds and clearly formed part of the same structure including a well-developed line of sandstone blocks, on occasions two stones high. In addition it was interesting to note the presence of decomposing red brick in association with these stones. It would appear that the store was built of both sandstone and red brick. Large numbers of gin bottle fragments, rusted iron objects and china were found on the inside (i.e. south) of the line of stones. Excavations, however, failed to locate any evidence of an interior floor within the structure.

After following the foundations in a westerly direction, further excavations were undertaken to the east. The excavation of 8 square metres revealed what would appear to be one corner of the store. The corner was well built and more substantial than the foundation stones in the other excavated areas. In addition, a roughly constructed stone wall angles out from this corner in a northerly direction. It is suggested that this roughly built stone wall is the remains of the fortifications of Fort Bromhead, built immediately after the battle and linking the ruins of the hospital with the store and well-built kraal. The stones used for Fort Bromhead were probably used in the construction of the church, mission house and school buildings. The highest concentration of bone and Martini-Henry cartridge cases was recovered from the rubble layer in this excavated area.

It would appear that the clearly defined row of stones relates to the British Commissariat store and Dr Webley believed that the foundation stones were probably those of the outer or front wall.

3 Excavations on the battlefield

After establishing the position of the 'hospital' and 'store' a number of trenches were excavated to bisect the outer lines of the battlefield. Some trenches were sited along the southern margin while others were intended to sample the top of the rocky ledge to the north. Although the barricades were of a temporary nature, it was hypothesized that particularly dense numbers of cartridge cases and other military debris might indicate these lines. The absence of a clear stratigraphy on the battlefield itself suggests that both the levelling of the site prior to the construction of the new mission house and church in 1882 and gardening activities over a period of 100 years have destroyed much of the original stratigraphy. The dark loamy soil contained fragments of yellow clay, red brick lenses and the densest concentration of artefacts at depths of 0.3–0.5m.

It was further hypothesized that artefacts relating to the battle and to the subsequent occupation of the site by British soldiers between February and March 1879 would have been dumped beneath the ledge and would thus be concentrated in this area. Three large areas were therefore excavated immediately below the ledge. Very little artefactual material was recovered from these lower excavations. The dark brown soil was very shallow and overlaid sterile yellow clay. The deposit consisted mainly of recent builders' rubble with virtually no historic material. An official from the Natal Provincial Association Works Branch office in Dundee informed Dr Webley that during the centenary celebrations at Rorke's Drift in 1979 a bulldozer had been used to 'neaten' the area below the ledge. The soil from this area may have been used to construct the ramp onto the battlefield so that visitors to the site could have more convenient access to the battlefield during the celebrations. In addition he reported that members of the public had dug extensively at Rorke's Drift and at Fort Melvill during 1979 in search of artefacts relating to the battle and this is confirmed by newspaper reports from that time.

4 The walls of Fort Bromhead

It was hoped that the area next to the ramp leading up to the rocky ledge on the battlefield would provide some evidence of the gate of Fort Bromhead. However, only recent builders' rubble was recovered, indicating that this area has been disturbed, perhaps during the construction of the ramp to the site during the centenary celebrations of 1979.

A number of areas were excavated in order to extend the stone 'pathway' first found in 1988. The first three areas contained some stone walling but were not very rich in artefacts. The next area, situated next to the concrete plinth, was rich in green bottle glass pieces. Two badges, a brass sphinx and a brass crown, were found here. It was initially thought that the presence of a .577 slug in this area probably indicated extensive disturbance to the deposit but this view has since been re-evaluated.

The most extensive evidence for stone walling was found in the next area where quartzite cobbles and red brick seemed to form part of a wall. The excavations were enlarged to expose more of this feature. Associated with the walling were several cartridge cases, glass, bone and iron objects.

It would appear that this might be the remains of the front wall of Fort Bromhead. This wall was left *in situ*, photographed and then covered in plastic sheeting and sand. Portions of Fort Bromhead were therefore found along the front (north) of the battlefield as well as adjoining the back corner of the British store.

5 A metal-detector survey of the slope of Shiyane (Oskarsberg)

One of the aims of the archaeological research had been to attempt to gain new insights into the Zulu side of the battle. No artefacts were recovered which could unequivocally be linked to them. With this in mind, Dr Webley and her team determined to survey the slopes of Shiyane, in particular examining the caves and ledges from which the Zulus are reported to have fired on the British. Most of the mortalities suffered by the British were as a result of Zulu sharpshooters firing from Shiyane. Since tourists have visited this area for over 100 years, the team decided that a metal-detector survey would be the most economical means of recovering buried spears and spent bullets. At least three slugs of a .577 calibre were recovered from a cave overlooking the battlefield. They were within a metre of each other and were probably dropped by the same sharpshooter. The calibre of these bullets matched those of a wax-moulded bullet recovered from the front ledge of the battlefield. Furthermore, during the construction of a car park in front of the battlefield similar wax-moulded, fired slugs were recovered. These discoveries suggested that the team were recovering bullets that had been used during the battle of 1879. The fact that many of these slugs were recovered from the car park area (to the north of the battlefield) confirms reports that the Zulus were overshooting their targets.

One of the spent bullets from the car park area had three rifling marks that suggested to a gun expert that it had been fired in an Enfield rifle. This would confirm observations in an article on firearms in the Zulu kingdom by Professor Guy[7] that muzzle-loaders were fairly common in the period up to the 1870s. The Zulus could purchase both percussion Enfields and Tower muskets cheaply from suppliers in Mozambique, but these weapons were frequently obsolete and ineffective.

It is tempting to link the percussion caps found on the front of the rocky ledge to muzzle-loaders used by the Zulus during the battle. However, Mechanick[8] has claimed that some of the Natal Native Contingent were still armed with muzzle-loading, percussion Enfields. The percussion caps may well have been dropped prior to the battle, before the NNC fled the scene. However, they may perhaps also be linked to James Rorke's occupation of the site. His will of 1876 lists 'a Rifle, a Dble [double-barrelled?] gun and a revolver with cartridges'. We may also assume that since Rorke was a trader he probably dealt in arms and ammunition.

The metal-detector survey also recovered a number of Martini-Henry slugs in the vicinity of the caves on Shiyane suggesting that the British soldiers were shooting at a distance of 400 yards or more with their rifles.

Artefactual Remains

Fauna

Large samples of faunal remains were recovered from the excavations. Areas around the mission house as well as close to the rocky ledge were particularly rich in what appeared to be sheep, goat and cattle remains. The historic accounts indicate that livestock was slaughtered for the soldiers at the front of Fort Bromhead. Dr Webley tentatively identified pig and baboon from the same site. Other finds included a piece of ivory tooth and a grooved and snapped bone tube.

Metal

Two iron hoes were recovered behind the mission house next to doorways which have since been bricked in. The hoes were planted vertically in the soil and were used as shoe scrapers by the missionaries. Rusted nails were most commonly recovered. Other finds include buttons, buckles, tins, a spoon and a fork handle, a penknife, a trowel, iron bars, the heel of a boot, watch chains, brass razor blades, regimental buttons, small brass containers and coins including an 1862 Queen Victoria halfpenny. The sphinx badge (of the 24th Regiment) would probably have been worn on the collar, while the crown badge had probably broken off a helmet.

A total of thirty-three Martini-Henry cartridge cases and seven unfired Martini-Henry bullets are all that bear testimony to the battle. Eleven percussion caps were found to the front of the rocky ledge. Unusual calibres include a .38 Smith and Wesson cartridge. One twelve-bore shotgun firing pin was recovered from Extension 5 among all the Martini-Henry cartridges suggesting that other firearms may also have been used during the battle. It is possible that this cartridge dates to the occupation of the site after the battle, as many officers owned their own hunting rifles. The wax-moulded slug of .577 calibre recovered from the rocky ledge matches slugs found both in a cave on Shiyane and in the car park area to the front of the actual fortified area. They present new light on the Zulu side of the battle.

Glass

Of interest were the many pieces of melted glass around the kitchen area of the mission house and under the floor in the excavated room. They suggest a high temperature that may be related to the fire in the hospital. Generally most of the glass fragments from the excavation were either olive green or aqua coloured. One bottle stopper bore the embossed letters of Lea & Perrins. The majority of glass fragments recovered near the store were dark green and probably derive from spirit bottles. Two square-based gin bottles were partially reconstructed; one had the name 'Schiedam' embossed on the side, another had 'Schiedam' embossed on a shoulder seal.

Ceramics

Large numbers of ceramic pieces were recovered, the majority from around the mission house and very few from the store area. Several pot sherds were found around the mission house. They are all undecorated and it is impossible to determine whether they pre-date 1849 or are contemporary with the historic occupation. However, the sherds are most common around the kitchen area and were found together with imported glass and china fragments. This may indicate that either Rorke or the later missionaries used locally fired clay pots or employed people who did.

Conclusions

All the aims of the archaeological project at Rorke's Drift were achieved but with varying degrees of success. Sections of the foundations of the hospital were recovered under the floor of the present mission-house-cum-museum. Charcoal pieces and fragments of melted glass confirm that this structure overlies the ruins of the field hospital burnt down by the Zulus.

The foundation stones of the front wall of the British Commissariat store were also located. It appears to have been largely situated underneath the present church, which would mean that the marker stones used to delineate the position of the store are incorrectly placed. They should be moved back (i.e. southward or towards Shiyane) some 8 metres. Excavations have uncovered 20m of the front foundations of the store and it is therefore quite possible that the store could have been 80ft in length as described by Otto Witt.

It is clear that the very intensive occupation of the battlefield for some three months after the battle probably resulted in a fairly complex stratigraphy. However, the deposit in and around the battlefield appears to have been subject to considerable disturbance right up to 1979 and it now seems unlikely that much would be gained by more extensive excavations of the area.

In addition to finding the position of the store, excavations also appear to have uncovered at least a portion of the walls of Fort Bromhead. A section of roughly constructed stone wall was found adjoining the back corner of the store while a substantial portion of walling was also uncovered on the edge of the rocky ledge.

One important discovery, which resulted from the metal-detector survey, is that it appears that the Zulu were indeed over-firing the battlefield. It was recommended that another survey be undertaken of the slopes of Shiyane once the grass has been burnt even though Dr Webley believed that most of the material has been collected by visitors to the site during the last 100 years.

Aerial photographs of the mission area have highlighted some unusual features such as cross-hatching in the field in front of the mission house and circular features near the turnstile in front of the rocky ledge. These features may be due to the British occupation of the area in 1879 but they could equally be ascribed to the agricultural activities of the missionaries; only archaeological research will solve this issue. Furthermore, Dr Webley felt that research should also be aimed at integrating the site with Fort Melvill, the military road to Isandlwana, May's Hotel, Sihayo's kraal and Isandlwana itself as Rorke's Drift should not be viewed in isolation.

The excavations at Rorke's Drift are a salutary reminder of the significant changes that can occur at a particular site over a very short period of time (archaeologically speaking). Despite the scale of the military conflict at Rorke's Drift, very few military items were recovered which support the historical accounts.[9]

CHAPTER 18

A Visitor's Guide to Rorke's Drift

This battlefield is the most famous of all the Zulu War locations. It covers a very small area, no larger than the size of three tennis courts, where eight officers and 131 British and Colonial soldiers held off an attacking force of 4,500 Zulus for over twelve hours. The British soldiers of B Company 2/24th (2nd Warwickshire) Regiment formed the guard of the Centre Column's supply base and temporary hospital at Rorke's Drift. The attacking Zulus had, earlier in the day, constituted the reserve of the attacking Zulu army at the battle of Isandlwana, some 10 miles (16km) away, but had not taken part in the battle. It is most probable that this force of reserves then attacked Rorke's Drift and neighbouring farms to redress this imbalance, to maintain their prestige, and to obtain supplies of food. The site was originally a trading post and had been established by James Rorke in 1850. He died in October 1875 and the site was quickly purchased by Swedish missionaries to be used as a mission station. The new missionary, Otto Witt, who converted Rorke's bungalow home into his own residence, turned Rorke's store into a church. On the day of the battle, the British commandeered the site and converted the church back into a store and the house into a hospital. Today the store has been rebuilt as a church and the hospital, Witt's home, which was rebuilt after the battle, is a fine museum. The local people are very friendly and helpful.

Location The nearest towns are Dundee 30 miles (50km) and Nqutu 16 miles (48km). It is 16 miles (26km) from Helpmekaar and 10 miles (16km) from Isandlwana by road. There are no facilities other than the tea room, toilets and post office.

Distinguishing features An impressive and emotionally inspiring small battlefield covering a tiny area that is linked to the battlefield of Isandlwana. The site is dominated by the Oskarsberg hill, named by Witt after the Swedish king; the Zulus know it as Shiyane, the 'eyebrow'. The actual Drift or river crossing is about half a mile (800m) by foot or 1 mile (1.6km) by car. The Orientation Centre sells light meals and drinks during the main part of the day as well as maps, books and souvenirs.

Points of interest at Rorke's Drift in suggested order

1   **The Rorke's Drift Orientation Centre and museum.** This building occupies the site of the hospital during the battle. See the excellent diorama in the museum, which has numerous pictures and artefacts.

2   **The central battlefield.**

3   **The British cemetery.** Note that the British deserter, Corporal Anderson, is buried in the cemetery, but not the civilian storekeeper, Mr Byrne. The centre cross was crafted by Private Melsop of C Company 2/24th; he had been a stonemason by trade before enlisting with the 24th Regiment.

4   **The church.** (The store during the battle). Visitors are always made most welcome.

5   **Zulu graves.** There are three marked mass graves, each with a memorial stone in English, Zulu and Afrikaans. The only other Zulu memorials are at Isandlwana and the site of the Ulundi battlefield.

6   **James Rorke's grave.** Rorke requested he should be buried under 3ft (1m) of concrete to prevent his remains being disturbed – he then, according to legend, committed suicide.

7   **The Oskarsberg Mountain.** This hill dominates the river crossing and is a commanding feature and a major landmark. One can climb it, starting at the visitors' centre at Rorke's Drift. The round trip should

take about seventy minutes. The view from the top is spectacular.

8   **Bushman paintings.** On the east face of the Oskarsberg, in the
    sandstone terraces of the lower slope, there are some bushman paint-
    ings in an overhang. They appear at first to be somewhat damaged
    and faded, but this is because of their great age. It is quite a trek to
    get to them and you will need a guide to reach them.

9   **The Oskarsberg terraces,** occupied by the Zulu marksmen during the
    battle. Following the battle, soldiers of the 24th carved their
    regimental number into the rocks.

10 **The Buffalo river.** The Buffalo river at Rorke's Drift at the time of
    the Zulu War constituted the border between Natal and Zululand,
    and an old trading track snaked its way from Rorke's Drift to Ulundi
    – the route that Chelmsford intended to follow on expiry of the
    ultimatum. At midnight on 10 January 1879 the ultimatum that had
    been issued to the Zulus expired. Chelmsford forded the Buffalo river
    at Rorke's Drift at the head of No. 3 column, made up of 4,850 men,
    220 wagons and 4,500 oxen. His objective was the Zulu capital,
    Ulundi, 65 miles (108km) away to the east.

11 **The 'Old Drift'.** The Old Drift is also the site of the infamous
    'Sihayo incident'. In the winter of 1878 the famous Chief Sihayo
    KaXongo Ngobese (of the Qungebe people who lived in the Batshe
    river area opposite Rorke's Drift) had two of his adulterous wives
    stoned to death in the river crossing there. This incident was seized
    upon by the British High Commissioner, Sir Bartle Frere, and woven
    into the preamble of the British ultimatum. It was made to look like
    a cross-border incident.

12 **Second British Military Cemetery.** This site was re-discovered in
    1999 by a local Zulu Petros Sibisi and Nicky von der Heyde who
    were searching for evidence of the wagon track built between 14
    and 20 January 1879 linking Rorke's Drift and Isandlwana. The
    overgrown cemetery was in the centre of an untended grove of gum
    tress. The site has since been restored. The cemetery contains graves
    of soldiers, part of the garrison of Fort Melvill, who died of fever.

There are also some more recent civilian graves in this cemetery.

13 **Fort Northampton** is still discernible, as it is well cut into the sandstone.

14 **The ferry pool,** just upstream from the present day low-level bridge, was where the British established their ponts. This position is commanded on the Natal (western) side by a ridge, upon which the British built a sandbag and palisade fort called Fort Melvill in honour of Lieutenant Teignmouth Melvill VC. This fort was garrisoned after the battle of Rorke's Drift. About 400 yards downstream from the bridge the river runs over a series of rock shelves which constitute the 'old drift' – a natural causeway where people and wagons could gain purchase when crossing – hence the importance of the site. Downstream from the drift on the bend in the river, two old pont stanchions marked with the date '1863 Camel steel' still stand today, but this site was probably used after the Zulu War.

Note that the road you will take from Rorke's Drift to Isandlwana is only approximately the route that Chelmsford took. The old track is still visible from the air, and some care was taken when situating the new road not to do too much damage to the old track. It is significant that the old wagon track used to run from the Manzimyama river onto the saddle of Isandlwana. The new road runs to the north of the mountain.

How to find it

Route 1. From Helpmekaar on Route 33
Good and dry weather conditions only. Take the dirt road sign posted to Rorke's Drift. After descending the steep pass, continue for 3 miles (5km) to the junction; turn right towards Rorke's Drift. As you approach the Oskarsberg hill, the red roofed buildings at Rorke's Drift will become visible. Continue to Rorke's Drift; the Orientation Centre and battlefield are situated on the left as you enter the settlement. Obtain your tickets from the gift shop before entering the Battlefield.

Route 2. Route 68

All weather. From Dundee, take route 68 towards Nqutu for 14 miles (20km) and then take the first turning right signposted to Rorke's Drift. At the first junction, turn left towards Rorke's Drift. As you approach the Oskarsberg hill, the red-roofed buildings at Rorke's Drift will become visible. Continue to Rorke's Drift; the Orientation Centre and battlefield are situated on the left as you enter the settlement. Obtain your tickets from the gift shop before entering the Battlefield.

Route 3. Route 68 from Babanango to Nqutu

All weather. When 8 miles (13km) from Nqutu, take the signposted dirt road to Isandlwana. This road follows the route of the attacking Zulu army and descends onto the Isandlwana battlefield from the Nqutu plateau. As the road drops down onto the plain, the Conical Hill will be immediately to the front with Isandlwana to the right. Follow the road into Isandlwana village and proceed past the Isandlwana mountain towards the signposted road to Rorke's Drift. After 3 miles (5km), turn left towards Rorke's Drift. After crossing the Buffalo river, turn left at the junction. On approaching the Oskarsberg Hill, the red-roofed buildings at Rorke's Drift will become visible. Continue to Rorke's Drift; the Orientation Centre and battlefield are both situated on the left as you enter the settlement. Obtain your tickets from the gift shop before entering the Battlefield.

Recommendations

Employ a reputable guide to obtain maximum benefit. Allow a full day to see everything at Rorke's Drift and the graves of Lieutenants Coghill and Melvill at Fugitives' Drift only 5 miles (8km) away – but do remember that this is on a game reserve – get permission from Fugitives' Drift Lodge before entering the reserve. If walking directly to the Buffalo river crossing, good walking shoes are essential. Spray legs and ankles against ticks if walking around in long grass.

APPENDICES

With regard to the reports by Chard, Bromhead and Glyn, a facsimile of the original document follows each transcript. These facsimilies have been included so that the reader can compare and contrast the handwriting in which each report is written and the signature at the end.

The Two Chard Reports

The first 'Chard Report' became the official report concerning the Zulu attack on the mission station. It was this report that Chelmsford forwarded to the War Office in the attempt to lessen the impact of the British defeat at Isandlwana. Towards the end of 1879, when Chard was safely back in England, he was commanded to submit a further report to Queen Victoria. Chard was required to include greater detail although nothing is known of the preparation or research that went into this second report, other than the fact that apologies for a delay were given to Queen Victoria as Chard claimed to have 'lost his notes'. The identity of the author of the two reports remains unknown although both documents were signed by Chard (see Chapter 9 for further details). Both reports are unabridged.

The second 'Chard Report' is reprinted by kind permission of HM The Queen.

The First 'Chard Report'

Rorke's Drift, 25th January, 1879.

I have the honour to report that, on the 22nd instant, I was left in command at Rorke's Drift by Major Spalding, who went to Helpmakaar to hurry on the company 24th regiment ordered to protect the ponts.

About 3.15p.m. on that day I was at the ponts, when two men came riding from Zululand at a gallop, and shouted to be taken across the river. I was informed by one of them, Lieutenant Adendorff, of Lonsdale's regiment (who remained to assist in the defence), of the disaster at Isandhlwana camp, and that the Zulus were advancing on Rorke's Drift. The other, a carbineer, rode off to take the news to Helpmakaar.

Almost immediately I received a message from Lieutenant Bromhead, commanding the company 24th regiment at the camp, near the commissariat stores, asking me to come up at once.

I gave the order to inspan, strike tents, put all stores &c., into the wagon, and at once rode up to the commissariat store, and found that a note had been received from the third column to state that the enemy were advancing in force against our post, which we were to strengthen, and hold at all costs.

Lieutenant Bromhead was most actively employed in loopholing and barricading the store building and hospital; and connecting the defence of the two buildings by walls of mealie bags and two wagons that were on the ground.

I held a hurried consultation with him, and with Mr Dalton, of the commissariat (who was actively superintending the work of defence, and whom I cannot sufficiently thank for his most valuable services), entirely approving of the arrangements made. I went round the position, and then rode down to the ponts and brought up the guard of 1 sergeant and 6 men, wagon &c.

I desire here to mention the offer of the pont-man, Daniells and Sergt. Milne, 3rd Buffs, to moor the ponts in the middle of the stream and defend them from their decks with a few men.

We arrived at the post about 3.30 p.m. Shortly after, an officer of Durnford's Horse arrived, and asked for orders. I requested him to send a detachment to observe the drifts and ponts, to throw out outposts in the direction of the enemy and check his advance as much as possible, falling back upon the post when forced to retire, and assisting in its defence.

I requested Lieutenant Bromhead to post his men; and, having seen his and every man at his post, the work once more went on.

About 4.20 p.m. the sound of firing was heard behind the hill to our south. The officer of Durnford's returned, reporting the enemy close upon us, and that his men would not obey his orders, but were going off to Helpmakaar; and I saw them, apparently about 100 in number, going off in that direction.

About the same time Captain Stephenson's detachment of the Natal

Native Contingent left us, as did that officer himself.

I saw that our line of defence was too extended for the small number of men now left us, and at once commenced a retrenchment of biscuit boxes.

We had not completed a wall two boxes high, when, about 4.30 p.m., 500 or 600 of the enemy came in sight around the hill to our south, and advanced at a run against our south wall. They were met by a well sustained fire; but, notwithstanding their heavy loss, continued the advance to within 50 yards of the wall, when they met with such a heavy fire from the wall, and cross-fire from the store, that they were checked; but, taking advantage of the cover afforded by the cook house, ovens, &c., kept up a heavy fire. The greater number, however, without stopping, moved to the left, around the hospital, and made a rush at our north-west wall of mealie bags, but after a short but desperate struggle, were driven back with heavy loss into the bush around the work.

The main body of the enemy were close behind, and had lined the ledge of rock and caves overlooking us, about 400 yards to our south, from where they kept up a constant fire, and, advancing somewhat more to their left than the first attack, occupied the garden, hollow road, and bush in great force.

Taking advantage of the bush, which we had not time to cut down, the enemy were able to advance under cover, close to our wall, and in this part soon held one side of the wall, while we held the other. A series of desperate assaults were made, extending from the hospital along the wall as the bush reached, but each was most splendidly met and repulsed by our men, with the bayonet; Corporal Schiess, Natal Native Contingent, greatly distinguishing himself by his conspicuous gallantry.

The fire from the rocks behind us, though badly directed, took us completely in reverse, and was so heavy that we had suffered very severely, and about 6 p.m., were forced to retire behind the retrenchment of biscuit boxes.

All this time, the enemy had been attempting to force the hospital, and shortly after set fire to its roof.

The garrison of the hospital defended it room by room, bringing out all the sick who could be moved, before they retired.

Privates Williams, Hook, R. Jones, and W. Jones, 24th regiment, being the last men to leave, holding the doorway with the bayonet, their own ammunition being expended.

From the want of interior communication, and the burning of the house, it was impossible to save all. With most heartfelt sorrow, I regret we could not save these poor fellows from their terrible fate.

Seeing the hospital burning, and the desperate attempts of the enemy to fire the roof of the stores, we converted two mealie bag heaps into a sort of redoubt which gave a second line of fire all round – Assistant Commissary Dunne working hard at this, though much exposed, and rendering valuable assistance.

As darkness came on, we were completely surrounded, and after several attempts had been gallantly repulsed, were eventually forced to retire to the middle, and then inner wall, of the kraal on our east. The position we then had we retained throughout. A desultory fire was kept up all night, and several assaults were attempted and repulsed; the vigour of the attack continuing until after midnight. Our men firing with the greatest coolness, did not waste a single shot, the light afforded by the burning hospital being of great help to us.

About 4 a.m. 23rd instant, the firing ceased, and at daybreak the enemy were out of sight, over the hill to the south-west. We patrolled the grounds, collecting the arms of the dead Zulus, and strengthened our position as much as possible.

We were removing the thatch from the roof of the stores, when, about 7 a.m. a large body of the enemy appeared on the hills to the south-west.

I sent a friendly kafir, who had come in shortly before with a note to the officer commanding at Helpmakaar, asking for help.

About 8 a.m. the third column appeared in sight, the enemy, who had been gradually advancing, falling back as they approached. I consider the enemy who attacked us to have numbered about 3000 (three thousand). We killed about 350 (three hundred and fifty). Of the steadiness and gallant behaviour of the whole garrison, I cannot speak too highly.

I wish especially to bring to your notice the conduct of Lieut. Bromhead 2–24th regt., and the splendid behaviour of his company, B, 2–24th; Surgeon Reynolds, A.M.D., in his constant attention to the wounded under fire where they fell; Acting Commissary Officer Dalton, to whose energy much of our defences were due, and who was severely wounded while gallantly assisting in the defence; Assistant Commissary Dunne; Acting Storekeeper Byrne (killed); Colour Sergeant Bourne, 2–24th; Sergeant Williams, 2–24th, (wounded dangerously since dead); Sergeant Windridge, 2–24th; Corporal Schiess, 2–3 N.N.C. (wounded); 1395 Private Williams, 2–24th; 593 Private W. Jones, 2–24th; Private McMahon A.H.C.; 716 Private Jones, 2–24th; Private Hook, 2–24th; Private Roy, 1–24th.

The following return shows the number present at Rorke's Drift, 22nd of January, 1879:

	Officers	N.C. & Men	Sick N.C & Men	Total
Staff		1		1
Royal Artillery		1	3	4
Royal Engineers	1	1		2
3rd Buffs		1		1
1-24th Regiment		6	5	11
2-24th Regiment, B company, 17 casuals sick	1	81	17	99
90th Light Infantry			1	1
Commissariat and Transport Department	3	1		4
Army Medical Department	1	3		4
Chaplain	1			1
Natal Mounted Police			3	3
Natal Native Contingent	1		6	7
Ferryman		1		1
	8	96	35	139

The following is a list of the killed:

Sergeant Maxfield, 2/24th; Private Scanlon 2/24th; Private Hayden, 2/24th; Private Adams, 2/24th; Private Cole, 2/24th; Private Fagan, 2/24th; Private Chick, 2/24th; 1398 Private Williams, 2/24th; Private Nicolls, 1/24th; Private Horrigan, 1/24th; Private Jenkins, 1/24th; Mr. Byrne, Com. Department; Trooper Hunter, N.M. police; Trooper Anderson, N.N.C

Private (native) N.N.C

Total 15

12 wounded* of whom two have since died, viz:

Sergeant Williams, 2/24th; Private Beckett, 1/24th

* List already forwarded by medical officer.

Herewith is appended a plan of the buildings, showing our lines of defence. The points of the compass referred to in this report are as shown in sketch approximately magnetic.

I have, &c.

(Signed) John R. M. Chard

Lieutenant R.E.

To Colonel Glynn, C.B., commanding 3rd Column.

Chelmsford added the following comment to Chard's report:

Sir,

It is with much satisfaction that I have the honour to forward the report of the successful defence of Rorke's Drift post on the 22nd and 23rd January.

The defeat of the Zulus at this post, and the very heavy loss suffered by them, has, to a great extent, neutralised the effect of the disaster at Isandhlwana, and no doubt saved Natal from a serious invasion.

The cool determined courage displayed by the gallant garrison is beyond all praise, and will, I feel sure, receive ample recognition.

As at the present moment the lesson taught by this defence is most valuable, I have thought it advisable to publish for general information the report in question which I trust will meet with your approval.

Chelmsford

Lieutenant-General

Rorkes Drift -
25th January 1879

Sir;

I have the honor to report that on the 22nd inst I was left in command at Rorkes Drift by Major Spalding, who went to Helpmakaar to hurry on the Comp? 24th Reg? ordered to protect the Ponts -

About 3.15 pm on that day I was at the ponts when two men came riding from Zulu-land at a galop, and shouted to be taken across the river - I was informed by one of them, Lieut Adendorff of Lonsdale Reg? (who remained to assist in the defence) of the disaster at Isandhlwana Camp, and that the Zulus were advancing on Rorkes Drift -

The other a Carbineer rode off to take the news to Helpmakaar -

Almost immediately I received a message from Lieut Bromhead, Comm? the Company 24th Reg? at the Camp near the Comm? Stores, asking me to come up at once -

I gave the order to inspan, strike tents, put all stores &c into the wagons, and at once rode up to the Comm? Store and found that a note had been received from the Third Column to state that the enemy were advancing in force against our post, which we were to strengthen and hold at all costs -

Lieut Bromhead was most actively employed in loopholing and barricading the store building and hospital and connecting the defence of the two buildings by walls of mealie bags and two wagons that were on the ground -

I held a hurried consultation with him and with Mr Dalton of the Comm? (who was actively superintending the work of defence, and whom I cannot sufficiently thank for his most valuable services) entirely approving of the arrangements made. I went round the position and then rode down to the ponts and brought up the guard of 1 Sergt & 6 men, wagon &c —

I desire here to mention the offer of the Quar. master Daniells and Sergt. Milne 3d Buffs to moor the ponts in the middle of the stream and defend them from their decks with a few men —

We arrived at the post about 3.30 p.m. Shortly after an officer of Durnford's Horse arrived and asked for orders; I requested him to send a detachment to observe the drifts and ponts to throw out outposts in the direction of the Enemy and check his advance as much as possible, falling back upon the post when forced to retire and assisting in its defence —

I requested Lieut Bromhead to post his men, and having seen his and every man at his post, he once more went on.

About 4.20 p.m. the sound of firing was heard behind the hills to our South. The officer of Durnford returned reporting the Enemy close upon us, and that his men would not obey his orders, but were going off to Helpmakaar and I saw them apparently about 100, in number going off in that direction.

About the same time Capt. Stephenson's detachment of Natal Native Contingent left us, as did that officer himself.

I saw that our line of defence was too extended for the small number of men now left us and at once commenced a retrenchment of biscuit boxes.

We had not completed a wall two boxes high when about 4.30 p.m. 500 or 600 of the Enemy came in sight around the hills to our South

and advanced at a run against our South
wall. They were met by a well sustained
fire but notwithstanding their heavy loss,
continued the advance to within 50 yards of
the wall when they met with such a heavy
fire from the wall, and cross-fire from the
store that they were checked, but taking advantage of the cover afforded by the cook-house
ovens &. Kept up a heavy fire.
The greater number however without stopping
moved to the left around the hospital and
made a rush at our N.W. wall of mealie bags
but after a short but desperate struggle were
driven back with heavy loss into the bush
around the work.

The main body of the enemy were close
behind and had lined the ledge of rocks
and caves overlooking us about 400yds
to our South from where they kept up a
constant fire and advancing somewhat
more to their left than the first attack
occupied the garden, hollow road and bush
in great force.

Taking advantage of the bush which we
had not time to cut down the Enemy were
able to advance under cover close to our
wall and in this part soon held one side
of the wall while we held the other.

A series of desperate assaults were made
extending from the hospital along the wall
as the bush reached, but each was most
splendidly met and repulsed by our men
with the bayonet. Corpl. Schiess N.N.C.
greatly distinguishing himself by his conspicuous
gallantry.

The fire from the rocks behind us, though
badly directed, took us completely in reverse

and was so heavy that we had suffered very
severely, and about 6 pm were forced to
retire behind the retrenchment of biscuit
boxes -

All this time the enemy had been attempting
to force the hospital and shortly after set
fire to its roof -

The Garrison of the hospital defended it
room by room, bringing out all the sick
who could be moved before they retired.

Privates Williams, Hook, & Jones 2nd Bn. 24th Reg.t
being the last men to leave holding the
doorway with the bayonet their own
ammunition being expended.

From the want of interior communication
and the burning of the house it was
impossible to save all - With most
heartfelt sorrow I regret we could not
save these poor fellows from their
terrible fate.

Seeing the hospital burning and the
desperate attempts of the enemy to fire
the roof of the stores we converted two
mealie bag heaps, into a sort of redoubt
which gave a second line of fire all
round. Asst. Commy. Dunne working
hard at this though much exposed, and
rendering valuable assistance -

As darkness came on we were
completely surrounded and after several
attempts had been gallantly repulsed
were eventually forced to retire to the
middle and then inner wall of the
Kraal on our East - The position we
then had we retained throughout -

A desultory fire was kept up, all night

and several assaults were attempted
and repulsed; the vigour of the attack
continuing until after midnight; our men
firing with the greatest coolness did not
waste a single shot; the light afforded
by the burning hospital being of great
help to us —

About 4 am 23rd inst the firing ceased
and at daybreak the enemy were out
of sight over the hill to the South West
We patrolled the ground collecting
the arms of the dead Zulus and —
strengthened our defence as much as
possible

We were removing the thatch from
the roof of the stores, when about 7 am
a large body of the Enemy appeared on
the hills to the S.W. —

I sent a friendly Kaffir who had come in
shortly before with a note to the Officer
Commanding at Helpmakaar asking
for help —

About 8 am the third column appeared
in sight the Enemy who had been —
gradually advancing falling back as
they approached I consider the Enemy
who attacked us to have numbered
about 3,000 (three thousand).

We Killed about 350 (three hundred & fifty)
Of the steadiness and gallant behaviour
of the whole garrison I cannot speak too
highly.

I wish especially to bring to your
notice the conduct of

Lieut Bromhead 2/24th Regt and the splendid

behaviour of his company B 2/24th

Surgeon Reynolds QMG in his constant attention to the wounded under fire when they fell

Acting Commt Officer Dalton to whose Energy much of our defences were due and who was severely wounded while gallantly assisting in the defence.

Asst Commy Dunne

Actg Store Keeper Byrne (Killed)

Col Sergt Bourne 2/24th

Sergt Williams 2/24th (wounded dangerously since dead)

Sergt Kendrick 2/24

Corpl Scheiss 2/3 Natal Native Contgt (wounded)

1395 Private Williams 2/24th   Private Hook 2/24th
593 ,, H. Jones 2/24th 716 ,, Jones ,,
—— Mr Mahon A.H.C. - Roy 1/24th

The following return shows the number present at Rorkes Drift 22nd Jany 1879

	Officers	NCO men	SICK Officers	SICK NCO men	Total
Staff		1			1
Royal Artillery		1		3	4
Royal Engineers	1	1			2
3rd Buffs		1			1
1/24th Regt		6		5	11
2/24th " B Company } S & Transport	1	81		17	99
90th Lt Infantry				1	1
Commy & Transport	3	1			4
A.M.D.	1	3			4
Chaplain	1				1
Natal Mounted Police				3	3
Natal Native Contgt	1			6	7
Ferryman		1			1
	8	96	0	35	139

The following is a list of the Killed

Sergt Mumford 2/24th Regt   1393 Pt Williams 7-24th
Pte Scanlan   Nicolls 7/24.
   Crawley   Horrigan 7/24
   Adams   Jenkins —
   Cole   Mr Byrne Comm: Sr:
   Fagan   Trooper Bender N M P.
   Chick   Anderson N N C
                     1 Pte (Native) ....

          Total 15

12 Wounded * of whom two have since died
Viz Sergt Williams 2/24th Regt
     Pte Beckett 1/24th —
making a total killed of 17

* List already forwarded by Medical Officer

Herewith is appended a plan of the
building showing our lines of defence
The points of the compass referred to in
this report are as shown in sketch
approximately magnetic.

       I have the honor to be
         your obedient servant
           Jno Rouse Merriott Chard
                 Lieut RE

To Col Glyn C.B.
Comg. 3rd Column

The report was then urgently forwarded to the Secretary of State For War, The Right Hon. Frederic Stanley, who promptly replied to Chelmsford:

From; The Secretary of State For War   20-3-79
To; Lt. Gen. Lord Chelmsford, K.C.B.

My Lord,

I have received with great satisfaction your despatch of the 8th Feb. last, and its enclosure from Lt. Chard, R.E., containing a narrative of the heroic defence of the Post at Rorke's Drift on the night of the 22nd Jan. last.

Having laid these documents before the Queen, I have received her Majesty's Commands to express to you her admiration of the gallantry of all who took part in that brilliant defence. The fertility of resource displayed in improvising defences and the cool and determined courage by which they were guarded and maintained have been especially remarked by her Majesty and will worthily take a prominent place in the annals of the British Army.

I have conferred with H.R.H. The F.M. C. in C., as to the recognition which those officers, N.C.O.'s, Privates and others who are specially mentioned should receive, and I shall lose no time in making the necessary recommendations to Her Majesty on the subject.

Fred Stanley

The Second 'Chard Report'

RORKE'S DRIFT
The Defence of Rorke's Drift, 22nd–23rd January 1879

An account of the defence of Rorke's Drift, written by Major J. R. M. Chard, V.C., R.E., at the personal request of Queen Victoria, and submitted to Her Majesty at Windsor Castle on 21st February 1880.

Early in January 1879, shortly after the arrival of the 5th Company, Royal Engineers, at Durban, an order came from Lord Chelmsford directing that an officer and a few good men of the R.E., with mining implement, etc., should join the 3rd Column as soon as possible. I was consequently sent on in advance of the company, with a light mule wagon containing the necessary tools, etc., and in which the men could also ride on level ground; with a Corporal, three Sappers and one Driver, my batman, who rode one, and looked after my horses. The wagon was driven by a Cape black man, with a Natal Kaffir lad as vorlooper. The roads were so bad that in spite of all our exertions, our progress was slow, and although we got a fresh team at Pieter-maritzburg, we did not reach Rorke's Drift until the morning of the 19th January 1879. The 3rd Column was encamped on the other side (left bank) of the river Buffalo, and the wagons were still crossing in the ponts. I pitched my two tents on the right (Natal) bank of the river, near the ponts, and close to the store accommodation there for keeping them in repair. On the 20th January, the 3rd Column broke up its camp on the Buffalo River and marched to Isandhlwana, where it encamped, and the same evening, or following morning, Colonel Durnford's force arrived and took up its camp near where the 3rd Column had been.

There were two large ponts at the river, one of which only was in working order, and my sappers were during this time working at the other. Late in the evening of the 21st January I received an order from the 3rd Column to say that the men of the R.E., who had lately arrived, were to proceed to the camp at Isandhlwana at once – I had received no orders concerning myself. I reported this to Major Spalding, who was now in command at Rorke's Drift, and also pointed out to him that the sappers leaving there were no means at my disposal for putting the ponts in working order, or keeping them so. Major Spalding had also received no orders respecting me, except that I was to select a suitable position protecting the ponts, for Captain Rainforth's Company 1/24th to entrench itself. I consequently asked, and obtained permission from Major Spalding, to go to the camp at Isandhlwana and see the orders.

On the morning of the 22nd January, I put the corporal and three sappers in the empty wagon, with their field kits, etc., to take them to the camp of the 3rd Column; and also rode out myself. The road was very heavy in some places, and the wagon went slowly; so I rode on in advance, arrived at the Isandhlwana Camp, went to the Head-Quarters Tent, and got a copy of the orders as affecting me, and also the road between Helpmekaar and Rorke's

Drift and the orders also particularly stated that my duties lay on the right bank of the River Buffalo.

A N.C.O. of the 24th Regiment lent me a field glass, which was a very good one, and I also looked with my own, and could see the enemy moving on the distant hills, and apparently in great force. Large numbers of them moving to my left, until the lion hill of Isandhlwana, on my left as I looked at them, hid them from my view. The idea struck me that they might be moving in the direction between the camp and Rorke's Drift and prevent my getting back, and also that they might be going to make a dash at the ponts.

Seeing what my duties were, I left the camp, and a quarter of a mile, or less, out of it met with Colonel Durnford, R.E., riding at the head of his mounted men – I told him what I had seen, and took some orders, and a message all along his line, at his request. At the foot of the hill I met my men in the wagon and made them get out and walk up the hill with Durnford's men. I brought the wagon back with me to Rorke's Drift, where on arrival I found the following order had been issued. The copy below was given me, and preserved from the fact of its being in my pocket during the fight:

Camp Rorke's Drift
22nd January 1879.

Camp Morning Orders.
1.   The force under Lt. Col. Durnford, R.E., having departed, a Guard of 6 Privates and 1 N.C.O. will be furnished by the detachment 2/24th Regiment on the ponts.
A Guard of 50 armed natives will likewise be furnished by Capt. Stevenson's detachment at the same spot – The ponts will be invariably drawn over to the Natal side at night. This duty will cease on the arrival of Capt. Rainforth's Company, 1/24th Regiment.
2.   In accordance with para. 19 Regulations for Field Forces in South Africa, Capt. Rainforth's Company, 1/24th Regiment, will entrench itself on the spot assigned to it by Column Orders para. – dated –
H. SPALDING, MAJOR,
Commanding.

The Guard as detailed was over the ponts – Captain Rainforth's Company had not arrived. I went at once to Major Spalding on arrival, told him what I had seen, and pointed out to him that in the event of an attack on the ponts it would be impossible with 7 men (not counting the natives) to make an effective defence. (According to the orders, Capt. Rainforth's Company should have been already at Rorke's Drift.)

Major Spalding told me he was going over to Helpmekaar, and would see about getting it down at once. Just as I was about to ride away he said to me 'Which of you is senior, you or Bromhead?' I said 'I don't know' – he went back into his tent, looked at an Army List, and coming back, said – 'I see you are senior, so you will be in charge, although, of course, nothing will happen, and I shall be back again this evening early.'

I then went down to my tent by the river, had some lunch comfortably, and was writing a letter home when my attention was called to two horsemen galloping towards us from the direction of Isandhlwana. From their gesticulation and their shouts, when they were near enough to be heard, we saw that something was the matter, and on taking them over the river, one of them, Lieut. Adendorff of Lonsdale's Regiment, Natal Native Contingent, asking if I was an officer, jumped off his horse, took me on one side, and told me that the camp was in the hands of the Zulus and the army destroyed; that scarcely a man had got away to tell the tale, and that probably Lord Chelmsford and the rest of the column had shared the same fate. His companion, a Carbineer, confirmed his story – He was naturally very excited and I am afraid I did not, at first, quite believe him, and intimated that he probably had not remained to see what did occur. I had the saddle put on my horse, and while I was talking to Lieut. Adendorff, a messenger arrived from Lieut. Bromhead, who was with his Company at his little camp near the Commissariat Stores, to ask me to come up at once.

I gave the order to inspan the wagon and put all the stores, tents, etc., they could into it. I posted the sergeant and six men on the high ground over the pont, behind a natural wall of rocks, forming a strong position from which there was a good view over the river and ground in front, with orders to wait until I came or sent for them. The guard of natives had left some time before and had not been relieved. I galloped up at once to the Commissariat Stores and found that a pencil note had been sent from the 3rd Column by

Capt. Allan Gardner to state that the enemy were advancing in force against our post – Lieut. Bromhead had, with the assistance of Mr. Dalton, Dr. Reynolds, and the other officers present, commenced barricading and loopholing the store building and the Missionary's house, which was used as a Hospital, and connecting the defence of the two buildings by walls of mealie bags, and two wagons that were on the ground. The Native Contingent, under their officer, Capt. Stephenson, were working hard at this with our own men, and the walls were rapidly progressing. A letter escribing what had happened had been sent by Bromhead by two men of the Mounted Infantry, who had arrived fugitives from Isandhlwana, to the Officer Commanding at Helpmekaar. These two men crossed the river at Fugitives Drift, with some others and as they have since reported to me, came to give notice of what had happened, to us at Rorke's Drift, of their own accord and without orders from anyone.

I held a consultation with Lieut. Bromhead, and with Mr. Dalton, whose energy, intelligence and gallantry were of the greatest service to us, and whom, as I said in my report at the time, and I am sure Bromhead would unite with me in saying again now, I cannot sufficiently thank for his services. I went round the position with them and then rode down to the ponts where I found everything ready for a start, ponts in midstream, hawsers and cables sunk, etc. It was at this time that the Pontman Daniells, and Sergt. Milne, 3rd Buffs, who had been employed for some time in getting the ponts in order, and working them under Lieut. MacDowell, R.E. (killed at Isandhlwana), offered to defend the ponts, moored in the middle of the river, from their decks with a few men. Sergt. Williams 24th and his little guard were quite ready to join them.

We arrived at the Commissariat Store about 3.30 p.m. Shortly afterwards an officer of Durnford's Horse reported his arrival from Isandhlwana, and I requested him to observe the movements, and check the advance, of the enemy as much as possible until forced to fall back. I saw each man at his post, and then the work went on again. Several fugitives from the Camp arrived, and tried to impress upon us the madness of an attempt to defend the place. Who they were I do not know, but it is scarcely necessary for me to say that there were no officers of H.M. Army among them. They stopped the work very much – it being impossible to prevent the men getting around them in little groups to hear their story. They proved the truth on their belief in what they said by leaving us to our fate, and in the state of mind they were in, I think our little garrison was as well without them. As far as I know, but one of the fugitives remained with us – Lieut. Adendorff, whom I have before mentioned. He remained to assist in the defence, and from a loop-hole in the store building, flanking the wall and Hospital, his rifle did good service.

There were several casks of rum in the Store building, and I gave strict orders to Sergt. Windridge, 24th Regiment, who was in charge (acting as issuer of Commissariat stores to the troops) that the spirit was not to be touched, the man posted nearest it was to be considered on guard over it, and after giving fair warning, was to shoot without altercation anyone attempted to force his post, and Sergt. Windridge being there was to see this carried out. Sergt. Windridge showed great intelligence and energy in arranging the stores for the defence of the Commissariat store, forming loopholes, etc.

The Reverend George Smith, Vicar of Estcourt, Natal, and acting Army Chaplain, went for a walk (before the news of the disaster reached us) to the top of the Oscarberg, the hill behind Rorke's Drift. Mr. Witt, the missionary, went with him, or met him there. They went to see what could be seen in the direction of the Isandhlwana camp. He saw the force of the enemy which attacked us at Rorke's Drift, cross the river in three bodies – and after snuff-taking, and other ceremonies, advance in our direction. He had been watching them for a long time with interest, and thought they were our own Native Contingent. There were two mounted men leading them, and he did not realize that they were the enemy until they were near enough for him to see that these two men also had black faces. He came running down the hill and was agreeably surprised to find that we were getting ready for the enemy. Mr. Witt, whose wife and family were in a lonely house not very far off, rode off, taking with him a sick officer, who was very ill in hospital and only just able to ride. Mr. Smith, however, although he might well have left, elected to remain with us, and during   the attack did good service in supplying the men with ammunition.

About 4.20 p.m. the sound of firing was heard behind the Oscarberg. The officer of Durnford's returned, reporting the enemy close upon us, and that his men would not obey his orders but were going off to Helpmekaar, and I saw them, about 100 in number, going off in that direction. I have seen these same men behave so well since that I have spoken with several of their conduct – and they all said, as their excuse, that Durnford was killed, and it was no use. About the same time Capt. Stephenson's detachment of Natal Native Contingent left us – probably most fortunately for us. I am sorry to say that their officer, who had been doing good service in getting his men to work, also deserted us. We seemed very few, now all these people had gone, and I saw that our line of defence was too extended, and at once commenced a retrenchment of biscuit boxes, so as to get a place we could fall back upon if we could not hold the whole.

Private Hitch, 24th, was on the top of the thatch roof of the Commissariat Store keeping a look-out. He was severely wounded early in the evening, but notwithstanding, with Corpl. Allen, 24th, who was also wounded, continued to do good service, and they both when incapacitated by their wounds from using their rifles, still continued under fire serving their comrades with ammunition.

We had not completed a wall two boxes high when, about 4.30 p.m., Hitch cried out that the enemy was in sight, and he saw them, apparently 500 or 600 in number, come around the hill to our south (the Oscarberg) and advance at a run against our south wall.

We opened fire on them, between five and six hundred yards, at first a little wild, but only for a short time, a chief on horseback was dropped by Private Dunbar, 24th. The men were quite steady, and the Zulus began to fall very thick. However, it did not seem to stop them at all, although they took advantage of the cover and ran stooping with their faces near the ground. It seemed as if nothing would stop them, and they rushed on in spite of their heavy loss to within 50 yards of the wall, when they were taken in flank by the fire from the end wall of the store building, and met with such a heavy direct fire from the mealie wall, and the Hospital at the same time, that they were checked as if by magic.

They occupied the Cook-house ovens, banks and other cover, but the greater number, without stopping, moved to their left around the Hospital, and made a rush at the end of the Hospital, and at our north-west line of mealie bags. There was a short but desperate struggle during which Mr.

Dalton shot a Zulu who was in the act of assegaing a corporal of the Army Hospital Corps, the muzzle of whose rifle he had seized, and with Lieut. Bromhead and many of the men behaved with great gallantry. The Zulus forced us back from that part of the wall immediately in front of the Hospital, but after suffering very severely in the struggle were driven back into the bush around our position.

The main body of the enemy were close behind the first force which appeared, and had lined the ledge of rocks and caves in the Oscarberg overlooking us, and about three or four hundred yards to our south, from where they kept up a constant fire. Advancing somewhat more to their left than the first attack, they occupied the garden, hollow road, and bush in great force. The bush grew close to our wall and we had not had time to cut it down to our wall, and in this part soon held one side of the wall, while we held the other.

A series of desperate assaults was made, on the Hospital, and extending from the Hospital, as far as the bush reached; but each was most splendidly met and repulsed by our men, with the bayonet. Each time as the attack was repulsed by us, the Zulus close to us seemed to vanish in the bush, those some little distance off keeping up a fire all the time. Then, as if moved by a single impulse, they rose up in the bush as thick as possible, rushing madly up to the wall (some of them being already close to it), seizing, where they could, the muzzles of our men's rifles, or their bayonets, and attempting to use their assegais and to get over the wall. A rapid rattle of fire from our rifles, stabs with the bayonet, and in a few moments the Zulus were driven back, disappearing in the bush as before, and keeping up their fire. A brief interval, and the attack would be again made, and repulsed in the same manner. Over and over again this happened, our men behaving with the greatest coolness and gallantry.

It is impossible for one individual to see all, but I particularly myself noticed the behaviour of Col. Sgt. Bourne, 24th, Sergt. Williams 24th, Corpl. Scheis N.N.C., Corpl. Lyons 24th, Private McMahon A.H.C., Privates Roy, Deacon, Bush, Cole, Jenkins 24th, and many others.

Our fire at the time of these rushes of the Zulus was very rapid – Mr. Dalton dropping a man each time he fired his rifle, while Bromhead and myself used our revolvers. The fire from the rocks and caves on the hill behind us was kept up all this time and took us completely in reverse, and although very badly directed, many shots came among us and caused us some loss – and at about 6.00 p.m. the enemy extending their attack further to their left, I feared seriously would get in over our wall behind the biscuit boxes. I ran back with 2 or 3 men to this part of the wall and was immediately joined by Bromhead with 2 or 3 more. The enemy stuck to this assault most tenaciously, and on their repulse, and retiring into the bush, I called all the men inside out retrenchment – and the enemy immediately occupied the wall we had abandoned and used is as a breastwork to fire over.

Mr. Byrne, acting Commissariat Officer, and who had behaved with great coolness and gallantry, was killed instantaneously shortly before this by a bullet through the head, just after he had given a drink of water to a wounded man of the N.N.C.

All this time the enemy had been attempting to fire the Hospital and had at length set fire to its roof and got in at the far end. I had tried to impress upon the men in the Hospital the necessity for making a communication right through the building – unfortunately this was not done. Probably at the time the men could not see the necessity, and doubtless also there was no time to do it. Without in the least detracting from the gallant fellows who defended the Hospital, and I hope I shall not be misunderstood in saying so, I have always regretted, as I did then, the absence of my four poor sappers, who had only left that morning for Isandhlwana and arrived there just to be killed.

The garrison of the Hospital defended it with the greatest gallantry, room by room, bringing out all the sick that could be moved, and breaking through some of the partitions while the Zulus were in the building with them. Privates Williams, Hook, R. Jones and W. Jones being the last to leave and holding the doorway with the bayonet, their ammunition being expended. Private Williams's bayonet was wrenched off his rifle by a Zulu, but with the other men he still managed with the muzzle of his rifle to keep the enemy at bay. Surgeon Reynolds carried his arms full of ammunition to the Hospital, a bullet striking his helmet as he did so. But we were too busily engaged outside to be able to do much, and with the Hospital on fire, and no free communication, nothing could have saved it. Sergeant Maxfield 24th might have been saved, but he was delirious with fever, refused to move and resisted the attempts to move him. He was assegaied before our men's eyes.

Seeing the hospital burning, and the attempts of one enemy to fire the roof of the Store (one man was shot, I believe by Lt. Adendorff, who had a light almost touching the thatch), we converted two large heaps of mealie bags into a sort of redoubt which gave a second line of fire all around, in case the store building had to be abandoned, or the enemy broke through elsewhere. Assistant Commissary Dunne worked hard at this, and from his height, being a tall man, he was much exposed, in addition to the fact that the heaps were high above our walls, and that most of the Zulus bullets were high.

Trooper Hunter, Natal Mounted Police, escaping from the Hospital, stood still for a moment, hesitating which way to go, dazed by the glare of the burning Hospital, and the firing that was going on all around. He was assegaied before our eyes, the Zulu who killed him immediately afterwards falling. While firing from behind the biscuit boxes, Dalton, who had been using his rifle with deadly effect, and by his quickness and coolness had been the means of saving many men's lives, was shot through the body. I was standing near him at the time, and he handed me his rifle so coolly that I had no idea until afterwards of how severely he was wounded. He waited quite quietly for me to take the cartridges he had left out of his pockets. We put him inside one mealie sack redoubt, building it up around him. About this time I noticed Private Dunbar 24th make some splendid shooting, seven or eight Zulus falling on the ledge of rocks in the Oscarberg to as many consecutive shots by him. I saw Corporal Lyons hit by a bullet which lodged in his spine, and fall between an opening we had left in the wall of biscuit boxes. I though he was killed, but looking up he said, 'Oh, Sir! You are not going to leave me here like a dog?' We pulled him in and laid him down behind the boxes where he was immediately looked to by Reynolds.

Corporal Scammle [Scammell] of the Natal Native Contingent, who was badly wounded through the shoulder, staggered out under fire again, from the Store building where he had been put, and gave me all his cartridges, which in his wounded state he could not use. While I was intently watching to get a fair shot at a Zulu who appeared to be firing rather well, Private Jenkins 24th, saying 'Look out, Sir,' gave my head a duck down just as a bullet whizzed over it. He had noticed a Zulu who was quite near in another direction taking a deliberate aim at me. For all the man could have known, the shot might have been directed at himself. I mention these facts to show how well the men behaved and how loyally worked together.

Corporal Scheiss, Natal Native Contingent, who was a patient in the Hospital with a wound in the foot, which caused him great pain, behaved with the greatest coolness and gallantry throughout the attack, and at this time creeping out a short distance along the wall we had abandoned, and slowly raising himself, to get a shot at some of the enemy who had been particularly annoying, his hat was blown off by a shot from a Zulu the other side of the wall. He immediately jumped up, bayonetted the Zulu and shot a second, and bayonetted a third who came to their assistance, and then returned to his place.

As darkness came on we were completely surrounded. The Zulus wrecking the camp of the Company 24th and my wagon which had been left outside, in spite of the efforts of my batman, Driver Robson (the only man of the Royal Engineers with us), who had directed his particular attention to keeping the Zulus off his wagon in which were, as he described it, 'Our things.'

They also attacked the east end of our position, and after being several times repulsed, eventually got into the Kraal, which was strongly built with high walls, and drove us to the middle, and then to the inner wall of the Kraal – the enemy occupying the middle wall as we abandoned it. This wall was too high for them to use it effectively to fire over, and a Zulu no sooner showed his head over it than he was dropped, being so close that it was almost impossible to miss him. Shortly before this, some of the men said they saw the red-coats coming on the Helpmekaar road. The rumour passed quickly round – I could see nothing of the sort myself, but some men said they could. A cheer was raised, and the enemy seemed to pause, to know what it meant, but there was no answer to it, and darkness came. It is very strange that this report should have arisen amongst us, for the two companies 24th from Helpmekaar did come down to the foot of the hill, but not, I believe, in sight of us. They marched back to Helpmekaar on the report of Rorke's Drift having fallen.

After the first onslaught, the most formidable of the enemy's attacks was just before we retired behind our line of biscuit boxes, and for a short time after it, when they had gained great confidence by their success on the Hospital. Although they kept their positions behind the walls we had abandoned, and kept up a heavy fire from all sides until about 12 o'clock, they did not actually charge up in a body to get over our wall after about 9 or 10 o'clock. After this time it became very dark, although the Hospital roof was still burning – it was impossible from below to see what was going on, and Bromhead and myself getting up on the mealy sack redoubt, kept an anxious watch on all sides.

The enemy were now in strong force all around us, and every now and then a confused shout of 'Usutu' from many voices seemed to show that they were going to attack from one side and immediately the same thing would happen on the other, leaving us in doubt as to where they meant to attack. About midnight or a little after the fire slackened, and after that, although they kept us constantly on the alert, by feigning, as before, to come on at different points, the fire was of a desultory character. Our men were careful, and only fired when they could see a fair chance. The flame of the burning Hospital was now getting low, and as pieces of the roof fell, or hitherto unburnt parts of the thatch ignited, the flames would blaze up illuminating our helmets and faces. A few shots from the Zulus, replied to by our men – again silence, broken only by the same thing repeatedly happening. This sort of thing went on until about 4 a.m. and we were anxiously waiting for daybreak and the renewal of the attack, which their comparative, and at length complete silence, led us to expect. But at daybreak the enemy were out of sight, over the hill to our south-west. One Zulu remained in the Kraal and fired a shot among us (without doing any damage) as we stood on the walls, and ran off in the direction of the river – although many shots were fired at him as he ran. I am glad to say the plucky fellow got off.

Taking care not to be surprised by any ruse of the enemy, we patrolled the ground around the place, collecting the arms, and ammunition, of the dead Zulus.

Some of the bullet wounds were very curious. One man's head was split open, exactly as if done with an axe. Another had been hit just between the eyes, the bullet carrying away the whole of the back of his head, leaving his face perfect, as though it were a mask, only disfigured by the small hole made by the bullet passing through. One of the wretches we found, one hand grasping a bench that had been dragged from the Hospital, and sustained thus in the position we found him in, while in the other hand he still clutched the knife with which he had mutilated one of our poor fellows, over whom he was still leaning.

We increased the strength of our defences as much as possible, strengthening and raising our walls, putting sacks on the biscuit boxes, etc., and were removing the thatch from the roof of the Commissariat Store, to avoid being burnt out in case of another attack, when at about 7 a.m. a large body of the enemy (I believe the same who had attacked us) appeared on the hills to the south-west. I thought at the time that they were going to attack us, but from what I now know from Zulus, and also of the number we put hors de combat, I do not think so. I think that they came up on the high ground to observe Lord Chelmsford's advance; from there they could see the Column long before it came in sight of us.

A frightened and fugitive Kaffir came in shortly before, and I sent for Daniells the Pontman, who could speak Zulu a little, to interview him. Daniells had armed himself with Spalding's sword, which he flourished in so wild and eccentric manner that the poor wretch thought his last hour had come. He professed to be friendly and to have escaped from Isandhlwana, and I sent him with a note to the Officer Commanding at Helpmekaar, explaining our situation, and asking for help; for now, although the men were in excellent spirits, and each man had a good supply of ammunition in his pouches, we had only about a box and a half left besides, and at this time we had no definite knowledge of what had happened, and I myself did not know that the part of the Column with Lord Chelmsford had taken any part in the action at Isandhlwana, or whether on the Camp being taken he had fallen back on Helpmekaar.

The enemy remained on the hill, and still more of them appeared, when about 8 a.m. the Column came in sight and the enemy disappeared again. There were a great many of our Native Levies with the Column, and the number of red-coats seemed so few that at first we had grave doubts that the force approaching was the enemy. We improvised a flag, and our signals were soon replied to from the Column. The mounted men crossed the Drift and galloped up to us, headed by Major Cecil Russell and Lieut. Walsh, and were received by us with a hearty cheer. Lord Chelmsford, with his Staff, shortly after rode up and thanked us all with much emotion for the defence we had made. The Column arrived, crossing by the Ponts, and we then had a busy time in making a strong position for the night.

I was glad to seize an opportunity to wash my face in a muddy puddle, in company with Private Bush 24th, whose face was covered with blood from a wound in the nose caused by the bullet which had passed through and killed Private Cole 24th. With the politeness of a soldier, he lent me his towel, or, rather, a very dirty half of one, before using it himself, and I was very glad to accept it.

In wrecking the stores in my wagon, the Zulus had brought to light a forgotten bottle of beer, and Bromhead and I drank it with mutual congratulations on having come safely out of so much danger.

My wagon driver, a Cape (coloured) man, lost his courage on hearing the first firing around the hill. He let loose his mules and retreated, concealing himself in one of the caves of the Oscarberg. He saw the Zulus run by him and, to his horror, some of them entered the cave he was in, and lying down commenced firing at us. The poor wretch was crouching in the darkness, in the far depths of the cave, afraid to speak or move, and our bullets came into the cave, actually killing one of the Zulus. He did not know from whom he was in the most danger, friends or foes, and came down in the morning looking more dead than alive. The mules we recovered; they were quietly grazing by the riverside.

On my journey homewards, on arriving at the railway station, Durban, I asked a porter to get me some Kaffirs to carry my bags to the hotel. He sent several, and the first to come running up was my vorlooper boy who had taken me to Rorke's Drift. He stopped short and looked very frightened, and I believe at first thought he saw my ghost. I seized him to prevent his running away, and when he saw that I was flesh and blood he became reassured. He said he thought I got away, he said (the solution of the mystery just striking him), 'I know you rode away on the other horse.' As far as I could learn and according to his own story, the boy had taken the horse I rode from the river to the Commissariat Store, and, wild with terror, had ridden it to Pietermaritzburg without stopping, where he gave it over to the Transport people, but having no certificate to say who he was, they took the horse from him but would not give him any employment.

During the fight there were some very narrow escapes from the burning Hospital. Private Waters, 24th Regiment, told me that he secreted himself in a cupboard in the room he was defending, and from it shot several Zulus inside the Hospital. He was wounded in the arm, and he remained in the cupboard until the heat and smoke were so great that they threatened to suffocate him. Wrapping himself in a cloak, or skirt of a dress he found in the cupboard, he rushed out into the darkness and made his way into the cook-house. The Zulus were occupying this, and firing at us from the wall nearest us. It was too late to retreat, so he crept softly to the fireplace and, standing up in the chimney, blacked his face and hands with soot. He remained there until the Zulus left. He was very nearly shot in coming out, one of our men at the wall raising his rifle to do so at the sight of his black face and strange costume, but Waters cried out just in time to save himself. He produced the bullet that wounded him, with pardonable pride, and was very amusing in his admiring description of Dr. Reynolds's skill in extracting it.

Gunner Howard, R.A., ran out of the burning Hospital, through the enemy, and lay down on the upper side of the wall in front of our N. Parapet. The bodies of several horses that were killed early in the evening were lying here, and concealed by these and by Zulu bodies and the low grass and bushes, he remained unseen with the Zulus all around him until they left in the morning.

Private Beckett, 24th Regiment, escaped from the Hospital in the same direction, he was badly wounded with assegais in running through the enemy. He managed to get away and conceal himself in the ditch of the Garden, where we found him next morning. The poor fellow was so weak from loss of blood that he could not walk, and he died shortly afterwards.

Our mealie-bag walls were afterwards replaced by loopholed walls of stone, the work making rapid progress upon the arrival of half the 5th Company R.E. with Lieut. Porter. As soon as the Sappers arrived we put a fence around, and a rough wood cross over, the graves of our poor men who were killed. This was afterwards replaced by a neat stone monument and inscription by the 24th, who remained to garrison the place.

I have already, in my report, said how gallantly all behaved, from Lieutenant Bromhead downwards, and I also mentioned those whom I had particularly noticed to have distinguished themselves.

On the day following, we buried 351 bodies of the enemy in graves not far from the Commissariat Buildings – many bodies were since discovered and buried, and when I was sick at Ladysmith one of our Sergeants, who came down there invalided from Rorke's Drift, where he had been employed in the construction of Fort Melvill, told me that many Zulu bodies were found in the caves and among the rocks, a long distance from the Mission house, when getting stone for that fort. As, in my report, I underestimated the number we killed, so I believe I also underestimated the number of the enemy that attacked us, and from what I have since learnt I believe the Zulus must have numbered at least 4,000.

As the Reverend George Smith said in a short account he wrote to a Natal paper – 'Whatever signs of approval may be conferred upon the defenders of Rorke's Drift, from high quarters, they will never cease to remember the kind and heartfelt expressions of gratitude which have fallen both from the columns of the Colonial Press and from so many of the Natal Colonists themselves.'

And to this may I add that they will ever remember with heartfelt gratitude the signs of approval that have been conferred upon them by their Sovereign and by the People and the Press of England.

JOHN R. M. CHARD,

January 1880.   Captain and Bt. Major, R.E

The Bromhead Report and Letters

Bromhead's report

This report, signed by Bromhead in his capacity as commander of B Company, was submitted to Colonel Glyn more than two weeks after the defence of Rorke's Drift. The identity of the author of this report is unknown although the report is signed by Bromhead. (See Chapter 9 for further details.) The report is produced unabridged and unaltered.

From: Lieut. Gonville Bromhead 2/24th Regt.

To: The Officer Commanding 2/24th Regiment
Rorke's drift
15th February 1879
Sir,
I beg to bring to your notice the names of the following men belonging to my Company who especially distinguished themselves during the attack by the Zulus on this Post on the 22nd and 23rd January last; and whose conduct on this occasion came under my personal cognisance.

<u>No. 1395 Private John Williams</u> was posted by me together with private Joseph Williams and Private William Horrigan 1/24th Regt. in a further room of the Hospital. They held it for more than an hour, so long as they had a round of ammunition left, when, as communication was for the time cut off, the Zulus were enabled to advance and burst open the door. They dragged

out Private Joseph Williams and two of the patients by the arms, and assagaied them. Whilst the Zulus were occupied with the slaughter of these unfortunate men, a lull took place, during which Private John Williams – who with two patients were then only men left alive in this ward – succeeded in knocking a hole in the partition, and taking the two patients with him into the next ward, where he found

No. 1373 Private Henry Hook. These two men together, one man working whilst the other fought and held the enemy at bay with his bayonet, broke through three more partitions, and were thus enabled to bring eight patients through a small window into our inner line of defence.

In another ward, facing the hill, I had placed

No. 593 Private William Jones & No. 716 Private Robert Jones: They defended their post to the last, until six out of the seven patients it contained had been removed. The seventh, Sergeant Maxfield, 2/24th Regt. was delirious from fever. Although they had previously dressed him, they were unable to induce him to move. When Private Robert Jones returned to endeavour to carry him away, he found him being stabbed by the Zulus as he lay on his bed –

No. 1240 Corporal William Allen & No. 1362 Private Frederick Hitch, must also be mentioned. It was chiefly due to their courageous conduct that communication with the Hospital was kept up at all. Holding together at all costs a most dangerous post, raked in reverse by the enemy's fire from the hill, they were both severely wounded, but their determined conduct enabled the patients to be withdrawn from the Hospital, & when incapacitated by their wounds from fighting themselves, they continued, as soon as their wounds had been dressed, to serve out ammunition to their comrades during the night.

> I have the honour to be
> Sir
> Your most obedient servant
> G. Bromhead
> Lieut. 2/24th Regt.
> Commanding B Company 2/24th Regt.

Note: It was to this report that Lord Chelmsford added the names of Lieutenants Bromhead and Chard.

Bromhead's letters

Both of the following Bromhead letters are unabridged:

Bromhead's letter to Lieutenant Goodwin-Austen

Rorke's Drift

19th February 1879

My Dear Austin, [sic]

I can't tell you how grieved I was to hear on the return of the Column on the 23rd of January that your brother had been left in that fateful camp. He had been attached to B Co at Freetown and we got on so jolly together that he told me he should ask the Col. to let him stay with the Company, but I am sorry to say it was not to be. The night before the Column transport crossed the river it came out in orders that B Company were to remain here and your brother was sent back to G Company and Griffiths who was Company Officer as usual was posted to the Company. Your brother who was knocked up from over work at the ponts, where he had been working day and night, to get troops across the river had to go sick, but still he march [sic] with the Column. I have not got over the dreadful news we received yet, in fact can hardly believe it. We had an awful night of it here as you may fancy. We heard the camp had been taken, and were also afraid that the Column had received a heavy blow, and the Zulus came at us in such force and with such fierce pluck. I thought we should never pull through it, but the Company behaved splendidly [word illegible] as our ammunition held out and we held them back till daylight. We were on the Natal side of the Buffalo but can do nothing as far as I can see until we are fitted up again. I hope they are going to send us out some more troops or you wont see many of us again. The Zulus are so strong we stand a poor chance against them, as it is we expect to be attacked any day.

I hope the wound is better, and that you do not suffer from it.

Yours sincerely,

G. Bromhead

Bromhead's letter to his sister

This was written towards the end of February and it received limited publicity in Britain:

> I fear you will be very anxious about me as no doubt we are rather in a fix. I am getting over the excitement of the fight and the sickness and fury at our loss. It is not so much the poor fellows being killed as the way the savages treat them. Having been left alone we have built a mud fort, which I think we ought to hold against any amount of Zulus, till we get help from England. I send you a paper with the report of the fight and the remarks of the General on the behaviour of my company which are flattering. If the Government gives all the steps [promotions] of the poor fellows killed I shall most probably get my company into the 1st Battalion who are to go home directly after the war is finished. I have not got over the wonder of there being one of us left. God was very good to us in giving us a little time to get up a defence, or the black fellows would have taken us by surprise, which they will find hard to do now.

From / Lieut. Gonville Bromhead 2/24 Regt.

To / The Officer Commanding 2/24th Regt:

Rorke's Drift

15th February / 1879

Sir/

I beg to bring to your notice the names
of the following men belonging to my Company
who especially distinguished themselves during
the attack by the Zulus on this Post on the
22nd & 23rd January last; & whose conduct
on this occasion came under my personal
cognizance.

No. 1395 Private John Williams was posted
by me together with Private Joseph Williams
& Private William Horrigan 1/24th Regt: in
a further room of the Hospital. They held
it for more than an hour, so long as they
had a round of ammunition left, when, as
communication was for the time cut off, the
Zulus were enabled to advance & burst
open the door. They dragged out Private
Joseph Williams & two of the patients by the
arms, & assegaied them. Whilst the
Zulus were occupied with the slaughter
of these unfortunate men, a hole was taken
place, during which Private John Williams
— who with two patients were the only

being left alone in this ward — succeeded in knocking a hole in the partition, & in taking the two patients with him into the next ward, where he found

No. 1373 Private Henry Hook. These two men together, one man working whilst the other fought & held the enemy at bay with his bayonet, broke through three more partitions, & were thus enabled to bring eight patients through a small window into our inner line of defence.

In another ward, facing the hill, I had placed

No. 593 Private William Jones &

No. 716 Private Robert Jones. They defended their post to the last, until six out of the seven patients it contained had been removed. The seventh, Sergeant Maxfield, 2/24th Regt. was delirious from fever. Although they had previously dressed him, they were unable to induce him to move. When Private Robert Jones returned to endeavour to carry him away, he found him being stabbed by the Zulus as he lay on his bed —

No 1240 Corporal William Allen &c,

No 1362 Private Frederick Hitch, must also be mentioned. It was chiefly due to their courageous conduct that communication with the Hospital was kept up at all — holding together at all costs a most dangerous post, raked in reverse by the enemy's fire from the hill, they were both severely wounded, but their determined conduct enabled the patients to be withdrawn from the Hospital, & when incapacitated by their wounds from fighting themselves, they continued, as soon as their wounds had been dressed, to serve out ammunition to their comrades during the night. —

I have the honor to be
Sir
Your most obedient servant

G. Wmhead
Lieut 2/24 Reg.t
Commanding B. Company 2/24

Colonel Glyn's Report

Following the defeat at Isandlwana, Colonel Glyn was removed by Chelmsford from command of the Centre Column and appointed to command the strengthened garrison at Rorke's Drift. Glyn was suffering severe depression following the loss of his regiment and he was fully aware that his isolation was deliberate – he was to be a scapegoat for the defeat at Isandlwana. He had no access to any information and he could not communicate beyond Rorke's Drift. Glyn was tormented by the events at Isandlwana and, nearly one month after the event, he personally wrote a highly emotive report to place his regiment and officers in as good a light as possible. Glyn's report is produced unaltered and unabridged.

Colonel Glyn's Report

Rorke's Drift,
Buffalo River.
February, 21st 1879.

Sir,

I have the honor to report that on the 22nd January last, when the camp of Isandlwanha was attacked by the enemy, the Queen's Color of 1st Battalion

24th Regiment was in the camp - the Head Quarters and five companies of the regiment being there also.

From all the information I have been since able to obtain, it would appear that when the enemy had got into the camp, and when there was no longer any hope left of saving it, the Adjutant of the 1/24th Regiment, Lt. Teignmouth Melville, departed from the camp on horseback carrying the Color with him in hope of being able to save it.

The only road to Rorke's Drift being already in possession of the enemy, Lt. Melville and the few others who still remained alive, struck across country for the Buffalo River, which it was necessary to cross to reach a point of safety. In taking this line, the only one possible ground had to be gone over, which, from its ruggedness and precipitous nature, would, under ordinary circumstances, it is reported, be deemed almost utterly impassable for mounted men.

During a distance of about six (6) miles, Lt. Melville and his companions were closely pursued or more properly speaking, accompanied, by a large number of the enemy, who, from their well-known agility in getting over rough ground, were able to keep up with our people though the latter were mounted. So that the enemy kept up a constant fire on them, and sometimes even got close enough to assegai the men and horses.

Lt. Melville reached the bank of the Buffalo and at once plunged in, horse and all. But being encumbered with the Color, which is an awkward thing to carry even on foot, and the river being full and running rapidly, he appears to have got separated from his horse, when he was about half way across. He still however held on resolutely to the Color, and was being carried down stream when he was washed against a large rock in the middle of the river. Lt. Higginson of the Natal Native Contingent, who had also lost his horse in the river, was clinging to this rock, and Lt. Melville called to him to lay hold of the Color. This Lt. Higginson did, but the current was so strong that both officers, with the Color, were again washed away into still water.

In the meantime Lt. Coghill 1/24th Regiment, my Orderly Officer who had been left in camp that morning when the main body of the force moved out, on account of a severe injury to his knee which rendered him unable to move without assistance, had also succeeded in gaining the rivers bank in company with Lt. Melville. He too had plunged at once into the river, and his horse had carried him safely across but on looking round for Lt. Melville and seeing him struggling to save the Color in the river, he at once turned his horse and rode back into the stream again to Lt. Melville's assistance.

It would appear that now the enemy had assembled in considerable force along their own bank, and had opened a heavy fire on our people directing it more especially on Lt. Melville who wore a red patrol jacket, so that when Lt. Coghill got into the river again his horse was almost immediately killed by a bullet. Lt. Coghill was thus cast loose in the stream also, and notwithstanding the exertions of both these gallant officers, the Color was carried off from them, and they themselves gained the bank in a state of extreme exhaustion.

It would appear that they now attempted to move up the hill from the river bank towards Helpmakaar, but must have been too much exhausted to go on, as they were seen to sit down to rest again. This, I sorely regret to say, was the last time these two most gallant officers were seen alive.

It was not for some days after the 22nd that I could gather any information as to the probable fate of these officers. But immediately I discovered in what direction those who had escaped from Isandlwanha had crossed the Buffalo I sent, under Major Black 2/24 Regt. a mounted party who volunteered for this service, to search for any trace that could be found of them. This search was successful and both bodies were found where they were last seen, as above illustrated. Several dead bodies of the enemy were found about them, so that they must have sold their lives dearly at the last.

As it was considered that the dead weight of the Color would cause it to sink in the river, it was hoped that a diligent search in the locality where the bodies of these officers were found might lead to its recovery. So Major Black again proceeded on the 4th inst. to prosecute this search. His energetic efforts were, I am glad to say, crowned with success, and the Color with the ornaments, case etc., belonging to it, were found, though in different places, in the river bed.

I cannot conclude this report without drawing the attention of H.E., the Lt. General Commanding, in the most impressive manner which words can command, to the noble and heroic conduct of Lt. Adjutant Melville, who did not hesitate to encumber himself with the Color of the Regiment, in his resolve to save it, at a time when the camp was in the hands of the enemy, and its gallant defenders killed to the last man in its defence, and when there appeared but little prospect that any exertions Lt. Melville [two words illegible] would enable him to save even his own life. Also later on to the noble perseverance with which when struggling between life and death in the river, his chief thoughts to the last were bent on the saving of the Color.

Similarly would I draw His Excellency's attention to the equally noble and gallant conduct of Lt. Coghill, who did not hesitate for an instant to return, unsolicited, and ride again into the river, under a heavy fire of the enemy, to the assistance of his friend; though at the time he was wholly incapacitated from walking and but too well aware that any accident that might separate him from his horse must be fatal to him.

In conclusion, I would add that both these officers gave up their lives in the truly noble task of endeavouring to save from the enemy's hands the Queen's Color of their Regiment, and greatly though their sad end is to be deplored, their deaths could not have been more noble or more full of honor.

I have the honor to be
Sir
Your obedient Servant

Commanding 3 Column

(As printed in the *London Gazette* on 4 April 1879)

Rorke's Drift
Buffalo River
— February 21st 1879 —

Sir
  — I have the honor to report that on the
22nd January last when the camp of Isandlwana was attacked by the enemy, the
Queen's Color of 1st Battalion 24th Regiment
was in the camp — the Hd Qrs and five companies of the regiment being there also —

  From all the information I have been since
able to obtain, it would appear that when
the enemy had got into the Camp, and when
there was no longer any hope left of saving it,
the Adjutant of the 1/24th Regiment, Lt Teignmouth
Melville, departed from the Camp on horseback
carrying the Color with him in hope of being
able to save it —

The only road to Rorke's Drift being already in
possession of the enemy, Lt Melville & the few
others who still remained alive struck across
Country for the Buffalo River, to reach which
it was necessary to cross to reach a point of
Safety. In taking this line, the only one possibly
open had to be gone over which, from its
ruggedness & precipitous nature, would, under
ordinary circumstances it is reported, be
deemed almost utterly impassable for
mounted men. —

During a distance of about Six (6) miles

Deputy Adjt Genl
South Africa.

32.7716)

Lt Melville & his companions were closely pursued or more properly speaking accompanied, by a large number of the enemy, who from their well-known agility in getting over rough ground, were able to keep up with our people though the latter were mounted. So that the enemy kept up a constant fire on them, & sometimes even got close enough to assegai the men & horses —

Lt Melville reached the bank of the Buffalo and at once plunged in, horse & all — But being encumbered with the Colour, which is an awkward thing to carry even on foot, and the river being full & running rapidly, he appears to have got separated from his horse, when he was about half way across. He still however held on resolutely to the Colour, and was being carried down stream when he was washed against a large rock in the middle of the river. Lt Higginson of the Natal Native Contingent, who had also lost his horse in the river, was clinging to this rock, and Lt Melville called to him to lay hold of the Colour — This Lt Higginson did, but the current was so strong that both officers, with the Colour, were again washed away into still water.

In the meantime Lt Coghill 1/24" Regiment, my orderly officer who had been left in camp that morning when the main body of the force moved out, on account of a severe injury to his knee which rendered him unable to move without assistance, had also succeeded in gaining the river

bank in company with Lt Melville —
He too had plunged at once into the river
this horse had carried him safely across but
on looking round for Lt Melville and
seeing him struggling to save the Color
in the river, he at once turned his horse
and rode back into the stream again
to Lt Melville's assistance —

It would appear that now the enemy had
assembled in considerable forces along their
own bank, and had opened a heavy
fire on our people directing it more
especially on Lt Melville who wore a red
patrol jacket — So that when Lt
Coghill got into the river again his
horse was almost immediately killed
by a bullet — Lt Coghill was thus
cast loose in the stream also, and
notwithstanding the exertions of both
these gallant Officers, the Color was
carried off from them, and they themselves gained the bank in a state
of extreme exhaustion —
It would appear that they now attempted
to move up the hill from the river bank
towards Helpmakaar, but must have
been too much exhausted to go on,
as they were seen to sit down to rest
again — This, I sorely regret to

Say, was the last time these two
most gallant officers were seen
alive —

It was not for some days after the
22nd that I could gather any information
as to the probable fate of these officers.
But immediately I discovered in what
direction those who had escaped from
Sandlwana had crossed the Buffalo
I sent, under Major Black's 2/24 Regt,
a mounted party who volunteered for
this service, to search for any trace that
could be found of them — This
search was successful and both
bodies were found where they were
last seen, as above indicated. Several
dead bodies of the enemy were found
about them, so that they must have
sold their lives dearly at the last.

As it was considered that the dead-
weight of the Color would cause it to
sink in the river, it was hoped that
a diligent search in the locality where
the bodies of these officers were found
might lead to its recovery — So Major
Black again proceeded on the 4th inst
to prosecute this search — His energetic
efforts were, I am glad to say, crowned
with success; and the Color with

the Ornaments, Case &c belonging to it,
were found, though in different places,
in the river bed —

I cannot Conclude this Report without
drawing the attention of H.E. the Lt
General Commanding, in the most
impressive manner which words
Can Command, to the noble and
heroic conduct of Lt's Adjutant
Melville, who did not hesitate to encumber himself with the Color of the
Regiment, in his resolve to save it,
at a time when the Camp was in
the hands of the enemy, & its gallant
defenders killed to the last man in
its defense; and when there appeared
but little prospect that any exertions
Lt Melville would ^anell masse enable him to
Save even his own life — Also later
on to the noble perseverance with which
when struggling between life and
death in the river, his chief thoughts
to the last were ~~best~~ bent on the
Saving of the Color —

Similarly would I draw His
Excellency's attention to the equally

noble and gallant conduct of
Lt. Coghill, who did not hesitate
for an instant to return, unsolicited,
& ride again into the river, under a
heavy fire of the enemy, to the assistance
of his friend; though at the time he
was wholly incapacitated from
walking & but too well aware that
any accident that might separate
him from his horse must be
fatal to him —

In conclusion I would add that
both these officers gave up their
lives in the truly noble task of
endeavouring to save from the
enemy's hands the Queen's
Color of their Regiment; and
greatly
^though their sad end is to be
deplored, their deaths could not
have been more noble or more
full of honor —

I have the honor to be

Sir

Your obedt. Servant

R.T. Glyn. — Colonel

Commanding 3 Column

Surgeon Reynolds's Report

During the 1870s the British Medical Association was an extremely powerful body that enjoyed great influence in Parliament. When the BMA realized that one of their members, Surgeon Reynolds, had taken part in the defence of Rorke's Drift and had performed a number of serious operations in darkness while under attack, they urgently sought and then published his report. It was first published in the Supplement to the *BMA Yearbook 1878–9*.

The British Medical Association Report of the Defence of Rorke's Drift 1879
[Unabridged]

On January the 22nd at about 12.30 p.m. we were surprised at Rorke's Drift by hearing big guns in our neighbourhood, and almost immediately I commenced climbing up the hill of Oscarberg in company with the Missionary Met [Witt] and Mr. Smith, Army Chaplain. We expected to get a view of what was happening, but on looking across the Buffalo River from the top, we discovered that Isandlana [sic] Mountain (five miles away) shut from our view the scene of action. The reports of three more big guns were distinctly audible after we completed the ascent, there being, I should say, a quarter of an hour's interval between each of them.

At 1.30 a large body of natives marched over the slope of Isandlana, in our direction, their purpose evidently being to examine ravines and ruined kraals for hiding fugitives. These men we took for our own Native Contingent. Soon afterwards appeared four horsemen on the Natal side of the river, galloping in the direction of our post, one of them was a regular soldier, and feeling they might possibly be messengers for additional medical assistance, I hurried down to the hospital and got there as they rode up. They looked awfully scared and I was at once startled to find one of them riding Surgeon-Major Shepard's pony. They shouted frantically, "the camp at Isandlana has been taken by the enemy and all our men in it massacred", that no power could stand against the enormous number of the Zulus, and the only chance for us all was by immediate flight. Lieutenant Bromhead, Acting Commissary Dalton, and myself forthwith consulted together, Lieutenant Chard not having as yet joined us from the pontoon, and we quickly decided that with barricades well placed around our present position a stand could best be made where we were. In other words, removing the sick and wounded would have been embarrassing to our movement, and desertion of them was never thought of.

Just at this period, Mr. Dalton's energies were invaluable. Without the smallest delay, which would have been so fatal for us, he called upon the men (all eager for doing) to carry the mealie sacks here and there for defences, and it was charming to find in a short time how comparatively protected we had made ourselves. Lieutenant Chard arrived as this work was in progress and gave many useful orders as regards the lines of defence. He approved also of the hospital being taken in, and between the hospital orderlies, convalescent patients (8 or 10) and myself, we loop-holed the building and made a continuation of the commissariat defences round it. The hospital, however, occupied a wretched position having a garden and shrubbery close by, which afterwards proved so favourable to the enemy; but comparing our prospects with that of the Isandlana affair, we felt that the mealie barriers might afford us a moderately fair chance. The patients, I must mention, were retained in the hospital, although situated at our weak end, as every part of the commissariat house was crowded with stores, and we did not consider either building would be taken unless with the fall of the whole place.

When our plans of temporary defence were nearly completed, I was relieved by seeing Mr. Met and Mr. Smith safely inside the laager. They had just then returned from the hill, where they remained up to a late moment, continuing to believe the natives I before alluded to were our own men, instead of which they were the very Zulus who fought against us later on at Rorke's Drift. Mr. Smith was at this time looking for his horse and told me afterwards he should have to remain as his Kafir groom had bolted, and apparently taken with him the horse. Mr. Met was making preparations to ride away.

About 3.30 p.m. the enemy made their first appearance in a large crowd on the hospital side of our post, coming on in skirmishing order at a slow slinging run. We opened fire on them from the hospital at 600 yards, and although the bullets ploughed through their midst and knocked over many, there was no check or alteration made in their approach. They seemed quite regardless of the danger, and, what struck me as most strange, they had no war cry, nor did they at this time fire a single shot in return. As they got nearer they became more scattered, but the large bulk of them rushed for the hospital and the garden in front of it. My attention being altogether directed for a while to these points, I cannot state with authority, whether the Zulus, whom I shortly afterwards saw in a larger number on the opposite or north side of our fort, got there by extending this body or if they came independently from the other direction, thereby carrying our their reputed mode of attack in a bull's horn fashion.

However it was, we found ourselves quickly surrounded by the enemy with their strong force holding the garden and shrubbery. From all sides, but especially the latter places, they poured on us a continuous fire, to which our men replied as quickly as they could reload their rifles; again and again the Zulus pressed forward, and retreated, until at last they forced themselves so daringly and in such numbers as to climb over the mealie sacks in front the hospital, and drive the defenders from there behind an entrenchment of biscuit boxes, hastily formed with much judgement and forethought by Lieutenant Chard, R.E. I discovered afterwards that this officer, when planning our defences, reckoned on the assistance of the Basutos who deserted at the last moment.

It followed from this, that our men at first had to be distributed over so large an area in proportion to our numbers as dangerously to weaken any one point and render it unequal to repel a determined rush, I am convinced, but for this entrenchment, our fort could not have held out five minutes longer.

A heavy fire from behind it was resumed with renewed confidence and with little confusion or delay, checking successfully the natives, and permitting a semi-flank fire from another part of the laagar to play on them destructively. At this time too, the loopholes in the hospital were made great use of, so that the combined fire had the desired effect of keeping the Zulus at bay. It was, however, only temporary as after a short respite they came on again with redoubled vigour. Some of them gained the hospital verandah and there got hand-to-hand with our men defending the doors. Once they were driven back from here, to find shelter again in the garden, but others soon pressed forward in their stead, and having occupied the verandah in larger numbers than before, pushed their way right into the hospital, where confusion on our side naturally followed. Everyone tried to escape as best he could, and, owing to the rooms not communicating with one another, the difficulties were insurmountable.

Private Hook, 2/24th Regiment, who was acting hospital cook, and Private Connolly, 2/24th Regiment, a patient in hospital, made their way into the open at the back of the hospital by breaking a hole in the wall with a pickaxe and then through the small window looking into what may be styled the neutral ground. Those who madly tried to get off by leaving the front of the hospital were all killed with the exception of Gunner Howard. He gained, with most extraordinary luck, a detached rear [position?] without being noticed by the enemy, and after dusk the Zulus still being close about him, he left this retreat to hide himself in the long grass 400 or 500 yards away. He did not rejoin us until daylight the following morning when it was no longer dangerous to move about.

Private Hunter, Natal Mounted Police, was the only one killed of those who made an escape through the small window. He was shot dead while crossing over to the biscuit boxes after his exit through the window, by a fire from the enemy from behind mealie sacks.

The only men actually killed in the hospital were three, excluding a Kafir under treatment for compound fracture of femur. Their names were Sergeant Maxfield, Private Jenkins, both unable to assist in their escape (being debilitated by fever), and Private Adams, who was well able to move about but could not be persuaded to leave his temporary refuge in a small room, and face the danger of an attempt at escape to the laager. During this partial success of the enemy, very heavy firing was being made on our fort from all sides, and it was in this period we lost a large majority of our killed and wounded. The engagement continued more or less until about 7 o'clock p.m. and then, when we were beginning to consider our situation rather hopeless, the fire from our opponents appreciably slackened, giving us some time for reflection. Lieutenant Chard here again shined in resource. Anticipating the Zulus making one more united dash for the fort and possibly gaining an entrance, he converted an immense stack of mealies standing in the middle of our enclosure and originally cone fashioned, into a comparatively safe place for a last retreat. I would explain that the top of the cone was removed and a number of sacks were taken out from the heart of what remained, forming a sheltered space, sufficient to accommodate about 40 men, and in a position to make good shooting. Mr. Dunne, Commissariat officer, assisted in this work. Just as it was completed, smoke from the hospital appeared and shortly burst into flames. The light given by it, however, proved advantageous to us (it being now nightfall), a matter which the Zulus themselves must have recognised, as no further attack was made from that quarter. During the whole night following, the enemy carried on desultory firing, and several feigned attacks were made, with much shouting of their war cry, but nothing of a continued or determined effort was again attempted by them. After 6 o'clock a.m. we found, after careful reconnoitring, that all the Zulus, with exception of a couple of stragglers, had left our immediate vicinity, and soon afterwards a large body of men were seen, at a distance in Zululand, marching towards us. For a long time, and even after redcoats were distinguished through our field-glasses, we believed them to be the enemy, some of them perhaps dressed in the kits of those who had fallen at Isandlana. Indeed, we could not think otherwise, as the Basuto officer who escaped with his men from Isandlana and retreated on our post the day before reported that the General's party had been broken up into small lots, each trying to get back into the Colony by any route.

Not until the mounted infantry, forming an advanced party, crossed the Buffalo drift, about a quarter of a mile off, were we convinced of our relief.

Then we raised a white flag (for they were not certain of us either, seeing the hospital still smoking) and gave three cheers, really feeling that it was all right for us. I do not think it possible that men could have behaved better than did the 2/24th and the Army Hospital Corps (three), who were particularly forward during the whole attack, as well as odds and ends of other regiments who happened to be present at Rorke's Drift on the occasion.

It would be difficult to pick out the heroes from our garrison, but Corporal Schiess of the Natal Native Contingent (a Swede [sic] by birth) came under my notice as the most deserving of praise and recommendation. Among the invalids from Natal are, as is known, men wounded in the defence of Rorke's Drift, or who were patients in the hospital there at the time of the attack by the Zulus. They are now at Netley, and all speak very loudly in praise of the gallantry and devotion of Dr. Reynolds of the Army Medical Department. According to their report, Dr. Reynolds took active measures for the defence of the hospital as soon as it was known the Zulus were about to attack the place, and never ceased to exert himself in helping to ward off the enemy, and in caring for the wounded, during the whole time the fighting lasted.

Signed by Surgeon Reynolds.

It is curious that Surgeon Reynolds praised himself in the report by using the third person technique.

The Bourne Report

In December 1936 Lieutenant Colonel Bourne OBE, DCM made a BBC radio broadcast concerning the battle of Rorke's Drift for a series entitled 'I was there'. It generated enough interest for 350 people to write to Bourne. It says something of the man that he replied to every one of them. Regrettably, the BBC scrapped the recording during the 1950s as being of insufficient interest. The following is a transcript of the broadcast:

In December 1872, when I was 18 years old, I enlisted in the 24th Regiment and received the princely pay of 6d. a day, of which 3d. was deducted for messing and washing, leaving 1s. 5d. a week – for luxuries. I went to bed every night hungry but quite happy, and it made a man of me.

The Regiment had just come home from India after fifteen years. Now the 'A' Company of any Regiment in those days was always called the Grenadier Company and was supposed to have the biggest men. I think the Sergeant Major must have been a wee bit humorous, for he posted me to our 'A' Company although I stood only five foot six inches and was painfully thin.

After five years of home service, in February 1878 the Regiment received sudden orders to proceed to the Cape of Good Hope to take part in the Kaffir War. This was my first experience of active service, and shortly after, my Colonel promoted me Color-Sergeant of 'B' Company – 100 strong. I was only twenty-three, very nervous, sensitive, and afraid of my new responsibilities. Several men of the Company were of my own age, other older, and some old enough to be my father, but after a few months I felt more secure and thought I was getting along quite well. I also found myself 'unpaid private secretary' to several men who could barely read and write, and I deciphered and answered their letters home, feeling quite happy in our relations. One day I heard a man named Wall ask my batman 'if the kid was in', a day or two later I asked Partridge casually who 'the kid' was, and received the answer, 'why, you are, of course.' My stock slumped at once. I think it does us all good to have our swollen heads reduced. But we were a very happy family. You can't live in tents, and on Mother Earth, for two years on Active Service without knowing your men intimately.

The Kaffir War ended in June 1878 and we were moved to Pietermaritzburg, Natal, to assist in raising the curtain on the Zulu drama. On January 11 we crossed the Buffalo River at Rorke's Drift – into the Zulu country. Our Commander-in-Chief was Lord Chelmsford. Our strength was four thousand five hundred men – including thirteen companies of my Regiment, the 24th, now the South Wales Borderers. Our company was left behind at Rorke's Drift, to guard the hospital, stores, and the pontoons at the Drift on the Buffalo River. This was my company, and at the time I was bitterly disappointed. We saw the main column under Lord Chelmsford engaged the enemy at once, and I watched the action, along with my four sergeants, from a little hill by Rorke's Drift. Then we saw them move on again, and they disappeared.

And now I must tell you what happened to them during the next ten days.

They made their camp under a hill called Isandhlwana, about ten miles away. Then a day later, on the twenty-first, Lord Chelmsford learned that the enemy was in force ahead of the camp, and he moved out on the morning of the twenty-second with nearly half his force to attack them. But as he advanced they disappeared, and in his absence his camp was attacked and overwhelmed by fourteen thousand Zulus. So swift was the disaster that the few survivors who got away could give no reliable account of it, but the evidence of the dead who were afterwards found and buried where they lay told the unvarying tale of groups of men fighting back to back until the last cartridge was fired. After the war, Zulu witnesses all told the same story.'At first we could make no headway against the soldiers, but suddenly they ceased to fire, then we came round them and killed them with our assegais.' According to one account, the last survivor was a drummer boy who flung his sword at a Zulu. This was the last occasion that Band or Drummer Boys were taken on Active Service, as it was also the last occasion that the Colours were carried into action. Lieutenants Melvill and Coghill lost their lives that day trying to save the colours. Fully twelve hundred men were killed. And by half past one no white man was alive in Isandhlwana camp.

Of course, back at Rorke's Drift we knew nothing of this disaster, although my sergeants and I on our hill above it could hear the guns and see the puffs of smoke. But an hour later, at two o'clock, a few refugees arrived and warned us what to expect. One man whispered to me 'Not a fighting chance for you, young feller.' Up to that time we had done nothing to put our small post in a defensive position, as our force in front was nearly five thousand strong and had six guns, and the last thing that we expected was that we should be the saviours of the remainder of that force. The strength of our small garrison at the Drift was two combatant and six departmental officers, and one hundred and thirty-three non-commissioned officers and men, thirty-six of whom were sick, leaving about one hundred fighting men. Remember that twelve hundred men had just been massacred at Isandhlwana.

Can you then be surprised that, flushed with their success, the Zulus were making for our small post confident that we should be easy victims to their savagery? Having had the warning – but only two hours in advance, as it turned out – we set to work to loophole the two buildings and to connect the front of the hospital with a stone cattle kraal by sacks of Indian corn and oats, and to draw up two Boer transport wagons to join the front of the Commissariat Stores with the back of the hospital. These proved excellent barricades, but by no means impregnable.

The native has often been credited with deep cunning, but luckily for us if the Zulu possessed any he did not use it, for as the sacks connecting the hospital had to be laid on a slope of the ground he could safely have crept along, cut the sacks open with his assegais, the corn would have rolled out and he could have walked in and I should not now be telling the story.

When Lieutenant Chard of the Royal Engineers joined us he approved of what we had done, but considered that our inner space was too big, and suggested a line of biscuit boxes. This was done and proved of great value when the enemy set the hospital on fire.

I was instructed to post men as look-out, in the hospital, at the most vulnerable points, and to take out and command a line of skirmishers. Shortly after 3.30 an officer commanding a troop of Natal Light Horse arrived, having got away from Isandhlwana, and asked Lieutenant Chard for instructions. He was ordered to send detachments to observe the drift and pontoons, and to place outposts in the direction of the enemy to check his advance.

About 4.15 the sound of firing was heard behind the hill on our front; the officer returned and reported the enemy close upon us. He also reported that his 100 men would not obey his orders and had ridden off. About the same time another detachment of 100 men belonging to the Natal native contingent bolted, including their officer himself. I am glad to say that he was brought back some days later, court-martialled and dismissed from the service. The desertion of these detachments of 200 men appeared at first sight to be a great loss, with only a hundred of us left, but the feeling afterwards was that we could not have trusted them, and also that our defences were too small to accommodate them anyhow.

We knew now that whatever might happen we had to fight it out alone, and at about 4.30 the enemy, from 500 to 600 strong, came in sight round the hill to our south, and driving in my thin red line of skirmishers, made a rush at our south wall. They were met, and held, by a steady and deliberate fire for a short time, then, being reinforced by some hundreds, they made desperate and repeated attempts to break through our temporary defences, but were repulsed time and again. To show their fearlessness and their contempt for the red coats and small numbers, they tried to leap the parapet, and at times seized our bayonets, only to be shot down. Looking back, one cannot but admire their fanatical bravery.

About 7 o'clock they succeeded, after many attempts, in setting fire to the hospital. The small numbers we were able to spare defended it room-by-room, bringing out all the sick who could be moved before they retired. Privates Hook, R. Jones, W. Jones and J. Williams were the last to leave holding the door with the bayonet when all their ammunition was expended. The Victoria Cross was awarded to these men, and they fully deserved it.

The Zulus had collected the rifles from the men they had killed at Isandhlwana, and had captured the ammunition from the mules which had stampeded and threw their loads; so our own arms were used against us. In fact, this was the cause of every one of our casualties, killed and wounded, and we should have suffered many more if the enemy had known how to use a rifle. There was hardly a man even wounded by an assegai – their principal weapon.

The attack lasted from 4.30 p.m. on the twenty-second to 4.00 a.m. on the twenty-third – twelve exciting hours – and when daybreak occurred the enemy was out of sight. About 7 o'clock they appeared again to the south-west. But help was at hand; Lord Chelmsford with the other half of his original force was only an hour's march away. On the previous afternoon he had learned of the destruction of his camp at Isandhlwana. A certain Commandant Lonsdale had chanced to ride back to the camp and had been fired at by Zulus wearing our men's uniform. He escaped by a miracle and was able to report the news to Lord Chelmsford.

Lord Chelmsford at once addressed his men and said: 'Whilst we were skirmishing ahead the Zulus have taken our camp; there must be ten thousand in our rear, and twenty thousand in front, we must win back our camp tonight and cut our way back to Rorke's Drift tomorrow.' 'All right, sir, we'll do it.'

They got back to camp that night, but they found a grim and silent scene as they cautiously approached. The next day they resumed their march and appeared at Rorke's Drift, and our enemy retired.

In his dispatch afterwards, Lord Chelmsford said: 'To out intense relief the waving of hats was seen from the hastily erected entrenchments, and information soon reached me that the garrison... had for twelve hours made the most gallant resistance I have ever heard of against the deter-mined attack of some 3,000 Zulus, 350 of whose dead bodies surrounded the post.' Our losses were 17 killed and 9 wounded, their 351 killed that we buried. Their wounded must have been between 400 and 500, which they removed under cover of the night.

There are two things which I think have made Rorke's Drift stand out so vividly after all these years. The first, that it took place on the same day as the terrible massacre at Isandhlwana, and the second, that Natal was saved from being overrun by a savage and victorious foe.

Seven V.C.s were awarded to this one company of the regiment which is now the South Wales Borderers. I have told you the names of four of the men who won the V.C.; the other three were Lieutenant Bromhead, Corporal Allen and Private F. Hitch. The Victoria Cross was also awarded to Lieutenant Chard, Royal Engineers, Surgeon Reynolds, and Corporal Schiess, but not one, I regret to say, of those VCs is alive today...

Lieutenants Chard and Bromhead and the men received the thanks of Parliament, the officers being promoted to the rank of Major. I was awarded the Distinguished Conduct Medal with an annuity of £10 – the same as awarded to the Victoria Cross – and awarded a commission, but as I was the youngest of eight sons, and the family exchequer was empty, I had to refuse it that time.

Now just one word for the men who fought that night; I was moving about amongst them all the time, and not for one moment did they flinch, their courage and their bravery cannot be expressed in words: for me they were an example all my soldiering days.

The following year, Queen Victoria received at Windsor Castle a Colour Party of the Regiment, and decorated the Queen's Colours with a silver wreath of immortelles in memory of Lieutenants Melvill and Coghill, 'for their devotion in trying to save the Colours of the twenty-second of January (that was at Isandhlwana) and for the noble defence of Rorke's Drift.' So if you ever have the great privilege of seeing the Colours of the South Wales Borderers uncased you will see the wreath. The original wreath presented by Her Majesty is now in the Regimental Chapel of Brecon Cathedral.

Article: Courtesy AZWHS, December 1998.

Assessment of Martini-Henry Rifle use by the Zulus at Rorke's Drift

Historians have persistently rebutted Colour Sergeant Bourne's assertions that the Zulus used British Martini-Henry rifles at Rorke's Drift. The following assessment supports Bourne's belief.

Four units of Zulus, approximately 4,500 warriors, took part in the battle of Rorke's Drift; those that constituted the reserves from Isandlwana were the uThulwana, iNdlondlo and uDoklo *amabutho*. The other Zulu group present were the iNdluyengwe *amabutho* who had formed part of the Zulu right horn behind Isandlwana and who had then sealed off the road between Isandlwana and Rorke's Drift while the British camp and its defenders were systematically destroyed by the main Zulu force. Having missed the battle and its associated glory, the leader of the reserve force, Prince Dabulamanzi, a half-brother of the Zulu King Cetshwayo, then led his reserve towards the river to raid and plunder farms immediately across the Natal border, albeit possibly disobeying Cetshwayo's orders not to do so.[1] It was a section of the iNdluyengwe that then pursued and harried the Isandlwana fugitives as they fled for their lives back towards the Buffalo river and Natal. All four groups met and amalgamated later that day for the attack on Rorke's Drift under the command of Prince Dabulamanzi whose force was not local to the area and had been 50 miles away at Ulundi when the British converted the mission station into a supply depot. Furthermore, because Dabulamanzi's Zulus initially raided across the border along a broad 6 mile front, it is possible that they were unaware that the isolated post at Rorke's Drift even existed – let alone that it would be defended.

However, between leaving the hidden Zulu position in the Ngwebeni valley and before arriving at the Rorke's Drift road, the three reserve *amabutho*, the uThulwana, iNdlondlo and uDoklo, had swung to the right of the advancing Zulu main army heading for Isandlwana in order to reach their own objective – the Rorke's Drift to Isandlwana road. In so doing, they had then run straight into a detached section of the 24th command-ed by Second Lieutenant Dyson of Cavaye's E Company – who had been sent from the camp to hold the high spur 1 mile from the British position. This spur led from the Nqutu plateau directly to the British camp at Isan-dlwana and formed a downward slope that provided the natural access route between the plateau and the camp. Cavaye's subordinate, Dyson, having reached the top of the spur with Cavaye's men had then placed his platoon-sized force some 500 yards to the left (west) of Cavaye and E Com-pany, presumably to cover the valley that led behind Isandlwana. Unfor-tunately for Dyson and his men, the Zulu reserve swept over the brow of the hill immediately to their front and, being unable to retreat in the face of such an overwhelming fleet-of-foot foe, Dyson and his men stood their ground and briefly fought to the last man. In a matter of moments the Zulus annihilated Dyson's small force and, there is little doubt, collected their rifles and ammunition. Although this incident is not recorded in any regi-mental records, Chelmsford later reported that he had lost two companies on the spur: this was partially incorrect as the bulk of the two companies, less Dyson and his men, did manage to effect a partial retreat off the spur before being caught and overwhelmed by the Zulus several hundred yards from the main camp position.

One of Chief Sihayo's sons, Mehlokazulu kaSihayo, left an intriguing account only weeks after the battle in which he referred to the possible fate of the British troops that had been detailed to defend the spur. He stated:

> The soldiers were at this time in the camp, having come back from the front, all but two companies, which went on to the hill and never returned – they

were every one of them killed. They were firing on the wings of the Zulu army while the body of the army was pushing on, the wings also succeeded, and before the soldiers knew where they were, they were surrounded from the west, attacked by the wings from the right, and the main body from the back. They were all killed, not one escaped; they tried to make an opening towards the camp, but found the Zulu army was too thick; they could not do it; it was impossible.

An account by a Colonial soldier appeared in the *Natal Witness* on 7 February, which touched upon the matter. The article was referring to the battle of Isandlwana and includes these provocative words:

If it had not been for the mismanagement, the Zulus would have been beaten off. Just fancy sending a company (70 men) out at a time to stop 20,000 Zulus. Barker, who escaped, says he saw one company which was sent onto the high hills, to the left of the camp to keep the Zulus back; they shot hundreds of them, but in five minutes there was not a man left. Two other companies were served the same way.

As late as 2 September 1880, when the matter was further discussed in Parliament, reference was made to the dispatch sent by Chelmsford immediately after arriving in Pietermaritzburg. Only five days after the disaster Chelmsford had stated that:

One company went off to the extreme left and has never been heard of since, and the other five, I understand, engaged the enemy about a mile to the left front of the camp, and there made a most stubborn and gallant resistance.

The most convincing material relating to this incident is found in the records of the noted South African historian George Chadwick, who was the guardian of the Isandlwana battlefield until 1986 and a member of the National Monuments Council until his death in late 2000. Chadwick always accepted that Dyson and his men had fought and died above the spur and he referred to the site of their graves in an article he wrote during his active tenure of office. He noted that in 1928 the graves and cairns immediately around the battlefield had been fenced off and these alone received any care or attention. Many graves outside the fenced area, including those of Dyson and his men, had become indistinguishable from other piles of stones that extensively littered the area. Later, in 1958, a graves curator had inadvertently destroyed a number of cairns and graves while renovating the battlefield; this process had exposed relics and human bones, which resulted in visitors registering a number of strong protests. Chadwick was requested to restore the cairns and graves *in situ* and whilst doing so, he decided to make a survey of the whole battlefield with the intention of restoring those distant cairns that had long since been lost or neglected. Relying on his memory, maps and old photographs he discovered forty such cairns; some were along the Fugitives' Trail and others were on the ridge in question; this was the very same ridge that led up to the Nqutu plateau where Dyson and his men were overrun. Chadwick knew that he was possibly alone in believing that British graves were on the ridge and, after diligently searching the area, he found several isolated cairns away from the ridge exactly where Dyson was believed to have made his last stand. Chadwick's examination of the cairns and graves revealed 24th Regimental buttons, boot protectors and human bones under the cairns. The site was dismantled, documented and rebuilt. It was the very same area through which the Zulu reserve of the uThulwana, iNdlondlo and uDoklo *amabutho* had sped to take up their allocated reserve position before moving on to Rorke's Drift. In the forty-two years since Chadwick's restoration on the spur, the area has rarely been visited except by herd boys; due to severe weathering and the growth of grass over the last forty years, the cairns are now no longer visible.[2]

These Zulu reserves, having now tasted blood and flushed with success, continued their rapid advance to their allocated position blocking the Isandlwana to Rorke's Drift road. There they came across Lieutenant MacDowell's small party of engineers who were busy repairing the damaged roadway across a watercourse 1 mile from Isandlwana. MacDowell was at the Isandlwana camp when his men were completely taken by surprise and swiftly overwhelmed and slain; and so a further ten to fifteen Martini-Henry rifles and ammunition were added to the Zulus' armoury of captured British rifles. It is always possible that the Zulus ignored and left Dyson's and MacDowell's Martini-Henry rifles and ammunition where they lay following each of the engagements; however, these items were prized by the Zulus above all other trophies and it is most unlikely that the warriors would have abandoned them.

Finally, with regard to this issue, if the Zulus had fired Martini-Henry rounds from the Oskarsberg into the British position, would the Zulus have diligently collected their spent cartridge cases or abandoned them where they fell? During archaeological excavations of Rorke's Drift during 1992, a metal-detector survey was conducted on the slopes of the Oskarsberg with special attention being given to the caves and ledges reputedly used by the Zulu marksmen during the battle.[3] No Martini-Henry cases were discovered although a number of Martini-Henry rounds were found; these, presumably, had been fired into the caves by the British defenders.

During April 2001, the author undertook a small survey of the area immediately above the caves and terraces; the possibility was that some of the Zulu marksmen could have fired into the British position from the cover of rocks beyond the caves. Indeed, by spending only one day searching the area, six spent Martin-Henry cases were discovered at a distance of 300 yards from the original British rear box-wall. It is therefore highly probable that a number of the Zulu marksmen firing from the Oskarsberg into the British position were marginally further away than previously believed: the area where the cases were found would have been the only protected area where the Zulus could have assembled before their attack on the mission station rear wall.

The gap in time between the lived event and its present-day examination is too great for conclusive proof that Bourne was right or wrong. If his belief was correct and the Zulus attacking Rorke's Drift used Martini-Henry rifles from Isandlwana, which the above factors tend to suggest, then, sadly, the implication is that a number of British soldiers at Rorke's Drift were killed by Zulus firing British rifles that they had seized only hours earlier.

Application from the Swedish
Government for Protection of its
Mission Station

This recently discovered document clearly indicates that the Swedish government was expecting war in Zululand as early as the end of 1878, which challenges the widely held view of historians that the British government were taken completely by surprise when British troops invaded Zululand in January 1879.

CC. – 2308 Item 10. Further Correspondence respecting the Affairs of South Africa. Request for protection of Rorke's Drift Mission Station by Swedish Government[1]

From: Lieut. Governor Sir H. Bulwer, Government House, Pietermaritzburg, Natal, February 18, 1879.

To: Sir Michael Hicks Beach

Sir,

With reference to your despatch of the 5th last,[2] transmitting copy of a correspondence with the Foreign Office, respecting an application made by the Swedish government that steps might be taken to afford protection in the event of a Zulu war to the Swedish mission of Oskarsberg, on the borders of Zululand, I have the honour to inform you that the mission station in question is in this colony, and appears to be stationed near Rorke's Drift, where the reverend Otto Witt purchased, a short while back, on behalf of his mission, the farm Tyeana, formally belonging to the late James Rorke, which, since the purchase, has been called by Mr. Witt, in honour of the king of Sweden, Oscarberg.

2 When Mr. Witt purchased the farm last year, there were two large substantial buildings on it, the one being the dwelling house, and the other comprising several rooms used for mission and farm purposes.

3 Before the Zulu war broke out, a column of Her Majesty's troops and of some Colonial forces, was stationed in the neighbourhood of Rorke's drift, which is one of the principal roads entering Zululand.

4 When the war broke out the troops belonging to this column crossed Rorke's drift, and had proceeded ten (10) miles, or thereabouts, into the interior to Isandula, where the attack was made on the 22nd January by the Zulu army on the headquarter's camp.

5 From the situation of the mission station at the entrance of Zululand, and several miles from any other house, the buildings of Oscarberg became of importance to the military column, as commanding the ford and as suitable for the purposes of a military depot. Permission was accordingly obtained by the military authorities from Mr. Witt for the use of the outer building as a depot, and more recently the dwelling-house was occupied as a hospital.

6 On the night of the 22nd January, after the disaster at Isandula, a large Zulu force attacked this post. The attack was most gallantly and successfully repulsed by a small detachment of troops stationed there. The dwelling-house was, however, destroyed by fire.

Signed;

H. Bulwer,

Lieutenant Governor.

Bibliography

P.E. Abbott, *Recipients of the Distinguished Conduct Medal 1855–1909*

Jack Adams, *The South Wales Borderers*, London 1968

Anglo Zulu War Historical Society Journals 1–10

C.T. Atkinson, *The South Wales Borderers 24th Foot 1689–1937*, Cambridge 1937

J.W. Bancroft, *The Zulu War, 1879: Rorke's Drift*, Tunbridge Wells: Spellmount Ltd 1991

Ian Bennett, *Eyewitness in Zululand*, Greenhill 1989

Sonia Clarke, *Invasion of Zululand*, Brenthurst: South Africa 1979

Richard Cope, *The Ploughshare of War*, University of Natal Press 1999

Sir Reginald Coupland, *Zulu Battle Piece – Isandlwana*, London 1948

M.J. Crook, *The Evolution of the Victoria Cross*, Midas Books 1975

Sir A. Cunynghame, *My Command in South Africa*, Macmillan 1879

F. Emery, *The Red Soldier*, Ball Paperbacks, Johannesburg 1977

The Hon. Gerald French, *Lord Chelmsford and the Zulu War*, Unwin 1939

P. Gon, *The Road to Isandlwana*, London 1979

Adrian Greaves, *Isandlwana*, Cassell 2001

A. Greaves and B. Best, *The Curling Letters of Zulu War*, Pen & Sword 2001

A. Greaves and I. Knight, *A Review of The South African Campaign of 1879*, Debinair 2000

J.J. Guy, 1971 'A note on firearms in the Zulu kingdom with special reference to the Anglo-Zulu War 1879', *Journal of African History* (4): 557–70

Hamilton-Browne, *A Lost Legionary in South Africa*, London 1890

Norman Holme, *The Silver Wreath*, Samson Books 1979

Ian Knight, *There Will Be An Awful Row At Home About This*, Shoreham 1987

Ian Knight, *The Sun Turned Black*, Watermans 1995, and Windrow & Green 1992

Ian Knight, *The Zulu War – Then and Now*, Plaistow Press 1993

John Laband, *Lord Chelmsford's Zululand Campaign*, Alan Sutton Publishing 1996

John Laband, *Oh! Lets Go and Have a Fight at Jim's*, Kingdom & Colony

J. Laband and P. Thompson, *Kingdom in Crisis. The Zulu response to the British invasion of 1879*, Pietermaritzburg: University of Natal Press 1992

Laband, Thompson and Henderson, *The Buffalo Border 1879*, University of Natal, Durban 1983

W.G. Lloyd, *John Williams, VC*, Glamorgan 1993

M. Lummis MC, *Padre George Smith of Rorke's Drift*, Wensome 1978

F. Mechanick, 1979 'Firepower and firearms in the Zulu War of 1879', *Military History Journal* 4 (6): 218–20

Medal Rolls 1793–1889 of the 24th Foot, South Wales Borderers, J.B. Hayward & Son

W.E. Montague, *Campaigning in South Africa*, Blackwood 1880

Donald Morris, *The Washing of the Spears*, Cape 1996

Morris and Arthur, *Life of Lord Wolseley*, 1924

Parliamentary Papers 1878–1906 (C 2222–2295)

Paton Glennie, and Penn Symons, *Records of the 24th Regiment*, London 1892

A. H. Swiss, *Records of the 24th Regiment*, London 1892

War Office, Précis of Information, 1879

A. Wilmot, *The Zulu War*, London 1880

W.B. Worsfold, *Sir Bartle Frere: a Footnote to the History of the British Empire*, 1923

Newspapers, Journals and Periodicals of 1878/1879

The Illustrated London News London

The Graphic London

Natal Colonist South Africa

Natal Mercury South Africa

The Natal Times South Africa

Natal Witness South Africa

Punch London

Standard London

The Times London

Daily News London

Notes

Introduction

1   A memorandum in July of 1878 from Chelmsford to the Duke of Cambridge at the War Office.

2   The regiment had two serving battalions and, most unusually, both battalions were serving in South Africa. For future easy reference throughout, each battalion is entitled as the 1/24th or the 2/24th.

3   *Hansard*, Lords, 13 February 1879, 1042

4   Parliamentary Papers C–1883 dated 15 May 1877.

5   **a.** Ultimate paragraph of a letter from Sir Henry Bulwer (Lieutenant Governor of Natal) to Sir Henry Barkly (Colonial Office) dated 1 April 1877. C–1776.

> *As the mail is closing, I have just received news from our borders that Cetywayo is collecting his men, and that he is very angrily disposed again against the Boers, and evidently contemplates the necessity of hostilities.*

b. A deposition taken by Mr Fynn, Resident Magistrate of the Umsinga Division, dated 29 March 1877 states:

> *That all the Zulus, with the exception of Sihayo's people, including all those in the western border, were assembled, as with the greater part already mustered for war with the Transvaal Dutch. C–1776.*

c. Another deposition by the same magistrate reports:

> *The Dutch had been informed secretly that the Zulu would enter the*

Transvaal yesterday or today (the 30th or 31st March 1877) for the
purpose of war with the Dutch. C–1776.

d. As if confirmation of Cetshwayo's intention was needed, he sent the
following message on 15 May 1877 to Shepstone:

I thank my father Somtseu [Shepstone's native name] *for his message.*
I am glad that he has sent it, because the Dutch have tired me out, and
I intended to fight with them once, only once, and to drive them over the
Vaal. You see, my Impis are gathered. It was to fight the Dutch I called
them together. Now I will send them back to their homes. C–1883.

6   C–2100.

7   C–2222.

8   An account by a Zulu deserter recorded by the Hon. William Drummond, a
Zulu speaking staff officer on the HQ Staff. See Frank Emery, *The Red*
Soldier, Ball Paperbacks, Johannesburg 1977.

9   C–2308 No. 10. See Appendix G.

Chapter 1

1   By the end of the war the invasion force would have used over 27,000 oxen
and nearly 5,000 mules to reach Ulundi for the final battle. (War Office
Précis).

2   John Laband, *Lord Chelmsford's Zululand Campaign*, p.xxxv, Introduction.

3   Composition of the Centre Column:

No. 2 Column – Commanding, Lieutenant-Colonel Durnford, RE Staff –
For general staff duties, Captain Barton, 77th Foot; for transport duties,
Lieutenant Cochrane 32nd Foot; senior medical officer, civil surgeon
Cartwright Reed. Corps – Rocket battery (mules), Captain Russell, RA;
1st Battalion 1st Regiment Natal Native Contingent, Commandant
Montgomery; 2nd Battalion 1st Regiment Natal Native Contingent, Major
Bengough, 77th Foot; 3rd Battalion 1st Regiment Natal Native Contingent,
Captain Cherry, 32nd Foot; Sikali's Horse; No. 3 Company Natal Native
Pioneers, Captain Allen.

No. 3 Column – Commanding, Brevet Colonel Glyn, CB, 24th Foot;
Staff – Orderly officer, Lieutenant Coghill, 24th Foot; principal staff officer,

Major Clery; for general staff duties, Captain Gardner, 14th Hussars; for transport duties, Captain Essex, 75th Foot; senior commissariat officer, Assistant Commissary Dunne; sub-district paymaster, Paymaster Elliott (hon. captain); senior medical officer, Surgeon Major Shepherd. Corps – N battery, 5th Brigade, Royal Artillery, Brevet Lieutenant Colonel Harness; Royal Engineers, No. 5 Company, Captain Jones, RE; 1st Battalion, 24th Foot, Brevet Lieutenant Colonel Pulleine, 24th Foot; 2nd Battalion, 24th Foot, Lieutenant Colonel Degacher, CB, 24th Foot; No. 1 Squad, Mounted Infantry, Lieutenant Colonel Russell, 12th Lancers; Natal Mounted Police, Major Dartnell; Natal Carbineers, Captain Shepstone; Newcastle Mounted Rifles, Captain Bradstreet; Buffalo Border Guard, Captain Smith; 3rd Regiment Natal Native Contingent, Commandant Lonsdale; staff officer, Lieutenant Hartford, 99th Foot; 1st Battalion, Commandant Lonsdale; 2nd Battalion, Commandant Cooper; No. 1 Company Natal Native Pioneer Corps, Captain Nolan.

Chapter 2

1 Some modern writers have used the term 'assegai' to mean a stabbing spear. In fact, the word 'assegai' has nothing to do with the Zulu language. The word is Berber and was widely used by the Spanish and Portuguese and later adopted by the French and English. In fourteenth-century French such a weapon was known as the 'archegaie', while in English, Chaucer used the term 'lancegay'. The word 'assegai' never existed south of the Sahara.

2 Zulus avoided swimming at all times for cultural reasons; the survivors, including the old men, were forced into the river or put to death. AZWHS, June 1997.

Chapter 3

1 Originally spelled *Helpmekaar* by the Boers and subsequently as *Helpmakaar* by British settlers and troops. In Dutch it means 'help one another' whereas it was popularly known as 'help m' cart up' by the British

troops due to the steep hill climb to the settlement. Following the defeat at Isandlwana and the defence of Rorke's Drift, Helpmekaar received numerous wounded soldiers. Due to the heavy rains, unhygienic conditions and lack of medical supplies (all lost at Isandlwana) which followed these battles, many of the troops suffered illness and disease. Those that died of their injuries or disease subsequent to these actions on 22 January 1879 are buried in the now neglected cemetery behind the modern police station. This work retains the original spelling throughout main text.

2   C.T. Atkinson, *The South Wales Borderers 24th Foot 1689–1937*, Cambridge 1937.

3   ibid.

4   A.H. Swiss, *Records of the 24th Regiment*, London 1892.

5   The following is an extract from the official orders issued by Lord Chelmsford in November 1878. Item 145 deals with 'Cattle and other prize' and reveals why all ranks had a vested interest in the price obtained from the contractors.

> The following rules, having reference to the capture of cattle, or other prize, will be adhered to by all forces serving under the orders of the Lieutenant-general commanding –
>
> On any cattle or other prize being taken, the officer commanding the corps or party making the same will at once report the circumstances and number or nature of the prize to the officer in charge of the operations, who will thereupon determine what troops will share, and will appoint prize agents to arrange for the disposal of the cattle, &c., and to distribute the proceeds according to the following scale, viz.–
>
> Private or trooper – 1 share.
>
> NCO – 2 shares.
>
> Captain or subaltern – 3 shares.
>
> Field officer – 4 shares.
>
> Officer in command of the operations – 6 shares.
>
> Officers of the staff – shares according to their rank.

6   Boys were permitted to join the regular army, but those under the age of 17 were enlisted as 'boy soldiers' and only entitled to half pay until reaching that age.

7   At the age of 18 years, Charles Robson was languishing in Bow Street police cells when he elected to join the Royal Engineers rather than go to prison.

8   Most of Chard's men remained sick at Durban suffering the after-effects of smallpox vaccinations.

Chapter 4

1   Pte Richard Stevens, Natal Mounted Police, who survived Isandlwana – letter to family dated 27 January. See Frank Emery, *The Red Soldier*.

2   A.H. Swiss, *Records of the 24th Regiment*, London 1892.

3   *ibid.*

4   *ibid.*

5   I. Knight, *There Will Be An Awful Row At Home About This*, Shoreham 1987.

6   I. Knight, *The Zulu War – Then and Now*, Plaistow Press 1993.

7   Adrian Greaves, *Isandlwana*, Cassell 2001.

8   Account by Mehlokazulu, 27 September 1879 *Natal Mercury.*

9   Richard Stevens, letter dated 27 January 1879.

10   Archibald Forbes, *The Daily News* 10 July 1879.

Chapter 5

1   Smith-Dorrien returned to Isandlwana in time for the Zulu attack, which he survived, being one of only five Imperial officers to escape the massacre.

2   Lieutenant W. Heaton of Upcher's Company, 1/24th Regiment later wrote:

      22 Wednesday January 1879

      Orders came in for Rainforths Coy to leave as well as ours. Col Hapard & Baxter came in for breakfast. All goods bar light field kit and one blanket stay with stores. A lot of canteen stores for both Battns came in, made arrangements to forward them to the Drift. Rainforths Coy left 2.30 ours just after 3. Met Spalding outside, after him, any number of mounted men from the camp of Col Glyn's Column, where the Zulus had cut up 5 Coys of ours. Killed Col Pulleine Wardell Anstey Daly Dyson White Pullen. Coghill & Melvill escaped with Battns Colour.

Hospital at the Drift and detachment 2/24th cut up. Got orders to retire to Helpmekaar got in about 11 and made laagar then put on outpost duty 12.30 to 3am.

3   Spalding justified his actions on 22 January when he wrote:

Capt Rainforth's Company 1/24th Regiment was ordered from Helpmekaar to Rorke's Drift by OC No. 3 Column for the purpose of taking up and entrenching a position commanding and defending the ponts on the Buffalo River.

I know of no other orders touching the erection of work for such a purpose.

This company should have been in the required position on the 20th January the day of the departure of No. 3 Column from Rorke's Drift for Isandhlwana. They did not arrive on that day nor even on the 21st. Seeing this on the 22nd I rode over to Helpmekaar with a written order in my pocket directing Capt Rainforth positively to reach the points by sundown on that day. I met his company together with that of Major Upcher of the same Regiment on their march down to Rorke's Drift. I accompanied them. The intelligence from Isandhlwana met us on the way.

4   See Introduction – Ref. 7.

5   Numerous primary sources reveal that Dalton strongly assisted with the command during the battle at Rorke's Drift – only to revert to his official subservient role the following day. Although his role was acknowledged by Chard, Dalton's role was overlooked in official reports and his actions officially 'downgraded' when medals were awarded. For further evidence on this aspect, see chapter 15. See also *Padre George Smith of Rorke's Drift* by Canon Lummis MC (Wensome, 1978).

6   By a surprising coincidence, on the following day Mrs and Revd Witt each learned from different sources that the Zulus had killed the other. Convinced by the news, both made their way to Durban in abject sadness – only to meet each other on the outskirts of the town.

7   It is popularly believed that Dalton had been a sergeant major in the 85th Regiment. He left the 85th in March 1862 having achieved the rank of

Sergeant. He then transferred to the Commissariat Staff where he reached the rank of 1st class staff sergeant before he retired in 1871 with the Long Service and Good Conduct Medal for nearly twenty-two years' service. He then emigrated to South Africa.

8   Corporal Anderson was buried with those killed at Rorke's Drift. By shooting him, the soldiers of the 24th had dealt with the matter to their satisfaction. Captain Stephenson was detained by the British two days later and returned to Rorke's Drift. He was informally court-martialled and dismissed from his position.

9   The attack on Rorke's Drift was initially unintended – the Zulus had crossed the river into Natal merely for short-term plunder. See – John Laband *Oh! Let's Go and Have a Fight at Jim's.*

Chapter 6

1   C. 2242.

2   Two separate supply wagons were in the vicinity of Helpmekaar when they learned of the British defeat at Isandlwana and the attack at Rorke's Drift. One was carrying Martini-Henry rifles and ammunition under escort by Colonel Bray and men of the 4th (King's Own Royal) Regiment. One or more wagons got stuck so, as a precaution, the escort offloaded the rifles and buried them to prevent them being lost to the Zulus. The escort marked the hiding place and retraced their tracks; but on their return several days later and after several heavy rainstorms, they could not find the location. The rifles were never recovered. The other wagon under escort was near Greytown and on receipt of the same information, they unloaded two extremely heavy boxes marked 'Horseshoes' and deposited them in the town store. Following the Zulu War a mounted troop halted outside the store. The troop captain entered the store and reclaimed the two boxes, which the store owner had meanwhile used as steps to reach his upper shelves. He reluctantly relinquished the two useful boxes and signed the necessary papers. As the two boxes were being carried out of his store, he noticed that the requisition paper stated 'two boxes of Gold sovereigns marked *HORSESHOES*'.

Chapter 7

1   Letter from Gunner Howard February 1879.

2   Many readers will have noticed the emphasis placed on horses in contemporary letters, diaries and journals relating to nineteenth-century warfare. Harness understood the position and importance of horses and gave meticulous attention to this aspect of his command. Through 1878 Stuart Smith, Harness's captain, scoured southern Africa to buy suitable horses. On 6 March of that year Harness wrote that his captain had returned the previous day with forty-eight horses at an average cost of £24 13s. 7d. The artillerymen who mastered the care of horses in southern Africa – with small feeds and the use of every opportunity for grazing – criticized the failure of the regular cavalry to adapt to local conditions during the Zulu campaign. On 19 July 1878 Harness wrote that he congratulated himself on the condition of the horses, and, 'if we get through the march as I hope we shall, it will be a creditable thing to the officers and men of the battery'. Colonel J.T.B. Brown, RA, complimented Harness on the condition of his horses on another march, to Ulundi, almost a year later: 'Lieutenant-Colonel Harness's horses were all native, and principally bought in the Orange Free State and Old Colony, before there had been so great a demand. They were useful and handy horses for the light guns, and Harness had them so well trained that they were very little trouble. A few mounted men used to drive them to water, or out to feed just like a herd of cattle instead of having a man to every two or three horses.'

3   Donald Morris, *The Washing of the Spears*, Cape 1996.

4   See Chapter 17, Archaeological Investigations at the Battlefield.

5   See Colonel Bourne's BBC Radio Transcription in Appendix E.

6   The Curling Letters – courtesy AZWHS.

7   Norman Holme, *The Silver Wreath*, reference Private 913 James Ashton.

8   Following the publication in the British press of letters from Sergeant Jervis 90th Light Infantry and Private Snook 13th Light Infantry reporting the massacre of hundreds of Zulu wounded following the battle of Khambula, numerous questions were asked in the British Parliament. For the full reports, see House of Commons Hansard, 3rd Series, vol. 246 cc. 1708–1718 of 12 June 1879; vol. 247 cc. 693–694 of 26 June 1879 and vol. 247

cc. 723–724 of 26 June 1879 and Frank Emery, *The Red Soldier*,
Johannesburg 1977. Although the British military commanders in Zululand
initially denied the routine killing of Zulu wounded, most subsequent reports
and letters from participants in these battles confirmed the policy – especially
following the battles of Khambula on 26 March and Ulundi on 4 July 1879.

9   Hamilton-Browne *A Lost Legionary in South Africa*, London 1890.

10 *Column Orders* Feb 2nd By Order Banister Act. Adj.2/24th Regt.
Until further orders, 3 patrols of 1 NCO and 1 section of fours each will
leave the fort immediately after Reveille sounds every morning and proceed
to reconnoitre as follows. One to the first sluit [ditch] on the road to
Helpmakaar. One round the North end of the hill behind the fort and one
round the south side of the hill. These patrols to reconnoitre for the enemy
not further than a mile from the fort and then return at once and report. The
parties to be detailed over night.

11 Letter from Captain Walter Parke Jones. See Frank Emery, *The Red Soldier*,
Johannesburg 1977.

12 Paton, Glennie and Penn Symons *Records of the 24th Regiment*, London
1892:

> On 4th February 1879, Lieutenant Colonel Black, who in a previous
> reconnaissance had found the bodies of Melvill and Coghill close to a
> large boulder, against which they appear to have stood to fight, for
> around them lay several dead Zulus, set out with a search-party, to
> endeavour to find the Queen's Colour. After erecting a cairn of stones
> over the bodies of the two officers where they lay, the party descended
> into a glen through which the Buffalo runs in deep curves, about four
> hundred yards below where Melvill crossed. First the case was found,
> then the crest; lastly, at a spot fifty yards higher up, the colour itself was
> lifted from the water where it had become wedged between the stones.
> The party returned to Rorke's Drift and handed over the colour to
> Colonel Glyn, the men of the 2nd battalion turned out and gave a hearty
> cheer as the trophy was brought in. Next day it was taken under escort
> to Helpmekaar and given over to the two companies then representing
> the 1st battalion.
>
> On 14th April 1879, the bodies of Lieutenants Melvill and Coghill

were buried beside where they fell. A marble cross was subsequently placed over the spot by Sir Bartle Frere and his staff, bearing the inscription:–

> In Memory of Lieutenant and Adjutant Teignmouth Melvill
> and Lieutenant N. J. A. Coghill, 1st battalion 24th regiment,
> who died on this spot, on 22nd January 1879,
> to save the Queen's Colour of their regiment.
>
> *(And on the reverse side)*
> For Queen and Country. Jesu Mercy.

While the 1st Battalion was at Gosport during the summer after its return home, Queen Victoria expressed a wish to see the rescued colour. Accordingly, on 28th July 1880, Lieutenant Colonel J. M. G. Tongue, with Lieutenants Weallens and Phipps, and an escort of four colour sergeants, carried the colours to Osborne, where Her Majesty attached a wreath of immortelles to the pole of the Queen's Colour. The case bears the following inscription:–

> This wreath
> was placed on the
> Queen's Colour of the 1st Battalion 24th Regiment
> by
> Her majesty Queen Victoria,
> to commemorate the devoted gallantry of
> Lieut. and Adjutant T. Melvill and Lieut. N. J. A. Coghill,
> who gave their lives to save the Colour from the hands
> of the enemy on 22 January, 1879, and in recognition
> of the noble defence of Rorke's Drift.
> As a lasting memorial of Her Gracious Act,
> a facsimile of the wreath in silver was commanded
> to be borne on the
> Queen's Colour of both Battalions of the Regiment.
> Authority dated 15th Decr., 1880.
> Queen and Country.

(NB The original wreath of flowers had been attached to the Colour by the ladies of Durban prior to the regiment embarking for England. Queen Victoria initially replaced their wreath pending the presentation of the silver wreath).

13 According to the incomplete diary of a passing traveller, a Mr Leyland. (See *The Buffalo Border 1879* by Laband, Thompson and Henderson, University of Natal, Durban 1983.)

Chapter 8

1 Adrian Greaves, *Isandlwana*, Cassell 2001.

2 Ian Knight, *The Sun Turned Black*, Watermans 1995.

3 Adrian Greaves, *Isandlwana*, Cassell 2001.

4 Later in the war, when rumours that Spalding had deserted his men began to spread, Chelmsford intervened on Spalding's behalf. He wrote a memo to the adjutant general in which he exonerated Spalding; Chelmsford believed that Spalding was acting correctly when he left Rorke's Drift to trace the overdue replacements. Chelmsford wrote that it was 'the non-arrival of this detachment that caused major Spalding to go to Helpmakaar to hasten its departure'. He went on, 'I refer to this latter point in justice to Major Spalding as I have heard that remarks have been made relative to his absence from this post at the time'. Chelmsford's letter dated 19 May 1879.

5 War Office Précis of Information. 1879.

6 Other participants were also badly affected by what they experienced, both physically and mentally. In an age when mental trauma was misunderstood, there was little sympathy or understanding for those who broke under the strain of witnessing the savagery of fighting Zulus. In an institution like the army it was expected that emotions should be kept on a tight rein, especially amongst the senior officers; the 'stiff upper lip' syndrome prevailed. It is well documented that Chelmsford underwent a period of severe depression in the aftermath of Isandlwana – see WO 32/7709 – and requested that he be replaced. Colonel Glyn suffered a breakdown at Rorke's Drift but eventually recovered sufficiently to take a limited part in the second invasion of Zululand. Colonel Hassard, Officer Commanding Royal Engineers, had such a severe nervous breakdown that he was replaced. Colonel Pearson, the

defender of Eshowe, was invalided home suffering from mental and physical exhaustion. By the end of September 1879 the last detachments of the British Army had left Zululand with their baggage. Durban became chock-a-block, with the bars doing a roaring trade. In the general confusion one story put the finishing touch to the war.

Lieutenant General Sir William Butler wrote that just before one crowded transport was due to sail home, the captain received an order to delay sailing; six soldiers found to be insane during the course of the war (including Rorke's Drift defender Private Wall) were about to be embarked under escort for consignment to a British lunatic asylum. The captain, nervous at losing a tide, waited impatiently. Presently a boat containing the six additional passengers arrived alongside. On the transport a mass of men of different units, many already demobilized, lined the sides, having a last look at Durban. The lunatics, still in their uniforms, scrambled up the ladder and immediately vanished into the crowd to the consternation of the escort and ship's captain.

The shore escort wanted to depart before the ship sailed and rapidly gave such descriptive details as they could remember before rowing back to shore. On board, the ship's officers held an emergency conference with the military. For fear of starting a general panic, news of the occurrence was kept a close secret. A select group of observers was enrolled, from men known to the officers or wearing decorations, and these were sworn to secrecy and detailed to watch different portions of the ship. All the way to Cape Town the observations continued. Any man sitting in isolation or in the throes of seasickness found himself under suspicion. At frequent intervals some man would be tapped on the shoulder and led to an inspection by a panel consisting of the ship's doctor, captain and an army officer. By the time the ship reached Cape Town there were twenty-six men in detention.

Accordingly an urgent request was sent from Cape Town for someone to come from Natal who could positively identify the lunatics. An asylum orderly was hastily sent down only to discover that none of the men detained were lunatics. On the contrary, six of the men detained had been engaged on the search for the lunatics and had been the most conscientious in reporting others as madmen.

Chapter 9

1   Norman Holme, *The Silver Wreath*.

2   See Appendix A for the initial 'Chard Report'.

3   Colour Sergeant Bourne receives no mention in Morris's classic *The Washing of the Spears*.

4   See Memorandum from Captain Fleetwood Edwards to Queen Victoria 21 February 1880. Archives of Zululand, Archival Publications International 2000. Vol. 2 p.136.

5   Curling Letters. Courtesy of the AZWHS.

6   In later stages of the war other nominations for the VC failed or were seriously delayed where protocol was not strictly followed – for example, see the case of Captain Duck of the Veterinary Corps who was refused a VC for his gallantry at Hlobane on the grounds that 'he should not have been there'.

7   The Bromhead Report and two Bromhead letters, see Appendix B, by kind permission of the 24th Regimental Museum, Brecon.

8   Clery Letter 16 May 1879 – see Greaves and Best, *The Curling Letters of the Zulu War*, Pen & Sword 2001.

9   Letter from Rorke's Drift by Lieutenant Banister dated 27 January 1879.

10 Adrian Greaves, *Isandlwana*, Cassell 2001.

11 The Glyn Report. See Appendix C.

12 The second Chard Report is reproduced at Appendix A, by kind permission of HM The Queen.

Chapter 10

1   Ian Bennett, *Eyewitness in Zululand*, Greenhill 1989.

2   Queen Victoria was a great believer in bestowing rewards for loyalty and merit, especially in the military where almost every campaign during her reign saw the issue of specially designed medals and ribbons in recognition of brave or loyal service. Although Queen Victoria had instituted the Distinguished Conduct Medal for other ranks at the start of the Crimean War, she acknowledged the need of an award for outstanding bravery, one that could be bestowed regardless of rank. The resulting bronze cross, fashioned from the metal of captured Russian guns from Sebastopol, was first presented in

June 1857, but there were very few opportunities to win this coveted award. Those officers who did found the road to promotion considerably easier and, as a consequence, many volunteered for active service with the possibility of a VC in mind. Considering the short duration of the Zulu War and its long periods of inactivity, the number of VCs awarded was exceptionally high. Apart from the politics involved, there was another reason. The Zulus did not possess artillery or effective firearms and so most of the fighting was highly visible and close combat, perfect warfare for the brave.

The award of so many VCs to one regiment for a single action was unprecedented. In earlier wars where there were several acts of bravery, a ballot was held amongst the soldiers themselves to decide who was the most deserving recipient.

3   Ian Knight, *The Sun Turned Black*, Watermans 1995.

4   AZWHS Journal, December 1997. Curiously, when Lord Wolseley presented Bromhead with his Victoria Cross, he did so in the mistaken belief that he was presenting the award to Bromhead's brother, who had served with Wolseley in Ashanti. See *Life of Lord Wolseley* by Morris and Arthur 1924.

5   Letter from Wolseley dated 16 July 1879. See WO327386 (Awards to Commissary Dalton and Dunne).

6   M.J. Crook, *The Evolution of the Victoria Cross*, Midas Books 1975.

7   ibid.

8   In order to understand how the medal and its bars were awarded, it may be helpful to show what was printed on the reverse of the medal application form.

The Medal will be granted to the Forces employed against:

(a) The Gcalekas, Gaikas and other Kaffir Tribes from 26th September 1877 to the 28th June 1878 inclusive. (Year on Clasp 1877–78)

(b) Against the Pokwane from 21st to 28th January 1878 (Clasp 1878)

(c) Against the Griquas from 24th April to 13th November 1878 (Clasp 1878)

(e) Against Sekukuni from 11th November to 2nd December 1879 and against Moirosi's Stronghold (Clasp 1879)

Clasps for those who served throughout the conflicts were entitled to fit 1877–78–79 or 1878–79 according to which campaigns they participated in.

Chapter 11

1   W.E. Montague, *Campaigning in South Africa*, 1880.

2   CO 879/17 no. 218.

3   W.B. Worsfold, *Sir Bartle Frere: a Footnote to the History of the British Empire*, 1923.

4   Richard Cope, *The Ploughshare of War*, University of Natal Press 1999.

Chapter 12

Material courtesy of the Anglo Zulu War Historical Society.

Chapter 13

1   See Ref. 6 Chapter 8.

2   Even more catastrophic, with regards to the numbers of casualties sustained, was the Italian defeat at the hands of Ethiopian tribesman at the battle of Adowa in 1896. The primitively armed Ethiopians killed some 8,000 well-armed soldiers in the barren mountains. The Italian general Baratieri, like Custer and Chelmsford, underestimated the native opponents and all suffered the fatal consequence.

3   For a comprehensive roll of members of the 1st and 2nd 24th Regiment involved at Rorke's Drift, see Norman Holme, *The Noble 24th*, Savannah 1999.

4   Donald Morris, *The Washing of the Spears*, Cape 1996.

Chapter 14

1   *Medal Rolls 1793–1889 of the 24th Foot, South Wales Borderers*, J.B. Hayward & Son.

2   P.E. Abbott, *Recipients of the Distinguished Conduct Medal 1855–1909*.

Chapter 17

1   AZWHS Journal, December 2000, Article by Dr Peter J. Mitchell.

2   Sheila Henderson, *The Turbulent Frontier* as quoted in *The Zulu War and*

the Colony of Natal, edited by G. Chadwick and E. Hobson, 1979.

3 ibid.

4 P. Gon, *The Road to Isandlwana*, London 1979.

5 Following the battle, Rorke's Drift suffered torrential rain and it could be presumed that the spent cartridge cases would have been trodden into the mud. During the archaeological excavations of the site during 1993 virtually none were found, even though excavations were conducted to a depth of 100cm. Visitors to the site would certainly have collected mementos lying around, and metal detectors have been used; yet the amount found by the archaeologists seems very low. Perhaps the spent rounds were collected up and deposited elsewhere, but this seems unlikely given the conditions prevailing at the time and that more urgent survival tasks needed to be performed.

6 J. Laband and P. Thompson, *Kingdom in Crisis. The Zulu response to the British Invasion of 1879*, Pietermaritzburg: University of Natal Press 1992.

7 J.J. Guy, 1971 'A note on firearms in the Zulu kingdom with special reference to the Anglo-Zulu War 1879', *Journal of African History* (4): 557–70.

8 F. Mechanick, 1979 'Firepower and firearms in the Zulu War of 1879', *Military History Journal* 4 (6): 218–20.

9 The fieldwork for this paper was undertaken while Dr Webley was employed at the Natal Provincial Museum Service who rendered their support, both financial and tactical, during the project. Mr G. Dominy, Mr D. Forbes-Milne, Mr F. Roodt and Ms R. Devereux of Museum Service may be singled out for their assistance in facilitating Dr Webley's fieldwork. Mr N. Ruddiman provided many of the photographs. Grateful thanks also go to the Evangelical Lutheran Community at Rorke's Drift in particular for their interest in the project and their assistance and support during Dr Webley's and her team's stay at the mission station. Mr Bresler kindly undertook an identification of the cartridge cases and spent bullets.

Appendix F

1 It is popularly believed that King Cetshwayo had ordered his generals to stay out of Natal but this belief overlooks Cetshwayo's address to his army. See

the account by a Zulu deserter recorded by the Hon. Drummond, a Zulu speaking staff officer on the HQ Staff. The Zulu claimed Cetshwayo had instructed his army to cross the border into Natal. See Frank Emery, *The Red Soldier*, Ball Paperbacks, Johannesburg 1977.

2   In March 2001, the author was able to trace an elderly Zulu, Bantubezwe Ntanzi, whose father had fought against the British at Isandlwana. Bantubezwe Ntanzi has lived his whole life at Isandlwana and he recalled seeing a number of British graves to the left of the spur when he was a young man. He also pointed out the location of several cairns, long since demolished, in the vicinity of the Conical Hill. If nothing else, his account supports the hypothesis that the modern-day cairns at Isandlwana are those that have been relocated since 1879.

3   See Chapter 17 Archaeological Investigations at the Battlefield.

Appendix G

1   The Swedish application was ignored by the British government.

2   Not published.

Index